ON TO THE SANUMÁS

"The personal sacrifices made by Don and Barb Borgman defy description. But this skillful compilation by Tom Sorkness goes a long way toward helping us fathom their willingness to sacrifice as necessary to bring God's message to the Sanumá people. We who are in their Crossworld family (previously called UFM) highly honor the Borgmans for their perseverance and recognize with them their dependence on the Lord throughout this journey."

—LUKE PERKINS,
president, Crossworld

"Since the time of the apostle Paul, God has used courageous men and women to bring His Word to the hardest-to-reach places on earth. This is one such account. Facing seemingly insurmountable obstacles, the Yanomami people of Brazil were brought the gospel and had the scriptures translated into their own language. It is, on the one hand, an amazing story of brave and resourceful missionaries. But more than that, it is an account of God's work in building His church with people from every tribe, tongue, and nation."

— JONATHAN MASTER,
president, Greenville Presbyterian Theological Seminary

"*On to the Sanumas* is a real-life adventure story about Don and Barbara Borgman, missionaries with Unevangelized Fields Mission. Along with author Thomas Sorkness's editorial notes, the reader is given a firsthand account of the Borgmans in search of tribes in northern Brazil that had never heard the Gospel. This is an inspiring story of how the Gospel changes lives, freeing people from fear and giving them hope."

—LINDA FINLAYSON,
children's author of *God's Timeline: The Big Book of Church History*
and *God's Bible Timeline: The Big Book of Bible History*

"A compelling account of faith and endurance through trials of primitive jungle conditions. The Borgmans' life and work showcase reliance on God's strength amid extreme obstacles. This carefully crafted historical record highlights God's steadfast mercy and his ongoing global activity. It is a poignant narrative offering needed encouragement to Christians who, as Don aptly puts it, are often 'afflicted by inertia.' The Borgmans preach God's word to us as they preached it to each other."

—ADAM PORCELLA,
senior vice president and provost, Cairn University

"This generation needs examples of men and women who have given their lives to the cause of Christ. In *On to the Sanumás,* Tom Sorkness has given us that. A teacher who spent his own career investing in the next generation, Sorkness has provided us with a labor of love that I trust will be used by God to inspire others to proclaim Christ to the ends of the earth until the end of the age."

—**JOHN CURRIE,**
professor of pastoral theology, Westminster Theological Seminary

On to the Sanumás
Sanöma töpö kulati hamö

*The Missionary Lives of Donald M. and Barbara H. Borgman
and the Translation of the Sanumá New Testament*

Edited by THOMAS J. SORKNESS

Foreword by PHILIP GRAHAM RYKEN

RESOURCE *Publications* · Eugene, Oregon

ON TO THE SANUMÁS: SANÖMA TÖPÖ KULATI HAMÖ
The Missionary Lives of Donald M. and Barbara H. Borgman and the Translation of the Sanumá New Testament

Copyright © 2024 Thomas J. Sorkness. All rights reserved. Except for brief quotations in critical publications or reviews, no part of this book may be reproduced in any manner without prior written permission from the publisher. Write: Permissions, Wipf and Stock Publishers, 199 W. 8th Ave., Suite 3, Eugene, OR 97401.

Resource Publications
An Imprint of Wipf and Stock Publishers
199 W. 8th Ave., Suite 3
Eugene, OR 97401

www.wipfandstock.com

PAPERBACK ISBN: 978-1-4982-9243-6
HARDCOVER ISBN: 978-1-4982-9245-0
EBOOK ISBN: 978-1-4982-9244-3

11/26/24

Figure 1, Map of Yanomami Regions, reprinted with permission by University of Toronto Press.

Figure 40, Colonel João Camarão Telles Ribeiro, reprinted with permission by *Instituto Histórico-Cultural da Aeronáutica* (INCAER).

"God Parts the Clouds," by William G. Born appears in Appendix F and is printed in full by permission of the author.

Unless otherwise indicated, all Scripture quotations are from The ESV® Bible (The Holy Bible, English Standard Version®), © 2001 by Crossway, a publishing ministry of Good News Publishers. Used by permission. All rights reserved.

Scripture quotations marked (TLB) are taken from *The Living Bible*, copyright © 1971 by Tyndale House Foundation. Used by permission of Tyndale House Publishers, Carol Stream, Illinois 60188. All rights reserved.

Scripture taken from THE MESSAGE. Copyright © 1993, 1994, 1995, 1996, 2000, 2001, 2002. Used by permission of NavPress Publishing Group.

Scripture quotations marked (NIV) are taken from the Holy Bible, New International Version®, NIV®. Copyright © 1973, 1978, 1984, 2011 by Biblica, Inc.™ Used by permission of Zondervan. All rights reserved worldwide. www.zondervan.com. The "NIV" and "New International Version" are trademarks registered in the United States Patent and Trademark Office by Biblica, Inc.™

Scripture quotations marked (Wms) are taken from the *NEW TESTAMENT: A TRANSLATION IN THE LANGUAGE OF PEOPLE* by Charles B. Williams. Copyright© 1937 by Bruce Humphries, Inc. Copyright© renewed 1965 by Edith S. Williams.

Scripture quotations marked (Ber) are taken from THE MODERN LANGUAGE BIBLE, THE NEW BERKLEY VERSION IN MODERN ENGLISH, Copyright© 1945, 1959, 1969 by Zondervan Publishing House.

Scripture quotations marked (KJV) from The Authorized (King James) Version. Rights in the Authorized Version in the United Kingdom are vested in the Crown. Reproduced by permission of the Crown's patentee, Cambridge University Press.

Scripture marked (NKJV) taken from the New King James Version®. Copyright © 1982 by Thomas Nelson. Used by permission. All rights reserved.

"And how are they to believe in him of whom they have never heard?"
"Cristo ta wäsä pole, ĩ töpönö ĩ ta hini paia mane maaki,
-Cristo a pitili- ĩ na ĩ töpö pi kuu totio kitä ta o?"
(Rom 10:14 KJV, Sanumá)

Dedicated to Don and Barb
and to their children: David, Stephen, Andrea, and Darlene
To the glory of God and the ongoing work of the Sanumá church!

Contents

Foreword by Philip Graham Ryken | xi

Preface | xiii

Acknowledgments | xv

Introduction | xix

1	Preparation (1949 to 1958)	1
2	Further Preparation and Jungle Training (1958 to 1959)	14
3	New Frontiers (1959 to 1962)	51
4	The Atroais and the Sanumás (1963–1964)	129
5	Transitions (1963 to 1968)	144
6	From Strength to Strength (1969 to 1973)	172
7	Location Change, New Contacts, and First Fruit (1973 to 1978)	190
8	Olomai, Part I, The Sprouting of Seeds Sown (1979 to 1986)	222
9	Olomai, Part II, Spiritual Growth and Challenges (1986 to 1991)	252
10	My Word Will Not Return Void (1992 to 1999)	269
11	The Fruit of Their Labor (2000 to 2018)	291

Afterword | 329

Appendix A: Yanomami Terms and Denominations, by Donald Borgman | 332

Appendix B: "Trail Song," by Donald Borgman | 335

Appendix C: Letter, by Arnold C. Borgman | 338

Appendix D: Subsequent Contacts with the Atroais by the Wai Wais,
    by Donald Borgman | 341

Appendix E: Reflections on Adjusting at Auaris, by Barbara Borgman | 349

Appendix F: "God Parts the Clouds," by William G. Born | 352

Appendix G: Reflections on Their Children's Education,
    by Barbara Borgman | 369

Appendix H: Sikoi Encounter, by Thomas J. Sorkness | 371

Appendix I: A Word about Don and Barb Borgman, by Rev. Stan Allaby | 377

Appendix J: Terms of Service, Furlough Dates, and Continued Work
    (1958 to 1999) | 380

Bibliography | 385

Subject Index | 387

Scripture Index | 393

Foreword

THE STORY OF DONALD AND BARBARA BORGMAN's long, faithful, and ultimately fruitful missionary work in Brazil participates in larger narratives.

Don Borgman was captivated in his teenage years by missionary accounts of gospel work among the Indigenous tribes of British Guiana. He went to college in the late 1940s and early 1950s—first to Moody Bible Institute and then to Wheaton College. At both schools he became part of the massive missionary mobilization that took place in the United States after World War II, when the eyes of many Americans were opened to the spiritual needs of the wider world. Both Moody and Wheaton were catalysts for the Great Commission, sending scores of graduates to mission fields around the globe.

Borgman was influenced by Young Life–a catalyst for personal evangelism–which enhanced his interest in world missions. He was also inspired by the sacrificial service of Jim Elliot, Nate Saint, Ed McCully, Pete Fleming, and Roger Youderian. Together with their faithful wives, these five martyrs gave lives they could not keep to gain a glory they could never lose. In January 1956, while on their mission to reach the Waodani in the jungles of Ecuador, all five men were slain by members of the tribe, who left their bodies to drift in the Curaray River or cast them aside on the riverbank. Like so many others, Borgman admired Jim Elliot and his coworkers; he too wanted to give his life to reach people who had never heard the gospel. This passion led him to participate in first contact expeditions to the Yanomami people of Brazil when he first arrived on the field in the late 1950s and early 1960s, thus helping to open a new region for gospel work.

The Borgmans, who married in 1964, served with Unevangelized Fields Mission (UFM) now known as Crossworld. The name of their mission agency fits another broader narrative: missionaries who were motivated—as Paul was (Rom 15:20-21)—to be the first witnesses to share the gospel with a particular people group.

In order to do this pioneering work, the Borgmans stationed in 1965 at the Auaris mission post in the far northwest corner of Brazil's Roraima State, near the Venezuelan border. They made first contact with the Yanomami people who lived there and spent decades learning the language of the Sanumá tribe, whom they served and befriended. It took nearly half a century, but the Borgmans persevered, and in 2006 they finished translating the New Testament into the Sanumá language. This too is part of a wider narrative—the story of worldwide Bible translation. Today the Scriptures that the Borgmans painstakingly translated in collaboration with Sanumá colleagues have a secure place on the shelves of the illumiNations exhibit at the Museum of the Bible in Washington, DC, alongside thousands of other Bibles from all over the world.

The Sanumás were not their only collaborators. Beyond their partnership with UFM, the Borgmans benefited over the years from their connections with Wycliffe Bible Translators, Missionary Aviation Fellowship, New Tribes Mission, and other agencies, both evangelical and governmental. Of course, they also depended on the support of churches back in North America. Even the most intrepid missionaries require the wisdom, expertise, gifts, and practical help of many others.

Because the Borgmans' story participates in these larger narratives, aspects of their story will sound familiar to people who know the history of North American missions. Thomas Sorkness's goal in this carefully researched history—based on journals, newsletters, interviews, and other sources—is to help their story come to life in its unique particularity. Who were the people who helped the Borgmans get to the mission field? Why did they go to Brazil? What happened when they got there? What specific hardships, unexpected blessings, and painful tragedies did they experience over the long decades of their ministry?

By answering these and many other questions, Sorkness adds to our understanding of worldwide missions. As importantly, he dignifies the gospel work of Don and Barb Borgman and honors their kingdom service by giving a detailed account of their life together in ministry—the life they offered so that others too could know the Savior they loved.

Philip Graham Ryken
President, Wheaton College
April 2024

Preface

In the spring of 1977, while a sophomore at Gordon College in Massachusetts, I had the privilege of participating in an expedition to make first contact with an Indigenous people group in far Northwestern Brazil. The group we were seeking to contact was known as the Sikois, part of the greater Sanumá tribe, a subgroup of the Yanomami. I went with a college acquaintance, Norman Allaby. Our host and leader on this expedition was Donald Borgman, a Bible translator with Unevangelized Fields Mission (UFM). Don had worked with the Sanumás for over ten years, and it had long been his desire to make contact with the Sikois. Two people from the neighboring Maiongong tribe, father and son Lourenzo and Komak (Alberto), were our guides. Our expedition was adventurous and successful, but over the intervening years, I have to confess that I didn't spend much time thinking about the trip, particularly of those involved, missionaries and Indigenous people alike.

Nevertheless, my participation in this expedition made a lifelong impression on me. In the summer of 2018, I decided to write an account of my experience, largely for my children and posterity. As I did, the feelings, sights, and even smells came flooding back to me. One day, as I was writing, I thought to myself, "If only I could ask Don about . . . " I didn't even know if he was still living, but I thought I would find out. I discovered that the name UFM had been changed to Crossworld and that its headquarters was in Kansas City, Missouri. I called and left a message, stating who I was, who I was looking for, and why. The next day, my wife, Lois, handed me the phone and said, "It's Don Borgman!"

The following summer, Lois and I traveled to Indianapolis to visit Don and his wife, Barbara, where they were now living. I had had very little contact with Don since the time of my trip to Brazil, and during our visit, my understanding of their lives together on the mission field was magnified in ways that I could barely take in. What had loomed so large in my mind, the expedition, now became microscopic in comparison. I was humbled. On the morning of our departure, I told Don that he, or someone, should write a history of their work. He told me that others had said the same, but he really didn't know who could do that. He was not inclined, besides the fact that he was still busy doing translation work and producing Bible teaching material for the Sanumás. At the time, he was eighty-seven! I asked him if he had kept any record of their time on the field. He went back to his office and brought out a box, neatly ordered chronologically, of journal entries, letters home, and newsletters beginning in 1949 and continuing to 2018. Sixty-nine years' worth! It was at that point that I realized why the Lord had sent me on that expedition so many years before. I told Don that I would write the story.

Over the next year or so, Don scanned and sent me all the documents, and we corresponded about the details, primarily for clarification, but also to gain some personal perspective from both him and Barb. The project has proved to be a huge task but a labor of love. So, why did I take this on? To begin with, it's a story of historical significance, not only for the missionary record, but also for the broader scope of Brazil's history and the history of the Indigenous people of the region. It needed to be recorded. Secondly, it demonstrates the commitment of Don and Barb, as well as the other missionaries involved, to get the Word of God into Sanumá hands. It was an arduous, lifelong task, but one to which they were fully dedicated. Next, it brings glory to God in countless ways. It demonstrates God's ongoing determination to bring in his harvest, adding to the church representatives from all the nations—every tribe and tongue. It also shows God's great mercy and love for his children: the Indigenous people, the missionaries, and all others involved. Finally, it shows God's power to overcome those who would seek to thwart his purposes.

In closing, I would like to say that it has been a blessing, honor, and privilege to complete this work. God brings circumstances and situations into our lives for which we may not see the reason until many years have passed. This work is an example of that.

Thomas J. Sorkness (Editor)
Wyndmoor, Pennsylvania
April 2024

Acknowledgments

Without the help of many friends and family members, including friends of Don and Barb Borgman, this account of the work among the various Yanomami tribes and especially the Sanumá people would never have materialized. When I first started this project, I thought I could accomplish it in one, perhaps two years, at most. At the time of this writing, it has now been over four. Also, I had very little understanding of what it would take to put it all together. That became evident as the project unfolded. It was complicated, and much of the project was beyond my capabilities. That being said, so many people pitched in enthusiastically to help me. I think the best way to acknowledge and thank various people is to lay things out as the project progressed chronologically.

First, I wish to thank both Don and Barb for the patience they have displayed as this project went on and on, never seeming to end. I am particularly grateful to Don for the countless hours he spent going through and excerpting all the letters, journal entries, and newsletters and then digitizing and sending them to me electronically. To both, I appreciate the insights and added narrative explaining and contextualizing all the episodes of their lives, some very personal. With those additions, the account was further elucidated and made more full. Thank you so much for entrusting to me the rendering of your story. I have been privileged beyond measure to relate it.

Digitizing and sending all the material was really only the beginning of the work. The various documents were originally written in different formats and script. Most of the early letters and journal entries were handwritten and needed to be transcribed. Later documents were typed on a typewriter, with some on onion skin type paper. Much later, newsletters were produced on computer and printed. All eventually needed to be transcribed. I wish to thank my friend and former student, Maty Ennis, for transcribing all the handwritten letters. This was a tedious task, and I am most grateful. Beyond the handwritten letters, however, all the rest needed to be put into a common font. My son, Erik, devised a program to convert all the text variants to this end. The problem then was that many parts of the text had become garbled and needed to be transcribed. I am indebted to my daughters Louisa and Rachael for laboriously reading through all the original text and making corrections as needed. Also, thanks to Louisa's husband, Larry Gant, for helping Louisa get set up to do the work. Transcribing in both contexts took hours upon hours to complete.

Technical help along the way came from not only Erik, but also son-in-law Omar and daughter Kristiana. Omar spent many hours enhancing images using his graphic design skills, and Kristiana helped with formatting suggestions. Without their general knowledge and computer skills, I would have gotten stuck and not able to move forward at many points. Also, Lois and grandson Isaiah Rose did all the work in producing the map of the many rivers, regions, cities, mission stations, and tribal groups that appear in the work. This required computer skills way beyond my capabilities.

Further thanks go to those who made contributions to the overall work including John Peters, Bill Born, and Rev. Stan Allaby. All played a role in Don's and Barb's missionary lives on the field. Their contributions were immeasurable in providing insight to the narrative and are mentioned along the way. Thanks also to Robin Brown and Gay Cable who provided insight and information as well as those who contributed photographs to include in the text. These were David Hawkins (son of Bob Hawkins), Claudia Glover (daughter of Claude Leavitt), Lydia Munn and Alice Hatch (daughters of Neill Hawkins), Lois Cunningham, and Diane Voth. I also wish to thank Emily Banas and Paul Ericksen of the Billy Graham Center Archives and Library Archives & Special Collections of Wheaton College for their help in finding early maps and references by MAF of the Yanomami territory. Special thanks to friend and former student, Sofia Lima, for finding information on Colonel João Camarão Telles Ribeiro through the Brazilian Air Force. I am also quite grateful to Dr. Philip Ryken who graciously agreed to take the time to write the Foreword for this story.

Of course, editing a big project like this is a huge task. A big thank you goes to Bethany Currie for her hours of work in not only making suggestions and corrections of what I wrote and included, but also for providing a basic formatting approach to the entire work. Her efforts and involvement have been absolutely invaluable. Also, thanks to Josh Currie for indexing the book. I am also grateful to Don and Barb for their eagle eyes for needed corrections as well as Lisa Ryken and my wife, Lois, who caught typos, left out words, and phraseology that simply didn't make sense. In regard to final editing, I wish to thank former students, mother and daughter team Nicole and Tegan Baldini, for their editing efforts to get the final draft to the publisher. Without all these folks, this project would never have seen the light of day.

Finally, I would not have been able to complete this project had it not been for the ongoing encouragement of my family, including all my children, along with friends who kept me going, but most significantly my wife, Lois. She not only has been a good critic along the way, even making me start completely over at one point, but also providing the needed prodding to simply stay on task. She has been the most helpful in the end, and I am ever grateful. I am thankful to the Lord for providing me with this opportunity to tell this story—an opportunity that originated almost half a century ago. It is Don's and Barb's story, but in the end, it is God's great story.

Introduction

STARTING IN THE LATE 1950S, missionaries with Unevangelized Fields Mission (UFM) began to penetrate the vast, largely unexplored region of Northwest Brazil to the west of the Rio Branco. Their objective was to make contact with various tribes of the Yanomami people who inhabited the area in order to learn about the tribes, their language and dialect, and eventually create a written language for translating the Bible into their own tongue. Along with this was the goal to present the gospel to the tribes, to see souls saved, and to plant a church or churches among them. The focus of this volume is about one of those missionaries, Donald M. Borgman, and his work among those tribes, but primarily among the Sanumá people. Don's work in relation to the Sanumás began in 1965 and continues today, but his story begins long before that.

More than a decade and half before the beginning of the Sanumá work, Don spent a number of years preparing for his life calling, first through formal training at Moody Bible Institute and then Wheaton College and Graduate School. During this time, he was determined to enter the mission field as a Bible translator. The following presents the context of Don's life work on the mission field including the people, setting, and time period. Next, is a consideration of the focus and significance of Don's work, and then, finally, a review of the organization and formatted presentation of this narrative.

The Yanomami and Other Indigenous Groups

The Yanomami[1] represent a collection of tribes and their countless villages found in an area of Roraima State of extreme Northwest Brazil and over the

---

1. The Yanomami language family has been called "Yanoama," "Yanomamö," and "Yanomamo." Ernest Migliazza (1972) suggested the term "Yanomama," as this term is not found in exactly this spelling in any dialect, but is understood by the great majority of speakers, and it will not be confused with any dialectical groups. We adopt here, however, the designation "Yanomami" which has been in use since about 1975 in

mountainous border into Venezuela. The Yanomami are generally subdivided into several tribes or dialects with many subgroups. There are five major divisions: 1) the Yanomam, also referred to as the Waicas; 2) the Ninam, who are divided between the Ninam along the Mucajaí River and the Yanam along the Uraricoera River and to the north; 3) the Aica who reside to the southeast of the Ninam (they are a branch of the Yanomam or Ninam); 4) the Sanumá who live along the Auaris River to the extreme northwest of the region and over the mountains into Venezuela; and 5) the Yanomamö who live mostly over the mountains in Venezuela to the south of the Sanumás.[2] The map below indicates the general locations of these tribes at the time of early contact in the 1950s. Note that the Rio Branco, untitled on the map, flows from the north to south alongside Boa Vista to the extreme right of the map. It joins the Rio Negro in the south. Also, note the rivers flowing west and north in Yanomamo and Sanumá territory. This is because they are on the other side of the Serra Parima mountains, and flow into the Orinoco River, Venezuela's major river. Along these watersheds make up the domain of the Yanomami people.

Brazil by the National Indian Foundation and journalists. (See Appendix A for further explanation.)

2. For anthropological studies of these groups, one should read the following works: *Life Among the Yanomami* by John F. Peters, *Yanomamö - Last Days of Eden* by Napoleon A. Chagnon, and *Sanumá Memories*, by Alcida Rita Ramos. Also, of interest is *Journey to the Far Amazon*, by Alain Gheerbrant. It is the story of his expedition from Venezuela to Brazil across the Serra Parima in 1948. He, purportedly, was the first to make contact with the Yanomami tribes, at least in modern times.

Introduction

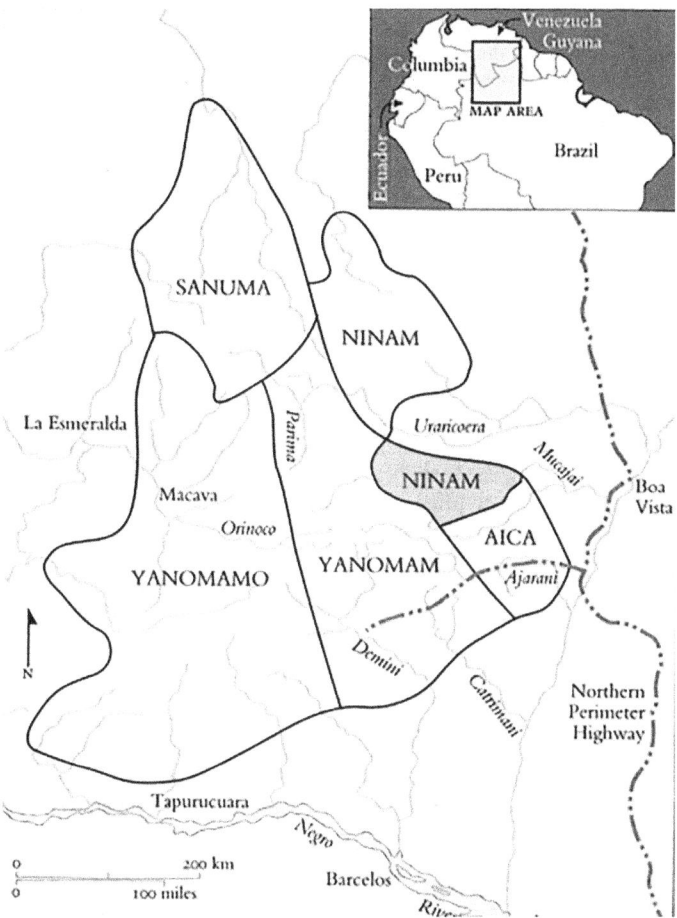

Map of Yanomami Regions (scale not given)[3]

The Yanomami people, collectively at the time, could be characterized as primitive, Stone Age, animist type people. Between the various groups there were only slight differences in material culture as well as religious beliefs and practices.[4] These people were primarily hunter-gatherers but also practiced some slash and burn horticulture, primarily for banana production and cassava (manioc). They fished as well. Villages were self-sufficient. Most lived in small communities of no more than sixty to seventy people. These villages were generally separated by at least a two-day journey along rivers or trails. Conflict sometimes took place between different tribes,

---

3. Peters, *Life Among the Yanomami*, 22.
4. Peters, *Life Among the Yanomami*, 23–27.

generally over the stealing of women, revenge killing, and reprisal for the use of magic root—a way of making one's enemy sick by placing a curse on an individual.

In addition to the Yanomami, there are numerous language groups and tribes of similar culture throughout South America. Several tribes in both Brazil and Guyana (British Guiana at the time) are part of the Carib speaking peoples and play important roles in this narrative. They are the Wai Wais, the Atroais, the Maiongongs, and the Macushis. One additional group referred to are the Wapishanas. They are of the Arawakan language family. With the exception of the Maiongong[5] people, the aforementioned Carib tribes primarily lived to the east of Boa Vista across the Rio Branco into Guyana. The Atroais resided in ancestral tribal lands between Manaus and Boa Vista to the southwest of Guyana in Brazil. The Atroais had a fierce reputation. Many of Don's early accounts refer to them directly.

The focus of this account, primarily, are the Sanumás, but many references are made to the Wai Wais and Atroais, as well as the Ninam/Yanam people, Yanomam/Waicas, and the Maiongongs.

The Missionaries

Various missionary groups have, over time, penetrated the far reaches of the Amazon as well as across the Andes. Of these are Wycliffe Bible Translators, New Tribes Mission, and Unevangelized Fields Mission (UFM), the latter being the group this account is most concerned with. UFM got its start in 1931 as a break off from Worldwide Evangelization Crusade (WEC). The story of the "Three Freds" in the 1930s introduced most students to the mission society and its quest to open up the Amazon region.[6] By the late 1940s, missionaries under UFM had reached the Wai Wai country of Southern British Guiana and by the mid-1950s Wai Wais started coming to Christ. During this time, one of the UFM missionaries, Neill Hawkins, who had played a prominent role in reaching the Wai Wais, had set his sights on the Yanomami region with plans to open it up to missionary endeavors. In the 1950s, Hawkins traveled to the United States to raise up missionary volunteers to help establish new bases in the region. It was through this effort

---

5. Like the Sanumás, the majority of Maiongongs reside in Venezuela, both at the time under consideration as well as today. In Venezuela, they were known as the Maquiritares. Today, they are generally referred to as the Ye'kuanas, a self-designation, which means "canoe people." The Ye'kuana were former enemies of the Sanumás.

6. For a full account of the story of UFM, one should refer to Homer Dowdy's book, *Speak My Words Unto Them*.

that Don Borgman was recruited along with John Peters and others. The earlier excerpts of Don's journals and letters catalog the initial expeditions into Yanomami country.

One important development was the inspiration and recruitment of young Brazilians to take up the mission work, not only among the Sanumás, but other Yanomami tribes. The UFM missionaries, including Don, felt it was important for the Brazilian church to take ownership of the propagation of the gospel among the Indigenous people of Brazil. This was out of principle but also for the very practical reason of preparing the tribes for the eventuality of the Brazilian government throwing American missionaries out of the country—a very real threat that surfaced from time to time. Through a variety of providences, God brought resolution to these possibilities.

In addition, it would be remiss not to mention those who made it possible for these missionaries to get in and out of such remote places. These people were the pilots of Missionary Aviation Fellowship (MAF). In many cases, their experiences were quite harrowing as they did their work as supporters of the overall operations of the mission. Finally, it is important to note, and Don mentions this many times in his letters, the support of those at home who upheld this work through prayer and financial support. The vast majority of these people are not known and will never be known. Yet, their sacrifices are of equal significance in this story—a story which has been ongoing for the past two thousand years. They are known by God.

The Setting

Much of this story takes place in the area of Northwestern Brazil known as Roraima State.[7] This is a region of vast tropical jungle. Unlike some parts of the Amazon rainforest which are so dense they are practically impenetrable, the forests where the Yanomami live tend to be a bit more open. It should not be assumed, however, that the forests of the region were not dense. From the air, all one can see for hundreds and hundreds of square miles is a carpet of green.

Besides the forest which predominates the region, the rivers and their innumerable tributaries play a major role, not only for the ecosystem, but for the different tribes and villagers who live along them. The rivers and streams are the life source for the people. The area is generally drained by

---

7. Prior to 1962, Roraima State was known as the Territory of Rio Branco, as indicated on the map. Prior to being established as a federative unit in 1988, Roraima was still designated a territory: the Federal Territory of Roraima.

two large rivers, the Rio Branco and the Rio Negro, of which the former is a tributary of the latter. The east flowing Uraricoera and the Mucajaí rivers, which largely parallel each other, are tributaries to the Rio Branco. In the accounts that follow, it is the Uraricoera and Mucajaí rivers, along with their significant tributaries, the Auaris, Parima, and Apiaú rivers that form the setting. All of these waterways are fed by countless small rivers and streams along the way. Eventually, all drain into the Amazon by way of the Rio Negro near the large city of Manaus in north-central Brazil.

One other dominant geographical feature of the region is the Serra Parima. The Serra Parima is a mountain range which separates this area of Northern Brazil from Venezuela. It is part of what geologists refer to as the Guiana Shield. The entire area of the Yanomami could be characterized as highlands since it is situated in the foothills leading up to the Parima Mountains.[8] Don's journal entries contain numerous references to rapids and waterfalls along rivers, many of which had to be portaged around.

The Serra Parima is of significance in this account for several reasons. To begin with, it separates two of the largest river systems of South America: the Amazon River in Brazil, of which various tributaries have already been mentioned, and the Orinoco River of Venezuela. These mountains also form a natural political divide between the two countries of which some Brazilian military interest was focused at the time. Of greater significance for this story is the fact that they divide people groups of the greater area. The Yanomamö people, a tribe of the Yanomami, live mainly in Venezuela with some living on the Brazilian side. Also, the larger portion of the Sanumá people live across the mountain passes in Venezuela as opposed to Brazil, thus making interaction infrequent. It should also be noted that most of the Maiongong (as referred to in this account, but also known as the Ye'kuana or Maquiritare) primarily live in Venezuela.

The map below, based on an early UFM depiction, shows the regions along with specific locations and references relevant to the account. Cropped and enlarged images of the same map appear at various points of the narrative in order to bring greater focus to locations.

---

8. Most of Roraima State is part of the Guiana Highlands.

UFM Works in British Guiana and Brazil (1950s to 1960s)
(based on an unpublished map by Don Borgman)

The Time Period

The time period of the work among the various tribes mentioned in this account is from the mid-1950s onward. Before Don's account and work, missionaries with UFM, starting in the 1930s, began making contact with tribes. As referred to earlier, in 1935 the "Three Freds" made their way up the Amazon to make contact with a tribe known as the Kayapós. They were martyred by them, the people they were trying to reach. This was only four years after UFM established itself in Brazil. Undaunted, more missionaries took up the work.

By the early 1940s, UFM missionary Neill Hawkins and his wife made their way to South America to work with the Macushis who lived in Northern Brazil and into British Guiana, straddling the Rio Takutu. By 1949, Hawkins—through information from the nearby Wapishanas—had heard of a Carib tribe known as the Wai Wais, a group living in Southern British Guiana and over into Brazil. Hawkins and others now concentrated their work among them. In 1955, a significant shaman of the Wai Wais by the name of Elká submitted his life to Christ. The large-scale conversion of the Wai Wais followed.

By the mid-1950s, Hawkins had made his way back to the States to raise a mission team to establish bases in Yanomami country. From the late 1950s to the mid-1960s, the various tribes and subgroups of the Yanomami were contacted and bases established including Mucajaí, Waica, Palimi-U,[9] Surucucu, and finally Auaris. Major players in these expeditions were Neill Hawkins and Bob Hawkins, Claude Leavitt, Rod Lewis, John Peters, and Don Borgman, along with various Wai Wais who agreed to accompany the explorers going into the tribes. It should be noted that this region was far from traditional Wai Wai territory and that the Wai Wais had little in common with these tribes. Their love of Christ and their desire to present the gospel to these unreached people was their chief motivation.

By the mid-1960s, with the tribes having now largely been reached and mission stations established, the earnest work of learning the native language, presenting the gospel, translating and teaching the Bible, as well as countless other aspects of missionary work—medical, dental, educational, hygienic, etc. now began. With the Sanumás, the missionary work was focused on producing the Scriptures in their language. In addition, the effort extended to establishing churches, increasing literacy, and creating schools. The Brazilian government has increasingly been involved in the work over time as well, although of a secular nature.

The Focus

The focus of UFM among the Wai Wais and their missionaries in Brazil and around the world was always to place the Word of God into the hands of

9. Palimi-U was established downriver from Waica Station in the mid-1970s.

Indigenous, non-literate people. This involved learning the language, creating a written language, and then translating the Bible into the native tongue. This endeavor takes years of focused, concentrated effort. Every Bible translator must be a trained linguist. As one will read in regard to Don's efforts over the years, the distractions were innumerable if not insurmountable, and yet the work progressed. Although Don would rely on outside help for further training and objective evaluations, the vast majority of his work was done by himself with the help of Sanumá people who agreed to aid him. In all, it is and was a very tedious task. For many years, Don was the only outsider that knew the language at a level that such translation work could be accomplished.[10] Don was first to produce the Sanumá language in Brazil in written form and the first and only grammar of this Sanumá language. Don was the leading expert in regard to the Sanumá language and also their culture. A couple of anthropologists arrived at Auaris station to study the Sanumá in the late 1960s. Don provided tremendous amounts of information and perspective to them.

Along with getting the Word of God into the hands of the Indigenous people, the gospel was shared: the saving work of Jesus Christ, leading people to repentance, teaching the Word of God in regard to discipling believers, identifying leaders within the group, and ultimately establishing churches under the leadership of the Indigenous Christians.

From the beginning of the work with the various tribes came the secondary, but no less significant work of ministering to the people's physical needs. Among these was medical help—nursing people with malaria and other deadly diseases, basic dental work, and fundamental hygiene, including dealing with prevention of the transmission of diseases. Teaching the people how to deal more effectively with parasites such as burrowing fleas and roundworms was also a focus going hand in hand with hygiene. In order to alleviate the possible outbreak of malaria, which was virulent from time to time, the missionaries would spray the thatched roofs of the huts to help control the malaria-carrying mosquitoes. Eventually, missionary nurses came and established themselves at various bases in the area. Today, the Brazilian government has a medical station to attend to the Sanumás at Auaris station, but it was the missionaries who paved the way with basic medical attention and even providing inoculations. This is not what they

---

10. Don stated that there was a missionary couple working with the Orinoco River Mission who had recently made entrance into the Sanumá territory on the Venezuelan side. Their names were Merrill and Louise Seely. He had met this couple in the States, and they encouraged him to go ahead with plans to work among the Sanumás in Brazil, and that they would communicate and compare notes.

were trained to do, but they had to learn in order to care for the people they had grown to love.

Over time, as the people in the various tribes wanted to learn to read and write, the missionaries taught them and established schools in different villages. Efforts to help with basic economy took place, all of which enhanced the standard of living among these people. One of the chief motivations for the Indigenous people in welcoming the missionaries was because of the opportunity to gain Western trade goods, especially metal utensils, pots and pans, axes, and machetes. This changed everything for the Indigenous people's economy. Today, although certain social patterns remain the same, the material culture of these tribes has gone through tremendous change. The ability to enhance the way of life for these people has been a byproduct of simply introducing Western ways to the culture. Although some missionaries, including Don, questioned whether changing the material culture in such ways was going against the primary principle of presenting the gospel, the conclusion was that change in this way was inevitable as the encroachment of Western civilization continued on these people.[11]

One last area of focus to mention is that the missionaries sought to be friends of these people. Don established deep and abiding friendships with members of the Sanumá tribe as well as some Maiongongs. Chief among these relationships was his friendship with Lourenzo, a Maiongong man who was married to a Sanumá woman. God used that relationship to ultimately bring many to Christ. Beyond this, however, is the sad fact that most Westerners, including the Brazilians, have been anything but kind and caring to the Indigenous peoples. With the encroachment of gold miners to Yanomami country over time, Indigenous people's lives have become of little importance. The interaction between miners and the Yanomami in general has not only been one of tremendous disruption, but tragedy. Although the government has sought to act as a buffer, at times, between the tribes and encroaching Brazilian exploitation of the resources of the region, it is the missionary who has generally been the friend of the Indigenous people.

---

11. In regard to the last point above, a simple illustration perhaps underscores the point of inevitable acculturation, even among indigenous people. The Maiongong or Ye'kuana people lived in very close proximity to the Sanumás at Auaris. In a simple comparison of the two traditional material cultures, there are some ways in which the Maiongong were more advanced. In native language, the Maiongong were sometimes referred to as the "canoe people" since they made excellent canoes and traversed the rivers and streams in this way. When these two tribes first encountered each other, the Sanumá did not know how to make canoes. Over time, however, through ongoing contact with each other, the Sanumá wanted to make canoes as well, so they didn't have to simply travel overland along the trails. They learned how to make them from the Maiongongs.

Introduction

The Significance

The greatest significance of this story is the completion of another chapter in the ongoing work of the Great Commission, inaugurated two thousand years ago by the Lord Jesus Christ. The account of gospel dissemination among the Sanumás and the other tribes is only a small part of the expansion of the church through the ages. The establishment of the church among the Sanumás is testimony that God's work and mission to found his kingdom on earth will not be thwarted.

Secondly, this story highlights the availability of eternal life for a people who were lost. The story of the gospel is one of salvation—salvation from the eternal wrath of God. Those Indigenous people who have, by faith, embraced Jesus Christ, now have this gift of and by grace. Furthermore, these people, including the Sanumás, have been lifted out of a life of degradation and fear. The Yanomami had at earlier times been warlike and threatening to people coming from the outside. Some have concluded that this behavior is simply a manifestation of these people's brutal nature.[12] What has been discovered by many missionaries over time is that these impulses have been rooted in fear of the outside world and the strange people they were encountering, as well as fear of the spirit world which controls their lives. Coming to know Christ has alleviated those fears.

The coming of God's law is gradually lifting these people out of moral degradation. The status of women has been raised. Lying, theft, gossip, spousal abuse, and many other behaviors common to mankind have been increasingly alleviated in the church. Many Indigenous people have said, much to the contrary of anthropologists and others, that they did not like their old way of life, under which they felt oppressed, and that now they feel liberated from those old ways.

Finally, the dedication of the missionaries to their calling over time is a testimony to their faithfulness and fidelity to the gospel work. There were many hardships and tragedies along the way. Much sacrifice took place. Distractions were overwhelming at times to the point that it is an amazement that the Sanumá Scriptures were ever translated and published.

---

12. There has been ongoing controversy in the anthropological world regarding assertions made by Napoleon A. Chagnon in regard to his work among the Yanomamö. This stems from his book entitled, *Yanomamo: The Fierce People*. For one report on this debate, see Tierney, "The Fierce Anthropologist," 50.

Introduction

Organization and Format

The organization of this account is generally laid out chronologically as the letters, journal entries, and newsletters were written. (Some exceptions were made in a few chapters in order to provide continuity of a particular topic. This is particularly the case with Chapter 7.) Editorial narration precedes each major part for the purpose of contextualization. Brief statements of the same sort are interjected at various points for further clarification of timeline and subject matter. All editorial statements are italicized. Each entry of material is in Don's own words unless otherwise specified. In order to keep the chronological approach intact, some entries may appear to be randomly dropped in, however, it is relatively easy to make references to other parts of the account as events and reflections unfold.

One major exception to the above is interactions with the Atroais. The accounts of preliminary attempts to make contact with this tribe are presented as a whole in Chapter 4 with post-1963 contacts, particularly by the Wai Wais, presented in Appendix D. The reason for the appendix entry is because Don's direct efforts to reach the tribe basically ended with his Uatumã River expedition in 1963. Nevertheless, the entries in the appendix are all from Don's journal entries and/or letters as conveyed to the early 1980s.

Along the way, the reader will find various maps and photos relevant to the narrative. All were provided directly by Don unless otherwise credited. Also, all Scripture entries are from the English Standard Version (ESV) of the Bible, unless otherwise stated. And finally, appendixes can be found at the end relating either supportive material or accounts that did not neatly fit into the narrative.

I

Preparation (1949 to 1958)

"I am reminded of your sincere faith, a faith that dwelt first in your grandmother Lois and your mother Eunice and now, I am sure, dwells in you as well. For this reason I remind you to fan into flame the gift of God, which is in you through the laying on of my hands, for God gave us a spirit not of fear but of power and love and self-control." (2 Tim 1:5–7)

Spiritual Seeds Planted at an Early Age

God has raised up his servants throughout the ages to spread the good news of the gospel and to establish and help build his church. Typically, those most effectively used by God have undergone extensive preparation for that purpose. As with Don Borgman, that training often begins early in life. As noted by Don below, seeds of faith, planted at a young age, provide a basis for service later on in life.

Email from Don to editor, August 6, 2020

My heritage was a godly one. The first five years of my life (1931 to 1936) we lived with my maternal grandparents there in Bridgeport, Connecticut. My grandfather was pastor of the church[1] and was instrumental in transforming the church from a liberal Congregational Church into an independent,

---

1. Don's grandfather was the Rev. Charles Haddon Spurgeon MacDowell, and the church was Black Rock Congregational, located in Bridgeport, Connecticut. Years later, Rev. Stan Allaby would pastor the church, and this would be the case for the majority of years that Don and Barb worked with the Sanumás. Black Rock Congregational Church would be the major sending church and supporter for Don and Barb's mission work over the years. (See "Black Rock Congregational Church – 1849–1999.")

evangelical one. My father became a Christian when he was twenty-six and soon after married my mother. Both of them were models of dedicated Christians, both in life and verbal teaching. I remember vividly that when I was nearing six years old my father went through the Wordless Book explaining to me the way of salvation. We knelt by the living room sofa as I received the Lord as my Savior. We had a lively youth group which met on Saturday nights, a group numbering up to 200. Our aim was to reach our peers with the gospel.

Rev. Charles and Sarah MacDowell (Don's maternal grandparents)

Arnold and Winifred M. Borgman (Don's parents)

Preparation (1949 to 1958)

Moody Bible Institute Days

Upon completion of high school, Don determined to pursue a calling in Gospel ministry. He had not decided what that calling might be, but whatever the Lord eventually led him to, he knew that he would need formal training in order to prepare. This decision would lead him to Moody Bible Institute in Chicago in 1949 and then to Wheaton College in 1951. The following relates those years of formal preparation for future ministry.

Email from Don to editor, August 8, 2019

On September 9, 1949, just before my eighteenth birthday, I left Bridgeport, Connecticut for Moody Bible Institute in Chicago, along with my friend Alan Christensen, traveling by train. Already I was thinking of transferring to Wheaton College after Moody, so I enrolled in the General Bible Course and added a Greek course, thinking that this would give me more credits in my transfer. The Greek course was taught by Dr. Kenneth Wuest, who had a genuine interest in the students and who would always start off the class with a "Greek nugget" and a short devotional period. My time at Moody gave me a solid spiritual foundation for the ensuing years of studying and maturing. Beside the Bible classes, there were the many top-notch speakers that inspired us.

There were other areas that filled up my schedule. I managed to get some part time jobs, first in the shipping department at Moody Press and then behind the food counter at a nearby Woolworth store. Also I was quite active in playing basketball on the varsity team and in an intramural league. The school required participation in "practical work assignments" which involved getting off campus and helping out in various youth programs. Of particular interest to me was taking a leadership role in a high school group in Chicago Heights, a good way south of Chicago. In all this I was forced to be bolder in leading groups and also in conversation with individuals with whom I shared the gospel of Christ. At Moody I spent a lot of time practicing cornet, playing solos and being in a trumpet trio that was part of a traveling "gospel team." Also, as the trio dissolved, I was part of a men's vocal quartet which traveled quite a bit.

Maybe one reason there was time for all these activities was that I had no interest in "dating." As far as I remember, I had no particular interest in girls throughout junior high and most of high school.

Letter from Don to his parents, March 21, 1950

We played the last of our intramural games tonight. We won tonight, but lost a couple of tough ones last week, so we ended up in about third. After the game we had a little birthday party for one of the kids on the floor. Most of the day yesterday I was at Montgomery with Dean. It was a real good time. They have some swell kids out there, and I could see the change since the last time I was out there. We didn't have too much time to talk during the day, but we missed the train and had to wait an hour for the next one, so we took a walk and talked, so I was glad for the extra time. You mentioned that you realize that we at school need constant prayer, and it's certainly true. I guess Dean[2] would sort of like to have me come out there and help out. A trumpet trio that travels around every week has one member graduating and would like to have me play with them (there aren't too many good trumpeters around school here). The kid with whom I went last week to the Hi-C club would like to get me into that work and said they needed somebody. Then there's the group that I'm on now as associate group leader. That means probably that I'm supposed to be leader next term. Please pray that I'll make the right decision—rather, that the Lord will lead me to make the right decision. There seems to be advantages for each one. I'd get good experience in playing if I went with the trio, and it would get me to practice more. However, you don't get to make many personal contacts doing this kind of work, and because of this, I'd like to go out to Montgomery although it would mean work. It seems as though I've never had to depend on the Lord for guidance like I have since I've been out here. I guess this is more true as we grow older and get out into the work—full time or not. Well, as I said before, it was good to see Dean and to hear of life at Wheaton.

Email from Don to editor, August 8, 2019

One other significant activity during my Moody days was what I could entitle "Silent Serving." One day, out of the blue, an African student came up to me and asked if I could help him in typing up some letters he had received which he would like to put into a book. I agreed, not realizing how much of my time this would take up. The man's name was Stephen Sitole, a heavy-set man from Southern Rhodesia. He had walked hundreds of miles to get to the coast and get a boat going to America. With much courage and

---

2. Dean was Don's older brother who was at Wheaton College at the time. He led a young people's group in Montgomery, Illinois.

Preparation (1949 to 1958)

determination, he finally got to Moody Bible Institute where he enrolled in the Pastors Course.

During this time he traveled in the South where churches had invited him to give his testimony. Back at Moody he received many letters from his contacts in the South and these were the letters I typed up for him. The time it took can be partially seen by my short mention of him in my letter back home.

Letter Excerpt from Don to his parents, March 26, 1951

I'd only have a short while there, and I don't know how much help I'd be to the young people. If we had meetings, we'd get out of school a little early. But now I'm getting off the subject. There are two main reasons why I feel I should stay here. First of all, I'd like to spend more time with the kids down in Chicago Heights and do a little more with the Hi-C work.

Then another thing—I've probably told you that I'm helping Steve, the fellow from Africa. Right now, I'm helping him type up some letters which he's going to compile and put into a little book for publication. This vacation would be a good time to get a large bulk of that out of the way. I need much wisdom and patience in working with Steve, for he's hard to understand at times, and he's very much misunderstood, too, so I hope I can be of some help to him. This second reason might seem very trivial, but it isn't. Further comments will be appreciated—I'll still be praying about it.

Wheaton College

Following his plans, Don transferred to Wheaton College in 1951, having finished two years of Bible training at Moody.

Email from Don to editor, August 8, 2019

Getting to and from school in the Chicago area was interesting. Sometimes I took the train, but more often I would hitchhike. This was before the days of interstate highways, and the trip would take me more than twenty hours.

For physical activity we had an intramural basketball team called "The Leftovers." We were mostly transfer students and did well in the top league (there were three). Along with basketball, there was tennis. I was able to make the number five spot on the Wheaton tennis team.

There was an opening for a college student to help with the young people at the La Grange Bible Church in La Grange, Illinois. With some fear and trembling I accepted this and would go out there each Sunday, teaching a class in the morning and then leading the youth group meeting at night.

While in Moody, I had been challenged in regard to Bible translation work though seeing a film put out by Wycliffe Bible Translators. It was the story of Marianna Slocum, engaged to be married to Bill Bentley, who was translating for the Tseltal Indians in Mexico and who died six days before their wedding. Marianna declared, "I'll go down and finish the job," which she did. A fact that struck me was that there were more than two thousand language groups in the world that had not even one word of the Scriptures.

Upon entering Wheaton College, I attended the Foreign Missions Fellowship meetings and joined the "East of the Andes Prayer Group." In a letter dated May 15, 1952, I wrote: "Naturally when I hear a missionary speaker—especially from South America—I start thinking about my own future and the place the Lord has for me, and about the preparation I should be getting in view of that place. As you know, I've been interested in translation work, and would like to spend a couple of summers at Wycliffe Translators in Oklahoma. This also would give me ten hours credit here at Wheaton . . . One thing that discourages me from the translating work, especially under the Wycliffe board, is that there wouldn't be much opportunity for other work such as teaching. Wycliffe has gotten into some places that have been closed to other missionaries with the agreement that no evangelistic work would be carried on —just translating."[3]

God proved to me his interest in me as an individual and proved his faithfulness in regard to supplying financial needs. The following entries in a small journal I kept were pretty much one-time happenings, but they stayed in my mindset for years to come.

---

3. Although Don's primary focus among the Yanomami would be translation, it was certainly impossible for him to see the myriad of ways he would minister to these people one day: befriending, sharing the gospel, teaching God's word, administering medical help, improving their standard of living, and the list goes on.

Preparation (1949 to 1958)

Excerpts from Don's journal, October 1953 and February 1955

Wycliffe policy: Do not ask for support

Looking back now, I see the importance of those nights when God moved my heart to seek him—when I lay alone under the stars on the baseball field—there to think God's thoughts and be taught of him through prayer.

"When are you going to begin to trust Me? When are you going to live with regard to the supernatural instead of the natural plane? Can you trust me to supply your needs? Why not put Wycliffe policy into effect now?

October 3, 1953

Little money—not enough for laundry and food for weekend. Check for $11.00 from Buildings & Grounds in late afternoon.

October 19, 1953

After walking to box with 3 cents in our pocket. Check from B & G for $12.00.

October 28, 1953

Ten cents in pocket. Installment of $87.00 due November 1. $104.00 for Dec 1. Check from Dad for $300.00 plus birthday money. "Praise the Lord for his goodness."

February 23, 1955

Was reminded concerning what I had written on previous page. Morning of February 22nd had $3.00, took car down and knew there would be $15.00 bill. (Had prayed definitely right before about financial situation—bill overdue—me in the hole.) That afternoon, at 3:30 p.m., went to box and prayed: "Great is Thy faithfulness. Lord, increase my faith" as I stood waiting for someone who was in front of box. As I opened it, I was surprised to see unexpected money order from insurance company for $7.50.

Next day letter from Dad starting, "It has occurred to me that you may be in very poor financial straits at the present time." Check for $2.00, 50 above first payment.

Foolish in a way when all I had to do at any time was to ask Dad—yet I felt God wanted to show me his faithfulness—and he sure did.

Email from Don to editor, August 8, 2019

Outside of studies and sports, quite a bit of my time was spent with the young people at La Grange Bible Church, and then in my senior year I had the opportunity to help lead a Young Life club in St. Charles, Illinois. The following excerpt from an August 9, 1954 letter summarizes inner struggles I had throughout my Wheaton experience: Spiritual vitality along with all these outside activities. This letter was written just before taking a carload of high school kids out to a Young Life Ranch in Colorado. I praise the Lord for the students who came to a saving faith in Christ as a result of our Young Life club.

Letter from Don to his parents, August 9, 1954

Hube Mitchell of Youth for Christ was speaker in the Wheaton Bible Church last Sunday night. He spoke on Christ—his difference than any other man—and the importance of personal witnessing; and did it in a fresh and vital way. I was encouraged very much to give all I have for the kids the Lord has given us to reach. I don't know why it is that in a meeting our hearts can be so stirred for those on the foreign fields, and even for those at home, but during the week these same hearts of ours are so cold and indifferent to the eternal issues; and yet I guess I do. We lose sight how wonderful Jesus is, the condition of those without him, and get wrapped up in our own activities and plans that won't finally amount to much.

WHEATON GRAD SCHOOL 1954–1957

Email from Don to editor, August 8, 2019

Feeling the need of more theological training, I dismissed the idea of seminary and decided on the Wheaton Graduate School. I already had had many Bible courses at Moody and Wheaton and didn't want to face another three years or more at a seminary.

While my dad helped me so much financially during these years, I tried to help out as much as possible by getting part-time jobs: outside construction during vacation time and school bus driving during the school year. (I was even a taxicab driver for a time!)

As I thought about my future place of service and which mission board to serve under, I learned that there were 180 tribes in Brazil without any translation work being done for them. My choice of mission boards had narrowed down to two: Wycliffe Bible Translators and Unevangelized Fields Mission (UFM). In high school I had heard presentations by three Hawkins brothers at different times. Neill, particularly, impressed me as he told about the work among the Wai Wai Indians in south British Guiana.[4] Now in grad school, I desired very much to have a talk with him, but here I was in Wheaton and he in South America. But I learned that he was presently in the States and getting together with him would be a big factor in my choosing to go with UFM.

Excerpt of letter from Don to parents, date undetermined

I had wanted very much to see Neill Hawkins and talk to him about the work, wanting even to get into Chicago to see him if he were passing through. I didn't know when he'd be out or where he'd be; and I didn't get to write to the mission board to ask them. The Lord arranged things, and Friday I got a letter from Neill saying that he'd been with you[5] and would like to talk with me. He'll be in Wheaton tomorrow.

In regard to the previous, Don relates the following:

Email from Don to editor, August 6, 2020

It was in March of 1955 while I was at graduate school that there was an episode which had a most important bearing on my future. Backing up to my high school years in Connecticut: Our church emphasized foreign missions and had invited various missionaries to speak. Among them was Rader Hawkins, who married a girl from our church. Through him we got to know two of his brothers, Neill and Bob. All of them were working in

---

4. For a full account of the work among the Wai Wais by the Hawkins brothers and UFM, one should read *Christ's Witchdoctor, the Story of Elka* and *Speak My Words Unto Them - A History of UFM International*, both by Homer Dowdy.

5. In reference to his parents, Arnold and Winifred Borgman.

northern Brazil and British Guiana and were members of the Unevangelized Fields Mission (UFM).

Neill, Rader, and Bob Hawkins on a Wai Wai Expedition, late 1940s (Courtesy of Alice Hatch)

Fast forward to 1955: In wondering where I should serve, I thought of Neill Hawkins and how great it would be if I could interview him. But he was in South America (I thought). Imagine my surprise when I received a postcard in the mail–from Neill Hawkins–saying that he was in the States for the purpose of recruiting twenty workers for a new work among an unreached tribe in north Brazil! (He had been speaking at our church in Connecticut and had met my parents, who told him of my desire to be a Bible translator.) In the postcard he asked if he could talk with me as he passed through Wheaton. I was excited as he sat down with me and showed me an aerial survey map that had been made by Jim Truxton of Missionary Aviation Fellowship. (The people of the area they surveyed were later known as Yanomamis.) MAF promised to serve that field if the leadership of UFM could recruit twenty workers.

People and even profs I had questioned regarding Paul's view on celibacy and marriage had given what I considered rather flippant answers, so I decided on this for my thesis topic. This would include the role of women, not only in marriage, but also in the church. Concurrent with this project was my starting a serious relationship with an undergrad girl. As for myself, knew that I definitely did not have the gift of celibacy the Apostle Paul spoke of in 1 Cor 7.

In reference to this young woman, Don wrote the following to his parents:

Letter Excerpt from Don to parents, October 1956

The Lord has brought us together. I love her more as the days go on. You know how uncertain I was for a long period while I was home. I'm glad for her sake and mine that there is none of that now (as of the last part of this summer, and especially when I was with her the first part of September). I thoroughly enjoy each time I am with her, even if it's a short breakfast. In many little ways we just "click" together, but the thing that has really drawn me to her is her devotion to the Lord, and I don't say this lightly. I know she'll be used of the Lord to keep my eyes on him and draw closer to him as the days go on. I guess it just had to take a long time of "re-orientation" for me in these past eighteen months or so. It'll be a great day when I can introduce her to the household. These short sentences have inadequately transmitted how I feel about it all, but maybe that's a sign that I'm in love.

Email from Don to editor, August 6, 2020

I took a year off from school to work as part-time staff with Young Life, living at home in Connecticut and helping out with the high school club in New Canaan where my brother Dean was leader. My thought was to also work on my thesis from there, a project which didn't get too far. So in the fall of 1956 I went back to Wheaton to finish up the thesis and graduate in the spring of 1957. It was during this time that my girlfriend relationship ended.

Letter from Don to parents, March 16, 1957

Dear Dad and Mother,

"But he knoweth the way that I take: when He hath tried me, I shall come forth as gold." (Job 23:10 KJV)

Robert Murray McCheyne wrote a letter to his congregation in which he recounts the experience of Job and his words in 23:8–10 particularly. Over a month ago, I read this letter in the *Memoirs*[6] which was loaned to me. At that time a separation from Nancy seemed inevitable, and these words from Job 23 gave me much encouragement. Because of the prolonged chastening, Job was bewildered, and yet still trusted the Lord. I suppose there is

---

6. From "PASTORAL LETTERS, NO. 3. How God works by Providences" as found in *Memoir and Remains*, Bonar.

no one who understands the working of the Lord in our particular case, and even I don't understand the way that is mine, but he knows, and my eyes and heart are toward him so that I may know the steps I should take right now, and especially that I may have a fuller trust on love for Christ. (Ps 25:15)

Much of the natural sorrow has been experienced already in the months that have preceded this final decision. Even before Christmas, I had serious doubts as to whether you would see Nancy. The leading of the Lord in all of this has been hard to understand. When I first met Nancy, I was not expecting the Lord to bring a girl into my life at that point. For a long time, there was a slight wavering, as you know, wonderings about the type of work I might be called to, and even slight wondering about my love for Nancy. One thing I know, I could never marry a girl I didn't love with all my heart. Last summer I came to the point where I decided it was doubting the Lord not to go ahead. There was a trust that he would take care of us even in difficult primitive work (if that were his place). And that he would certainly cause me to love Nancy with *all* my heart.

As I met Nancy at the end of the summer, and was with her this fall, there was no doubt that I did, and do, love her as a husband should. That love has continued and is in my heart as I write. And this has made the "way" seem very hard to understand. Sometimes I wonder if I didn't grow *too* attached to her and didn't continue to love the Lord as fervently as I should have.

At any rate, my heart has been toward the Lord all the while I've gone with Nancy, and I do love him right now more than ever. As Nancy and I read and prayed and talked last night there was a strange peace that filled both our hearts, knowing that he was leading us in a way that would most bring glory to Christ, in and through our lives.

As to the cause, there just wasn't the mutual peace about going ahead in marriage. I realize this is a most general statement, but at the time perhaps that will be enough explanation. As I mentioned on the phone, this is no spur of the moment decision. I have weighed it carefully and prayerfully for a long time. Since a definite unrest continued, I took this as the Lord's way of blocking plans to be engaged and married. I have no assurance as to the way he will lead our paths and hearts in the future; enough to follow at the present and take the steps he orders right now. He *can* and *will* bring us together if *he* wants, but if this has not been his match, then I am content and joyful to walk with Christ alone, until he brings something else to pass. And then I know it will be still a continuance of walking with Christ, in the fullness of his presence and blessing.

One thing you might be wondering about is whether the subject of my thesis had anything to do with all of this. It didn't. Many will greatly misunderstand our separation as they know the title and content of my thesis, and this fact has been one *little* factor in adding to my great desire not to leave her. But certainly peoples' thoughts and opinions have no place in a matter like this (Prov 29:25). I do realize however that the "time is short," that "the fashion of this world is passing away," and that "our light affliction, which is but for a moment, worketh for us a far more exceeding and eternal weight of glory." All that matters is that we are completely his, completely sold out to the service of Christ, married or single.

"Thou shalt guide me with Thy counsel, and afterward receive me to glory. Whom have I in heaven but Thee? And there is none upon earth that I desire beside Thee." (Ps 73:24–25)

Love you all,
Don

Decisions and Transitions— Early Training Complete

As Don's relationship with Nancy ended, his years at Wheaton ended as well. He now turned his attention to the pursuit of mission work in South America. While enrolled in Wheaton Grad School, Don attended the Summer Institute of Linguistics (SIL) in Norman, Oklahoma. This provided the fundamental training needed to pursue his eventual work as a Bible translator. At his second stint, in 1957, he states that he met several other students who were interested in joining with UFM. Soon after, he applied to that mission board and was accepted. He was now well trained to begin the work ahead. His training for this calling, however, was really just beginning.

2

Further Preparation and Jungle Training (1958 to 1959)

"Therefore, preparing your minds for action, and being sober-minded, set your hope fully on the grace that will be brought to you at the revelation of Jesus Christ." (1 Pet 1:13)

By the end of this time at Wheaton, Don had decided to join with UFM and head to South America to begin mission work as a Bible translator. This decision was a direct result of his conversation with Neill Hawkins. Hawkins served under UFM in South British Guiana working with the Wai Wai tribe. It had been Hawkins, and his brothers, who many years before had inspired Don with stories of working with these people. Neill now had a plan to expand the work of UFM. It was to this plan that Don would answer the call.

Donald M. Borgman

Further Preparation and Jungle Training (1958 to 1959)

Portuguese Learning and Jungle Training

Letter from Don to editor, August 16, 2019

Neill Hawkins, together with a pilot with Missionary Aviation Fellowship (MAF), had made an aerial survey of the area in Brazil west of the town of Boa Vista, an area of many Indian villages living close to the Venezuelan border, with almost no contact with the outside world. Little was known about what language group or groups they belonged to, and Neill's dream was to raise up a team to reach these people. MAF agreed to set up a program to service that area if UFM could recruit twenty couples to support such a program. It was for this purpose that Neill had gone to the States in 1955, and it was his visit to me in Wheaton that had influenced me. As he laid out the aerial survey map with the various villages marked, I was deeply challenged to be part of this team of twenty. (I happened to be number seven.)

Neill purchased land across the river from Lethem, British Guiana, and it was there, in the place called Bonfim, that the mission built a base for Portuguese language learning as well as a base for the MAF plane which was to service the Indian work both in British Guiana and Brazil.

It was to this base that I was headed as I left the States in February of 1958. On the way I stopped over to visit a Wheaton friend, Wayne Bragg, in Puerto Rico. He was a staff member of Inter-Varsity Christian Fellowship, working in the Caribbean area. It was my privilege to attend their Bible study group at night and also to say a few words through an interpreter.

My entry into Brazil was to be through British Guiana, and so on I went to the city of Georgetown where I was met in the middle of the night by UFM worker Claude Leavitt. Rader Hawkins had settled here in the city with the purpose of buying supplies for the Wai Wai missionaries in the southern part of the country. While here he had been instrumental in founding a church and Bible school.

Letter from Don to parents, March 8, 1958

Claude met me at the airport in the wee hours of the morning. It was good to get to know each one of the Leavitts—they're a great family. He is easygoing and much fun, with an ability to keep things and people from getting too serious. He's a practical man from whom I could learn a lot. His wife is sweet and desirous of pleasing the Lord in all things. There are four and a half kids: 3 boys and one girl.

I stayed across the street with a couple who will be going to the interior in June or so. The first night I realized that I would not naturally decide on Georgetown for a permanent home if it were just a matter of living. As soon as I crawled under the mosquito netting, the fifty million (scroungy looking) dogs outside had some sort of a party and barked like crazy. As soon as this outburst subsided, the twenty-five million roosters started to crow (about 3:30 a.m.). Houses are very close together. You never know whether the voices and footsteps are coming from your own house or from the one next door. We must have been eight feet from our neighbors.

But there are plenty of people in the city in need of the gospel. And this factor makes any differences in living conditions seem very unimportant. The people don't stay in hiding. They swarm the streets on foot, donkey cart, and mostly bicycles. The few cars slither in and out with the skill that surpasses a New York taxi driver. Without a doubt, it's worse than any place in America as far as driving is concerned. Driving on the left-hand side of the street helps to confuse for a while.

Email from Don to editor, August 16, 2019

Before moving on to Brazil we had some special meetings at the church, and also I had an interesting couple of days going out with a man from another mission to "Number Two Canal," about fifteen miles away from Georgetown. There was a small colony of "East Indians" living there (Indians from the country of India). We held meetings at night with about forty in attendance and with several making confessions of faith in Christ. On March 25th I wrote: "Had an encouraging little note from an East Indian boy at No. 2 canal. He mentioned that '... the people ... were asking me if I could get you down here to tell them more about Jesus.'"

A British Airways plane took a couple of us down to Lethem and from there we went by Jeep to the banks of the river opposite Bonfim, the river that divided British Guiana from Brazil. Crossing the river by boat I at last arrived at the place where I, along with about twenty others, would begin Portuguese language study.

Along with the team that had been raised up to enter the tribes, there was another important team back in the States who were standing behind me with their prayers. Following are copies of some of the letters sent back to this team, starting in February 1958.

Further Preparation and Jungle Training (1958 to 1959)

Letter from Don to support partners, February 1958

Dear Friends,

Less than two hundred years ago, the enthusiasm and perseverance of William Carey, "the father of modern day missions," aroused an unconcerned church to the need of those in heathen lands. In considering India's thousands without Christ, one of Carey's friends remarked, "There is a wealth of lives to be mined down there, but who will go down to mine it?" Carey turned to the small group and responded, "I will go down, but you must hold the ropes."

Many of you are "holding the ropes" for me as I arrive in South America. It is a great encouragement to remember that some of you have promised to pray for me every day. Many have emphasized the fact that they want to help in any way possible and have already sacrificially done so. In the words of the Apostle Paul, "I thank my God upon every remembrance of you . . . for your fellowship in the gospel." (Phil 1:3–5) It is my prayer that God might cause you to enter into the joy of seeing your prayers answered.

After a trip filled with delays, I met the smiling face (a welcomed sight at 3:00 a.m.) of UFM missionary Claude Leavitt here at the Georgetown airport. Unevangelized Fields Mission is helping to minister to this city's crowded, cosmopolitan population, and it will be my privilege to participate in some of their work here for two weeks. Then will come eight months of Portuguese language study at UFM's base in northern Brazil: Bonfim.

One more tribe recently has been contacted on the Uraricoera River. The accounts of this trip made by two missionaries and two converts from the Wai Wai tribe (who are now themselves missionaries) are thrilling testimonies to God's wonderful protection in the upriver journey and of his provision for a friendly contact with the Waicas. These reports encourage us to look forward to contact with other tribes located farther up this river. Pray that this will be done in God's time and in his way, and that the work among the Waicas will experience his blessing.

Letter from Don's father, Arnold Borgman, to support partners, June 1958[1]

This letter is to enclose one of Don's prayer cards and to bring you up to date concerning his activities and plans.

---

1. There were two extant versions of this letter. Rather than placing one in an appendix, the two were combined a bit. Left out of one of the versions was reference to possible forays into new territories by various UFM missionaries, including Don.

Don left the States in February. (He) spent about a day with a missionary friend in Puerto Rico, and then was met by Claude Leavitt in Georgetown. Some special meetings had been arranged in Georgetown and among some East Indians in a little village. These were real blessings at this village. After about ten days, he flew into Lethem, a small border town where Neill Hawkins met him, and then across the river to Bonfim, Brazil. There his main job has been studying Portuguese—with such incidentals as helping build the airplane hangar. His cornet went along with him, and he says it plays good Portuguese. He also took along a guitar, which he hasn't really mastered, but the boys around there like it.

There was a missionary conference at Bonfim, which gave him the opportunity of meeting some of his fellow laborers in the mission. Don has the opportunity of working with some of the Wapishana Indian boys, who are working at Bonfim as they know English fairly well. Also there are English speaking people over in Lethem.

He and another young missionary, John Peters,[2] are scheduled to go to Kanashen, the village of the Wai Wai people, for training among the Indians.

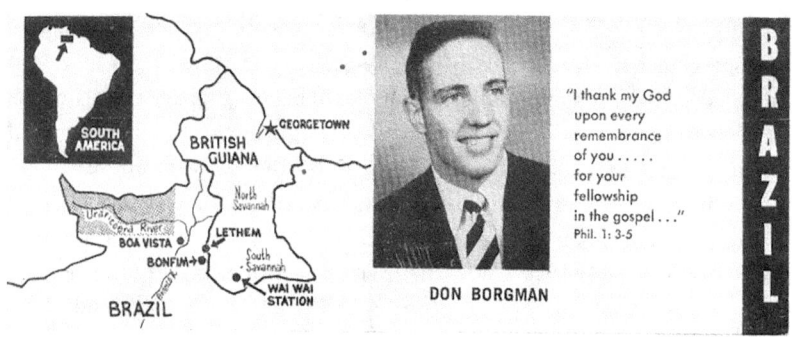

Don Borgman prayer card

---

2. For a personal account of John Peter's call and work among the Yanomami, one should read his book, *Amazon Jungle Life Among the Yanomami*. John, a few years later, would marry Lorraine Neufeld with Neill Hawkins officiating. Don served as John's best man. The two were married in the MAF hangar at Bonfim and would serve for several years at Mucajaí station, working with the Ninam. A few years later, they would return to Canada. Later, John would receive a Ph.D. in sociology and eventually publish a book, *Life Among the Yanomami*. The work is an anthropological study of the Ninam tribe. He has taught for many years on the university level.

Further Preparation and Jungle Training (1958 to 1959)

Don's journal, 1958

These last two weeks Neill has been feeling the force of that verse of Paul's, "For a great door and effectual is opened unto me, and there are many adversaries." (1 Cor 16:9) He has prayed and worked long for this work here in Rio Branco, and the Lord has worked in a marvelous way in opening up doors—in gaining permission to enter the territory after so many years of IPS (Indian Protection Service) ill will toward missionaries entering tribes. Now, the present governor has taken a definite stand against Neill and the work of Bonfim.

The father of one of his strongest political backers is a neighbor here who wanted the property of Bonfim and was much perturbed when Neill beat him to it and has shown animosity since. Finally, the governor understandably is fearful of foreigners getting too much of a foothold in these frontier territories which is as of now unpoliced. "Politics" is the big factor, though. He made a special visit to Bonfim and spoke of many "grave irregularities" present here. One of the big things was having a foreign airplane hangared here. [The mission also needs permission for the use of radio, which is very important.] Neill made that special trip to Boa Vista to work on the problem more. Things are still bad. The governor has ordered "no more expansion until further notice." I believe this means no more expansion of the building program here at Bonfim and know that it means that there is to be no more expansion into the tribes until he gives the okay. This would cut out the expeditions and also the occupation of the Waica territory.

[Neill Hawkins has the main burden of working with these officials. He had, of course, secured all government sanction that should have been necessary, but the local man claims he finds some irregularities. Do pray!]

Journey to Kanashen—Home of the Wai Wais

Following Don and John's initial language training at Bonfim, the two headed to South British Guiana to a place called Kanashen, the home of the Wai Wai people. To get there, they would be guided by a Wapishana boy by the name of Sammy.[3] The following journal entries record that journey as well as their introduction to the Wai Wai people.

---

3. The Wapishanas are an Arawakan speaking tribe that lived south of Lethem in British Guiana and across the Rio Branco in Brazil, south of Boa Vista at the time. Of the various tribes in the region, they were the most acculturated to Western ways. No Protestant mission works were allowed among them at the time in British Guiana, but that has now changed.

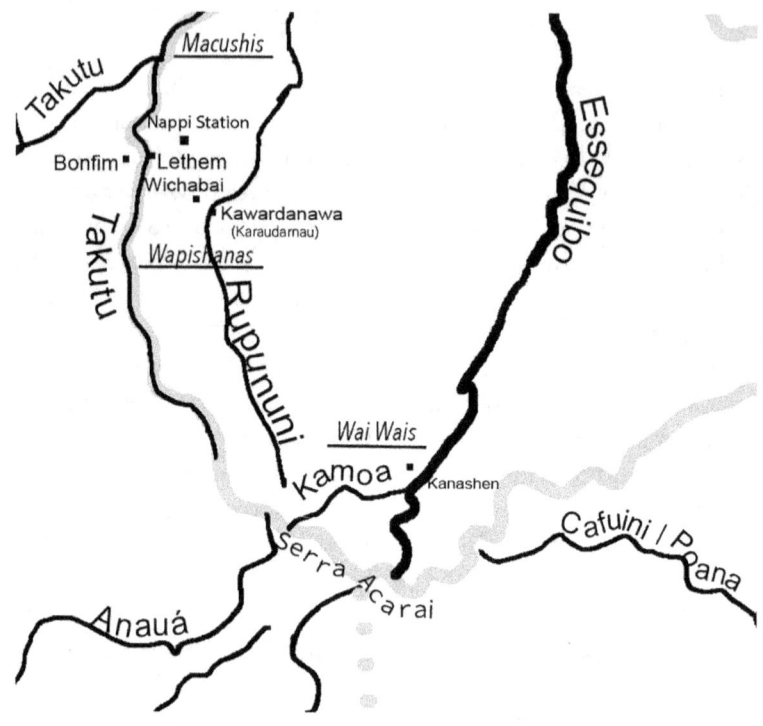

Map of the Lower Rupununi and Essequibo Rivers

Don's journal, 1958

Sammy was keyed up. A seventeen-year-old Wapishana Indian finds it hard to forget his South Savannah home village in which he had spent the first twelve years of his life. He was now anxious to leave the work at Lethem and Bonfim, make the one-hundred-mile trip back to his home, Kawardanawa, and visit once more with his family and old friend. Neill H., director at Bonfim Mission Station, had stalled him off for a month, asking him to wait to go with John and me as guide through the savannahs on our way to Wai Wai country. Here was the plan: My roommate (John Peters) and I were to spend two months in jungle training at the UFM base among the Wai Wai Indians who are located in the jungle on the southern border of British Guiana.

Further Preparation and Jungle Training (1958 to 1959)

Sammy, the Wapishana Indian boy, Don and John's guide

We proposed taking the Jeep as far as Wichabai, and then walking on from there over the road which would be impassable by vehicle. Another factor prompted John and me to encourage the overland trip. Perhaps this would be our only opportunity to see the South Savannah with its seven thousand Wapishanas. Possibly by walking through the villages and visiting with the people, we would know better how to pray for them and maybe even offer suggestions on how best they might be reached. It was decided that we should travel by Jeep to Wichabai, or close to it, then walk the rest of the way to Kawardanawa with Sammy where John and I would be picked up by plane for the remainder of the trip to Kanashen.

Monday, August 11

Today was rainy, and the prospects were dim for leaving, but by 10:30 a.m. the rains had let up, and we were on our way. Low, foreboding clouds hovered overhead, and knee-deep water covered long stretches of the road beneath us, but we churned on, much in the fashion of an amphibian. By noon it had cleared up slightly, and the three of us fellows disembarked with the Hawkins family to enjoy the picnic lunch by the side of the road.

Right after lunch, we hit another creek which had overflowed. But that wasn't all. Blocking our way was a huge tree that had fallen. I thought this was the end of our Jeep ride, but thanks to a machete, we managed to slither around it. Then we hit the deep part of the creek. Neill was just about to turn back, but then decided to give it a try, and we just did make it. Those Jeeps are amazing. It seemed as though the water was up over the motor. We are thankful for the extra ride which took us to a Macushi village where we started walking at 2:30 p.m. We were still twenty miles from Wichabai, but with only feminine aid left, Neill thought it best to turn back at this point, lest he spend the night with Jeep wheels anchored to the bottom of some mud hole.

We started at a fast pace, keeping it up for two hours. This brought us to Mountain Point, where we were glad to sit down, wash our feet, socks, and sneaks (which were mixed with mud, sand, and water, and not to be dry again for the next three days and nights)! The stop at that creek reminded me of Ps 23:2, "He maketh me to lie down in green pastures. He leadeth me beside the still waters ... He restoreth my soul." My body and soul were both restored.

Wanting to hit a shelter at Wichabai for the night, we kept walking hard, and what a walk! Sammy knew a shortcut off the road, which probably saved time but certainly not comfort. We hit thick, muddy swamps. To make matters worse, mosquitoes started gnawing at us as the sun set. The rest of the stretch to Wichabai was a nightmare. I was thirsty, my legs ached, the mosquitoes were driving me crazy, and I wondered why in the world we were doing this. I lost all youthful enthusiasm and thought that it would never again be regained. I had hardly enough gumption to even think, but I did meditate on the verses I had quoted during a testimony Sunday night in the Portuguese service, "Rejoice in the Lord always, in everything give thanks."

At 8:00 p.m., we sat down long enough to eat a candy bar, which was our supper. I was already thirsty, but it was a good excuse to sit down for a minute, and maybe pick up a little energy, too.

At 9:00 p.m., we reached the vacant garage at Wichabai. The Melville house was another quarter of a mile down the road, and after having thrown off our packs, we hobbled over like three hounds who had just come over the Sahara Desert. The first glass of water was just enough to soak up the pores in our mouth.

After reading Phil 1 together, we hung up our jungle hammocks in complete darkness (Sammy had his Wapishana hammock), and we sank into coma. About 1:00 a.m., it started blowing a terrific gale, and it rained the hardest I have ever seen. The noise was terrific, for we were sleeping under aluminum sheet roofing. I felt somewhat rested and, for the first time since walking, had the energy to sing and desire to talk. All three of us had a short conversation on how thankful we were to have hit shelter for the night. Sammy and John also joked about how weird my singing sounded as the rain was abating. Our spirits were up, but my legs—I thought I'd never be able to go on in the morning!

Tuesday, August 12

Read Phil 2 and prayed together, after which we ate some farinha (which is cassava, ground to the consistency of corn mush.) This is made from the cassava root and is the staff of life for those on the savannahs. It is ideal food for travel as it is easy to carry, preserves well, and swells up in the stomach. With the sack of farinha we had put in little chunks of dried beef. And to supplement our diet, we had some cookies and peanut butter.

At 8:00 a.m., we started on our way with legs that could hardly move. We picked up speed and at 10:30 came unexpectedly upon a Wapishana hut. (Sammy usually told us all that was ahead but hadn't mentioned this resting place.) This was the first sign of life that we had seen since Wichabai. We sat down, and a little girl brought us a bowl of drink that looked like muddy water and tasted like I think battery acid would. But it was delicious; we were thirsty.

Arrived 12:45 at the next Wapishana house, just before a heavy rain. I was exhausted. My legs were hurting very badly, and I couldn't even eat some corn that was offered, for the lack of lubrication for swallowing. Could hardly bend down to take off sneaks. They were cooking a special kind of corn mush cake out in the kitchen on a mud bottom stove, and I started to get up to watch but decided that the empty bench in the reception room was more profitable at the time. I never felt so unsociable in my life, but right then, as I lay across the bench, I didn't care too much about sociability, or much else, except to just lie there. Those corn cakes were delicious, especially with some peanut butter spread over them.

By 2:30 we were ready to start again—or as ready as we would ever be. We started off like a freight train, hardly moving at first, but gradually picking up speed. I walked behind the other two and was amazed that I was actually moving and amazed that I felt as good as I did. Thought much about the Wapishanas and about the best way they could be effectively reached.

That afternoon we had to cross three creeks. Each one presented a real project of undressing, tying all our stuff in a plastic bag, swimming across, and reassembling ourselves. Each operation took about one and a half hours. I believe this time in the swiftly moving creeks with their rapids was a tonic to my muscles, for after each one, I felt a little more like going on.

We arrived at the third creek about sundown, and had planned to camp there for the night, but Sammy's optimism figured we might be able to hit the ranch that night. For the next few miles we walked close together and at a fast pace. This time John lagged a little behind as we crossed through swamps with tufts of grass that wrought havoc with our ankles. The next creek was a doozy, wide and swift, and we were all glad to call it quits for the day. There was a big flat rock next to the creek that had been used before for slinging hammocks, and so we picked this spot to build a fire and hang our beds. By the time we had eaten, there was just enough space to put my foot on the rock and jump into my hammock. The rest was water. The water kept rising, but I went to sleep figuring that I'd move only when I felt water. The boys couldn't sleep, and watched the water rise to within four inches of the lower sag in my hammock and within three feet of our supplies. That was the peak, and the next morning we were all on dry ground again.

Wednesday, August 13

Sammy especially was rejoicing greatly, praising the Lord for his goodness to us during the trip. Read Phil 3 together, ate, and crossed creek at 7:30 a.m.

The morning before, my legs felt like they had four charley horses. I never would have thought that we were to make thirty-five miles that day. This morning it was my ankles which were swollen.

At 9:00 a.m., we reached the ranch. And again the Lord timed it just right, for about fifty yards from the house, it started to rain. The first man we met was Mr. Juner, a government ranger whose sons had been with Rader H. in Georgetown. Sr. Avilino was the man in charge of the ranch, and he showed us all Brazilian hospitality. After tea and crackers (the tea was strictly English influence) and a dry change of clothes which he gave us (which weren't soaked), the three of us lay down in his Brazilian hammocks, sang, and reviewed Ps 91:15, a verse that Sammy had learned and liked some time ago: "He shall call upon me and I will answer him. I will be with him in trouble: I will deliver him and honor him."

After a much-welcomed lunch we moved on, crossing three more creeks, and arrived at the Rupununi River and Kawardanawa at 4:00 p.m. Sammy's folks weren't home, which was a letdown for him. Most of the village people were out in their fields for the vacation months when their children could be with them. To reach them, Sammy would have to walk two more hours, so he stayed with us for the night. We bought part of a pig from the store (a five-by-five room run by a woman from up on the coast), and fried that up with some boiled rice to soak up part of the grease.

Further Preparation and Jungle Training (1958 to 1959)

Thursday, August 14

After reading Phil 4, Sammy was off to the fields. John and I got some firewood just before another rainfall (found out later it was the wrong kind of wood for burning well; Sammy and his brother got a big kick out of this.) By the time we finished fixing the fire, cooking, and eating, it was 10:00 a.m. Spent the rest of the morning reading Jas 1, writing, and taking a few minutes out to talk with two little girls who appeared in the door. They must have been about 12 and 14 years old. Tarsillia was the daughter of the schoolteacher, and was very kind to us, wanting to know all about our visit.

After a nap in the afternoon, I was sitting at the table writing, when Tarsillia again appeared in the doorway, this time with a loaf of fresh, hot bread in her hands. I think it was one of the best presents I have ever received. She seemed thrilled that I was so appreciative. May we be always eager to present the Bread of Life to those who are hungry and are starving their souls with the meat that perishes.

By nightfall, Sammy had returned with his 15-year-old sister and little brother, who took good care of us for the next few meals. We had a great time in the evening playing "Battleship" together and reading Luke 11.

Friday, August 15

Had a banquet of oatmeal, doughnuts (fried Wapishana style), corn, and melon. Spent most of the morning sewing up my pants, washing clothes, and shaving. That time at the creek was worth a million dollars. In the afternoon, for the first time in three days, I put on clean, dry clothes, and had the same feeling as a young man who steps out with a new suit. Because the plane hadn't come for us the afternoon before, we didn't expect it now till Monday, but to play it safe we thought it best to visit the teacher's house, thank his wife for the bread, and be ready to go. Sure enough, just as we were thanking her, the plane came, and we went out of that house like missiles leaving Canaveral!

After a walk like we had had, that plane was a dream come true. Before we had time to realize it, we were soaring past the savannahs, and over jungle territory. As we landed at Kanashen, it seemed as if there were a huge green wall on either side of us, and that we were lighting upon another planet. Even though I had seen many pictures of the Wai Wais, there still was a feeling of unreality as I peered out the window and saw in turn one hundred peering eyes of those who never ceased to marvel at the huge bird from another world with its strange traveling companions. The missionaries weren't as fleet-footed as the Wai Wais, and for five long minutes we might as well have been deaf and dumb, for we were alone among a people with whom we could communicate only with a smile.

That night at supper, we were surrounded by Indians. There were so many of them that I couldn't help but think of Bible conference days, and the crowd that would press in at the door just five minutes before chow call. And to a certain degree it was to be like this during our stay at Kanashen. The presence of Indians—everywhere and at all times—is something the missionary must not only get used to, but also enjoy. "Enjoy," I can hear some older missionaries say, "just wait till you've been on a station for a few years." As we discussed this around the table, Bob had some good advice for us, and advocated making a waist-high partition in the kitchen, giving elbow room for the one cooking, and yet not keeping the Indians completely away. Also this added contact with the Indians who had visited had proven invaluable for him in picking up the language. The main thing is to welcome the Indians in our own heart and mind. And it isn't only in Indian work that missionaries face this. How many mornings back there in Bonfim I would be rushing through to finish studying a "grupo" when a little fellow would come into the room wanting to talk. The natural tendency is to feel disturbed because of the "interruption." But especially when learning the language, it seems to me that we must put time visiting with the people right on the top of the list of importance.

Saturday, August 16

Morning was spent with Leonard Harris, director of the British branch of UFM. Profitable time discussing Indian work south of the Amazon (the region he had worked in and had just visited), and the future plans for the work there. Also we discussed the problems here in Kanashen, the matter of clothing especially.

Many of the Indians were hanging around in the afternoon and trading at the store. They asked us to play the horn and crowded around. It was a joy to be able to communicate to them in this way, for although I didn't know the words of their hymns, the tunes were based on English hymns. There is a real advantage in using English hymn tunes, modified for the different tribal group, for it gives a bond of fellowship for newcomers which would be lost otherwise.

Sunday, August 17

Each village meets for its own Sunday morning service, then all come together here at Kanashen for the afternoon service. The Wai Wais take charge of the Sunday meetings, with the missionaries leading and teaching in the Wednesday believer's meetings.

Wai Wai leaders (from left to right): Klemtu, Kirifaká, Elká, Mawashá, and Yakutá

That first Sunday morning I attended the meeting in a Wai Wai constructed church building. One of the elders gave a missionary challenge. He mentioned that it was hard to leave wife and children and hard to cross the many rapids in the rivers. And well he knew this, for he had already been on two four-month missionary trips to other tribes. He announced that the following Wednesday would be the time when the men would be given the opportunity to volunteer for three missionary trips which would be in operation soon. Also, he encouraged the others to bring food and trade goods for these trips.

It was my privilege in the afternoon to witness the first Wai Wai baptismal service. Bob and Claude baptized the four elders, and they in turn baptized the rest, each elder questioning a candidate. It was a thrill to see Elká, the present chief, baptizing the old chief, both of whom had been shamans. It was heartwarming to see Mawashá and Kirifaká baptizing their wives. There were twenty-one men and five women who were baptized that afternoon.

First Wai Wai Baptism Service (from left to right): Bob Hawkins, Elká, Kirifaká, and Claude Leavitt (Courtesy of Claudia Glover)

That night around the table, Mr. Harris told of the hazardous type of Indian work in which he had been engaged. We all realized that advance to the Maracanãs, and the tribes on the Anauá River might be fraught with dangers, as both these tribes are reportedly unfriendly. We heard from Mr. Harris a firsthand account of the martyrdom of the "Three Freds" (with UFM in 1935), and of other lives which barely escaped the arrow. May God give us supernatural wisdom and courage as we move ahead.

Monday, August 18

Wash day for some, but house-building day for us. There were Wai Wais to help us in gathering bush-rope, poles, and palm leaves. With bark strapped around our heads, we were able to drag six or more branches of palm out through the jungle to the site of our framework. From a monkey's viewpoint, we must have looked like giant ants, carrying prodigious bits of leaves along the path. The only tools we had for construction were machetes. The Wai Wais helped us considerably in showing us the tricks of the trade. They sure were an amiable bunch. What a contrast to the construction gangs back home in the States: Work going along smoothly, nobody getting ulcers, and nobody yelling when something went wrong.

The next day all was complete with table, benches, and all. Jungle hammocks provided mighty comfortable sleeping. The only things that seemed

Further Preparation and Jungle Training (1958 to 1959)

strange were sleeping under heavy wool blankets; the nights are cold here, although the days hit in the 90 degrees. Wai Wais keep a fire going beneath them all night in their houses, but John and I decided a blanket would be easier.

Wednesday, August 20

Observed reading and translating sessions.

Thursday, August 21

Split some heartwood for uprights in preparation for new station house.

Friday, August 22

Helped the Wai Wai men cut a field. First the underbrush gets slashed, then the little trees are cut halfway through. After about eighteen of these little ones are cut, the big tree is worked on, and as it falls, all the rest comes with it. After about six weeks of drying, the field is burned.

Sunday, August 24

Sunday afternoon, Elká told the story of Shadrach, Meshach and Abednego in a very graphic manner, giving the application of not fearing when the men go off on missionary trips, for Jesus will be in the midst of them. Mawashá then spoke regarding the three trips and the goods which the people had brought into the church that afternoon. The offering must have been well-pleasing in the sight of the Lord. Cassava bread was piled high; knives, scissors, beads, and other trade goods were lined up. The people had given sacrificially. Mawashá then exhorted the men to live lives of purity while the other men were away on the trips.

Formerly, as I had read through Deuteronomy, I had compared the conquest of Canaan to the appropriation of the land of rest that God has for those who believe and obey him. There is a land of promise, a place of victory in the Christian life which many Christians lose because of disobedience and lack of trust. Even during this short time on the foreign field, I have received letters which have made my heart sad for those who have trusted Christ for their salvation, and yet who have not "Wholly followed the Lord." What lives of sadness, what family mix-ups, and what frustration comes from failing to enter that promised land in our spiritual experience.

But today as I was reading through Deuteronomy, I couldn't help but compare possessing the land to "possessing the tribes." As soon as I had landed in Kanashen, I was met with the usual enthusiasm of Claude Leavitt who told me of plans to reach out to new areas to the south of here. One area was to the southeast, with tribes reported to be on the Trombetas River. At first Wai Wais would go alone to make contact. Another area was to the southwest in the region of the Anauá and Jauaperi Rivers. It was this latter region especially that caught my attention and interest, for I had had a special interest in this area ever since I had first heard about it from Neill. The third area was to the south, where a group of Wai Wais was to go within a week.

It was now that I saw the Lord's leading in a clearer light. Back in April at the annual field conference at Bonfim I had been confused. Another missionary was keyed up about an expedition up to the Maiongong country, in the extreme northwest corner of the Rio Branco territory. This was a big territory with many Indians, counting those over the border in Venezuela, and numbering in the thousands. Naturally speaking, this would be an ideal setup: An expedition with a missionary from whom I could learn a lot and then settlement in among such a numerous people. But my heart was uneasy. I had heard of another mission working in the more civilized section of the same tribe over on the Venezuela side, and couldn't stand the thought of overlap, when manpower seems to be so short in reaching the tribes. Allocations were soon to be made by the Field Council, and they had called me in, telling me of the plans for that region up to the northwest, and I gave agreement to go. Yet there was no peace in my heart. That night down by the river I spent a long time thinking and praying. My natural disposition wanted to "get going" and here was the opportunity. Besides this, the Field Council had thought it best to move in. I had already agreed to go. But still there was not peace, and I knew I must "let the peace of God rule." The next morning I got alone again and thought of Prov 29:25: "The fear of man bringeth a snare, but whoso putteth his trust in the Lord shall be safe." It was a hard thing to do, but I called Neill aside and told him that I did not feel right about the expedition. Subsequent events confirmed the indication that we should not push ahead to Maiongong country this fall.

Thus an "amen" sounded within me when I heard that Bob and Claude had been thinking seriously of the Anauá sector. But wherever God's place is for me, I believe that right now he wants me to have an enlarged vision for all the unreached tribes and to pray for a firm foothold of the Gospel among them. For our own mission, I pray that we might never hold back, but ever reach outward, thinking and praying "big," attempting great things for him, and expecting great things from him.

God's promise and warning in Deuteronomy are very appropriate for such a time and circumstance as this. He wants us to "possess the tribes" for his glory. In Deut 7, we see four attributes which should characterize the life and attitude of the conqueror:

Purity

"When the Lord thy God shall bring thee into the land whither thou goest to possess it . . . thou shalt smite them, and utterly destroy them . . . Neither shalt thou make marriages with them . . . ye shall destroy their altars and break down their images . . . For thou art an holy people unto the Lord thy God: The Lord thy God hath chosen thee to be a special people unto Himself." (Deut 7:1–6 KJV)

There is to be no compromise with the world, with that which pertains to the enemy, Satan. There must be hatred of sin, and an abhorrence of evil. The tendency of the day is to gloss over sin. Sin is exposed or even exonerated in anthropological circles. But even though sin is so open and common, even though we can see "reason" for sin (with our natural understanding), there must never come into our hearts the spiritual anesthetic of understanding sin to the point of excusing it. In our preaching to the people we must come out openly against it. Bob feels that this kind of preaching was an important factor in the success of their work in the early days among the Wai Wais. Although he was accused of not preaching the grace that is in Christ, he felt strongly that there can be no appreciation of grace without a realization of sin first.

Secondly, there must not be any relaxation in the battle against sin in our own lives. After going into a tribe, and after God brings victory, there might be the tendency to let down, spiritually. There might be the love and desire for comfortable living once again. This very desire might lead us to spend much time on ourselves and forget the people to whom God has sent us. There might come too, a loosening of the "loins of our minds," which, in the period of reaching out to the new tribes, had been kept girded.

We hear sad stories of great men who compromised later in life and who ended with much less a powerful testimony than when they were younger in years. We have two outstanding examples of this in the Biblical characters of Saul and Solomon.

Praise

"The Lord did not set His love upon you, nor choose you, because ye were more in number than any people . . . But because the Lord loved you, and because He would keep the oath which He had sworn unto your fathers, hath the Lord brought you out with a mighty hand." (Deut 7:7–8 KJV)

Three reasons are given for God's allowing Israel to conquer the land of Canaan. These three facts should cause ceaseless praise to flow from our hearts to the Lord.

1. One is found in Deut 9:4, "Speak not thou in thine heart after that the Lord thy God hath cast them out from before thee, saying, 'For my righteousness the Lord hath brought me in to possess the land; but for the wickedness of these nations the Lord doth drive them out from before thee.'" In a region such as the Anauá River, Satan has the ruling hand. God is jealous, righteous, and will have his power and holiness and love to be realized in such a region. He will take a servant who is unworthy, send him out to such a region, that the righteousness in and through Jesus Christ might be made manifest. Remembering the hymn, "My hope is built on nothing less than Jesus' blood and righteousness. I dare not trust the sweetest frame, but wholly lean on Jesus' name."

2. Consider Deut 7:8, "But because the Lord loved you . . . " Why had God chosen me and not someone else? How could He ever be so patient with me? I don't know, but my questioning ceases as I read these words, "because the Lord loved you."

3. Consider Deut 7:7–8, ". . . and because He would keep the oath which He had sworn unto your fathers." (See also Deut 9:5b.) We sons and daughters will probably never know nor start to know all that has been wrought on our behalf because of the dedication and prayers of a godly mother and father. This is a third thought which should humble us and move us to praise the Lord. Before I was ever born, I was dedicated to the Lord and his service; and through the years this initial dedication has been followed through with earnest prayer on my behalf. Many times when my thoughts were far from God-ward, strangely the Holy Spirit would put in my heart a restlessness, and during many of these times, I was aware that someone must have been praying for me. Praise the Lord for the volume of prayer going up from family and friends. The Lord will perform his word.

Possessiveness

"If thou shalt say in thine heart, these nations are more than I; how can I dispossess them? Thou shalt not be afraid of them... Thou shalt not be affrighted at them, for the Lord thy God is among you, a mighty God, and terrible." (Deut 7:16-27 KJV)

One of the men who has most impressed me with the importance of attempting great things for God and expecting great things from God has been Dawson Trotman. Billy Graham has said of him, "Dawson was a man of vision. When our God is small, the world looks big; but when our God is big, the world looks small. And Dawson saw the world as conquerable for Christ. No project was too big and no undertaking too great to tackle, if he felt that God was in it . . . his God was big and the world was little."

Before me right now is a printed message of Dawson's—a message which reminds me of the summer when it was my privilege to take some of the Young Life Camp work crew over to Glen Eyre to hear Dawson speak. This was the summer before he drowned, and those on the staff have said that he never spoke with more power than that summer. Constantly he exhorted and illustrated from his own experience, that we should call upon God and that we might see great and mighty things accomplished for his glory. In this printed message, after enumerating some of the things upon which the church erroneously places great importance, he states what he believes to be the great "need of the hour." Here it is: "Maybe I shall call it the *answer* to the need of the hour. I believe it is an array of soldiers, dedicated to Jesus Christ, who believe not only that He is God, but that He can fulfill every promise He has ever made, and that there isn't anything too hard for him. It is the only way we can accomplish the thing that is on His heart . . . getting the Gospel to every creature."

Patience

"And the Lord thy God will put out those nations before thee by little and little: thou mayest not consume them at once, lest the beasts of the field increase upon thee." (Deut 7:22 KJV)

In our spiritual growth, God usually does not give us more light than we can assimilate. As we go on, we see more clearly his will and plan. Deeper truths dawn upon us as day by day we walk in the light of his Word. And might it now be so in possessing the tribes? What are tagged as "delays" by us might very well be his perfect strategy, so that we might possess well the land which He has already given. We might be directed to pray for big things, and yet see the answer being performed "little by little." May the Lord give us patience in understanding his timing.

Trail Cutting with the Wai Wais

After some time among the Wai Wais, Don and John along with several others participated in two trail cutting expeditions. These were led by Wai Wai tribal members whose express purpose was to reach formerly uncontacted tribes with the gospel. Such experiences would provide invaluable learning opportunities for both of the new missionaries on the field, particularly in regard to jungle survival and Indigenous people's ways. The destinations of these expeditions were the Cafuini River which lay to the south of Wai Wai territory and the Anauá River which lay to the west. Both were across the border into Brazil.

Cafuini River Expedition, Don's Journal, 1958

Monday, August 25

Trail-Cutting Trip to Cafuini River.[4] Started in the morning by dug-out canoe with Claude, John, and four Wai Wais (Kafiena, Wanawa, Yakutá, and Klemtu). There was a two-fold purpose for this trip: 1) To cut a trail to the Cafuini so that soon after, a group of Wai Wais could travel down this river to the Trombetas River and contact another Carib tribe of Indians. 2) To provide a valuable chapter in John's and my jungle training period. We would learn many survival techniques from those who had lived off the forest all their lives. The only food we took was cassava bread. This is made from the cassava root which is grated and squeezed. The pulp is then sifted and baked in disc-shaped cakes which are cardboard thin (and about as tasteless). One of the men took along a cake of starch, and we missionaries splurged by taking a couple of cups of powdered milk. Aside from this delicacy, we were going strictly Wai Wai style. We had plenty of shot for game and expected that opening up a new trail would offer us plenty of meat. Traveled downstream about four miles, then up Onoro Creek another three.

About the middle of the afternoon we approached a swamp where we met a herd of wild bush hogs. The Indians stopped short, loaded their guns,

---

4. The Cafuini River, which is in Brazil, flows to the east and is a tributary to the Poana which flows into the Trombetas and then the Amazon. These rivers are in Para State. In a letter to friends in May 1963, Don relates that one reason why the Wai Wais were pressing toward the Cafuini was to make contact with a Carib speaking tribe, the Tunayana, which, despite failed initial attempts, they eventually accomplished.

and took off. If I had had a motion picture camera, I could have taken a picture that would have duplicated scenes of the American-Indian War days. One Indian would stop to shoot, and the others would dart on and soon disappear through the jungle. They picked off seven and immediately set to work weaving palm "knapsacks." Special trees were located which rendered bark which was suitable for straps. Three of the Wai Wais loaded up with two pigs each over their backs and returned to their villages. I helped load up one of the men and estimated that the pack weighed at least 125 lbs.

John and I took turns carrying the other pig and found that the Wai Wai method of a strap around the head was the best one. That one pig gained weight as we climbed one hill after another, and we wondered how the other Wai Wais could ever make it back to their villages before sundown.

Kafiena was a hero for the next couple days. He's the one who remained with us, led the way, and brought us to a shelter which he had made previously. Upon arrival, we were all in—except Kafiena, who proceeded immediately to get firewood, make a fire, and then prepare the pig. He sweated like a fireman aboard ship as he hustled to singe the hair off the hog and then scrape it off. John and I had only enough energy to sit and watch him, but I did muster up enough strength to hold part of the pig as he cut it up and cleaned it. Probably a year ago this would have turned my stomach, watching and smelling our future meal. I washed each piece, put it into the pot to boil, and then sat down to wait for chow call. Kafiena squatted and started singing all the songs he knew, seemingly with no loss of energy at all. We laughed out loud as he enthusiastically asked for one chorus after another. And as we sat around the fire, I was really thankful when I looked over at this young Wai Wai. Here was an Indian who had been formerly learning all there was to know about shamanism in preparation to take his position as a shaman. Like so many other Wai Wais, his life had been completely transformed, and now after singing, he was asking all about the tribes that lay "on the outside." The Holy Spirit had put it into his heart to reach them with the Gospel, and at this moment I realized that in so many ways the Wai Wais were in a much better position to do this than we missionaries.

After supper and a time of prayer with Kafiena, Claude joined John and me for a time of prayer in which our hearts were united for the unreached tribes.

The shelter was small. All of the temporary shelters which we built on the trip were triangular in shape with slanted, palm leaf roofs. A fire right in the middle of the shelter kept us all warm, as long as those in the bottom "bunks" kept it going. We all slept in Wai Wai hammocks, which are made of string tied together in fishnet style. I thought sure I'd fall through the holes if I spread it too much, and as I stretched out as much as the hammock would allow, I felt like a tightrope walker who had decided to lie down for a quick nap out in the middle of the rope. But we all slept well.

Tuesday, August 26

As I woke up, Kafiena was praying aloud. Each morning we had a time of private Bible reading and prayer before breakfast. The menu this morning was the same as the night before—bush hog and cassava bread.

That morning we climbed a high mountain in order to see the country but could only see back to Kanashen. Another part of the mountain blocked our view to the southeast, but we decided to return and meet the other Wai Wais who would soon be coming along the trail. At the foot, we did meet them, sat down and had a banana lunch and moved on, spending the afternoon climbing and descending the highest part of the mountain which had blocked our view in the morning. Previously, the Wai Wais had made a trail only as far as to the top of this mountain, and from now on we were to hit all new territory. We climbed a tree at the top, took a good look at the lay of the land to the southeast, took our bearing with compass, and continued on. Going down was almost worse than coming up. Huge, slippery rocks made going slow and hazardous as there was nothing to grab but some rotten pieces of wood. During the descent, I thought of the words of "The Ninety and Nine," ". . . and although the road be rough and steep, I go to the desert to find my sheep."[5]

Finally we leveled off, thankful for no sprains or broken bones. Soon we set up camp for the night, and we there learned how to construct one of those triangular shelters. Bush hog and cassava bread satisfied our appetites.

I was on the top berth that night and right in line with the smoke. Thought I'd have lung cancer for sure, but too tired to do much but wrap my head in a towel and drift off to sleep.

Wednesday, August 27

Bush hog and cassava bread for breakfast. At noon we found a Brazil nut tree and had a few for lunch. Prospects were good for supper, for one of the boys shot two spider monkeys.

In the afternoon we spent most of our time hacking our way through a thick stretch of bamboo. Our only consolation was a jungle milkshake (coined by Claude). We cut off sections of bamboo and inside was cool,

---

5. From the hymn by Elizabeth C. Clephane, 1868.

clear water. With such a stretch of bamboo, we thought maybe we'd hit the river that afternoon, but we were proven to be slightly optimistic.

Another creek, another shelter, another fire or two, some more cassava bread, and some more meat, but this time monkey. The part which wasn't boiled for supper was put on a little rack over the fire to roast all night. My hammock was about the same level as this rack and the upper half of a monkey was reclining in the same position as I was, with an arm stretched out ready to grab me if I should start to fall out of the hammock in the middle of the night!

Thursday, August 28

Breakfast: Monkey meat and cassava bread. After a Bible lesson with Wai Wais, Claude decided to climb one more hill and climb a tree. If we saw the river, we'd go on; if not, we'd get hammocks and supplies which for the time we would leave at the shelter. Wanawa climbed trees like a monkey, and he gained the position of official tree climber for the rest of the trip. He could see only another hill. We moved on; he climbed another tree but gave the same report. Kept going like that till noon at which point John and two Indians returned back to camp, and then on to Kanashen. Claude, Yakutá, Wanawa, and I kept going, traveling light, but hitting heavy hills. I was glad for a light load—tee shirt, shorts and a machete. As we climbed each hill, we thought it would be the last. What a disheartening sight to reach the crest, start descending, and see another high hill ahead. The position of the sun warned us that the next mountain had to be the last, at least for that day. After this one, we started walking on level ground. As Flo told us later, back at Kanashen right at that time, as we were hacking our way through the vines of that flat land, they were praying that if we had not found the Cafuini yet, that we might find it before dark.

We reached the Cafuini just as the sun was going down. There's not a long period of twilight in the jungle, so we had to move fast. The Wai Wais rushed off to hunt. Claude and I sat down and had a short praise service then got together materials for a shelter and gathered firewood. We heard the guns go off in the distance and thanked the Lord that we'd have some meat.

I wasn't hungry, even though I hadn't eaten since breakfast (we never stopped at noon). We had traveled hard all day, and I was more tired than hungry. Munched on a small piece of cassava bread. Then mustered together all my strength to reach over, get a few leaves to cover the dirt, and then lie down close to the fire.

About midnight I woke up surprisingly refreshed, but cold. The others were beat too and were sleeping soundly. Usually one of the Wai Wais would wake up and stir up the fire from time to time, but tonight even they were out of this world. I kept the fire going the rest of the night and profited by this time in talking to the Lord and thinking through some of the things I had been reading in James. Especially did the phrase "faith without works is dead" take my attention. Besides its primary meaning and application, I thought of how little we really "believe" what God has said in his Word. How can we say we have faith in the power of prayer, and yet spend so little time in intercession? How can we say we believe in hell, and yet have so little concern for the souls of men? Those truths which are written down in the doctrine books we've read need to be transferred from the page to our head, there to be re-thought; and from the head to the heart, there to be planted for the purpose of bearing fruit.

Because of the fact that darkness had settled in upon us quickly, we had not taken the time to gather much firewood. About 3:30 a.m. our fuel ran out, and although I hated the thought of it, I got up and felt my way through the darkness to a place where I thought I had seen a nice dead limb the afternoon before. If there happened to be an owl nearby, I'm sure he died laughing when he saw me climbing that tree, trying to balance myself hanging on all fours, upside down. But the mission was accomplished.

One of the weirdest sounds in the jungle at night is that of the red holler monkey. We had heard them just about every night on the trip, but tonight they were especially close. It's a sound that goes beyond description, but the closet I can come is to label it as a cross between an air-raid siren and a hurricane. The first night of the trip, Claude had said, "If you wake up during the night and think the jungle is walking out on you, it's the red holler monkey."

Friday, August 29

Ate quite a bit of marudi (curassow) bird for breakfast. We went south for a while to see if the river made a turn farther ahead. Supplemented our diet with some palm cabbage which we cut along the way. After a flat stretch and one hill, we turned back and steamed up and down the twenty-five big hills which lay between us and the next shelter. At the bottom of each hill was a cool creek, and I'm afraid I broke all training rules by drinking too much during these time outs. With a stomach full of water and a steep hill to climb right ahead each time, I felt a little worse for it by the time we hit camp that night. My stomach wasn't up to another meal of meat, so I feasted on some powdered milk which John had left in this shelter, dove into my hammock just before sundown, read an article in "Prairie Overcomer," and slept soundly till daybreak. I had to laugh when I read a statement in that article by a well-known missionary leader. Here I was looking up past the little roof of our lean-to, and out into virgin jungle, thinking over what I had just read, that "the day of the grass hut on the edge of the jungle are past."

Saturday, August 30

The other fellows had left plenty of monkey meat for us, so we filled up on this before setting out. Claude got thinking about his wife's cooking that morning and put his legs into higher gear. We had packs over our heads now, but the hills leveled out some. As we tramped through the bamboo swamp where we had spent so much time hacking, I had the same feeling I did when I traveled over the Connecticut Turnpike for the first time.

We hit the next shelter by noon and pressed on. The other crew were to have cut a new trail around the bad mountain but met with little success, so we spent the afternoon climbing back over the rocks.

Slept at the first shelter we had come to at the beginning. By this time, meat had lost all its appeal to me. I thought of the children of Israel and knew a little better how they must have felt when they got sick of the quail. The idea of being a vegetarian didn't strike me as a bad idea right then. Another item Claude and I really missed was sugar. It was a real treat to go down to the creek and swish some Colgate toothpaste around in our mouths. It was the only thing sweet we had tasted since Monday morning. The other treat came by surprise that night. One of the men left a handful of starch at this camp. He gave some to me. I wrapped it up in a leaf and baked it. Right then it tasted better than any doughnut I had ever had. I wondered then how anybody could ever complain about food. I thought back to a student assembly in college in which a fellow had complained about the starchy diet and ended by asking resentfully, "Why don't they just give us a box of starch as we enter the dining hall?" I grinned as I realized that I was drooling over a hunk of baked starch—the same stuff they use to stiffen clothes with up in Georgetown!

Claude and I talked a long time that night regarding the future of the work in this and surrounding areas. As I lay awake a long time that night, sometimes staring into the fire, sometimes gazing out at the moonlight that was filtering down through the mass of flora, I told the Lord how thankful I was to be part of such an advance into enemy territory for his glory.

Sunday, August 31

Very early start. Some hard but enjoyable walking, knowing that the end was near. Claude kept praising the Lord over and over for having hit the Cafuini—and for a soon return to his family. As we hit the level stretches, I thought of the folks back home who were in a church service now. The environments were quite different, and the distance very great, but I had a special sense of closeness and "sameness" through the fellowship and prayer.

One cassava field, and then the canoe. I pranced along those felled trees just like a Wai Wai. And I guess I got to thinking too much about this and was humbled sufficiently as I slipped on a charred limb and found myself six feet under—sprawled out on the ground floor with pack resting right on top of my head.

Reached Kanashen at noon. Poor Barbara said she had never seen Claude look so awful; he had lost 20 lbs. I had lost a few myself. One week back at Kanashen rectified this, however.

Monday, September 1

Class in medicine was interrupted by the news of a new arrival into the Wai Wai tribe. We went through the village to the edge of the woods, where there was a group of women and children looking and jabbering. Past them we saw the recent arrival, only a few minutes old, lying on two broad leaves on the ground. The other was sitting on a small log, waiting for the afterbirth. Flo cleaned out the baby's mouth and nose and later tied the cord.

As Flo handed the baby to the mother's husband, (who was not the baby's father), he queried, "Shall I love it as my own?" The many family mix-ups make one's heart sad. Even though recently many have turned to Christ, so that there are very few who are not Christians in the tribe, still there remain the scars of past life.

Further Preparation and Jungle Training (1958 to 1959)

Elká and Florence Reidle at Kanashen (Courtesy of Claudia Glover)

September 2–14

Worked on phonemic statement for the Wai Wai language, and had classes in medicine, motors (with much practice on the outboard, trying to get it to work for the next trip), tropical gardening, dealing with Indians (payment for work, trading, etc.), how to keep physically, mentally, and spiritually awake during the weeks and months on a station, and other miscellaneous subjects which were discussed outside of actual class.

Saturday, September 14

To combat the enemies of fear, fatigue, and frustration, God gives us this promise which I lingered over in Deut 33:27.

1. Fear—Fear of the unexpected. Maybe not so much the fear of being killed, but fearfulness that comes from the multifarious troubles and problems which barge in upon a missionary to rattle him. "The eternal God is thy refuge."

2. Fatigue—Physical and mental (Darlene Rose's testimony of feeling herself going mentally and then realizing the reality of this promise). "Underneath are the everlasting arms."

3. Frustration—As we move forward, the foes at times seem so formidable. "And he shall thrust out the enemy from before thee, and shall say, destroy them.

Anauá River Expedition

Monday, September 15

Anauá Trip.[6] We praise the Lord that the motor was fixed in the nick of time. We had to take along the biggest syringe we could find in the infirmary in order to keep blowing out the carburetor, but the motor ran, and we enjoyed every moment of not having to paddle. Left at 8:30 a.m. in two dugouts, the one being towed.

Read Ps 91, which was to occupy my thoughts for the next couple of days. We were on our way to cut a trail to the headwaters of a river on which lived a wild tribe. They were known to have killed two American flyers, but little else was known about them. It was natural for me to stop at Ps 91:5, "Thou shalt not be afraid for the terror by night; nor for the arrow that flieth by day." Every precaution would be taken in approaching such a group of Indians, but it seems that in this case, there would be no precaution that would preclude the possibility of attack.

Two shelters had been built before us, and we stopped at this point for the night. It was a perfect camp site. Big, flat rock protruding out into the water, plenty of firewood around, and good food. Claude, Frank, John and I formed a singing quartet that night. What could be better than lying in a Wai Wai hammock, stomach full, fire beneath, seeing five contented Wai Wais swinging close by, and singing the old hymns in four-part harmony?

Tuesday, September 16

The Kamoa River was about fifty feet wide most of the way up. Numerous trees had fallen across, and a log-cutting crew had preceded us by a week to make navigation possible. Even so, there were many tree trunks submerged just beneath the surface of the water, deep enough for a canoe to pass over,

---

6. The Anauá River lies across the Brazilian border of Guyana to the west of the Wai Wai territory at the time. The Anauá is a tributary of the Rio Branco.

but not deep enough for the motor. As a result, running that motor took energy and alertness all through the day. One of the Indians would stand in the bow, point out the course, and help steer with his paddle. For logs just beneath the surface, the motor would have to be lifted. Even with all this, we must have broken about a dozen or more shear pins that day.

In the early afternoon we met the tree-cutting crew on their way back. We stopped to talk for a while, and they explained that "the wood is more than we," meaning that it wasn't worth going on any longer for them. Besides this, they had met a fork in the river and decided it was a good place to return. They had been traveling in typical Wai Wai style. In all, there were ten of them in the small dug-out: three Wai Wais and seven dogs.

Again we camped on the banks of the Kamoa. Just before camp, an alligator was shot and captured, and we all enjoyed some of its meat. While the rest of us were building the shelters and getting ready to cook, one of the Wai Wais set an ingenious trap which caught two arapaimas right in succession. The trap was so constructed that as soon as the fish bit, a pin was released, and the fish was pulled right out of the water by a pole which had been bent over and secured by the pin.

Wednesday, September 17

Reached the port of departure about noon. Walked two and a half hours over ground which was a maze of dried-up riverbeds. It was an endless network of trenches and holes which were about six feet in depth. Traveling down in one of these trenches was fast, but they didn't always go in the direction which we wanted. Thus quite a few times we had to climb up and down the banks. Pitched camp early for the Wednesday afternoon Wai Wai Bible study.

Thursday, September 18

As usual, started off about 8:00 a.m. after quiet time and breakfast (which consisted of turtle meat this morning). Hit same kind of terrain, but thankful for no hills as yet. Wai Wais climbed a few trees and reported that there were mountains on either side of us. We headed for the edge of one range and pitched camp by a large stream at 4:00. Claude and I climbed the mountain while others hunted and set up camp. We saw we couldn't make it to the top before dark, so climbed a tree and got a look at the area we had covered. Upon our return, we spent a little time fishing. It was a virgin stream and a fisherman's paradise. Within a short time we had hauled in seven good sized arapaimas. Mine was three feet and twenty pounds. This was about the only fish I'd caught since flat fish days back in Long Island Sound.

Soon the hunters came in: Nawya with a turtle and Wanawa with a monkey.

Friday, September 19

Headed northwest up the mountains, and with much hacking in spots, we didn't reach the top till four hours later. Had a good view looking NNW. Saw huge mountains directly west across the valley and were thankful that mist had rolled away just in time for us to see the landscape. Otherwise we would have headed west. Neither of the two maps which we had corresponded to what we saw, but we took a good guess as to where we were and charted our course. Two hours down the slope, across a little valley, and it was time to call it quits for the day.

That night as I lay in my hammock, I thought of how many things which I was seeing would be impossible to put into pictures or even describe adequately (had left my camera behind to make for easier walking and cutting). The hunters coming in with their catch; the Wai Wais sitting in a circle and eating in the near darkness; the picturesque streams that we had crossed and fished in; and now seeing hammocks which seemed to be slung everywhere and at every level, with two or three fires dimly lighting the scene. Chatamchá was playing his flute, and a few were repeating Scripture verses.

Thought of the faint possibility of hitting Indians on the Anauá even on this trip. It's a little different thinking about this at night, but again Ps 91 came to my attention. "Making the Lord our habitation" is better than any earthly comfort or protection.

Saturday, September 20

Claude had ribbed me about eating my candy bar the first day out in the boat. Now he offered me his if I'd climb a tree to see the lay of the land. With an incentive like this, I couldn't resist. What a way to start off the day! When I got down, I felt finished before we had even started.

Hit level country for a while, then a mountain. At this point there was a difference of opinion as to which direction we should travel, and after consultation and prayer, we decided to head southwest (instead of northwest). Traveled long and hard that day, hitting bamboo and vines on the downward slope of almost every mountain.

In the afternoon we had a little cause for excitement and also thankfulness. Kai was in the lead and came up to the face of a huge rock. As he was looking off to the left, deciding which way to go, a jaguar rushed him from the right. He let out a blood-curdling yell which I couldn't duplicate but which I would recognize vividly if I should hear it again. The Wai Wais say that's the way they always yell when they see a jaguar. Providentially there was a barrier of thick bush rope which stopped the jaguar within two feet of Kai and made him slink off. Kai had a gun slung across his shoulder but didn't have time to get it into shooting position. He merely jabbed it toward the jaguar and said that he nicked it. As we sat for a minute to recuperate, I realized how much this place looked just like a jaguar habitat in the zoos—but with a few more vines and a little more "atmosphere."

Stopped at 5:30 with hardly enough strength left to cut firewood.

Sunday, September 21

Read Ps 90 and went through some of the hymns in the back of the Testament. Spent longest on Isaac Watts' hymn from this same psalm, "Our God, our help in Ages Past."

Then came the special treat we had all been waiting for—pancakes! The Wai Wais laid down poles for benches and had their Sunday morning service which I joined with much pleasure. Walked on for three hours in the afternoon.

Monday, September 22

Hit the worst mountain yet. By noon I thought I was in Tibet instead of the jungle of Brazil. Claude talked of turning back. The Wai Wais were discouraged. They were tired, sore, and had had no meat since Saturday. We ourselves were running out of food. Claude himself climbed a tree and saw only mountains ahead—far ahead and on all sides. He decided to turn back, and we all agreed that this was the thing to do.

I had a sinking feeling all through me—something like you have walking off the basketball floor after having lost a game in which you had been leading all the way through. Suddenly I felt myself just dragging along. At the previous camp we had read and talked about Rom 8:28. I believe it now, but my feelings hadn't yet quite gotten in line with my faith. God has his reason, which we will probably see in the future. My own desire to reach the Indians on the Anauá and Jauaperi Rivers has not diminished.

Coming back over those mountains was rough. The afternoon sun just about "conked" us. Revived both in body and soul that night. Frank, John, and I had a profitable season of prayer as we thought over our turning back and as we asked the Lord to continue to perfect our hearts.

Tuesday, September 23

In the afternoon, at one point I lagged behind the first four, but was still ahead of the last four Indians. Heard a noise like a bounding of a Saint Bernard. I knew it couldn't be a Wai Wai mutt, and as I looked thirty yards to my left, I knew that I was right. It was another jaguar, and although he didn't stay long enough for me to get a good look, I wasn't disappointed.

Reached the camp before the first highest mountain. Not much food.

Wednesday, September 24

Crossed mountain sooner than we had expected. Sat down at camp long enough to eat cassava bread and peanut butter which had been left. Hadn't had much breakfast that morning, and this unexpected feast was "the most."

Then we charged off like bulls and made it all the way back to the Kamoa by nightfall. When we hit the trenches we just about ran. I lost Claude one time and took the Lexington Avenue subway instead of Broadway, retraced steps and brought up the rear with some Wai Wais. The trail was poorly marked in spots, but the Indians are uncanny in their ability to follow markings without even hesitating.

That night it seemed as if the trip were over. As we reminisced back over the past days, we had some memories that wouldn't soon be forgotten. We had had our share of aches and pains and tiredness, but also had had a good share of laughs. There were little things that could have been annoying, but were too funny to bother us, like the time:

- When John fell out of the canoe with Wanawa holding on to his leg for fear that he would drown; with the result that water poured in and we all almost drowned. I jumped overboard to make the boat lighter while Claude and Frank bailed like crazy.
- When somebody would cross a creek on a fallen tree and fall in, just before hitting the bank.

Further Preparation and Jungle Training (1958 to 1959)

- When John threw the soap to me with a little too much arc. It hit the top of the shelter and dropped neatly into the pot of oatmeal which Claude was stirring.
- When Claude couldn't get over how good his cup of tea was, until he was finished and was told that it was coffee.
- When somebody's hammock was too close to the fire and we could smell roasted flesh.
- When the fire got out of hand in the middle of the night and burned off the canvas from one of my sneaks.
- When John was coming back from the creek late at night, groping his way along. Claude yelled for him to head more to his right, thinking that John was still on his way down. (He made it back by dawn.)

Thursday, September 25

Had a huge breakfast, for we had left some supplies. Wai Wais had caught a few alligators the night before, and they ate well, too. We softies finished up the oatmeal, and pancake flour, with turtle eggs for dessert.

In spite of motor trouble much of the way back, we made it to Kanashen just before sunset. As we came putting around the last bend, what a sight met our eyes! Wai Wais were lined up along the bank, waiting to greet us and hear the news. It was hard to break the news to them, but Acts 27:25 came to me as it had back in the mountains: ". . . I believe God, that it shall be even as it was told me." In God's time and manner, those on the Anauá and Jauaperi will be reached with the Gospel.

Letter from Don to support partners, October 1958

Wai Wai Country
Dear Friends,

In my last letter I requested prayer in regard to Satan's attacks against the advancement of the gospel in Rio Branco Territory. Allow me to share with you some encouragement and instruction which God has given in the book of Ezra.

"The Lord had made them joyful, and turned the heart of the king . . . to strengthen their hands in the work of the house of God." (Ezra 6:22)

God had raised the spirit of some of his people in captivity to return and build his house in Jerusalem (Ezra 1:5). There they met with opposition; first, from the people of the land (Ezra 4:4), then from the governor, who sent a letter of accusation to King Darius (Ezra 5:6). But the building of the temple was God's work, and "the eye of their God was upon the elders of the Jews, that they could not cause them to cease." (Ezra 5:5) God had control of the king's heart and decisions, with the result that the work was finished (Ezra 6:14).

We believe that the advance into the Indian tribes of north Brazil is God's plan and God's work. It is to be expected that Satan will oppose, but also that God will overcome for his glory. The governor of Rio Branco visited Rio de Janeiro and made formal complaint against our work to four departments: Indian Protection Service, Civil Aeronautics, Frontier Commission, and Security Division. The first two departments apparently disregarded the complaints and are friendly toward the work. The latter two combined forces and sent seven top army officials to investigate the work of Unevangelized Fields Mission. Field leader Neill Hawkins tells us that the result of their visit to Bonfim "exceeded what could have been hoped for." The officers made a public announcement encouraging support of the work. We are joyful, and that you for praying "for those in authority." This now means the opening of the Waica station (Uraricoera River) sometime in November and an expedition to the Indians of the Mucajaí River, south of the Uraricoera, during the months of November and December.

". . . They gave after their ability." (Ezra 2:69)

Some of those who are most concerned for the outreach of the gospel into new tribes are found here among the Wai Wai Indians. During these weeks of jungle training, there has come one thrill after another. One of the first was witnessing the initial Wai Wai baptismal service, in which the missionaries baptized four elders, the elders in turn questioning and baptizing the rest. Then came the first Wai Wai communion service for the baptized believers. Another "first" was the ordination of one more Wai Wai elder, with the four elders exhorting, laying their hands on the head of the new elder, and praying.

But one of the biggest thrills was to see the missionary emphasis of this native church. In a Sunday service, one elder poured out his heart to his people, preaching from Mark 16:15, the verse which is written on a large plaque in front of the church. He told of the sacrifice involved in leaving wife and children for an extended period and of the hardships in crossing river rapids and steep mountains. Then he reminded them of Christ's command

and asked for volunteers for three different missionary trips. Also, he asked those who were to stay behind to bring food and trade goods for the men. By the next Sunday, men had volunteered to go, and before the afternoon service, food and trade goods poured into the church. These gifts were given by those who had first given themselves to the Lord, and then gave very sacrificially of their means.

Three of us missionaries and a few Wai Wais spent a week cutting a trail to the head of the river which will take one group far to the southeast. Another group of Wai Wais has already left to reach a tribe to the south. The trip to the third region probably will involve not only Wai Wais, but Claude Leavitt and myself. I might add here that in preparation for jungle living, these two trail-cutting trips with the Wai Wais were invaluable. We slept in Indian hammocks (resembling fishnets), learned their art of building fires, putting up shelters, hunting, fishing, cooking, weaving and carrying packs made out of palm leaves, and climbing trees which have no limbs for the first fifty feet. I look forward to coming back to take part in an expedition with those who love the Lord, love us, and have such a desire to see other tribes won to Christ.

". . . That we might afflict ourselves before our God, to seek of him a right way for us." (Ezra 8:21)

We spent two weeks cutting a trail in the direction of the Anauá River, which is southwest of here. Maps of that area are extremely inaccurate, and unexpectedly we found ourselves battling with a tough mountain range. Because of this, we are calling upon MAF for an aerial survey of the whole area, in order to pinpoint the Indian villages and to mark out the best possible way to continue the trail to the Anauá.

Pray much for this survey flight which will take place about November 1. Sometimes it is difficult to locate dwellings which are situated in clearings that are small. Also, begin now to pray for friendly contacts later on. Nothing much is known about the tribe(s) of this region except that they are reportedly fierce. We will need special wisdom and protection if we are to approach these who have demonstrated animosity toward outside intrusion. We believe that as the hand of our God is upon us, "He will deliver us from the hand of the enemy, and of such as lay in wait by the way." (Ezra 8:31)

Jungle Training Complete—On to the Yanomamis

The introduction to jungle exploration and life would prove indispensable for both Don and John in the years to come. Having the experience and knowledge of their Wai Wai friends, not only for these expeditions but for future forays into Yanomami country, would be God's provision for the next expansion of the gospel. Had it not been for the missionary zeal of the Wai Wais, it is doubtful that this expansion would have gotten very far. It was now time for expeditions into Yanomami country, an area in which few outsiders had ever set foot.

3
New Frontiers (1959 to 1962)

"A voice cries: 'In the wilderness prepare the way of the Lord; make straight in the desert a highway for our God . . . '" (Isa 40:3)

NEILL HAWKINS HAD A desire and ultimately developed a plan to open up the Yanomami territory to UFM work. The initial foray was to ascend the Uraricoera River in order to make contact with the Yanomam or Waicas who lived along the river. This was accomplished following an arduous journey upriver traversing rapids and waterfalls. Members of this expedition were Bob Hawkins, Rod Lewis, Elká (former shaman and now Christian leader of the Wai Wai tribe), and another Wai Wai Christian elder by the name of Mawashá. The expedition began in November of 1957 and took about four months.[1] After making contact with the local people, they built an airstrip for an MAF plane to get in. The first UFM station was then established at this point along the river. It became known as Waica Station, named for the tribe living in the area. Rod Lewis and his wife, Louise, would be the first missionaries at that location.

Later, in November of 1958, a second expedition was launched, this time up the Mucajaí River. Members of this team were Neill Hawkins, John Peters and two Wai Wai men, Marawenare, and once again, Mawashá. This trek was similar to the previous one up the Uraricoera River and resulted in another airstrip and mission station.[2] This second station would be called Mucajaí. The people living in this vicinity were Yanomami, but of a different dialect from the Waicas. These people were Ninam or Shirishanas, relatives of the

---

1. Dowdy, *Speak My Words*, 131.
2. Peters, *Life Among the Yanomami*, 11.

Yanam, who lived north of the Uraricoera River. Eventually, John Peters and his wife, Lorraine, would establish themselves at this new station in 1959.

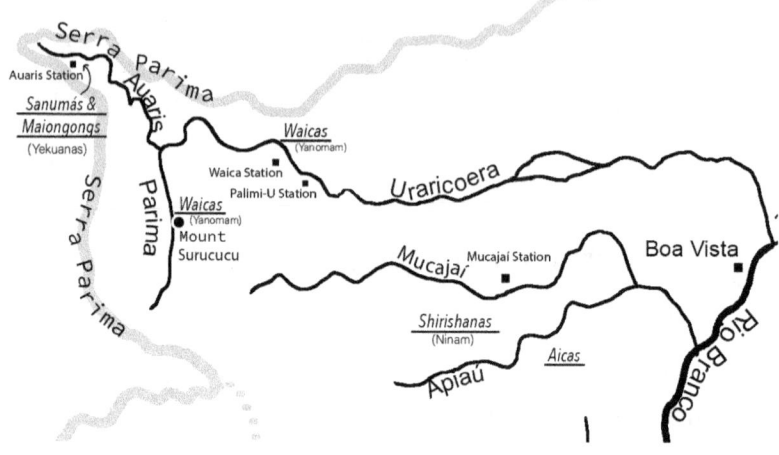

Map of Yanomami Territory

THE APIAÚ RIVER EXPEDITION

Don's involvement in these new works began in January 1959 when he was brought into Mucajaí Station. Following a brief period there, he and several others launched an overland expedition from the station to reach the Apiaú River to the southeast. The Apiaú is a tributary to the Mucajaí far downriver from the station. Aica people purportedly lived along this river. Earlier, MAF aerial surveys had turned up villages as well as individuals, one of whom aimed a bow and arrow at the plane as it flew over. Members of the expedition were Claude Leavitt, John Peters, two Wai Wais, a number of Shirishanas (Ninams) and Don. The overland trip to find the Aicas would prove to be quite challenging.

Email from Don to editor, September 24, 2019

There was considerable hesitation as to the launching of the trip at this time. Adverse pressure from the government was gaining momentum and had made us very cautious as to not let our advance into the Apiaú be known by the Brazilians. Then the lack of water along the trail added to our wariness. A half-day out on the trail convinced us that the creek beds were dry as a bone, but Claude wrote saying that he felt certain that by digging in the creeks, water would be found. He felt that the expedition should be made before the field conference in April. Claude soon arrived and was followed shortly by two Wai Wais, for we thought their presence and help would be an extra precautionary measure, as we still couldn't communicate fluently with the Shirishanas.

John Peters with Shirishana Man[3] (printed with permission by John F. Peters)

Don's Journal, 1959

Tuesday, February 24

Yakutá and Wahne looked dazed as they stepped off the plane into the midst of a jabbering, back-slapping mob. With their arrival we were now ready to move. A light rain was falling, and this answer to prayer raised everybody's spirits. We traveled only a couple of hours that afternoon, pitching camp by a good-sized creek bed. To ensure a minimum drinking supply, we were packing four tins and one rubberized bag of water, the latter only for the first afternoon. It was an encouragement to see Yakutá sitting in his hammock, writing down Shirishana words in his own Wai Wai script. He looked and acted like a trained linguist.

---

3. From the book cover to Peters' *Amazon Jungle Life Among the Yanomami*.

Wednesday, February 25

We commenced this day's trip with Claude minus his long pants and belt, and me without my leather shoelaces. Ants had invaded us during the night and chewed to bits the above-mentioned articles.

Traveled pretty hard this day, covering at least sixteen miles. We all were very thirsty. Claude and John prepared the campsite while I dug for water. Hit clay after one foot and continued on to depth of five feet but did not break through the layer. The Shirishanas were digging with their hands, munching on the moist sand that they found just before the clay. Food and other things were irrelevant; there was a desperation for water. Is there this same kind of desperation for spiritual water in our lives? Can we say with David, "Ps 42:1–2?" Or can we pray: "Ps 63:1, 2a, and 8a?" Do other things become irrelevant as we thirst for God? Even the essential things such as food occupy little of our attention when we reach the desperation point of spiritual thirst. May we, with Job, "esteem the words of His mouth more than our necessary food." (Job 23:12)

Thursday, February 26

At 1:00 p.m. reached the one creek which Harold had seen from the air. The men's morale ran high as we drank and bathed (at opposite ends of one of the pools). Some continued cutting the trail, as progress had been slowed up considerably because the old trail was hard to be found. Yakutá and Wahne went off hunting and brought back a small jaguar.

Friday, February 27

Found honey in a tall tree. Two of the men climbed up with axes, then chopped their way to the liquid treasure. Bees were swarming in their hair and all around them, but it was worth it. Pure, sweet honey dripped in abundance from the combs. Words can't express how good that tasted. I can appreciate better now those verses in Ps 19:10 and 119:103 "(in the law of the Lord) sweeter also than honey and the honeycomb" and "How sweet are Thy words unto my taste! Yea, sweeter than honey to my mouth." Digging for water, Claude and I had a friendly argument as to who was the more tired. So, to decide, we had a race down the creek bed. Crazy!

New Frontiers (1959 to 1962)

Don and Claude Leavitt on the Apiaú Expedition

Saturday, February 28

Ma'ama and I left early to cut trail, but the carriers caught up to us by 10:00 a.m. John and I took turns carrying pack. Passed creek where four Shirishana women had died from colds. Hills got worse from then on, and at 1:45 p.m. we came upon a mountain creek, spotted with water, so this was the terminal point for the day. Thus far the trip had been fairly easy, and I thought that somebody must have been praying that we don't go too hard.

A couple of us had shot monkeys during the day, and then at night we heard something that sounded like a jaguar (so the Indians thought). We sure had a laugh when it and its mate turned out to be pacas. The paca is a large, good eating rodent, and we enjoyed this change in diet.

Sunday, March 1

Services and rest for the morning. In the afternoon I found a jungle cathedral downstream. How good the Lord was to make such a spot for me to enjoy at that time. A water hole was surrounded by huge rocks. The quietness was broken only by an occasional chirping or by my own voice: as I was the only occupant, I sang aloud from the I.V. Hymnal. The songs echoed against the forest wall enclosing the creek. Read Ps 27 and Ps 109. Went jaguar hunting at night with Claude and Wai Wais. Big tracks, but no jaguars.

Monday, March 2

John had gone half a day cutting trail, so we traveled quite a way; enough to be tired and thirsty. Creek beds were getting drier now that we were hitting more level country. We hit water after digging three feet in sand. Tick bites were worse than usual (tick-picking was a continual necessary diversion). Have to admit that I was slightly disgruntled by these things, besides the regular day after day duties of walking, cooking (many times in the dark), putting up hammocks, repacking in the morning, etc. I was ashamed as I thought of the many who really suffered during war years for a cause not nearly so glorious as the one set before me. I thought of the life of Paul and of David. I thought of Jesus who knew what it meant to hunger, thirst, and be tired. (As I copy this from my brief notes written on the trips, the comparison seems absurd, but there on the trail, it was a real experience, and I remember that I did feel much like David of old in the wilderness, and I was in need of much encouragement.)

Tuesday, March 3

Saw blood on the trail which led to the place where Shatro had put an arrow into a jaguar. This was the first night that we had to depend solely on our own cans for water, and even this supply was low. All day long we had encountered few creeks, and these yielded no water. We gave a cup of water to each of the Shirishanas. It was almost pleasant to have nothing to do except sling our hammocks and lie down; no digging for water, not much firewood to get, no cooking. However, the thought of no more water took the edge off the enjoyment. As we sang hymns together, our spirits brightened and then we fixed what was probably the most appreciated meal of the trips, a cup of milk, farinha, and sugar . . . woke up a few times during the night with a very dry mouth.

Wednesday, March 4

One cup of water for breakfast with nothing else, so that the water wouldn't be needlessly absorbed. The men expected to hit the Apiaú by noon, and at 1:30 were very discouraged. We sat down and prayed, and within a minute we found a twig cut by a knife. It was the first time all day that I saw any one of the Indians smile. It was the knife mark of a Waica, for the last time the Shirishanas had crossed the trail, they had no knives.

In the afternoon, the boys were dying of thirst. Every so often one of them would let out a loud wail of agony. One Indian would plow on in front then drop down on the trail while another took his place. About 4:30 p.m. some of the cargo was dropped. I was following the lead man, Waytiri, and together we ploughed on, cutting trail. Suddenly he stopped and said we were near. As he broke out in a smile, I almost broke out in tears, but I guess there wasn't enough fluid left for that. Soon after, John caught up, and said that some of the men had just dropped on the trail. I'll never forget his words of encouragement, "Keep plugging and praying."

When we continued on and still didn't hit the river, I couldn't help but think of the agonies of hell. The men were dazedly going on, sometimes crying out, sometimes enduring it silently. The cries of the rich man in Luke 16 seemed to be very clear to my ears, and I wondered if it could be possible that men would suffer like this in hell. Never before had I come so close to disbelieving Christ's own words. And yet I did believe that He was true, that I must believe that destruction was to be eternally, consciously suffered by those dying without Christ. I had a lump as big as an orange in my throat, and I promised the Lord that never again would I want comfort and ease while there are souls dying without a saving knowledge of him. "Lord, keep the remembrance of that afternoon always in my heart, that I may be spurred on to endure any suffering or loss, to the end that some might be spared the lake of fire and torment, prepared for the devil and his angels."

At 5:30 we all stopped. All were about finished. We could hardly talk, and when we did, it was as if a fire had burned out our tongues. In desperation, we again prayed. Within fifteen minutes, we saw the most beautiful sight this world can offer—water! Just before John and I reached the banks, we saw a blur of speed and determination. It was Shatro, soaking wet, carrying a can of water back to some of the older men who were prostrate on the trail. At the river I jumped in and drank and soaked. This bliss was abbreviated by the rude greeting of an electric eel shocking my leg and by the news that there was an alligator up ahead.

Thursday, March 5

Preparations for the supply drop. We had just made it in time to get ready at the day previously set. There was a smoke signal all set right next to our campsite and another just downstream a ways near the site where we wanted the drop. Much of the river had dried up, and we were able to walk on the bed. There was a good stretch of shallow water where the plane was to drop the goods. Plane came at 2:15. Russ was the bombardier and at first missed the big stretch of water, making a direct hit on the big rock at the end. The rice in the cans shot up like a geyser.

There were some items that would be better dropped onto dry land, over the loudspeakers Harold (Berk) told us that there was a clearing about one hundred yards in from the South banks. Things sure look different from the air. The clearing was cleared of trees all right, but was a maze of thorns, thistles, and briars.

We recovered the goods okay and then started the fun with the bucket-drops. The wind wasn't helping Harold, but he did manage to put down the cloth bucket at one edge of the clearing. In the process of getting to it we were clawed and gashed mercilessly by the thorns. I said, "That's enough for me." I wasn't that anxious to send mail out, but Claude had a wife and family and was determined. A couple more attempts, but each time the bucket had to go up before Claude got to it. One more try, and this time he made a dive for that bucket as though it were a loose football in the end zone in a tied up ball game. He made it! Off went the bucket with the letters inside. But to our (mostly his) dismay the line caught in a tree, depositing the rest of the cut line and bucket. One more pass by Harold, a "Sorry, boys" over the loudspeaker, and off they went. (Russ was sicker than a dog.)

In all the excitement, someone had let the fire next to the camp get out of bounds. Result: one charred bundle that was a hammock the night before. It was a jungle hammock, and the net was left dangling on the ground.

Found out that John had just relinquished his hammock. In the excitement, one of the Indians had left the signal fire which had spread and gone through our camp. John's single hammock was hanging upside down, and all that we found were two knots tied to the trees. (We had brought along an extra hammock for just such an emergency.)

Heard yells down river that night and wondered if the plane had scared the poor Indians to death. We prayed that they wouldn't be frightened off. Eager to get to them the next morning.

Friday, March 6

Off to the Waica trail and the Indians we had heard shouting the night before. Found the Waica trail on South bank at 10:30. Soon lost trail and started cutting but found old trail again. At 3:15 hit village. Nobody home.

The "Waicas" turned out to be two Brazilians who were hunting for otter skins. After talking about the difficulties of travel in the dry season, exchanging other words of information about ourselves, and giving them some medicine, we left them and at 10:30 headed along the trail which we knew would bring us to the village. A trail which led to a number of Brazil nut trees took us off the track for a while, but we circled back. Wahne found the right trail even as Yakutá was climbing a tree to locate the mountain.

We passed quite a few Indian camping sites, and each one gave us encouragement. Soon we were ascending the mountain, in back of which lay the village. At 3:15 our delegation arrived, but there was nobody to receive us. Claude thought that when they heard us call, they went into hiding. So we stayed and waited, noting the interesting features of this, another tribal group.

The clearing was about ninety by fifty feet. At either end was a shelter like half a roof, fifteen to twenty feet high. Under these there were a couple little shelters made of a few banana leaves which sheltered them from the wind. Along the side of the clearing there were two more of these little shelters, five feet in height. Hammocks were only four feet long and made of strips made from reeds. The cooking boards were beautifully shaped into a perfect oval. The field we had passed through contained bananas and cassava.

At 4:45 some little boys unsuspectingly emerged from the "mats" but quickly turned around when they saw us. We all called out and motioned. The mothers were now peeking through at us. I can still see the Shirishanas jabbering and beckoning them to come. The four women did come, shaking slightly from nervousness and fear.

Probably the most noticeable thing about these women at first sight is their clothing. In each ear was a stick about ten inches long. This was the extent of their dress, except for a string around arms, legs, and chest.

Sunday, March 8

Because there were no men around, we headed off the next day in the direction of another village Harold had reported. None of the young boys of the village wanted to guide us, so we left on a trail heading southwest. When we started going south and past the mountain to our west, we knew we were headed wrong. Back to the creek where trail had burned, and then down another trail going west. Soon the path led to the creek, and we decided to climb a hill to get bearings. The men were grumbling and wanting to go back. Their cassava bread had given out, and their feet were hurting on the rocks. So we started down creek, promising to return soon to (the) campsite on the Apiaú. Four of the men returned via the Waica village to retrieve knives they had left near the trail before coming into the clearing. Yakutá shot a monkey while the other men were batting fish over the head in a small creek pool.

The group made its way back to Mucajaí. Thus ended a somewhat disappointing trip to find a sizeable Aica population along the Apiaú. Although no mission station would be established along this river, it was helpful to know who was living in the area, since the point of this and future expeditions was to survey the various tribes and their locations in the greater region. Not too long after this, some of these people along the Apiaú came to Mucajaí Station and settled among the Ninam people living there, thus providing continued contact by the missionaries. On another note, during the group's long trek back to Mucajaí, Don composed a hymn in this head regarding the arduous hike. It is entitled "Trail Song."[4]

Stuck at Mucajaí Station

Following the Apiaú expedition, Don and Claude Leavitt were flown out to Boa Vista for a field conference in Bonfim. A few days later, Don was then flown back out to Mucajaí to replace John Peters. It was at this time that government troubles began. All MAF flights were grounded; Don was stranded as the only missionary at Mucajaí. On top of that, since the government had not allowed two-way radios into these stations, he had no way to communicate with the outside world. The following reflects Don's thoughts and experiences about that time period. Don would spend four months here, living in a small, thatched roof shelter with no walls.

Letter from Don to support partners, January 1959

Mucajaí River, Brazil
Dear praying friends,

In the past year many plans have been laid in preparation for advance into unreached tribes. Also there have been many plans changed, sometimes at the last minute. I had no idea when last I wrote that the next place of writing would be an isolated spot on the Mucajaí River; but here I am. I am happy to be here and happy to be observing the movements of the Lord throughout this territory and following his path for me.

---

4. Both the lyrics and musical notation can be found in Appendix B.

New Frontiers (1959 to 1962)

Walking along a jungle trail yesterday, I thought again of the importance of always taking an Indian guide when venturing any distance from home base. There are some deceptive side-paths, and at times even the main trail is not clearly seen, being hidden by a mass of foliage. I thought, too, how wonderful it is to have the Guide who never falters, the Lord Jesus himself. As we meet deceptive side-paths which appear to be the better way, as we encounter a mass of confusing circumstances in God's way for us, we have the promise that "a man's heart deviseth his way: but the Lord directeth his steps." (Prov 16:9 KJV)

We thought that there were Indian villages on the Anauá River to the southeast of Boa Vista, and we tentatively were planning an expedition there; but an aerial survey failed to find villages. This means that the tribe must be on the next river south and that God's answer for advance into this group is "not yet."

This focused our attention on two rivers southwest of Boa Vista, the Mucajaí and Apiaú. In November Neill Hawkins, John Peters, and two Wai Wais traveled two weeks over rocks and rapids to contact the Indians on the Mucajaí. The Lord gave an exceptionally friendly reception. The people showed no fear, were eager to receive medicine and trade goods, and helped considerably in the construction of an airstrip.

Neill Hawkins was flown out January 1st to resume his many leadership responsibilities at Bonfim. Three days later I was flown in to join John Peters in setting up a new station. We need your prayers as we: 1) tackle the language (all the people are monolingual), 2) administer medicine, and 3) construct buildings, to the one end of communicating the gospel of Jesus Christ to these who for so long have been cut off from civilization and a chance to hear about the true God.

Continue to pray for radio permission. Until this is granted, our only means of contact with the outside is the biweekly flight of the MAF plane. It is possible that I will be here until September, but even now we are formulating plans to reach the tribe to the south of us on the Apiaú River. Pray for the Lord's timing for this expedition. We believe that the next steps will be in that direction and that God will be preparing the way before us.

Don jotting down Waica words and phrases

Email from Don to editor, September 2019

In connection with the intense thirst we all felt during the trip to the Apiaú River, there was one incident that gave us a good laugh. The river had all but dried up, but there were pools of water in which we jumped, cooling off and satiating our thirst. I found a pool I could have all to myself, jumped in, and was promptly shocked by an electric eel!

After this trip, my cohort, John Peters, flew out to Boa Vista to await his future bride. Before his replacement, Frank Ebel, could be flown in, the plane was grounded, for two months, leaving me with only Indians as companions and with no radio communication. My dad wrote a letter to the supporters of our work, telling something of our plight.[5] There were no serious injuries or sickness during that time, but there was one accident that gave me a scare. One day we were sawing a log with a pit saw, and I was on the top side when my foot slipped. One of the teeth of the saw caught my leg just above my knee and produced a deep gash. Thankfully, it missed any major veins, and I was able to heal with plenty of sulfa powder and a butterfly patch.

---

5. See Appendix C.

John and Lorraine Peters

I didn't go hungry during that time, but the diet was certainly different than that which I had been used to. When the plane finally came, I was able to treat the pilot and passenger Ernie Migliazza to a celebratory meal of monkey meat which had been boiling in the pot. (Ernie audaciously commented that it tasted spoiled!)

Letter from Don to support partners, June 1959

Mucajaí River, Brazil
Dear friends,
For more than two months our ears had been tuned to hear the motor of the MAF plane, but each day registered a blank. Then on June 11th came a buzz which unmistakably was not a nearby bug, but the one-and-only little yellow plane—our only means of talking to the outside world. As Pilot Harold Berk nosed in for a trial run, he gave me the thumbs-up signal, which meant that once again God had been working a miracle.

Helping Together by Prayer

Thanks to a letter from my father, many of you were brought up to date with our situation here, and never before in my life have I felt such a concerted effort of prayer on my behalf. One lady wrote that when she received the letter, she phoned other prayer partners who all "pulled the plugs of their washing machines" and gathered to intercede for us missionaries. With such united supplication and faith on your part, it was certain that God would answer, "... in Whom we trust that He will yet deliver us; ye also helping together by prayer for us." (2 Cor 1:10–11)

He Preserveth the Strangers

After the MAF plane had been grounded in Boa Vista, the pilot and our field director, Neill Hawkins, went to Rio de Janeiro to talk with officials. They found out that the former governor of this territory and his party have continued their attacks against us. This whole affair has gained wide publicity with false reports and fantastic rumors being spread throughout Brazil. Mr. Hawkins writes that "there is a strong current of narrow nationalism in Brazil, and the governor has based his attacks on that. Evidently many of the men in high position had not been influenced by these currents, for thus far they have not taken drastic steps to oust us. We praise God for this, but I urge you to continue praying for these who are in authority, for the situation is still delicate.

As I have been reading the reports, I realize that in a very real sense we American missionaries are strangers and foreigners in Brazil. But I ask you to claim a promise in God's Word which came to me the morning I learned by the shortwave radio that the plane had been grounded. I turned to Ps 146, and these verses seemed to be written just for us at this time: "Happy is he that hath the God of Jacob for his help, whose hope is in the Lord his God . . . The Lord preserveth the strangers."

Table in the Wilderness

The shortwave broadcast mentioned was the semi-weekly conversation between UFM missionaries in Georgetown and the jungle station in southern British Guiana. For reasons which we still don't fully understand, the commercial plane which was to make a supply drop kept delaying and never did come. Knowing the food supplies must be low, Claude Leavitt gave us these words spoken by Israel in unbelief: "Can God furnish a table in the wilderness?" (Ps 78:19) That very morning one of the Wai Wai boys chased an armadillo and rode it horseback till he could dig his knees firmly into the ground and kill it. Each week we had meat. Sometimes it was only a small rodent about the size of a rat, but at other times we banqueted on monkey or tapir. With everything gone but salt and a little rice, we thoroughly enjoyed the native cassava bread and palm fruit drink. The Indians even brought in some bird eggs (in various stages of development). Yes, God had provided a table in the wilderness and had kept us all in good health.

Palm Fruit in Heaven

This time alone with the Indians has meant a push ahead in the language. The Wai Wais learned phrases quickly, so we conversed mostly in Shirishana. Together we would share new phrases, and together we spent much time with the people. For two weeks the river was extremely high and swift, so that the number of visitors from across the way dwindled down to a normal-sized crowd. Taking pity on our lonely existence, a few of the teenage boys asked if they could bring their hammocks and stay for a week or so. I wish you could share with me some of our fireside chats at night. Every truth about God and Jesus Christ is news that they have never heard before.

Letter from Don to support partners, September 1959

Bonfim, Brazil
Dear friends,
    Past memories, future plans, petitions, and praise mingle together and reach a zenith when one takes off in the Missionary Aviation Fellowship plane. At least it was that way with me as we whizzed past a group of motionless Indians, hit the last bump, and soared up into the heavens. The end of the richest experience of my life—eight months of getting to know the heart of an Indian and of learning a little more of his heart which was moved with compassion upon those who were "scattered abroad as sheep without a shepherd."
    I had grown to love this group as my own family. Together we had hunted, trekked, worked, visited, laughed, and sorrowed. I thought of the Sunday mornings when nearly everyone would gather and squat on the freshly swept floor of the big communal house. Still struggling for phrases, we would tell them of creation, sin, and stories of Jesus.
    These times were all over for me now, but I praised God that for them it was just the beginning. Frank Ebel had dug right in on the language, and

now could continue telling the good news. Good old Frank. How did he ever endure "batching" with me while waiting for his wife and boy to join him? A series of circumstances made the delay longer, the last of which was waiting for a new motor for the plane. But now they were together and being watched by at least seventy pairs of eyes as they were getting ready to eat. Strange new sights to these forest dwellers: a stove, a bed, and other such items. Strangest of all was that little boy with white hair. This family needs your prayers as they settle in to learn in order to teach.

As the plane leveled out at an altitude of seven thousand feet, my eyes turned to the south and my mind to the future. A small range of mountains stretched along the other side of the Apiaú River, thirty miles away. Another thirty miles beyond that was the Ajarani River with other mountains whose blue tint made the peaks merge into the horizon. We knew that at the edge of the nearer range lay two villages of Waica Indians—the Indians we had contacted a few months before. The location of other villages farther on still needed to be known before a station could be established. Would the Lord open the way for us in that region as He had done on the Mucajaí? I believed He would.

Letter from Don to support partners, December 24, 1959

Bonfim, Brazil
"But the Master comes, and the foolish crowd never can quite understand *the worth of a soul* and the change that's wrought by the touch of the Master's hand." (From a poem about the difference that an old violin makes in the hands of a master violinist.)
Dear fellow-laborers,

The realization of the value of the human soul hits me with new force today as I contemplate the birth, ministry, and death of Christ. Are we giving all we have, "toiling, wrestling with the energy with which so powerfully He energizes us–so that we may present every person complete in Christ?" (Col 1:28–29 Ber)

I think of the miners who have given all they have in their search for gold and diamonds. How well I remember the words of one prospector who passed by us on the Mucajaí River. "We've staked all our future on this venture," he said. "We've sold most our possessions and left our families, but gold is our life for the present." Suffering much physically and socially, men like this press on, propelled by the love of money. How we Christians need the love of Christ for souls, that we gladly might spend and be spent in an all-out effort to gain precious lives for the Savior.

Many of you have been "wrestling for us in your prayers" (Col 4:12), and this has been much appreciated in these days of delays and uncertainties. Ever since the last expedition was called off, we have been waiting for a government commission which was to look over our whole work. There have been continual postponements, and January 24th is the date they have now set. No new permission can even be asked for until these men give their report to Rio.

With the permission we do have to work on the Uraricoera River and its tributaries, we have planned an advance into the upper Parima River. This is about the farthest one can get from civilization here in Brazil, but there is a good-sized concentration of Indians in this area. Reports from the Indians at Waica Station are that these people, the Parahuris, are to be feared, and stockades were seen around the houses on an aerial survey. However, on the lower part of the Parima there is a miner, Mr. Koch, who has sent out word that a few Parahuris came down river and are helping in the building of his airstrip. We expect to make friendly contact with these few who are on the fringe of the group, and then see from their reactions the possibilities of moving farther upriver.

Even now there are those who are ready to move into the area as God opens up the way. After the two-month trip, the Bob Cable family and Sue Albright will be at Waica Station, studying the language in preparation to occupy a future post among these Parahuris. My main responsibility on the expedition will be the collecting of all language data possible, so that these other missionaries can begin learning phrases.

As you remember the general needs that such a trip as this entails, pray for us as we meet the miner who is at the lower Parima. His coworker has deserted him, saying that living conditions have been unbearable. We expect to meet a very needy man, both physically and spiritually, and we need wisdom in ministering to him.

Also there is no telling what will be of the reports he sends back to Boa Vista as we pass him by and move up into the area which is his ultimate destination. Brazilian airmen have reported that the headwaters of the Parima River look like an area rich in gold and diamonds, and to this region are heading miners from both the Mucajaí and Uraricoera Rivers. You can see our situation. Many in the civilized society here look down on the Indian; some believe that he has no soul. It is no wonder then that our motives are held under suspicion. Even though many government officials are favorable to the missionary work here, some are still actively opposing us, believing that we are out for the riches of the land. Now as we are seen moving up the Parima, you can imagine the stories. But we must move ahead. If we were to wait until rumors and opposition ceased, we probably never would reach these forest dwellers for Christ.

Ultimately, the immediate problem with the government was resolved, MAF flights were reestablished, and Don was brought out. Problems with the Brazilian government would be an ongoing issue for years to come, however. Through Neill Hawkins' tireless efforts to deal with government officials and through God's providential hand the mission to the Yanomami tribes was sustained.

The Parahuris Expedition

In January 1960, another expedition was launched up the Parima River to make contact with a group of Yanomamis (Waicas, presumably) referred to as the Parahuris. The Parima River meets the Auaris River some distance up the Uraricoera. Villages had been spotted during an aerial survey of the region led by Bob Hawkins in 1959. In addition, it was hoped that contact could be made with another group called the Maitas who lived in the area of Mount Surucucu which lay to the east of the Parima.

The expedition, consisting of Rod Lewis, Bob Cable, Don, and two Wai Wai Christians— Klemtu and Mawashá—commenced on January 4 and would last a little over six weeks.[6] The Wai Wai men had been indispensable in these expeditions and would be in future ones as well. Although they could not speak the language of the people they would be encountering, their jungle skills and common knowledge of Indigenous people's ways would prove to be invaluable to the UFM missionaries.

Don's Journal, 1960

Monday, January 4

We had loaded almost all the cargo on Saturday to see if the canoe would take it all, and we must have been optimistic in our figuring. This morning we had to take out some of the rice and farinha in order to make safe traveling through the swift water upstream. It was good those two Waica boys backed down and decided not to go along. Good, too, that two Wai Wai boys were with us. They were to prove a real help throughout the whole trip.

---

6. Donald M. Borgman, email to editor, August 23, 2019. "From Mucajaí I moved on up to Waica Station on the Uraricoera River. It was from there that we launched a two-month trip to survey the upper Parima River."

The rapids weren't bad the first day, although we did have to get out a few times and drag the canoe. There are a few things desirable for a good campsite: a good landing for the canoe, a place that is not too thick with growth, and a spot where ample "banana" leaves are available for the roof of the shelter. So any time after 4:30 a good location is sought, and it must be the same experience as looking for a motel. You don't want to stop too early and waste the daylight, nor do you want to travel too long and end up having to settle for a poor spot.

The expedition begins

Tuesday, January 5

Met four Maiongong Indians at midday. The Brazilian miner, Koch, had received word from the Waicas that a whole planeload of foodstuffs had arrived at the mission station for him. In his letter to Rod, he said that he thought this could not be true, reminding us that the Waicas "lie even when they sleep" (no pun in Portuguese). But just in case, he was sending the Maiongongs to pick it up. Koch had spent time at the mission station more than a year ago. Originally the mining party consisted of four, but some disagreement split them into two groups. Two of them had prospected in this region, while Koch and Rogerio located themselves at the mouth of the

Uauris River at its junction with the Parima. Rogerio majored in the planting and had made the field. Koch had been overseeing work on an airstrip which was located on the top of a mountain. Rogerio, in late November, figured he had had enough and left Koch alone, joined the two other miners who coincidentally were just on their way down to Boa Vista.

You have to hand it to these men. How different are their motives from ours, yet how they put up with hardships to get their desire. They are after material and possibly social prestige and fame. We are seeking the precious souls of men who have never heard the gospel, and never even heard of God.

Koch had been up there on the Uauris (later named Auaris) for more than a year and had only one supply drop, which was largely a failure. Fortunately he had met up with the Maiongongs as he stopped at the mission station, and I believe these ambitious workers had been his salvation.

Maiongong Indians at Koch's location

The Maiongong tribe is located in southern Venezuela. (Name of the tribe is Maquiritare in Venezuela.) There are just a few families who live on the Brazil side, way up in the northwest corner of the Rio Branco territory on the Uaris River. This tribe is exceptionally advanced in many ways. In Venezuela they have had much contact with the Spanish-speaking people and many of them are bilingual, living in the small towns. However, there are many who live back in the bush with little clothing and only occasional contact with the outside. Yet even these have made their name for being a highly advanced tribe. Their craftsmanship is unsurpassable. The Maiongong baskets, grater boards, and canoes are traded far and wide and are admired by many Brazilians.

Those on the Brazil side have been great travelers for many years. Recently they have made annual trips out to Brazilian civilization near Santa Rosa on the Uraricoera River. There they have sold grater boards and canoes in return for salt, clothes, and tools. Thus some of the men have acquired a good knowledge of Portuguese. These trips are long and hard, with many rapids having to be bypassed along the way. This means unloading the canoes in some sections, and carrying cargo by land while the canoes are carefully lowered down through the fast-falling water. In other places the drops are so severe that the canoes have to be dragged overland. We were to meet a sample of both these situations on our way up the Parima.

The thing that thrilled me as I met these boys on the river was the knowledge that they had had some contact with the gospel. In their visits to their people on the Venezuela side, they had met missionaries of the New Tribes Mission as well as believers of their own tribe.

The New Tribes group is doing a great job linguistically and spiritually among the Maquiritares. One of the boys always carried with him a reading primer that was given to him over there. Quite an amazing thing. Here was a group that lived in one of the remotest places in Brazil, yet they had much more than many Waicas who lay closer to Brazilian civilization. Materially speaking, they were far ahead of the Waicas, and with their being so close to believers in Venezuela (ten days from their village), their spiritual opportunities were far greater than those of the Waicas.

Wednesday, January 6

One of our first objectives was meeting the Tucushim people who lived in a village just below the bad falls on the lower Parima River. We arrived at the village about noon, found the place empty, but not entirely. There were hundreds of burrowing fleas that latched on to our feet. These little bugs seem to be in abundance in empty Indian houses (no dogs to cling to). They bury themselves in the foot and lay their eggs, making a sac one-eighth to one-quarter inches in diameter.

With a little scouting around, Rod and Mawashá found where they had moved. They were making a new field nearby and had made huts up there. A few of them were up at Koch's strip helping in the work.

These people struck me as being slight in stature, and one of their significant features was the haircut. Most of them had shaved off a round section on the upper back part of their heads, leaving a ring of longer hair around the bottom. Usually a few scars could be seen in this shaved area— scars probably made by the shamans who cut with sharp stones to get rid of sickness.

Their language was somewhat different, but we got along fine. They were fairly quiet but very friendly. They brought us some cassava drink right away and helped us in putting up our shelter. It was a nice spot right on a little beach at the foot of the rapids. And I was very thankful it was sandy terrain. In the middle of the night I awoke abruptly by a thud on the ground: me hitting it. The hammock rope suddenly had snapped.

Don in hammock

Thursday, January 7

One of the Tucushim men went up to the airstrip to call for five men to help us carry cargo to the top of the falls, five miles away. In the meantime Bob, Klemtu, and I, along with the Maiongongs carried some of the provisions up there to the top, at which point the Maiongongs returned while we overnighted.

Many times during the trip it was a joy to observe the Wai Wais. Tonight Klemtu was lying in his hammock, reviewing the many Bible verses he had learned. What God has done among the Wai Wai tribe there in south British Guiana, we pray that He will do here among the Waicas.

Mawashá and Klemtu

Friday, January 8

At 9:00, our five carriers arrived from the airstrip. Undoubtedly the cream of the crop: the chief of the village down below who made sure he never carried anything, and four very young boys. But downriver, Rod was receiving unexpected enthusiasm from those at that end. Even the women and children wanted to carry something, and as a result he got everything on the move before we ever reached the village.

We met the gang along the trail and had a good chat with some of the young fellows while everybody was resting. One of the eight boys that had come down from the airstrip claimed to be a Shamatari and another a Koatateri. These two groups, as well as the Tucushim people and the Parahuris, belong to the Waica language group, but have slightly different dialects. I had a lot of fun with the two boys mentioned above. I obtained a small word list of body parts and a few objects from them, and they in turn seemed to be interested in learning the names in my language.

Rod and John Peters had previously contacted a Shamatari village and stayed but a short time. They are said to be a very friendly and jolly bunch.

Most of them had never seen white men before Rod and John entered. One of the men kept saying jubilantly, "I have seen a white man up close; I have seen a white man up close." There were about eighty in that one village, and the people had told of many other villages one or two days away. Their dialect seems to have more differences from that spoken at the station than even the Tucushim people (Parahuri) we were to meet up on the Parima.

Shot down a whole flock of marudi birds just before supper time. These were enjoyed most heartily.

Rod Lewis teaching with Don in foreground

Saturday, January 9

The Maiongongs had left the previous day with our canoe. Instead of dragging their canoes the five miles up along the rapids, they had found it easier in their former travels to use a creek that paralleled the river and emptied into the Parima about a mile below the falls. They had cut a beautiful wide trail from the creek to the river at the top of the rapids. Usually a one-day operation, it took a day and a half this time because of low water level in the creek.

Left camp at noon, shortly after the canoe arrived. We hopped out of the canoe and dragged through one small rapid and had to unload everything at a second. Camped at the base of another set of rapids about a mile in length.

We had a very good talk with Francisco, one of the Maiongong boys. We told him the story of Jesus once again in Portuguese, and then we sang together. He liked especially "Nothing but the Blood of Jesus," for he had been taught this song in his own language when he had visited the missionaries in Venezuela. He certainly knows enough and understands enough of the message to be able to become a new creation in Christ, but he, as well as some of the other Maiongong boys, have raised up a barrier of resistance.

Rained hard during the night. Discovered that the coverings of our jungle hammocks were sadly in need of repair. Rod had long ago on a previous trip decided in favor of a Brazilian hammock; he just couldn't comfortably fit his huge frame in a jungle hammock. Bob's hammock was peppered with holes. So for the rest of the trip he slept in mine, and I used my Shirishana hammock which was brought along for an extra.

Sunday, January 10

Left camp at 11:00 a.m. with five more Waica carriers who had arrived. Traveled three-quarters of an hour through the rain to top of rapids. It poured some more as we went upriver to Koch's place.

Koch had lived at the river's bank for a month or so before moving up to the top of the mountain where he was to construct his airstrip. The Maiongong boys had built two houses on a knoll down by the river, and Rogerio had cleared an area for planting bananas, sugarcane, and beans. By this time most of the Maiongongs had come down to this site and were living (who lived on the Brazil side) in the two houses by the river. They provided most of the manpower for help on the strip as well as supplying quite a good amount of farinha.

Great meal of fish and rice. Afterwards we sat around and sang for the Maiongongs. There were about twenty of them in all.

Monday, January 11

Visited with Koch at the airstrip which looked like it still needed a lot of work. The recent rains made things look a little more soupy, but at best, Koch's plans to shape things up in a week or so seemed to be optimistic. He had found a good place for a strip, a scrubby area on a nice flat-topped mountain. The cleared area was five-hundred meters in length.

Had a hard time understanding this educated Brazilian from the south. He was full of conversation and was happy to have receptive ears at the listening end, even though these ears weren't picking up much of what he said. He appreciated very much the few provisions we had given him the previous day down at the river. Especially did he rave about the dehydrated spinach. He was sure that this would give him strength to carry on for the next few days. A year living alone with the Indians, eating much as they eat, had understandably as left its mark, and he complained of being very weak.

Rainy and late when we returned, but it cleared up nicely so that we could enjoy the full moon. We played various games outside with the Maiongongs and joked around in general. What a happy group. What is it that keeps them from accepting the gospel message?

Tuesday, January 12

Two of the Maiongongs hitched a ride and were towed by our canoe as we motored upriver. Rod's gun and an Indian lance combined to kill a huge rodent in the afternoon. This "capivara [capybara]" is supposed to be the largest rodent in the world; it must have been two hundred pounds. It lives along the riverbank and spends much of the time right in the water. We kept a leg, and the boys were happy with the rest as they turned around and started off downriver.

Wednesday, January 13

The journey upriver was slow going, for the river was now filled with bends. Hit the Maita creek at 2:30. Another hour and a half brought us to a bridge and trail. Set up camp in the rain.

Our plan was to first contact the Maita village and have them introduce us to the people they called the Parahuris over on the Parima River. Some of the Maitas had visited the mission station and had received trade goods. They had told Rod that they had trading contact with the Parahuris, and we felt that it would be the wise thing to reach the Parahuris through the friendly Maita group. Both the Waicas from around the station and the Maitas said that the Parahuris were fierce.

Bob Hawkins had seen the Maita village on the previous air survey, identified by a fellow he recognized as having seen at the station, "Fatso" by name. We knew that the Maita trail crossed this creek, but had we hit it so soon? It seemed unlikely.

New Frontiers (1959 to 1962)

Thursday, January 14

Inspected the trail for a short way, but it didn't go in the right direction to suit us, so we decided to go one more day up the creek. Here again the creek was very winding, and progress was slow. Hit rain much of the day. Inspected another trail which we pronounced to be a hunting trail—either Maita or Parahuri. Made camp late and in a downpour. Got soaked during the night. Everything wet and dirty.

Friday, January 15

Since we were low on gas and travel was so slow, we decided to paddle down the creek, with the idea of possibly heading up one of the trails that we had seen. Passed both trails, thinking that they might lead to the Parahuri houses anyway, in which case we could better travel by water. One Indian at Koch's, who said that he lived somewhere up in this neck of the wood, reported the Waicas upriver friendly, so we unanimously agreed to go straight to the Parima and contact the village.

Creek was swift and we made good time. Hit the Parima at 2:30 and at 4:30 saw a canoe and well beaten trail. Walked it for a while but no house. With darkness falling fast, we turned back and pitched camp in a place we soon found to be teeming with a multitude of biting ants.

Saturday, January 16

Klemtu and I waited at camp while the rest went up to find the house and meet the people. I was glad for the opportunity to wash clothes but didn't get too far with this project. As I was rigging up a bush rope clothesline, I heard a call from the other side of the river. My guess that the call sounded like a friendly one was verified as I paddled across and met with six men. Was able to talk to them enough to tell them that I was friendly and that there were others of our party up at their house. I understood enough to know that they too were friendly. They called themselves "Tucushim" and I never did hear any of the groups we met from then on call themselves "Parahuri" (later in talking about this to the Maitas and Waicas up on the Uraricoera River, we learned the possible reason. Those to whom we were talking laughed and said that the Parahuris were scared and didn't want to reveal their real name, but instead used the name of those who we passed there at the base of the falls on the Parima.)

These six Indians were very much afraid. I offered them some rice, but they politely refused, saying that they "didn't know" about that stuff. I told them that I was waiting for the other white man to return, and they left.

Soon Rod returned and told of his good contact up above at the house. When we arrived, they were already busy making us a shelter. Not much of a shelter, but the thought was good. They really spared the leaves, and we got soaked during the night.

Bob Cable with Parahuri couple

The first day with them we saw twenty-five men, seven women, and some children. The people were slight of build, fairly light in color, and some, like the Tucushim people down below, had that shaved circular spot on the crown of their heads.

The shelter they had built was right next door to their own, and they didn't spare the visits. They took turns keeping our fire going during the night. We never did decide whether this was just a friendly gesture, or whether they wanted to keep constant watch on us.

Sunday, January 17

Had a short service. All stood around and all chimed in on the singing. Rod spoke. People still fearful, especially at night. Kept asking whether we were friendly and good. They wouldn't allow us to go down the other side of the hill on the main trail, even though we told them that all we wanted was water. They offered the services of one of the boys. We figured that this path must lead to another house, probably the main house, and that they were fearful to show us the place lest we discover their young women.

The things we owned scared them. They told me more than once to put my notebook away. (Though I was a little less conspicuous with it, I continued to use it, and they grew accustomed to it and didn't mind.) They never did get used to the camera, and I quit taking pictures. Sure, the people back home would like to see the people and their habitat; but there'll be other trips back up in here, and our purpose right now isn't to take pictures, but to win the hearts and confidence of these victims of fear.

Our guns were a constant source of amazement to them. This morning Rod picked up a gourd the size of a grapefruit, hummed it way up in the air, and popped it off with the .22 right in midair. The bits came flying down at our feet. In the following days as some went hunting with the Wai Wais, they must have concluded that these shooting irons never miss. A few trips with me must have convinced them that the guns weren't completely magic.

My constant thought and prayer during these days is this: "May we show the perfect love that casts out fear."

Monday, January 18

Cooked cassava bread in the frying pan while Rod, Bob, and Mawashá were getting ready to take a jaunt upstream. They wanted to push up as far as possible through the rapids and maybe even get to the canyon that had been seen by air.

We moved our base of operations from the top of this steep hill to the bottom so that we could be near the good water supply at the river. This was a better all-around site, but that hike up and down the hill was a battle, especially in those beginning days when there was so much rain. The path led through an old field and in spots it was steep and muddy. It was like trying to climb up a greased playground slide. And usually in the slickest places there was neatly placed a thorn palm—very poor handrail. Every time I went up and down this hazard I thought of the words of the second verse of the Portuguese hymn, "Where He Leads, He I Will Follow." Translated it would be something like this:

> Though the road be hard to endure;
> Full of thorns and insecure;
> In His arms I'm safe and sure;
> Where He sends me, I will go.

But back to the cassava bread and cooking. It could be considered a chore and waste of time for a fellow, but on these trips it's really not much of a burden. In fact, it's a great help in making conversation with the people. It's a bad language learning situation at first to just sit in their house with pencil and notebook in hand. But as they come around your fire and watch you cook or grind out cassava flour, they talk in a relaxed manner. In this atmosphere they don't seem to notice the notebook.

Tuesday, January 19

Enjoyed the addition to our little house which was made the day before. Klemtu cut down some trees which not only gave us some good sunlight, but more importantly, gave us a few runways down to the river.

This is a good situation at the bottom of the hill. The people visit in little groups and are more relaxed than when we were right on top of them in their house. Three men came in the morning and brought cassava. A couple of them brought their hammocks to make their visit more enjoyable. Also brought their own lunch—bananas for roasting. Thankful that they seem "at home" here. Fished with one of the men in the afternoon.

Bob Cable hauling water

Wednesday, January 20

Rod, Bob, and Mawashá returned from upstream. They had hit rapids just twenty minutes out of camp, and by this our location on the map was pretty well settled. We were in the village which was seen and marked out on the aerial survey. They had found the rapids tough and had not been able to reach the canyon area.

I had a great visit with the people on the top of the hill in the afternoon. They were friendly and talkative, and loaded me down with papaya fruit as I left. I believe they finally trust us, but they still insist that there is only the one house.

Don teaching Parahuri boys

Thursday, January 21

Bob and I went hunting with two of the Parahuris. We saw tracks, and one of the boys smelled something or other, but that was all. Came across an eight-foot snake which was taken in stride by the leader. He calmly broke off a small branch and killed it. The thing was squirmy and wouldn't wrap up too well, so finally they tied the head and let the rest drag behind. Boys soon got discouraged and settled for the snake meat instead of going on. Had a meal that beat all meals. Rod boiled up some sweet cassava, red beans, and a bush chicken. Don't think I've ever enjoyed eating so much as I did that meal.

Parahuri man with snake

Friday, January 22

Five more Parahuri men arrived from another village downriver and inland to the west. They had visited with other Parahuri or Tucushim people down below and had learned we were here. Quite a time getting any language material from them. We don't know too much to start with, and each one helped out by talking with a big wad of tobacco between the lower lip and teeth. Bob and I took a walk and saw their new fields in the afternoon. Lots of bananas and sugarcane. Tried to travel incognito but met up with a couple of the men.

Saturday, January 23

Memorized language data in the morning. Met more Parahuris in the afternoon and traded with them.

Sunday, January 24

The old chief came down informing us that two Maitas had come over. It turned out that they were two of the same group—Parahuri. It might have been that we misunderstood, and that the old man had said that two men had just come over from visiting the Maitas, but this, too, was false as we found out later. Making allowances for misunderstanding, we still have to come to the conclusion that these people major in telling the untruth. They said they only had one field, the one on the way to our house. Bob and I had seen four or five more good-sized ones. As to the trail to the Maita house, some said it was ten sleeps, others four. (Later when they saw that we were on our way, they informed us that it was only one sleep away.) They still say that there is only the one house, but we know better. Already we had seen many more people than would fit in the one house.

Rod got on them for lying so much, and this greatly sobered them. We even got some boys to say that they'd go with us to the Maita house. As we went into the service, the attention was good. Later we stayed around and talked. Two boys had malaria, and we got medicine for them. One poor teenager nearly choked trying to get down his pills. Good time of fellowship between us Americans in the afternoon as we read, sang, and prayed.

Monday, January 25

The gang up on the hill had gotten together and decided they didn't want to take us to the Maitas. The reason? Probably the same reason most Indians don't want to take the white man on further—they want all the trade goods.

Not too hopeful, I went up the hill and finally a boy, a man, and his wife said they'd go. Later one more fellow joined the party. Klemtu and I stayed at camp again and went fishing in the afternoon. Klemtu shot one of those huge rodents, but it submerged before we could get to it.

Tuesday, January 26

Klemtu went out again after the rodent which by this time had come to the surface. He came back with it and almost simultaneously about ten Waicas were here wanting some of it. They must have some sort of ingrown telegraph system that we don't know about. The Wai Wais don't count this rodent as one of the chief delicacies, so we gave away all but some of the ribs—and I do mean ALL. They eat about everything.

Longest informant session I've ever had, and the best. There was a group sitting around all afternoon. They never seemed to tire of talking and repeating phrases whenever I would ask them. One fellow especially is helpful. At times he would sit right next to me and put words into my mouth to use in conversation with somebody else.

One man from downriver told of other houses upstream and to the west. The other men had gone, and he felt free to talk. He said that the one(s) to the west are fierce; those upstream are friendly. These upstream were only three days away, he said. This got me keyed up. Would he go with us? Would his toe get better? (A mean snip on his big toe, inflicted by an alligator.)

A great day. Realized that someone or many were praying in a special way. May the Lord give them the assurance that their prayers are heard and answered. It is not easy to pray with faith and fervency when we cannot *see* the actual situation.

> The weary ones had rest, the sad had joy
> That day, and wondered "how?"
> A ploughman singing at his work had prayed,
> "Lord, bless them now."
> Away in foreign lands they wondered "how"
> Their simple word had power.
> At home, the "Gleaners," two or three, had met
> To pray an hour.
> Yes, we are always wondering "how?"
> Because we do not see
> Someone, unknown perhaps, and far away,
> On bended knee.
> —Unknown

Friday, January 29

Boys returned from the Maitas at 10:00 a.m. They found a big, round, enclosed house with eighty people. Big fields with bananas, cassava, sugarcane, and cotton. The Maitas told Rod of other groups from there on up to the canyon. Five specific groups were mentioned, each a day's journey one from another, the last group being close to the canyon.

Saturday, January 30

Language study and work with tape recorder. Some have fear of this machine, but for the most part each one is willing to talk into it. The recorder has given much trouble, sounding out a great big buzz when ready to record. Rod and Bob, with more mechanical ability and curiosity than I, spent much time looking at the insides, but we never did get the thing working. Thankful for most of one side of one tape that is usable.

Working on the tape recorder

Sunday, January 31

Prov 27:7 (KJV), "The full soul loatheth a honeycomb; but to the hungry soul, every bitter thing is sweet." How true this is. Better to be hungry and enjoy the simplest of food than to be full and not really appreciate "the king's meat." We haven't had to eat anything bitter yet, but we've eaten simply, and have enjoyed to the hilt everything that we have eaten. This principle that Solomon noted is true in other areas as well. We don't appreciate Christian fellowship fully until we are forced to spend some time by ourselves. We don't fully realize the blessing of health until we spend a period in which we can't move without effort and discomfort.

And I think of the testimony of Augustus Mariweh, an African fellow I met at Wycliffe summer school. He had grown to the age of twelve, way off in the bush, without ever having heard about God. Then one day he heard the news of Jesus Christ. He told us jubilantly, "Oh, how sweet is the Word of God to those who hear it for the first time!" We Americans listen to the Word of God being proclaimed on the radio and from the pulpits with hardly an ounce of emotion being stirred up in our veins. We fall under Paul's condemnation as he wrote with a touch of sarcasm to the Corinthians: "Now ye are full, now ye are rich, ye have reigned as kings without us, and I would to God ye did reign, that we also might reign with you." (1 Cor

4:8 KJV) The trouble is not that we are "full" spiritually speaking, but that somehow our spiritual appetite has been deadened. "Blessed are they that hunger and thirst after righteousness."

Monday, February 1

We sure have a million-dollar campsite. I have often thought that many people in the States would give anything if they could come to a place like this and see the things we are seeing. Up this far on the Parima, the river is narrow and always fast moving. The hills and mountains hug the river closely, and as we move out on the tree that was felled, we can see one mountain upstream to our left and one high one downstream to our right.

Parima River rapids

Parahuris, February 1960

In the afternoon the sun beats against our side of the river, making for ideal swimming. The nights are crisp and clear with a bright moon shining overhead these days.

Usually we finish eating after sunset, and these last few nights we've cleared the "table" and enjoyed sitting out there in the clearing underneath the moon and stars. Rod is never lost for words and keeps the conversation lively when it bogs down. He's a fellow you like to listen to. Six foot three, well over two hundred pounds, and with a Southern accent. There he sits on a log, telling all about his days as a professional baseball player and then later as worker in the oil fields. Best of all were his reports on the invasion of Normandy and the push on Paris.

Thursday, February 4

Bob and I decided to find the other house of the people. We thought it must be in the vicinity of the new field that we had seen previously. On the way back from the Maita house, Mawashá had started up a well-beaten path before being called back by the Parahuris. This path probably led up to the house, and to this path we headed. It was a long way around, but a sure one. Heard voices as we came to the creek and as we passed, we met a fellow we'd never seen. We moved on quickly as we didn't want to get sidetracked now that we were so close. Climbed up a big hill, came to a field, and there right on the top was the clearing and house—the charred remains of it. How long it had been burned down we didn't know but knew that the other shelter or shelters must be nearby.

Maita Dwelling

The view from here was tremendous, but we didn't stop long to look. A couple of good trails led from the clearing, and after starting down one, decided upon the other. Soon found that we were on the right track, for we met two new women with babies. Their baskets were empty, so we knew that they were coming from the house and not to it. Surprisingly, they didn't act too fearful. They told us the house and men were on up ahead, and I'm sure they were relieved when we moved on.

Soon we hit an area with four or five little shelters. The women scattered into the bush as we were arriving, and we visited for a while with the boys, all of whom we knew. Surmising that there was another shelter up ahead, we took off, much to the consternation of the fellows. They kept trying to divert us off on the side paths, but we kept down the main road. Finally, when the boys saw they were fighting a losing battle, one of them said, "I'll go first and lead you into camp." He did a great job hooting our arrival and then yelling to the women not to be afraid and to come back. There were about thirty hammocks in this area. This was the chief's headquarters.

A few of the boys who had run up from working on their field offered to show us the way home, but they made sure it was a circuitous one, detouring around their fields. Even though we had to push through brush and cobwebs in some places, they still insisted that this was the "one and only" path to our place. I wonder if they really thought we believed them. Those characters! As soon as we hit our camp, they headed off up the other path which we knew went directly back to their house.

Friday, February 5

Worked with the tape recorder some, and then thought seriously about trying to find the house which the pilot had marked on the map as being due west, about a day's walk away. Since the recorder was on the blink, I felt this would be the next most profitable thing to do. The Parahuri (or Tucushim) people, with the exception of that one man from another village, had continually told us that there were no other villages to the west or south, that the whole region was "empty," so we knew it was useless to try to get a guide. But Mawashá had seen a pretty good path which crossed the river upstream a little. Klemtu and I had gone about three hours down this path (down and up!) and it did go west, showing encouraging signs of use. So Bob, Klemtu, and I decided to take our hammocks and enough supply for one night's sleep.

Saturday, February 6

Started out early, hitting it pretty hard along that up and down trail. At 10:30, we came down to a huge, beautiful creek. It was wide and shallow with a pebbly bottom. This sight was a complete surprise to us as no creek was marked on the map. The signs which we saw were encouraging. A bush-rope had been strung across a log bridge (one tree felled across river), and we saw the feathers of a bird that had been killed recently—probably that very morning. Crossed bridge, lost trail, but after scouting around found one that led to the main trail.

Came to an arm of the creek, which was still wide, but with a sandy bottom. At this spot we could see where someone had dug for worms for fishing, so our anticipation mounted. Two or three more hills and then we could see a mountain in front of us, and figured that they might live on top of it, although it seemed a crime for people to leave a nice creek like the one we had seen to live way up where water is scarce. If this wasn't a mountain, it was a long, high hill. As we hit the ridge, the path widened out and it wasn't long before we heard the welcomed sound of children's voices down in the valley to our right. Immediately after rounding the ridge, we came in sight of the house.

Another Maita Dwelling

We heard the women scatter as we called out. Keeping our distance from the house, yet staying out in the cleared area, we kept calling, telling them we were friendly, not to be afraid, and that we would give them knives. After fifteen minutes an old woman emerged from the bush, pathetically telling us that she was the only occupant of this big house. We gave her a comb and told her we had heard others, asking her to go call the rest. She insisted that she was the only one there, but we kindly told her we would sit down and wait for her to call the rest. Off she went.

While we were waiting, I decided to look inside the house, wondering whether this might be the only chance we would have to get inside the house. It was old, and vines had grown up on the sides of the stockade or high fence that encircles the oval ring of shelters. There were only two entrances and I managed to wiggle my way through one of these. I counted twenty hammocks and saw other fires which had been in use recently. On one side of the oval, the shelter was about fifteen feet high with huge, long leaves draped across the face to make for warmth. The rest of the circle was enclosed by smaller shelters six feet in height. In the middle was an open area. I saw no cassava plates or graters and saw only a few pieces of sweet cassava. There was an abundance of bananas and cotton.

Forty-five minutes later the woman returned, perspiring and out of breath. "She hadn't seen anybody," so took off in the other direction, down the path we had come up. I was tired, and lay down across the trail, using my sneaks for a pillow. It was the time to be excited, I guess, but I felt more in the mood to catch a few winks.

Another half hour and five men appeared on the trail with bows and arrows. They approached the same way we had, and evidently had circled around to see if there were others in our group. When they saw us, they threw their bows and arrows down to the side of the trail and came up to greet us.

They were scared to death and kept nervously jabbering at us as other men came in one by one. Soon they invited us inside the house. To each of the men we gave a few fishhooks, and to the women we gave combs. Only three elderly women appeared at first, but gradually the younger ones presented themselves to receive their combs. Possibly, too, the men believed us when we told them that we didn't want their women. Told them also that we didn't want to plunder their fields, but they never did let us see them. We did get to see their water hole, a swampy place. Had to dig a small hole to get clear water. Thought again of that nice, wide, clear creek down below. It must be fear of attack that drives these people to settle on the top of high hills. I don't think the bugs are any less numerous up higher.

We suggested that we build a little shelter down by the water hole, but they wanted us to stay with them in their house. They were ready to do anything to help us. We mentioned a fire and pronto, some boys went scurrying for wood and mustered up a blaze in no time flat. Cooked up some rice with a little soup for gravy. Also made a banana drink from the bananas they had given us. We shared this with the people, and they gulped it down and enjoyed it, but if they had known we had sprinkled in some powdered milk, they probably wouldn't have touched the stuff. Milk to Indians is strictly for babies.

What a privilege! People all around us, enjoying watching us eat. Later most of them left, but there was always a group of two or three close at hand. After a while we lay in our hammocks faking sleep, in this way getting a chance to think and pray. If we made much of a move at all during the night, one of the boys would be over us asking if we were good. I slept well, but Bob said the boys intermittently would wake him up, asking him whether we were friendly and good.

The next morning they all gathered to hear for the first time the message that there is one God Who created all things, loves them, and has a wonderful place in heaven for all who want him. As we said goodbye, they responded with an invitation to come back.

Sunday, February 7

After we were through with our oatmeal, we cooked up what was left and gave it to the people. Had service out in the opening. We couldn't tell them much but could say that God had made all the things about them, that He was friendly, and liked them.

Don teaching Maita boys

Three men and a couple of kids accompanied us down to the creek as we returned. Klemtu shot a bill bird, and they received it as a farewell present.

We had seen a complete change in their attitude. The one young man who had come up to us trembling and with a glassy stare in his eyes was one of those who accompanied us to the creek. Now he was like an old buddy to us. It was well worth the trip just to witness the transformation of attitude in this one man.

Monday, February 8

Sunday afternoon the old chief had come down and asked us to come up for a service the next day. We praised the Lord for this invitation and waited for them to come to show us the way. When they came, they also insisted that we bring up the tape recorder. We were actually going down that forbidden trail, with an entourage of Indians before and behind. It was like a grand parade celebrating victory. They led us through their new field and to an area of shelters that we had not yet seen. Noticed some new people, mostly women. A huge pot of bananas was boiling, and two big baskets were filled with the ones already cooked.

Rod tells about God

New Frontiers (1959 to 1962)

Pot of Bananas and a Barrel of Fun

I wondered about the man who had said he would take us to the other village. Knowing he'd probably not want to talk about it with all the others around, I asked him to come down to get a new bandage on his toe. He said he'd come a little later and kept his promise, making his way down to our camp alone. Prospects didn't look too good for getting to see another village. The rest of his gang from downriver had gone back home, and beside this, he said his toe still hurt. The verdict: he was going back home tomorrow. Again I told him how much we wanted to see the other village, and again we promised him a ride down river in our canoe if he'd wait for us. We talked a little more and then all was quiet. Suddenly he looked at me with those big bright eyes and said he'd go with us.

Tuesday, February 9

Started off in the canoe fairly early. We didn't know where the path started, so we were at the mercy of our guides. A boy of ten years also came along with the older man. It turned out that he knew the way a lot better than his elder. We soon came to the conclusion that the man just wanted a ride in the canoe, and with the rapids fairly swift, we told him that this was the end of the joy ride. He had said that there was no trail along the shore, but we hit one fifteen seconds after we got out of the canoe. Mawashá took back the canoe, and Bob, Klemtu, and I moved on.

It's always interesting to follow a small boy on the trail. They keep themselves amused by popping leaves with their mouth or by cutting down a branch and whittling on it. This boy's specialty was making spears and throwing them at fish, birds, or just a stump along the way.

The hills were low with the exception of the last one which was very high and long. It was slightly past noon, and we were now on a ridge which curved around making a cup-like valley in which was the big field. Our guide told us to wait while he went on to announce our coming. As we entered the clearing inside the house, we were mobbed by a big group of teenage fellows. The women soon appeared. The whole group showed less fear than either of the other two villages we had visited. Gave fishhooks to the men and beads to the women—a good method of counting how many are in a village. We counted about sixty in this one which was comprised of two oval type houses located right next to each other.

We recognized two men who had been at the other village and had told us they were from downriver. One of them was the chief. The boys showed us all around the place and were buddies from the start. Just a few of this group showed fear. The view from this summit was the best yet. A little east of north we could see the mountain by our base camp and village. Far across the way to the northeast we could see the mountain on which the Maita house was located. Swinging around a little more to the south lay the canyon which they said was one sleep away. The ridge on which we were standing continued up to a higher peak, and this would explain why this village hadn't been seen by the plane which had come from the south on the survey.

This was a tremendous bunch of teenage fellows. All afternoon they swarmed around us. Poor Bob didn't feel too good when he arrived, and then he had to be in the middle of this group of interrogating Indians for the rest of the day. An initial contact with a group like this is fatiguing. There's the physical tiring of the trail, but more noticeable is this social tiring that comes from being surrounded every moment by a group continually conversing. From arrival time to departure we answer questions and quiet their fears.

Don teaching teenage boys

But this teenage gang. They reminded me of the boys back home, full of life and fun. After supper we had a great time playing "ring on a string" hollowing out a piece of sugarcane to use for the ring. Then they gathered around our hammocks till we told them we were tired and wanted to sleep. Still at intervals they'd come and start talking. The whole set-up reminded me of a camp back in the States. The old chief who was sleeping next to us kept telling the boys to be quiet and go to their hammocks, pleading for the well-being of the guests.

There was quite a procedure for the one who wanted to go outside during the night. The doughnut-shaped house was encircled closely by a ten-foot heavy poled fence. At night the two openings were closed up. Someone was always half awake and at the portal if there was any rustling of the poles which were used to barricade the entrance. I had the fortune of experiencing one of these nocturnal procedures in which my bodyguards kindly dismantled part of the wall for my exit.

Wednesday, February 10

Possibly the purpose of this high wall around the house is for safety. But I wondered if part of the reason wasn't for warmth. As I stepped outside in the morning, I was met by a stiff, cool blast of wind sweeping across the ridge.

The boys had caught on to the songs well and wanted to sing them over and over. After a short service we bid goodbye. They told us to be sure to come back. They didn't know how much we really wanted to, nor did they know the many opposing forces that would seek to thwart our promise of return. Nor did they know the power of our God to bring such a promise to pass.

The route home was a different one—direct. Crossed river on bush rope bridge. All in all, this was the best trail I've been on yet; a gradual slope down and fairly level the rest of the way.

Rope bridge

Thursday, February 11

I visited the folks on the hill, telling of our planned departure. Said they would really miss us. We knew there would be a sense of relief that we were gone; they must have had some fear.

Friday, February 12

Learned a lesson today. Don't kid with the people unless you're positive they know you are kidding. Some of the boys asked to go for a ride in the canoe, so five of us took off. Jokingly I told the rest on the bank that we'd be gone for five days. Of all things, they believed us. Rod said that one of the women almost cried.

One last hunting jaunt in the afternoon. Missed a couple of birds. Must have been out of range of the gun—as good an excuse as any.

Saturday, February 13

Motor started on the first pull. Canoe had been loaded the night before, so we got a good early start. Let the downriver Parahuri man off about noon at the mouth of creek going off to the west. He said he'd make it home by nightfall. There he stood on the bank of the river with a smiling face, stroking his chest and then motioning downstream—his way of telling us that he was our friend and wishing us a good voyage downstream.

He was quite the man. It was no strain at all to sit, watching and listening to him. His storytelling was animated by all sorts of gestures. I'll never forget him showing us how he approached a Shamatari house once, only to be met with a shower of arrows.

Parahuri man with bow and arrow

The night before we left, he was sleeping with us and had hit the hammock early. Just as we were dozing off, he terminated his little beauty nap and felt inspired to rehearse some bird calls. Rod tells me he woke up a few more times during the night and the old boy was going through the same thing. Rod was about ready to ask one of the Wai Wais to stick an arrow in the bird making all the noise.

But of all the Parahuri people we had seen, this one was my favorite. He seemed to understand us more than the rest and was open with us, telling us what he knew of the region. He didn't beg, although we did trade together. Beside some of these tangible qualities, there was an indescribable something in the gleam of his eyes that captivated my liking for him. I pray that those eyes soon be turned upon the face of Jesus, bringing joy to his heart Who longingly awaits the day when someone will be able to point out the way.

Arrived at Koch's place at 2:00 p.m. Especially the Wai Wais were disappointed that the Maiongongs had already left to go downstream with Koch. It would mean a lot more lugging and extra time spent packing around the falls. Stayed long enough to pick up Mawashá's blow gun and a good dose of burrowing fleas. Went on and camped at the head of the first set of rapids. It rained as soon as we stopped. History was sadly repeating itself as far as the weather was concerned.

Sunday, February 14

The Wai Wais took enormous loads. We all packed all we could on our backs and plowed through the trail as fast as we could. Came back for another load while the Wai Wais took the nearly empty canoe through the rapids.

As far as I was concerned, I had exerted all my energy for the day by 10:30 in the morning. Sat on a rock feeling like I'd just been through a rough game of basketball. Started to rest up and dry off when the Wai Wai boys came back saying that the rapids were bad, and they couldn't get through.

All of us went back. Bob carried the motor, and the rest of us started carrying the canoe, but didn't get too far before we found out it was too heavy. We slid it back into the water and made it back to camp, sometimes carrying the canoe over rocks, sometimes guiding it through the rapids with the ropes.

Rapids along the Parima

Rod and I made ourselves a nice shelter with the tarp and what a relief it was to lie down and look out over the surf-like water.

Gal 1:24 struck me in a new way. Of the churches of Syria, Cilicia, and Judea Paul wrote: "And they glorified God in me." How is it with me? Is it my sole desire that people glorify God in me, or do I want it turned around to read, "And they glorified me in God?" A slight, subtle change, but all the difference in the world. So often we glorify personalities instead of the God who is operating in them. It might be a converted movie or baseball star. It might be a youth worker, pastor, or missionary. May eyes be focused upon Jesus Christ with each one of us in the fuzzy background.

In all our human, earthly relationships this correct focus is essential. We can get our eyes upon a friend or mate, with too much attention and focus upon that relationship. God is closely linked in this "glorying," but still out there in the blurred background. In regard to our service, here again we can fix our eyes on the work with all its attendant blessings—physical and spiritual. Certainly Christ is vitally a part of it all and yet it is possible that He be out of focus.

A short verse. Let's not get the words twisted around. "And they glorified God in me."

Monday, February 15

Paddled half a day down to the top of the falls. Wanted to go down to get some Waica (Tucushim) carriers, so we took off with loads, leaving Mawashá behind to get some supper ready for us in case we came back late. The trail seemed longer this time than the first time we had come across it. Maybe our strength was waning a bit. It's a good four or five miles.

Down at the bottom of the falls we saw no sign of canoe and received no answer as we called. I swam across the river and went up trail to their house, but this was empty and showed no signs of having been lived in recently. This was discouraging as it might mean that we'd have to lug all the stuff ourselves. There was a ray of hope however, for Rod noticed smoke downriver and figured that these Tucushim people were living down there at the mouth of a creek. It was this creek down which we planned to take the canoe the next day, hoping to meet the people then and ask for their services.

Darkness was fast creeping up on us, and so we started to hightail it back to the top of the falls. Klemtu kept charging along and we kept getting closer together so that we could see one another. One of our crew had back trouble and this slowed us down so that we didn't quite reach camp before darkness overtook us. It was pitch black now, but Klemtu unbelievably kept on the trail. I noticed he put a shirt around his shoulders and when I mentioned something about this, Bob recalled that Klemtu had left it on the trail on the way down. I thought we had left the trail long ago, but here we were still on course. We had a gay time keeping up with one another. Bob followed Rod's white hat, Rod kept an eye on my white shorts, and I would try to listen to Klemtu's footsteps. He helped out by talking to himself about there being no trail anymore. Once in a while I'd catch a glimpse of his camouflaged body, but usually only after knocking my head on the gun he was carrying, or stubbing my finger as I reached out to see if he was there.

The inevitable happened. We got off the trail and couldn't pick it up. We knew we were fairly near camp, so hooted and then shot the gun. Mawashá had already started out on the trail with a flashlight and heard the shot, hollering back at us.

As I had been following Klemtu, I thought of an incident back in Bonfim. Little Brian was following me one dark night, and I asked him if he could see the trail. "No," he replied, "but I can see you." Now I was in the same situation. I couldn't see the trail but made it my business to keep close to Klemtu and follow him. Don't we find ourselves in this situation in life? Well may we say, "Lord, I can't see the way and don't know where to place my next step, but I can see you, and I'm following close behind."

Tuesday, February 16

The canoe and the others started over the trail the Maiongongs had cut to the creek. I finished cooking the rice and cleaned up camp. I was to carry the hammocks, blankets, gun, and food while the others grunted with the canoe. They made good time, for I started three-quarters of an hour later and breezed right along, but never did catch them till the creek.

At first, the creek was ankle deep with just a few deep pools. We'd lift the canoe over some stretches, half drag it through others. At times we could hop a ride and coast for a few yards. Much of the way was this in-and-out process. Unfortunately the "outs" were more numerous. Many times we'd have to drag over logs and cut our way through vines and brush of fallen trees. One time I ripped into some branches with a cutlass and got a bee sting which puffed up my eye and closed it completely.

Late in the afternoon we hit a trail and figured that we must be near the village and mouth of the creek. Mawashá was out looking at it and called for me to follow on foot with him. Anything was better than that creek travel, so I jumped at the invitation.

Passed through a field but still there was no village in sight. I was beginning to doubt the wisdom of having started off like this so close to dark (especially with vivid memories of last night still in my head). The Lord has his angels watching over us, for just then a shotgun blast way off in the distance stopped us short. We looked at each other in surprise, for the noise was way off behind us. We realized then that the boys with the canoe were way back and that we'd better go back to meet them.

Mawashá veered off the trail and hit the creek at a spot just in front of the oncoming canoe. In getting there I had gone through another bee's nest.

Not only had the gunshots brought us back to the canoe just in time before dark, but also, they provided us with two birds. With other circumstances somewhat miserable, these birds and the little farinha we had were a real cause for rejoicing.

It had rained enough in the afternoon to soak our clothes. There was no good firewood in the area, and Klemtu had to work hard to start a fire. Rain and tiredness blunted the edge of any desire to make an elaborate camp. The shelter was narrow, just wide enough for hammocks to be hung one under the other. The rain had let up, and Mawashá was outside with his hammock, hoping that it would clear up for the night. But it rained. And it was cold. No fire, no dry clothes, and the rain was dripping down into our hammocks. We would have frozen if it were not that we were hung so close together. Mawashá joined Rod, Klemtu, and me "inside." The only trouble with hanging hammocks in this dresser drawer style was that there was nobody to pull us out. We couldn't even turn over or change positions without a major cooperative effort. Mawashá managed to ease out a couple of times and when he did, a cold blast of air penetrated my back.

Wednesday, February 17

I don't know about the others, but I didn't feel going anywhere. We were tired, cold, and wet. My feet felt like grater boards, sliced up a little from having gone barefoot in the creek. The extraction of some burrowing fleas also had left a few holes.

Once we were in the canoe again, conditions bettered. The sun came out and the creek was up higher because of the rain. At noon we hit a trail, but this time it was good news. There were some boys at the trail who told us that both the village and the river were "real close."

I followed the boys and was glad to see the same gang that had helped us up through the falls. They seemed like old friends and gave us a good greeting. We quickly negotiated for their services, and they were all set to go. Half the village piled into our canoe, and with a scull team like this, it didn't take us long to paddle up to the base of the falls.

In canoes along the river

Thinking of the foodstuffs up at the top of the trail, I was feeling pretty chipper and offered to go back up with the gang to bring down the rest of our supplies. By the time we arrived, I was starved and right away filled up on milk and farinha. After that the people crowded around asking for everything. I was pretty tired anyway so that I lost all joy for cooking anything else.

These Tucushim people were flippant as we talked about God. Some fellows laughed among themselves. This, coupled with their demanding attitude hit me the wrong way that night, and I was content to swing in my hammock and mind my own business. Not that minding one's own business is wrong, but when contacting new Indians, I feel we should talk with them as much as possible, especially on a short trip like this.

The Lord used a little boy to cheer me up and warm my heart. He came over and sat in my hammock, asking me to sing the new songs with him. Finally I had to tell him I was tired, and he graciously left, but I could hear him singing as I fell asleep. The next day on the trail he was in front of me carrying a shot box, gun, and my Brazilian straw hat. Every once in a while, he'd stop, call the next two in front of him back, and then he'd ask me to sing one of the choruses. Things like this make it all worthwhile.

Thursday, February 18

Got off surprisingly early with our caravan of twelve strong and some not so strong. Had a half-hour coffee break along the way. Some of the boys who had taken the lead had stopped and climbed up some tall trees, and they were breaking off the branches laden with berries.

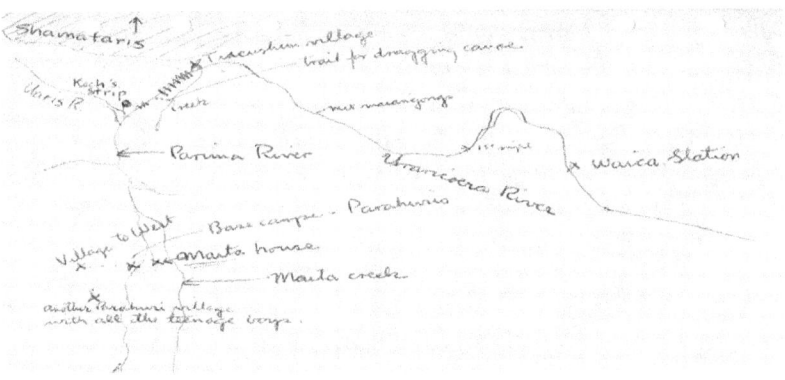

Map of Parahuri Territory by Don Borgman

Paid the carriers, loaded, and left by 10:00 a.m. Once again, the motor started on the first pull and purred right along. We couldn't have enjoyed a plush yacht more than we did that canoe. A bright sun above and a jungle hammock for padding beneath. The recent rains had made a good current, and it seemed as though we were flying low. By noon we started wondering whether we might not make it all the way to the station, but no one mentioned the thought. By 3:00 p.m., we knew we could make it.

No one objected. We got out the razor and scraped off the week's stubble. I started fumbling in the dregs of the duffle bag to see if there might be some cleaner clothes. At 6:00 p.m. we rounded the last bend. In a wonderful way, God had "preserved our going out and coming in."

Email from Don to editor, August 31, 2020

In March of 1960 Pastor Stan Allaby, from our home church in Connecticut, went to Georgetown, British Guiana, and spoke at meetings in the Kitty Bible Church. He was hosted by Rader and Ann Hawkins. While in Georgetown, he was joined by my dad and then together they traveled on to Lethem and crossed the border into Brazil, spending time at the mission base in Bonfim. While at Bonfim, Pastor Allaby was the speaker for our annual mission conference. By now it was April, and both Pastor Allaby and my dad met me at Mucajaí to encourage me and get a taste of jungle life among the Ninam Yanomamis.

Establishing a Base on the Upper Parima

Following the Parahuri expedition, Don was transferred out to Georgetown, British Guiana for six months. After this time, he would return to Yanomami country. Once back, problems with the Brazilian government emerged again, this time under threat of shutting down the entire UFM operation with possible expulsion of the missionaries from Yanomami territory. Once again, however, God moved in a way that would provide protection for the work—the Upper Parima in particular, through an unlikely source.

Email from Don to editor, August 13, 2020

We were standing on the small airstrip at Waica Station, talking over a mission in which we were to cooperate with the Brazilian Air Force in opening up airstrips along the border between Brazil and Venezuela. A telegram had just come to us stating that our mission was to evacuate Indian areas immediately. The Air Force colonel asked to see the telegram, read it and promptly tore it up asserting, "You are now under the wings of the Brazilian Air Force."[7]

Colonel João Camarão Telles Ribeiro, Força Aérea Brasileira[8]

The events and unusual partnership to unfold would prove to be the way God would continue the dissemination of the gospel to the Yanomami people. Once again, God's plan for the extension of his kingdom would not be thwarted. One is reminded of Prov 21:1, "The king's heart is a stream of water in the hand of the LORD; he turns it wherever he will." Don was ready to launch into another expedition far into Waica country on the Upper Parima River to participate in establishing a missionary base of operations. He and others would not be taking the conventional means for getting to the location, however.

Email from Don to editor, September 10, 2019

After the trip to the Parahuri Waicas on the upper Parima River, I spent six months in Georgetown, British Guiana, serving as purchasing agent, buying and packing supplies for the jungle stations both in British Guiana and Brazil. Mucajaí Station had already been established among the Shirishana Indians, as well as Waica Station, located on the Uraricoera River. By the end of 1961 the fields of UFM in British Guiana and Brazil had been separated

---

7. This man was João Camarão Telles Ribeiro. He would play a pivotal role in the years to come in helping the missionaries with their efforts in Brazil. Some of these are highlighted in Homer Dowdy's book, *Christ's Jungle*, a sequel to *Christ's Witchdoctor*.

8. Cambresis, "*João Camarão Telles Ribeiro: a notable Brazilian citizen.*"

administratively, and the base of operation for our mission in Brazil had been moved from Bonfim to the capital city of Boa Vista.

The Indian Protection Service had not yet given permission to settle down for any length of time in these areas, and Neill Hawkins continued dealing with officials in South Brazil regarding the registration of our organization. Along with much opposition, he did find favor with a colonel in Belem who was in charge of the whole Air Force operation in the Amazonian region. This Air Force colonel told Neill that he would like our cooperation in planting an airstrip in the area of the upper Parima, and I was privileged to be chosen to take part in this operation.

Letter from Don to parents, October 1960

This next project, upriver, that of building a strip and getting settled in among the Parahuris, is starting to take shape. In this project we are really serving the Brazilian Air Force (FAB) and while this has some disadvantages, the advantages in the present era of superstition and attacks far outweigh the disadvantages. FAB very badly wants an airstrip up in the Parima River Area, and they have asked us if we would cooperate with them, chiefly because of our knowledge of the Indians and their language. We have gladly consented to do this, praying for permission from the Indian Protection Service to settle in among the Indians once the strip is complete. Traveling with FAB men will be a bigger operation—more canoes, motors, supplies, etc., but FAB is supplying small aircraft for frequent drops, etc.

A week ago Friday (November 18), Ernie Migliazza,[9] the three single girls, two Indian boys, and I started downriver for a one-day trip to visit the downstream folks—the Parimiter Tuxaua and his gang. On the way down, we went through a couple of swift currents and figured we'd better get out and drag the canoe over the rocks at these points on the way back. It took two hours to get to the maloca, and we stayed for about three hours and had a good visit while it poured down rain outside.

We shoved off for home a little before 1:00 p.m. with the addition of stalks of bananas which the Indians were bringing back. Also a young

---

9. Email from Don to editor, September 10, 2019. "While waiting for the Brazilian Air Force personnel to arrive at Waica Station, we continued language study and Ernie Migliazza came to compare notes. He was a missionary from another organization working in a dialect north of Mucajaí. While he was with us, we took a trip downriver which could have ended in tragedy." Notes, largely by Ernie Migliazza, regarding names and terminology about the Yanomami can be found in Appendix A. Presumably he and Don were discussing these very terms during the time of his visit.

Indian mother and her very young baby (less than six months) hopped in with their basket full of belongings.

We hit the first bad place and I thought to pull up to shore, but the Indians encouraged me to go on pointing out a channel. Foolishly, I went ahead. The channel turned out to be a cross stream with rapids above and below. At the other end all I could see was bad rocks and swift water, but it was too late to turn around. As we proceeded, a downwash hit us broadside and over we went.

My first concern was the little baby, and the mother who was holding it above water by its little arm. We took the baby from her, knowing she couldn't make it to the rocks. Praise the Lord, we did get the baby safely on the rocks, and there Sandy comforted the wailing mother. Our next concern was Sue who could not swim, but she had on a life jacket, and Fran was taking charge of her and the canoe. All three were drifting downstream with Fran and Sue holding on to the capsized canoe, which by now was right side up. We men were swimming across and downstream for them when we spotted the gasoline can and a cartridge box floating, so we recovered these on the way to the girls, who we saw were safely near the shore.

Miraculously Ernie and Fran got the water out of the motor and got it to splutter while an Indian and I went to recover the gasoline which had been dumped on the opposite shore. After pulling ourselves and few belongings together, off we putted on one cylinder. We had lost the Indian's basket, most the bananas, and two guns: the station double barrel and Fran's .22. And with only one paddle, we were sure thankful for that one cylinder and for the Penta.

I never thought we could have made it home that same day, but the motor never failed, and we arrived just as darkness was thickening. To me the incident vividly showed me the Lord's mercy in the face of my own failure of good judgment. It could have been a real tragedy.

Email from Don to editor, September 10, 2019

At Waica Station each day we wondered if this might be the day that the men from the Brazilian Air Force would arrive. In the eyes of the public, the purpose of the FAB going into the area where we were was to verify if we were indeed missionaries or just gold miners posing as missionaries. Therefore we figured that this was the reason they wanted to "take us by surprise," and not announce the date of their arrival. The pilots of the FAB had not even contacted the mission pilots of MAF to find out about the condition of the airstrip at Waica Station.

Finally, after waiting since October, early in January we heard the buzz of the planes. The FAB had arrived, first with two L-19 canvas-covered small planes. The airstrip was only about three hundred yards in length. One end started at a small stream, and the strip went uphill and ended with a sharp drop-off. The MAF pilot always entered at the small stream, and the hill helped him to brake before the drop-off. The first plane of the FAB entered from the end of the drop-off and because of faulty (or no) brakes, the pilot veered off the strip into a planted field in which the wings of his planes were severely damaged.

The pilot of the second plane realized that he should enter from the opposite direction, but he touched down, not by the stream, but in the middle of the strip. As he was headed near to the drop-off, a few of us bystanders ran out and grabbed the struts of the plane to keep it from plummeting down the steep hill. Quite an exciting arrival!

Letter from Don to support partners, March 1961

"Prepare ye the way of the Lord, make straight in the wilderness a highway for our God." (Isa 40:3 KJV)
Waica Station, Brazil
Operation Airstrips
Dear friends,

With only ax, cutlass, and hoe, the preparation of an airstrip in jungle country is a slow, laborious process. How often I have thought of the above verse in Isaiah while hacking away at logs, brush, and soil. Monstrous trees must be felled, the whole area burned, remaining branches cut and burned again. Limbs and trunks are then cut and carried off. Huge trunks are extracted. Then another seemingly endless process of scraping off the top layer of roots and ashes, leveling mounds and filling in holes—all in preparation for that grand day when the bi-motor plane can make its entrance.

As we face the task of preparing the way so that Jesus Christ can enter Indian hearts, our path often is beset by a tangle of obstacles which must be cleared away by prayer and patience. One of these is the delay of government permission to enter new areas.

Cooperation with the Brazilian Air Force

One strategic new area is located in the headwaters of the Parima River where lies a heavy concentration of Waica Indian groups. The Brazilian Air Force has been wanting to build an airstrip there in hopes of both opening and protecting this frontier. We believe it was of the Lord that officials have invited our mission to cooperate with them in making initial contact into the region and in dealing with the Indians. Two of us fellows expect to be accompanying the Air Force team.

New Air Strip at Waica Station

Because of the vast expanse of virgin jungle between Boa Vista and the Parima, it was decided that the new strip already in process here at Waica Station should be lengthened to eight hundred meters and should serve as a supply base for the expedition upriver. Since the early part of January, I have been assisting in this project, supervising the Indian workers.

There are also eight Brazilian workers along with a telegraph operator and "enfermeiro" (male nurse). Most of these have been attending the Sunday evening service planned especially for them. Living right with the men has afforded opportunity for further individual witness, and we are thankful for the response shown by two of them as they have told of putting their faith in Christ for salvation.

On to the Parima

The strip here is nearly completed, and soon we expect to be on our way to the new area. We would solicit your prayer especially in regard to the initial contact with the Indians. Their houses have been spotted from the air, and we suppose that occasionally there are battles between the villages, for each of the communal houses is enclosed by a barricade. In all probability, these people have never seen a white man and will be very frightened upon our arrival.

As a result of recent aerial survey flights, a grassy, level area has been located on top of one of the mountains.[10] The Air Force plans to dispense with the long, hard river-land trip by dropping an incendiary bomb in order to burn the grass and prepare for an "emergency" landing in a light plane. This might entail damage to the plane, but not to passengers (we trust). With hoe in hand, the pilot and one passenger could then clear the way for a safer landing for the next plane.

What concerns us as a mission is the reaction of the Indians to this fire and sudden appearance of plane and strangers. If this method is of the Lord, then He can protect both Indians and us. If not, then pray that plans will be

---

10. Mount Surucucu, to the east of the Parima River (see map).

changed. There is the remote possibility that a helicopter will be brought up from Rio de Janeiro. Another possibility is that after the burning, rocks and mounds will be seen, thus making a river trip necessary.

As we enter new territory we will be faced with the problems and the opportunities of civilization. To the eyes of these primitive people will be revealed many new wonders. Our constant prayer is that in all the Waica groups there will be a fulfillment of Isa 40:5, "And the glory of the Lord shall be revealed."

Basing atop Mount Surucucu

The following relates the establishment of the mission station atop Mount Surucucu with the help of the Brazilian Air Force. Don would spend several months at the location from late 1961 into early 1962. This map shows the locations of sites mentioned.

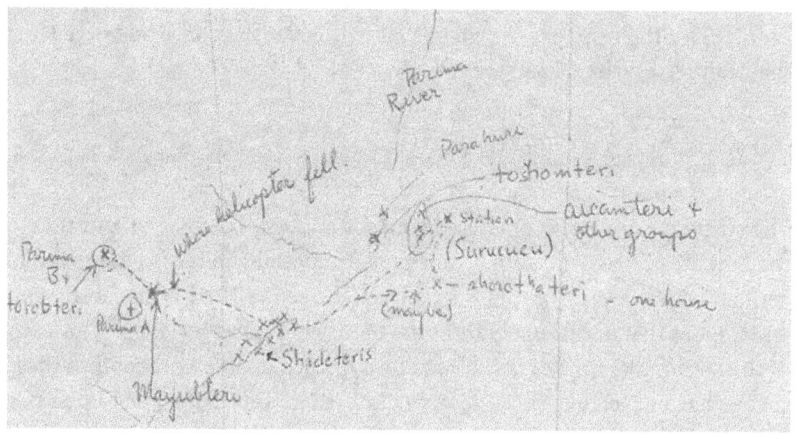

Map of Upper Parima Contacts by Don Borgman

Letter from Don to support partners, June 1961

Mt. Surucucu, Brazil

Dear friends,

A year ago we had just finished a short survey trip to the Parahuri Indians who live on the lower section of the Parima River. This was the fringe of a large Waica group, but we were prevented from going farther because of reported fierceness of the upriver people. Our prayer and planning were for a temporary station among this first Parahuri group.

Now we find ourselves holding down stations in two strategic points right in the midst of those "fierce" groups. After months of waiting and seeming standstill, the move of the past two months has happened so fast and miraculously that we have had the feeling of just watching on in wonder, witnessing God do the "exceeding abundantly above that which we asked or thought."

Imagine embarking out on a venture to contact unknown Indians by means of a helicopter, two Piper Cubs, a Grumman trainer, and a huge Catalina. That was our formation the morning of March 30th as these Brazilian Air Force planes headed far up the Parima in hopes of establishing two new airstrips along the frontier. The helicopter crew was to land first and mark out a short strip for the following Pipers. The larger planes were for coverage in case of mishap. Two grassy areas had been burned previously by incendiary bombs as an added precaution for a safe landing. Our first destination was the clearing farthest away, close to the Venezuela border.

As our Piper Cub reached the appointed spot and banked for a turn, I heard the colonel mutter, "The helicopter has disappeared." Ten minutes back we saw its remains sprawled out on a hilltop, but with the four men alive and seemingly unhurt. The other planes returned to Waica Station, but the colonel decided to try a landing back at the burned area. This was well executed, although we narrowly missed a half-hidden stump.

In the process of marking all danger spots and measuring the usable strip, we stopped to comment on the beauty of the surrounding hills and mountains. In my own heart was pulsating the truth of Ps 121, "I will lift up my eyes unto the hills. From whence cometh my help? My help cometh from the Lord." The helicopter had gone down, thus making our landing more risky. Our Indian guide was flying back home, and this made for greater uncertainty in confronting Indians who might appear. But the Lord was our Keeper.

The next day back at Waica Station seven of us piled into a bi-motor plane, eager to return to the same area, find or cut a trail to the stranded men, and contact the Indians en route. What a contact it was. Two dozen frightened Parahuris prancing up and down beating their chests, waving their lances and arrows, shouting continually, "I'm friendly, I'm friendly." After one night with them, we had to push on.

Two days later, Easter Sunday, we found the helicopter and crew, and that night around the fire there was a time of serious thinking as we read and commented on a portion of God's Word.

After returning to our encampment on the site labeled "Parima," we were ready to experience one more venture which was anything but orthodox. The other proposed airstrip lay thirty-five miles to the east on flat-topped Mt. Surucucu. Having located a cluster of Indian houses on a slope far across the valley, the Air Force colonel suggested that our Indian helper, Primeiro, and I drop in on this group in order to gain friendship and possibly help with the strip work. "Drop in" we did—literally. A new helicopter had arrived, and after a few practice sessions we were ready to climb out on one of the helicopter skids, hang, then drop to the ground.

As we boarded this strange "grasshopper," how thankful I was for Primeiro, who had proved himself a first-class diplomat among the Parahuris, and who was soon to introduce me to another group, the Aicamteris. More heavily was I leaning on Ps 121:8, "The Lord shall preserve thy going out and thy coming in from this time forth, and even for evermore."

All went well as we dropped among the high ferns on the hill above the village. That first visit will long be talked about by these Indians. To me it will be a constant reminder that God alone is the Planner and Protector in the mission he has given us in this jungle area. Give him thanks for letting us settle in among the Aicamteris here at Surucucu as well as the Parahuris and Shamataris surrounding the Parima station. (The Bob Cables and Sue Albright will be at Parima. The Sasscer family and I will be working together here.)

We continue to work with the Brazilian Air Force personnel stationed at these posts which are officially Air Force installations. Pray that there will be a harmonious working together. Praise God for the way he has raised up the Air Force to advance our work at a time when naturally speaking we would have been expelled from the territory by other government agencies.

There will be busy months ahead—building, planting, maintaining the airstrip, along with our main job of learning this new dialect. We anticipate almost continual contact with Indians as already three different village groups have stayed for at least one-week periods, working for trade goods. At present, it seems as though our chief function in their eyes is the dealing out of desperately needed material goods such as knives and axes. There is a deep concern in our hearts that there might be manifested among them an intense thirst to know and serve the true God.

Aftermath of the helicopter crash. Parahuri reviewing "survival" manual

In the meantime, as all of the aforementioned was happening, issues and conflict behind the scenes were taking place, as can be seen by the following report from Neill Hawkins. Neill had been the point person for UFM and the Brazilian government in relation to the overall mission in both Brazil and British Guiana, which was a burden he would carry for a number of years into the future.

Excerpt of newsletter from Neill Hawkins to support partners, July 11, 1961

Only a day or two after mailing the last prayer letter I received news of an order to evacuate all our missionaries from Indian lands. We asked for time to deal with the matter and to pray. The Lord answered by sending the Brazilian Air Force just at that time to begin the long-awaited push into Parahuri Indian country along the upper Parima River, and the Air Force wanted UFM missionaries to help deal with completely primitive Indians they would meet during the operation.

The ensuing missionary adventure story is too long to tell here. A helicopter was forced down in the jungle. Don Borgman and an Indian from Waica station took part in the rescue expedition. Contacts there and elsewhere with the Indians were friendly, and the work of the missionaries gained the gratitude and the strong backing of important officials in the Air Force.

Two new airstrips were opened in the Parima region, and the Air Force asked us to locate missionaries there. As God would have it, six missionaries, the last of the twenty who were prayed out to the field, were rather marking time until new opportunities should open, and thus two new mission stations were begun, Parima[11] and Surucucu. Pray for the missionaries and their families at these posts among primitive people and primitive living conditions. Pray too for the MAF pilot who flies up to two hundred fifty miles from Boa Vista, over jungle and into mountainous regions where navigation is dangerous in the rainy season.

Yet with all the new backing, authorizations were still needed from the Indian Service and from the military organization which controls the frontier zone, and it took much waiting here in Rio to see the end of the Lord's working there. But as you prayed, various members of the military were transferred, an Air Force officer openly and effectively championed our cause, and security restrictions that had weighed against us for three years were removed, so that our missionaries can now carry on without fear of an order removing them from the frontier zone. Formal permission from the Indian Service still awaits completion of reorganization there, but the situation is hopeful.

One price we have had to pay for a stabilized situation has been the voluntary removal of all missionaries from Bonfim, which is directly on the frontier with British Guiana. The territorial government is taking preliminary steps toward the purchase of the property. Pray with us that the Christian testimony there may be maintained.

---

11. As related by Don in correspondence with the editor: "After a year of establishing mission stations at Parima B and Surucucu, a pilot followed the river that passed by Parima B and found that it headed south and was a tributary that eventually emptied into the Orinoco River. Finding out that we were actually located in Venezuela, of course we got out of there. We then contacted an evangelical mission in Venezuela informing them that there was an airstrip waiting to be occupied."

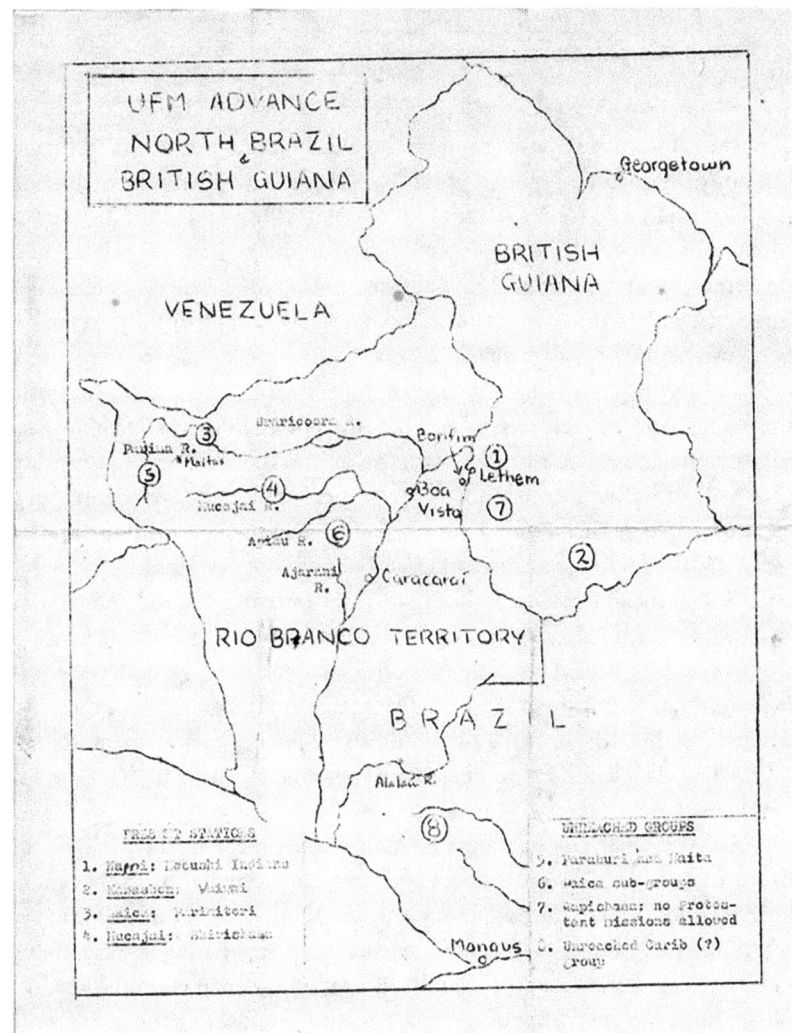

UFM Advance into North Brazil and British Guiana, by Don Borgman[12]

12. This map indicates the extent of UFM work in NW Brazil and British Guiana by about 1961. Within a few years, a station along the Auaris River would be established to the northwest of the Parima. This would be called Auaris Station. Also, a new station, Palimi-U, would be established downriver from Waica Station.

Don's journal, August 1961

Stay at Surucucu

The transition of my moving out of the "FAB" ranks was a little difficult, but now it has worked out well, and I will feel free to spend more time on language analysis. From January on till April, I felt my number one responsibility was to serve the FAB gang and be one of them. Then they all left, and the sergeant came here, and I felt obligated to help him as he was alone. And there was much work to be done on the "pista" (landing strip). I didn't mind living with him (the sergeant), but I felt the time had come to spend more time in the villages and in language analysis. When I was out in Boa Vista the old sergeant was replaced by another, and upon my arrival I promptly set to work on a little shack for myself on this side of the creek where coworker Russ Sasscer is. Right from the start I took meals at the Sasscers, so although we work together well, I don't believe this FAB man is dependent upon us or me at all. The Maiongongs being here is helping him quite a bit, too.

Sometime in October, I'd like to take one or two of the Aicamteris over to Parima in the plane and start out from there to here. I'm looking forward to this trip and expect to meet many Indians en route. In between these jaunts, I plan to buckle down to the language analysis. Pray that the Lord will help in this. I'd like to make a preliminary phonemic statement, so that I can check data while I'm still here with the Indians. This will make time at Wycliffe all the more valuable.

On the other side is a map of the route I expect we'll be taking, although I'm not positive of a direct path from the Mayubteris to the Shideteris. Besides visiting the people, another good purpose in this trip is to see where the most direct trail is between here and Parima B—in case of any plane mishap. I'm pretty sure that this drawn on the map is about the most direct. Elmer, the pilot, has never seen any sign of houses on the direct route over there.

Don's journal, 1961

Thursday, September 14

About my favorite Indian here is Ishofi or Tishofi, as he is also called. He's about nineteen years old, very intelligent, and quick to respond to things. He didn't want to make the trip when I mentioned it a few weeks prior, because of this "momocook" fruit, which is in season. I guess it would be like us taking a hitchhiking trip to the North Pole during the Christmas and

New Year's holidays. But he had been about a week out in the forest getting his fill of momocook and consented to take the airplane trip to Parima B and then return with us on foot by way of the Shideteris. He got in the plane without hesitation but was scared to death the whole trip.

Arrived at Parima in time for lunch, after which we went out and up to visit a couple of the houses. All the Indians (practically all) live way up in the summits of mountains, probably because of fear of attacks from other groups. But I must say it is almost worth the climb because of the view. Going up to the second house, we had to cross a small ravine tightrope-walking across a huge log, then scrambling up the mountain side, having to use all fours a lot of the way.

Was glad for the visit, because there happened to be a man and his boy visiting there who lived over at the Mayubteris, the very place we wanted to go the next day. They, too, were going back home, so our party was complete.

These people at Parima B are about the lowest that I've seen, living in sloppy shelters and with not a stitch of clothing, not even on the women.

There are about four groups of Indians living right around the station; I would imagine maybe five hundred in all. The nearest village is about a half hour away or a little less. Indians are at the station all the time. It's a hard situation at present, although things have improved 100% since the beginning. When Indians come to the station, most always they have trade goods in their minds, and this bargaining and bickering can get one down. Getting out into the villages is the best tonic in the world for one who has been cramped down to station life. Bob is able to get around more now that Sue has come, but the girls can hardly do much visiting. The Indians are still very demanding and rambunctious, so that Sue can hardly stay alone there while Bob and Gay are out. And Sue couldn't go out to the villages alone. Sue could well use a partner over there.

The FAB part of the picture is made up of one radio man (with no radio to operate there) and a civilian Brazilian worker (who wants to go home very badly). The new radio man there is very gentlemanly and easy to get along with. This isn't always the case. The one before would be constantly sending over to Bob's house for batteries, food, and what have you. We face the same thing here, and I blame the FAB. When they do things, they do them big, but then there's the long, long period in which they seem to forget about their personnel here. Supplies have been short for them, and we've gone months without hearing anything from headquarters in Belem. One of these months I expect that they'll roll in again with big planes, tractors, and all sorts of supplies. The confusion in Quadros leaving is partly a contributing factor to all of this. Well, this is getting off the subject of the trip.

Tarimu, Tishofi, and I slept in Bob's house with a fire between us. Finally the whole roof is now covered with "palha," or thatch, but Bob and family are still in the one half. They've sure been cramped underneath that tarp all these months. It seemed funny even for me not to see Bobby and Karen around and how much their parents must miss them.

Friday, September 15

Only one Maiongong was left at Parima, and the boys here asked me if he could travel here with us. I was more than glad, for it would mean extra help for us along the way. I didn't have too much confidence in the Waicas we might or might not pick up along the way. So Joao went with us.

The elderly Shamatari man and his son went with us. I would classify all the Indians of both Parima A and B as Shamataris—a different dialect from Parahuri or the brand of Waica we have here—but similar and understandable. The young ten-year-old boy carried a load of bananas, and the man carried a big old clay cooking pot. This amused me as they make a fuss about carrying along their little straw hammocks, usually leaving them behind and sleeping on the ground along the trail or making some bark hammocks. But here was the old man lugging a twenty-pound pot back to his village. I imagine the right kind of clay is hard to find and that pots are scarce.

I was going to take some good pictures this trip, and so carried the camera out of the sack, slung around my shoulder. Going under and over logs on the trail it must have slipped off without my knowing it. When I discovered it was gone, Joao and I went back to the spot where I last remember having it. Searched the trail but didn't find it. There is a slim possibility that it will turn up—very slim. (Camera came in from Parima on plane today.)

In spite of the lost time, we made it to the Mayubteri by dusk and were welcomed with the same kind of "giddy," wild welcome that we had received from these people when we made that first contact with the FAB. Tarimu didn't say much, but Tishofi was great, doing a lot of talking and making friends.

Their little village of about one hundred and fifty was a series of shelters joined in a huge circle and enclosed with a high barricade of logs. It was still under construction, but we managed to find an area with a roof over our heads.

Saturday, September 16

Spent most of the morning visiting a couple of sick people, giving penicillin shots, and then sitting down and singing and talking with them, and then with the little group that always gathered around 3:00 in the afternoon. An old man came up the latter part of the morning and asked us to come visit over at his little village (or communal house). So after eating, we all went over there and met some Mayubteris I had never seen before. There are three big communal houses close together at Parima A, and I judge that there are three hundred Indians.

Sunday, September 17

Three strong Mayubteri young men said they'd go over as far as the Shideteris with us and help carry some of our gear. Along with them went about four other younger boys to carry bananas for the three that were carrying our stuff. (Green cooking bananas are their food supply on trips. They depend on getting some game, and the bananas roasted supply their bulk food—something like potatoes.)

The most beautiful section in all this Waica area, in my opinion, is the grassy, woody area around Parima A with patches of woods, but for the most part rolling hills carpeted in light green. The colonel referred to it as a gigantic golf course, and this is a pretty good description. Most of the day we traveled through this area, and it was a good setting for me to learn a couple of verses of "How Great Thou Art" in Portuguese.

It was a circuitous route, but the Indians assured us that it was the only trail to the Shideteris. They had already insisted that there was no trail at all from their place to the north and over to Surucucu. I was determined not to open up any new trails, knowing what this means, and the Indians with me (Tarimu and Tishofi) certainly wanted to take the fastest, easiest route home.

We hit the jungle again and the trail seemed to peter out. Late in the afternoon we passed by a beautiful waterfall and not far past this we made camp. That day we had seen a deer escape us in the grassy area, and one of the boys had bagged a monkey. Now at camp they found some honey, and I shot a sloth.

Monday, September 18

What a blow, at noon the Mayubteris said they were going back. They were determined in this, so I dealt out their pay, and we rearranged the carrying packs. I was sure grateful for the other three with me. The trail had been terrible all morning, but the Shamataris told us it got better on ahead, because there was another trail that ran into it. We went up to the fork, and the trail didn't seem much better, but there was no turning back as far as we were concerned. The boys told Tishofi all the hills and creeks we'd hit and the general direction, so he took the lead. How he ever kept on that antique trail is beyond me.

Sunday afternoon it had showered, and again this afternoon we had to make a shelter in the rain. We got to expect these afternoon cloudbursts for the rest of the trip. Traveling and making camp in the rain is about the most discouraging thing.

Tuesday, September 19

The boys had told us that the trail went straight east, but we found it heading almost northeast. Tishofi was getting more and more discouraged as he beat down the brush. As we hit the fern areas, there was no trace of trail at all, and he just had to calculate where the trail might go, and then try to find knife marks as we hit the woods again. At noon he gave up and was ready to go back. He was sure we were on some hunting trail that ended in the middle of nowhere—a good description of that fern area. Not just ferns as we know them, but high six-foot affairs that are bristly and tear you all to shreds.

Tarimu was getting a cold and had a sore throat, so Joao and Tishofi took turns hacking a trail, heading just a little south of east. Toward the end of the day, from on the crest of one of the hills, we saw the end of the fern area.

The days were long and fatiguing, but always we were refreshed at night as we cuddled into our triangular shelter. We slept double-decker with a warm fire in the middle. We never went hungry at night. Usually we had soup and farinha or cassava bread. In the mornings we always had a bowl of oatmeal or banana mixture when we were in the villages.

New Frontiers (1959 to 1962)

Wednesday, September 20

Strength started giving out earlier and earlier in the day now, but by noon we had summited one of the highest ridges in the area. Atop this mountain were scrubby trees with low branches so that even I could climb them. What a spectacular view. We could see the mountains of Surucucu, Parima B, the mountain of the Parahuris where we visited last year. Tishofi got his bearings and was encouraged. He set off in another blaze of energy cutting us a trail. We put in a long day and hurriedly put up a shelter and got firewood just before dark.

Thursday, September 21

Climbed a couple more very high hills; the second one kept going up and up. Once again, we encountered a beautiful vista there on top of the world and this time we saw a field of bananas across the valley; we were actually entering Shideteri country. As we started to descend, we bumped into another trail and took it down the mountain side, almost 90 degrees. It wasn't long before we were on the four-lane highway trail that connected the Shideteri houses. I don't know where Tishofi got all his umph; he practically ran with the heaviest pack on his back. We hadn't gone too hungry, but these last couple of days it had been white man's food, and he was eager to get at those bananas and cassava bread again.

It was nearing noon as we approached the first maloca. Tishofi wanted to go ahead and allay the fears of the women, for he thought that the men might be off hunting. Sure enough they were, and the rest of our party was ushered into a house full of women and children.

It was sure good to rest, eat bananas, and just talk a bit. Tishofi learned that his father had just been there the day before, taking the two-day hike up to this place to carry back a clay pot to momocook territory (right near our station, by the way). We pushed on to the next maloca after giving each of the women a spoonful of beads and singing just a bit.

At this next settlement we found some men, too. Spent the afternoon talking with them and resting while the women ground up some cassava and made some bread for us to take along the next day.

Most of the Shideteri men, and many of the women, were off in the woods hunting and eating momocook, but we had a short and sweet visit at this one place. I was disappointed we didn't get to spend more time up in in this region, but Tarimu and Tishofi both were in a hurry to get back. Tarimu still wasn't feeling well, and now Tishofi was flagging. But the Indian philosophy is to keep pushing hard till you get home, even if you're half dead. They weren't half dead yet, and although I thought it might be better to stay one more day, I consented to push off the next morning.

Friday, September 22 and Saturday, September 23

We had made the most of the bananas and cassava bread while at the village. Tishofi especially was glad for the change in diet. He would eat our dried soup at night because he was hungry, but always complained of all the salt in it. Early in the morning the women brought down more cassava bread, and so we packed enough to last us for the two-day trip back to Surucucu.

Tishofi had the heavy pack and led the way. Reluctantly, three men agreed to go with us for one day then turn back the next. It was a great relief to be freed of my pack. Tishofi led a grueling pace, and the trail was one of the worst I've been over. It was well beaten all right, but we went over some steep hills. When there were no hills to climb, we found ourselves treading through a creek bed, which meant picking up irritable sand in the shoes or else plodding through the muddy embankments.

About 1:00 p.m., the Shideteri men said they had had enough and were going back, assuring us they had accompanied for a long way and over the worst spots. They were right. The terrain leveled out considerably after this. We were exhausted though as we made camp that night. Tishofi came down with a bad cold as a result of the trip's fatigue. He seemed a little better in the morning, and we set out, dividing his load between the rest of us. By noon he had gotten worse and said that he couldn't go on, so we decided to hit the next creek and make camp. He was shivering (although it wasn't cold), and I pulled out my blanket for him to wrap himself in as he walked along. Just then we hit a downpour, and my spirits were pretty low, in just an hour more we could all have been under a shelter.

It cleared up by the time we hit the creek; Tarimu and Tishofi recuperated and dried off in the sun as Joao and I made a shelter, Joao doing most of it. I'll tell you there's nothing more comforting and comfortable than a nice shelter at the end of the day. With the dripping and the cold all around, to be tucked in a hammock next to a fire is the greatest. We spent the afternoon enjoying this atmosphere and finishing off the cocoa and much of the cassava bread. I gave Tishofi a cold shot, and he was a new man in the morning, although not back to normal.

Sunday, September 24

I would have been content to stick another day right at the shelter, but Tishofi said it wasn't far at all now. Although we had traveled only a half a day the day before, the terrain was level and we had come a long way.

Soon we hit the base of the mountain where the Rokoteris live. The path to their establishment led over a high mountain and our guide said the trail was "lousy." So we took another trail that led to the Aracaiteri house (to the side and in back of the Aicamteris). The trail went up, and up, and up. Halfway there was a fork and at this point we met the Aracaiteris who had been away from home for three months out in the forest hunting and picking fruit. It was good to meet some who had never shown their faces before, and good, too, to rest a bit, for the trail still went up and up. There on the ridge, almost at the top, lay the house which I had seen before. I recognized it as the first maloca that met my eyes after landing in the helicopter last April.

Didn't stay long here since there was no food on hand, and I knew for a fact that the Aicamteri house was just over the next ridge. Russ and I had left some canned food at the Aicamteri house on our last visit, and I was counting on getting there shortly after noon and calling it quits for this day. Also I wanted to hold a little service for any of the Indians who still remained in camp.

The trail didn't go around the ridge but straight up over it. Once again, our recompense was a fabulous view, but I wasn't too grateful for the high price paid. On the way down to the house, Tishofi cut some sugarcane from his field, and we spent an enjoyable half hour chewing and sucking this.

Only one old man had remained in camp while the others were out in the forest. Tishofi said we could stay if we wanted to, but that he was going home to Dad, and to the cherished fruit drink. I couldn't keep him back although he could have profited from the extra rest. The rest of us were going to stay, but the myriads of burrowing fleas in the house discouraged me from this plan, and so we tramped on. Wouldn't you know it, we got to enjoy another drenching shower halfway home.

We were beat, but by now more or less in condition, and the walk seemed not nearly so bad as it had the first couple of times I had crossed this trail. We made the best time yet. After a long trip, there's something about the thought of "home" and "rest" and "food" that excites the adrenalin glands or whatever organ it is that gives that extra boost. It was about 4:00 p.m. when the famous Surucucu airstrip opened up before us.

Postscript

It took me about a week to fully recuperate from this jaunt. For the next days it felt all the time that I had just played a hard game of basketball. And did I ever eat. My appetite was unbelievable. I've said it many times before, but always I'm reminded of it as we go out on the trail. The simplest food and the simplest shelter are highly appreciated under such circumstances. I'll get home and take meals as a matter of course, but don't think I'll ever enjoy food as much as I have down here, and when I get home, if I had to live with the same diet I eat here, I'd probably not enjoy it much at all.

I hadn't expected to do so much hard trekking and had wanted to spend more time bumping into Indian villages. We would have hit more villages if we had headed more south from the Mayubteris and taken a more roundabout way to the Shideteris, but the Mayubteris encouraged us to take the direct route, saying they would carry our stuff for us along this trail but wouldn't go by way of the villages because they were fearful of being shot at by this people. I was disappointed in the attitude of our boy from Waica station. He wasn't feeling too well, to be sure, but he encouraged the Aicamteri fellow to not stay long at the Shideteri villages. Although most of the people were off hunting, I believe we could have had a profitable time with those in the malocas. We did have very good visits with the Mayubteris and with one group of Shideteris, and we did find the most direct route between here and Parima Station, and I did have good contact with the Indians, both of the villages and with Tishofi.

I am convinced more than ever that our main job here is to stick right here with these Aicamteris and live with them as much as possible. It will be for Aicamteri boys and men who have been touched by the gospel to spread the Word to these other villages. There are many, many out-of-the-way villages that we could reach only with much time and effort. Evangelization of the area will be the job for the Aicamteris. Pray that we will be "Pauls" and that the Lord will raise up his "Timothies" and other "Pauls" among them. There are very slight differences in dialect up through here, but communication is good. The Shideteris are very close to this dialect; it could be considered the same, I think. Starting with the Mayubteris and going west there are the Shamataris with a different dialect, but still understandable. I think that right now our purpose in visiting the villages, or at least the main groups around here, is to let them get acquainted with us. Any day now, or any month now, I expect a flood of miners in here, and I believe we as missionaries have a duty to gain the confidence of the Indians soon, so that they will trust us. Another purpose or advantage in these trips is the good time spent with the Indians who travel with us.

At least one more trip I'd like to make before March is down through the Maitas, over to the Parahuris we visited last year and then up here. Almost every night we should be sleeping in an Indian village, meeting at least five groups in all.

In the meantime, I'd like to spend as much time as possible with the Aicamteris as they hunt and go traveling right around here. Also, as I've mentioned, I'd like to do quite a bit of language analysis.

Russ is still in Georgetown, but we heard on the radio this morning that he'll be coming to Boa Vista on Saturday and then in here the middle of next week. When he arrives, both Sandy and Tarimu will be going back to Waica Station. Sandy's a good kid, but I've concluded that probably there will never be anything serious between us two. There hasn't been up to this point, although I've considered the thing.

The FAB has continued forgetting its responsibility here. No pilot in Boa Vista and no supplies for the men. As a result, it is our lot as missionaries to see that the sergeant and the Maiongongs don't starve. The FAB has helped us in bringing in things and in the future will no doubt help us, but it sure has been a sloppy set-up thus far.

Since getting back from my trip, I've been making a table and shelves for my room here, fixing the roof on the Sasscer house, and a few more odd jobs. I'm champing at the bit, wanting to get down to language study, and I believe when Tarimu goes out, the chance will be here.

Email from Don to editor, September 10, 2019

The following incident occurred when I was alone in my little hut near the edge of the airstrip at Surucucu. My next-door neighbors, both the Sasscers, and the Air Force sergeant were gone for a week or two, and there I was —*alone*—except for an occasional group of Indians who would come by. One of those days that I was alone, along came a group who lived a couple of hours away. They were my friends, and evidently, they wanted to show me hospitality in their own special way. Suddenly they all disappeared—all but one. They left in my presence a lovely teenage girl. Immediately the story of the biblical Joseph came to my mind. I grabbed a shovel and headed out of the hut, telling the girl that I was going out to work on improving the airstrip. Thankfully she was gone by the time I came back.

Letter from Don to support partners, January 1962

Mt. Surucucu, Brazil

Dear partners in prayer,

After two weeks of having gone "Indian," I admit that a change of diet and clothes is welcomed. It's a relief to escape the dirt and smoke of the big communal houses to which our neighbors are accustomed. But to the jungle Indian, the most conducive atmosphere for discussing spiritual matters is by his hammock and fire, and some of my most joyous moments have been spent right here. These past days God has been answering your prayers as we have seen a definite interest in the teaching of God's Word as well as an increased freedom on the part of the Indians to share the burdens of their hearts. Having listened to their stories, once again I am impressed with the fear that reigns in most lives.

Fear of the Civilized World

One day while hunting, we came across a small clearing out in the thick of the bush and away from the trails. The boys told me that this was one of the spots to which they had fled when the planes first came. "We were afraid that you would throw fire on us and burn us all up," they confessed. "Even after you came to meet us, most of us stayed in hiding for fear of your thunder-bows (shotguns)." This fear of the white man still exists in the more remote villages.

Fear of Neighboring Groups

Continuing feuds and battles are the topic of many a community discussion. House walls are fortified against attack. One man showed me the tree which shielded him from enemy arrows. Another showed me the deep scars that spears had left. I have seen the tears of widows whose husbands have been killed and whose daughters were carried away.

Fear of the Spirit World

There is much yet to be learned regarding belief in spirits among this group, but we do know that much of its life is centered on shamanism and superstition. Under certain conditions specified foods may not be eaten. The breaking of taboos is supposed to bring death or severe sickness. Many deaths have been attributed to the curse or spell of an enemy shaman. The spirits of the deceased are said to roam through the forest, sometimes in the form of jaguars or other beasts.

Fear of God

Because of the stealing that has taken place here at the station, we have been able to drive home the fact that the all-seeing God is displeased with sin in all its forms and that He is truly to be feared. Some have told us that they don't want to face God's punishment and will steal no more, but we are concerned that they comprehend God's love and forgiveness through Jesus Christ.

The past days have seen a different attitude on the part of many, as for the first time there are signs of a real desire to know more about our God. Often during the visits to the various houses, the head man would squat beside my hammock and ask questions such as these:

- "You speak of God the Son. Are there two Gods?"
- "Does God the Father have a wife?"
- "You mean the white man dies, too, just like us? Aren't you reincarnations?"
- "The airplane doesn't go off to God's House?"

Because the questions came from their own group, the other men, women, and children that had gathered around listened attentively to the answers and heard that Jesus now lives in heaven, but that He also lives with those who admit their guilt, asking for his cleansing; that when Jesus abides in us, He removes all fears.

These concepts are all so strange and new to these who have never heard God's message before. Pray that we might have an ever-increasing grasp of the language, and that the Holy Spirit will convict and instruct. We are convinced that as God's people take up the burden of these people in prayer, that soon there will be those singing with David, "The Lord is my Light and my Salvation; whom shall I fear? The Lord is the stronghold of my life; of whom shall I be afraid?"

First Term in Retrospect and First Furlough

Following his time at Mount Surucucu, Don returned to the States for his first furlough which would last from March 1962 to January 1963. During his first term on the field, Don had learned and experienced much. Not only had he gained knowledge about life in the jungle and the people who inhabited it, but he had grown spiritually as well, learning to trust his Heavenly Father for both his physical and spiritual needs. Furthermore, it should be noted that Don was part of a historical situation by participating in opening up the Yanomami country to exploration as well as initial contact with the tribes. Heading home, it would be time to rest and recuperate, renew acquaintances, provide information to supporters, and receive more training for his translation work at SIL. It would also be a time of unexpected and happy change.

4

The Atroais and the Sanumás (1963–1964)

"It is the Lord who goes before you. He will be with you; he will not leave you or forsake you. Do not fear or be dismayed." (Deut 31:8)

The Cafuini Once Again

During Don's early jungle training days, he had participated in a Wai Wai led expedition to reach the headwaters of the Cafuini River in Brazil, near the border of Southern British Guiana. The Cafuini would give the Wai Wais access to other unreached Carib tribes. A second expedition was to reach the headwaters of the Anauá River. The goal with this effort was to make future contact with the Atroai people. (This attempt to reach the Anauá had failed.) Even though Don's attention had been diverted to the Yanomami region and people, neither he nor the Wai Wais had given up hope of one day reaching the Atroais.

Another opportunity came in 1963 when the Brazilian Air Force, having seen the successes of building airstrips in Yanomami country, now turned to the Wai Wais and Don once again. God was continuing to use his own means to expand the kingdom. As a result of this new endeavor, Don's thoughts turned once again to the Atroais. A new plan would be hatched to try to reach this fierce group of people, but from a different direction. The following two letters highlight Don's work with Wai Wai young men to build the Cafuini airstrip and then his subsequent plans to reach the Atroais.

Letter from Don to support partners, January 1963

Boa Vista, T.F.R.B.
Dear friends,

Where In the World Are You Going? This was a missionary conference theme. It is not a trite question as we apply personally Christ's command: "Go ye into all the world and preach the gospel to every creature."

Right now I am going—at the rate of 575 mph—back to the Indians of Brazil. Soon it will be good-bye to jets and thruways as the canoes and trails are greeted once more. This means leaving the land where everyone, everywhere, speaks English. (This was my first shock when returning to the U.S. from Brazil.) It means a retreat from the culture in which people consider themselves social failures if they let the company go to bed before midnight.

But I am grateful for those hours of fellowship by the light of the midnight oil. My heart has been refreshed and refueled in the realization that, while many Christians are afflicted with inertia, there are many in the States who are moving and reaching out into needy places. In the rural areas I have been with pastors who are working hard and living sacrificially. Youth leaders are reaching teenagers in every strata of society. Laymen are entering the hearts and homes of their spiritually hungry neighbors.

Our location in North Brazil presents new open doors, and we re-echo the words of the songwriter, "To the regions beyond we must go." A subsequent letter will map out in detail two major areas for your prayer.

Presently I will be helping to open up a third area in Brazil, just south of British Guiana. This is a joint effort of our mission and the Brazilian Air Force. Wai Wais will be doing most of the manual labor. These Indian Christians are enthused about the whole project in that a base will be established from which they can move out to contact other Carib Indian groups for the sake of the gospel.

Pray that I will be able to do a capable job as the middleman between Wai Wais and Brazilians and that some of these Air Force men might yield their hearts to Christ.

Letter from Don to support partners, May 1963

Dear friends,

Our supply of food, strength, and desire was depleted. Across mountainous terrain and through thick growth and swamps we had hacked out a trail, but not far enough to reach our destination, a river that might open up the way for Wai Wai Indian Christians to contact the notedly unapproachable Atroais. This was 1958, during our jungle training, and this was our second unsuccessful trail-cutting trip. The other had been in search of the headwaters of the Cafuini, a waterway which would give access to at least four other unreached Carib tribes.

Subsequently, the Cafuini was found, and a group of Wai Wais suffered a long, arduous expedition in fulfilling their desire to reach the Tunayanas for Christ. Still, they prayed and planned about someday going to the other far-distant tribes.

Today I am sitting on the bank of the Cafuini River, in an encampment which is also host to my twenty-one companions, all of them Wai Wai young men. In cooperation with the Brazilian Air Force, we are constructing an air strip which for the Air Force will help open up the Brazilian frontier. For the Wai Wais this spot, two weeks of hard travel from their present village in British Guiana, will serve as base for their further missionary ventures. A few Wai Wai families plan to settle here permanently.

Recently I read Homer Dowdy's *Christ's Witchdoctor*, an account of the remarkable conversion of Elká, chief of the Wai Wais. So, it has been an even greater thrill for me to have this close contact with many mentioned in the book. Elká's younger brother, Yakutá, was here for a time. Now Mawashá, another elder, has taken his place and leads the boys as they gather for prayer, singing, and instruction. Another whose life is a challenge is smiling Tamokrana, the man who spent a night in prayer pleading for his friends outside of Christ.

For me, this is a temporary assignment terminating in June. In July and August, I plan to be traveling from Boa Vista to Manaus visiting Brazilians who live nearest the Atroai Indians. After gaining information in this way, we tentatively plan an aerial survey in September, and then a possible attempt for contact in October or November. Start praying now for the Atroais. This is one of the tribes that has been on our heart ever since that jungle training experience. Also, there are Wai Wais who have had a desire to go to the Atroais and who are ready to take part in the attempt to enter.

I shall be grateful for your prayer support in this whole project and will keep you up to date on developments. We look to the Lord to open or close doors, knowing that by following his method and timing we cannot fail. Promises from Isa 40–43 have been an encouragement, especially Isa 43:12–13: "You are my witnesses, says the Lord; I am God . . . When I act, who can impede?" In this, our might.

You have prayed for our relationship with the Air Force personnel, and I am happy to report that a radio operator received Christ last August as the result of personal witness and reading the New Testament. During the month of February, he and I were alone together at Surucucu Station.

Leandro evidenced definite spiritual perception and desire for further growth in Christ. Lately he had a 14-day break from the isolated jungle post and testifies that even in the city he found victory over former temptations.

"Back Door" Effort to Reach the Atroais

Following Don's contributions to the Cafuini project, a plan was developed to take a different approach to reach the Atroais. The new plan was to come up the Uatumã River, the mouth of which is at the Amazon to the east of Manaus. In the previous letter, Don indicated that his intention in July and August was to meet with Brazilians who had had contact with the Atroais over the years to gain detailed information about them. Having accomplished this, plans now were laid for this next expedition. The idea was to come to the tribe by the "back door," hoping to make contact with members of the tribe to the extreme east of their traditional territory. Members of the expedition would include Don, John Peters, and several Wai Wais, including Elká. The following records both the plan and execution of the expedition.

Locations of the Atroais Expedition

The Atroais and the Sanumás (1963–1964)

Letter from Don to support partners, September 1963

Dear praying friends,

"Atroai; Jauaperi River; Isolated." That is about the extent of information found in anthropological journals regarding the Atroai Indians. From time to time come reports of killings in the region of the Jauaperi, the river that separates our territory on Rio Branco River. To our knowledge these jungle people forcibly ward off any attempted entrance by those representing the civilized world.

Last year Neill Hawkins visited Brazilians living near the mouth of the Jauaperi and learned more of the sickening history of this tribe. South American Indians in general started killing only after having been attacked or mistreated by those from the outside, and the Atroais seem to be no exception. For more than twenty years there have been attacks and counterattacks. Some of the more talked-about incidents:

1944—One American lieutenant, one sergeant, and three Brazilians killed on a tributary of the Jauaperi.

1949—More than fifty Indians massacred as they were crossing river in canoes.

1961—Twelve Brazilians killed, supposedly because of a misunderstanding about taking produce out of an Indian field.

Amidst this dark picture filtered through one ray of encouragement. A peaceful contact had recently been made on the Uatumã River with a group thought to be Atroais living on the eastern extremity of the tribe. In July and August it was my assignment to learn more about that region. Praise the Lord for a fruitful time imparting the gospel to Brazilians along the way and for a profitable time gathering information about contacts with Indians on the Uatumã.

More than twenty years ago rubber hunters were ordered to kill any Indians who got in their way on this river. They did. Then about 1945, a few rubber men and their families settled far up the Uatumã. For a while there were peaceful dealings with the Indians, but relations became strained, and a sudden attack liquidated the sixteen Brazilians in the settlement. I talked with one man whose wife had sensed the coming trouble and had persuaded him to leave just a few days before the killing.

There were no further contacts up until two years ago when three different fishing parties met Indians at three different points along the river. These Atroais demanded almost all that the white man had but showed no signs of wanting to cause trouble. They even offered their bows and arrows in payment. The fishermen were afraid and stayed just long enough to execute a friendly exit.

From September to December the river is low, and it is said that during this time the Indians leave their inland villages in order to fish and look for turtle eggs on the sandbars. Last dry season fishermen and hunters steered clear of Indian territory, and there have been no further contacts.

At least two factors make us feel that now is the time to push forward in the direction of the Atroais. The present government permission for our mission to work among the Indians of the Uatumã River could be revoked with the coming change in directorship of the Indian Protection Service. Then, too, possible unwise actions and dealings with this suspicious, revengeful jungle community on the part of a hunting or fishing party could provoke animosity which would hinder a missionary's entrance to the tribe.

To gain further information as to the size and location of the Atroais, we plan an aerial survey within the next few days. Immediately following will come preparations for a three-month trip to the headwaters of the Uatumã. John Peters and I will be accompanied by three Wai Wai Indian Christians, one of whom will be Elká, the chief.

As the history of hate, revenge, and bloodshed was unfolded to me, the natural man asked, "Why take interest in this area? Those from the civilized world, interested only in material gain, started the trouble here; let them try to do the pacifying. Besides, there are other easier places to work!"

It was then that the basic purpose of missions became more meaningful to me personally than ever before. "Jesus came and spake . . . 'All power is given unto Me in Heaven and in earth. Go ye therefore and teach all nations . . .'" (Matt 28:18–20 KJV)

Many uncertainties present themselves as we embark on this trip, but we are assured of the prayers of many of you faithful ones. Pray that we will find the Indians and that the contact will be both peaceful and profitable. The greatest assurance is that as we go and teach all nations, He is faithful who promised, "Lo, I am with you alway, even unto the end . . . " (Matt 28:18–20 KJV)

— For Praying Friends —
EXPEDITION TO CONTACT THE ATROAI INDIANS
September 30 to about December 15

DON BORGMAN

ELKA

JOHN PETERS

ALSO TOMHAWA AND CAYUKUMA, WAI-WAI INDIANS
"The effectual fervent prayer of a righteous man availeth much."
JAMES 5:16

Personnel: DONALD BORGMAN and JOHN PETERS, missionaries with the Unevangelized Fields Mission. ELKA, Chief and Christian leader of the Wai-wai Indians, whose remarkable story is told in the book, "Christ's Witchdoctor". TOMHAWA and CAYUKUMA, Wai-wai Christians.

Mission: To reach the Atroai (Ah-tro-*ah*-ee) Indian tribe with the Gospel. Location is North Central Brazil. Contact must be made carefully and prayerfully as there is a history of killings of Indians, Brazilians and Americans.

Why go? Why go now? God's command is "Go ye therefore and teach *all* nations—". This particular field has been laid on the hearts of the missionaries and the Wai-wai Christians. They feel the Lord would have them go at this time. It is very desirable that this contact be made by missionaries rather than other groups who might provoke further animosity.

PRAY THAT CONTACT WILL BE PEACEFUL AND PROFITABLE

Prayer card for Atroai Expedition

The Atroais Expedition

Letter from Don to his parents, Barbara Hughes,[1] and her parents, November 27, 1963

Dear Barb, Mother and Dad, Mr. and Mrs. Hughes:

With so much news to write, I trust you'll understand and forgive this less personal carbon copy system. There *is* much to relate, and I don't see

---

1. Barbara Hughes, later to be Don's wife, is introduced in Chapter 5.

any extensive time that I can give to letter writing. You should see the stack of letters (this is not new) that I should answer.

I believe I left all in Manaus as I was making last-minute purchases and getting ready to shove off to the lower Amazonas and then up the Uatumã River. I had gone alone to Manus from Boa Vista to make most of the purchases. John Peters arrived in B.V. one Saturday afternoon, and just about had time to kiss his wife and three kiddies goodbye before taking the Sunday morning plane to Manaus with the three Wai Wais. We were pressed to get to the Uatumã to take advantage of the dry season when the Indians were reporting to be hunting turtle eggs.

What a stir the Wai Wais caused in Manaus! There are a lot of people there with mixed Indian blood but who cut their hair and dress like us. Here came the Wai Wais with their bare feet, bead collars fastened to decorated earrings, and to top it off that long decorated pigtail all the Wai Wai men use. The three boys wanted to see the center of town one day, and I made the mistake of complying. It looked like a parade with multitudes following them. Back in the early days when the missionaries first arrived at the Wai Wai village, it was the Wai Wais who spent many hours peering at the foreigners. Now the situation was reversed. Crowds hanging around our house, climbing up to the windows, crowding the door, wanting to get a squint at these living museum pieces. Kids would go along babbling some gibberish, trying to mimic the Indian talk (just like the Waicas did with us). One lady kept talking and asking questions in Portuguese, even after we told her they didn't understand (just like the Waicas and Shirishanas acted with us). With all of this, and with the running around for purchases, and with the hot, muggy weather, we were glad to be on our way as far from Manaus as possible.

We took a regular ferry line to Itaquatiara—almost a day down the Amazon. Oh, civilization! It was terrible. You wouldn't believe how many people could pack in and sleep in such a small place. Hammocks all over the place. If one has the unhappy necessity to get up during the night, usually at least three of your neighbors get an elbow or foot in the head. You have to be a contortionist to get to the deck, and then you have to crawl beneath the hammock. And the "W.C."—I won't even go into that—none of us did, in fact.

On the boat with us was a Baptist pastor from Itaquatiara, and he was very cordial, inviting us to overnight with him. This was a provision from the Lord, for we had a lot of baggage with us. From Itaquatiara (another Manaus experience as far as the curious crowds) we caught another launch to a little burg of Itapiranga. There we bought a canoe but had to wait a couple of days till it was available. It was election time, and the owner was one of

The Atroais and the Sanumás (1963–1964)

the candidates for mayor, so he was using the boat to transport extra votes. Elections can get quite heated in South America; one man was stabbed during one of the speeches there. (And we were going to "uncivilized" Indians.) The main impression of Itapiranga was the filthy drinking water. As we were leaving, we learned that the drinking water (we were fed at the candidate's house) was drawn from the port—and the port was filled with everything from oil to . . . it was filthy.

John had bought a 10-horse Evinrude in Georgetown for use at Mucajaí station, but we used it for the trip, and it was great. In one day, we made it to the mouth of the Jatapu River and camped on a beautiful beach with clean water and cool breezes, wow. In the next two days we made it up above the first rapids. One and half more days and we were up to the Abonari (not on map) one of the main tributaries of the Uatumã. This was the tributary that was our main destination, as the Brazilians had told us that most of the Indian traces centered there. No one had ever seen the Indian houses, but it was assumed that they lived up the Abonari. Well, the aerial survey had not turned up any fields or houses on the Abonari. By river, we had not yet seen any signs of Indians. We decided to wait at the Abonari's mouth, so that we could meet any Indians who would come either down the Uatumã or the Abonari. Timing was good, for we were all down with intestinal upset at that point and were able to rest without feeling we were losing time. I was hit the hardest, with a slight fever and weakness. My cough was bad, too. While I was recuperating, John and two of the boys went up the Abonari for a day but found no trace at all. After two weeks, I was strong, and we all went up the Uatumã for three days. Found a design on a tree which was old and might have been Indian or Brazilian.

By that time, it was getting time for the supply drop. We had thought there would be many sandbars, but there weren't, even though the river was low. There were only a couple of places from the Santo Antonio up where there was sand enough for turtle eggs, and these were close to shore. It was starting to rain a lot and the river was rising, so we decided to go down to the mouth of the Santo Antonio (tributary of Uatumã) and make our drop area there. Eldon was coming down the S. Antonio from Boa Vista and then was going north along the Uatumã in search of us.

As we were clearing away a little island for the drop of supplies, we found an old encampment that probably was three years old and probably Indian and also old Brazilian fields. Further on down the Uatumã we saw another encampment—definitely Indian and at least a year or two old.

We were somewhat disappointed, naturally speaking, that we didn't contact Indians, but never were we discouraged. We had prayed and planned much, and there were many, many others praying, so that we are confident that it was God's plan that we do not try the Uatumã door again. We concluded that there are no Indians living on the Uatumã or its tributaries, that if Indians do come out to the river some dry seasons, that they travel there from distant points—possibly from as far away as the Alalau—where the Atroais live. They might have small hidden fields near the Abonari, for the Brazilians report that they had bananas and cane with them.

I have thought that the Lord might be sparing our missions much expense and time by closing the Uatumã "back door." Even before the trip we had agreed that if Indians were found it would be only a steppingstone to get over to the populous Alalau.

On this trip, more than others, I have been impressed with some of the dangers of the jungle and of answer to prayer in God's protecting us. At the mouth of the Abonari, John and I were unloading a very heavy box. I asked to have it set down on a half-sunk log near the shore for a better grip. Then John looked further and saw a huge boa constrictor or anaconda stretched out with its head right in our path, right between the log and the shore. It was in the water and camouflaged well; we would have stepped right on it had we not rested the box.

Another time, Shayukuma woke up at night to find a big jaguar snooping around our camp. In the morning, they found its tracks within ten feet of our hammock—blissful sleep. I thought of how many times people were praying for our safety and their prayers were answered. Safety from Indians was not needed on this trip, but I feel we were spared from serious sickness and these attacks from animals.

My cough recurred just before the drop, and I thought to myself that it would be great to go south after Manaus to get treated and also to talk to Neill concerning our trip and future plans. We made it back to Manaus after the drop, in record time, but found that Neill had left for Sao Paulo that very morning. Later in the day, who should I bump into on the street but Neill? He postponed his flight to see an army general who was passing through. So, we had ample time to talk over plans with our field director.

John and Wai Wais flew to Boa Vista the next day. Isobel Ebel's health is so bad—so bad that the doctor told her not to live in the jungle anymore. So, we have lost the Ebels to the work; they have probably arrived in the States by now. It was a bad liver condition. So, John and family are alone at Mucajaí.

With the back door closed to the Atroais, I was thinking of a direct approach through the front, maybe using Wai Wais and no foreign missionaries for the first contact. But we have no permission to work on the Alalau River, and the new Indian Protection Chief in Brasilia is not favorable toward missions. Neill doesn't want to approach him at this time for we have calm in the rest of the region, and he doesn't want to wake up the sleeping giant by contacting the IPS man at this time. We have not forgotten the Atroais and still plan for our mission to get in there, but now is not the time evidently.

The Shamataris[2] have long been my second choice—the group that lives up in the northwest corner of the Roraima territory. A survey trip or preliminary language gathering trip is probably next on the agenda for me, and the Shamataris probably will be our home, Barb. I am very happy for this—for even naturally speaking, I have wanted to split myself in two and work with the Atroais and this Shamatari group.

I was going to get my cough checked in Manaus, but one morning Neill, out of the blue, asked me if I wanted to come south with him. He was thinking mainly of the good medical attention but might have had also in the back of his mind that I could be used some in contacting those who would be interested to enter our Indian work—Brazilian young people. Neill's second flight south had been canceled so this gave me time to pack up some things going by boat to Boa Vista and join him in the jet flight south. We both feel this delay was ordered of the Lord and that this is the place for me now.

Letter from Don to support partners, December 1963

Dear faithful friends,

The identity and present whereabouts of Indians on the Uatumã River remains a mystery, but the powerful volume of prayer for the Atroais within the last three months has dismissed any discouragement.

On the September aerial survey, we found seven Atroai villages close to the Alalau River, but there was not a sign of a field or house near the Uatumã. The question which faced us was whether to continue plans for a river trip up the Uatumã. Those who travel the upper part of this river and who had had peaceful contact with Indians there just two years ago had affirmed that we would be sure to meet Indians in October when the river is low. (Since that contact, Brazilians have kept away from the headwaters in the dry season for fear of another contact which might not be friendly.) With this assurance, we felt that we should explore this region which might prove to be the "back door" to the wild Atroais who lived on the Alalau. Perhaps the Indians contacted were a small group who had friendly relations

---

2. Don is referring here to the Sanumás. The term Shamatari is a Yanomami designation given to tribes living west of themselves, in this case, by the Yanomams or Waicas. See Appendix A.

with the Atroaís, or maybe they were a group of Atroaís who appeared on the Uatumã during prolonged hunting parties.

But the back door has been shut. The Wai Wais, John Peters, and I spent over a month in the headwaters without seeing another Indian. There were signs of a couple old Indian encampments, but nothing recent.

Even though there were no Indians to attack us, we praise God for protecting us in definite ways, once from a huge anaconda and on two other occasions from jaguars.

All of us profited from the rich fellowship together. I think for instance of Elká, who night after night patiently explained to Tamhawa that which he had heard and seen of Christ and His Word. This young Christian, Tamhawa, is from another tribe but has learned Wai Wai. With the teaching he has received, he plans to go back to his own group to be a witness there and possibly to organize a missionary trip to still another tribe. He needs prayer for strength and faithfulness.

Where do we go from here in regard to the Atroaís? God has not disregarded them, nor have we forgotten them. Elká is ready to take some Wai Wais to try an entrance through the "front door," if God so leads.[3] This would need to be backed and followed up by some of us, and at present we do not have Indian Protection Service permission to work in the region of the front door, the Alalau River. There has been a change in the leadership of the IPS, and there is not much natural hope of getting permission from the present director.

Along with the Atroaís, the Shamatari Indians have been on our hearts for some time. They live northwest of the Waicas among whom we presently work. The Shamataris belong to the Waica language family but are a distinct, major dialect. They have come down to Waica Station and repeatedly have invited us to live among them, so the door there is wide open. In February, I plan to make an initial survey trip with thoughts of permanently locating in that area.

Till then I am soaking up the luxurious civilized life here in Sao Paulo, the largest city in Brazil. Primarily, I have come to investigate the cause and cure of a cough that is in its last stages, but which had been hanging on for over five months. The doctor diagnoses it as a bronchial condition but assures me that I should be ready for the jungle again after a short rest.

Another unexpected reason for being here has very evidently been ordered of the Lord. Our field director had had it upon his heart to introduce Brazilian young people into the Indian work to labor with us on an equal

---

3. For subsequent contacts with the Atroaís, as referenced by Don over the ensuing years, refer to Appendix D. And for a full account of Wai Wai efforts to reach this tribe, one should read *Christ's Jungle*, by Homer Dowdy.

footing, Here in South Brazil there are dedicated, well-trained youth and also prospering churches who could support workers. For the past week Neill Hawkins has been talking to various Brazilian leaders in the churches, and interest in this new project is keen.

There are pressing duties which force Neill back to Boa Vista now, but he plans to return in April to lay concrete plans. For this next month there will be opportunities for me to speak in churches and interview young people interested in tribal work.

Keep with us in prayer for these important areas of outreach:

1. The unreached, untamed Atroais. Needed are government permission, new workers, and continued direction as to the time and method of contact.
2. The friendly Shamataris[4] whom we plan to contact in February.
3. The God-chosen Brazilians who will feel the call and who will fit into the Indian work in our territory.

"With God nothing shall be impossible . . . Be it unto us according to Thy word." (Luke 1:37–38 KJV) May we experience this submissiveness and expectancy in 1964.

The Sanumás

Email from Don to editor, August 13, 2020

The Impetus for the Sanumá Work: the Maiongong at Surucucu

The Maiongongs were a Carib tribe and were known as Maquiritares in Venezuela. Today they are known by the name they give themselves: Yekuanas. They are skilled in building houses and canoes and extremely industrious workers. At least annually some of them would travel many days downriver to work for and trade with Brazilians. In 1961, a group of them met up with Brazilian Air Force workers at Waica Station and were employed by them in the arduous job of cutting down the jungle and making an 800-meter airstrip. This would serve as base to move on to places like Surucucu and Parima B.

This group of Yekuanas pleaded with the (Brazilian) colonel to go up to their village in the headwaters of the Auaris River and give medicine to the many who were physically in need. "Okay," the colonel replied, "you go up and make an airstrip, and I'll go up there with our Beechcraft plane." And

---

4. The Sanumás.

that's what the Yekuanas did, without outside supervision, they made an airstrip. True to his word, the colonel landed there with a male nurse, who gave out medicines.

Now we were at Surucucu with the Yekuanas still working with the Air Force. Chico, one of the Yekuanas, came up to me and asked if I wouldn't go up to their village to live and to help them, especially with medicines. He said that the Air Force had made only that one trip and evidently weren't going to continue to do so. I told Chico that my own purpose was to settle in a Yanomami village, to which he replied, "We have a Shirishana [Yanomami] village right next to ours, and you can live there." Fortunately, there was a "Shirishana" man from that very village who was there working alongside the Yekuanas. He called himself a "Sanumá," and I could tell it was a different dialect. So it was that I decided to accept Chico's invitation, and I set my sights on this new area, eager to live and work among the Sanumás. This would take time, for I had a furlough coming up and with that the meeting of the young lady who was to become my wife.

In June of 1964, together with some Yekuanas and a mission candidate, Silas Coutinho, I took a survey trip down the Auaris River to identify possible Sanumá villages. I decided that the best place to set up a mission base would be back at the airstrip the Yekuanas had made.

Letter from Don to support partners, June 1964

"The steps of a good man are ordered of the Lord, and he delighteth in his way." (Ps 37:23 KJV)
Belem, Brazil
Dear faithful friends,

Someone has added to the above verse: The steps *and stops* are ordered of the Lord. In the past few months I have had both, one month traveling in the jungle and the next two trying to get rid of a persistent cough and fever.

Samatali Region Surveyed

For our survey trip we were able to enlist the capable help of three Maiongong Indians and one Samatali.[5] The latter turned back at the first village when he heard that the relatives of a man he had recently killed in that region were after him. We visited most of the Samatali groups on the Brazil side, obtaining information about the greater number of villages which are

---

5. As noted earlier, "Samatali" was a term used by the Waicas to refer to the Sanumás as well as other tribes to their west.

just across the border in Venezuela. Thanks to a couple of sharp, patient Samatali boys, we received abundant language material which we are analyzing at present.

Impressive to us were the numerous rapids along the way. At least thirty times we had to unload the canoes, carry the baggage around the falls, and then either shoot the falls in the empty canoes or drag them over rocks or along the trail. Toward the end of our trip our canoe flooded in what looked like an easy pass. My Brazilian companion could not swim but had always worn a life preserver. Ironically, he was without it at this point. How we give thanks to God for preserving our lives in that whirling current, allowing us to reach shore and safety. There were moments when I thought the battle was hopeless.[6]

As soon as health permits, we plan to make another visit to the nearest Samatali village which is upriver from Waica Station. Then in the beginning of the dry season we would like to think in terms of building a station farther upriver among these Samatalis. Pray concerning the location for this station.

Health Problem Continues

For almost a year now, I have had repeated occurrences of coughing accompanied at time by fever and weakness. The worst siege came after this last trip. Treatment thus far has been without lasting results, and so I have come to Belem in order to have more thorough laboratory tests. Do pray that God will guide and bring complete recovery if it be his will.

THE MACEDONIAN CALL

It was no doubt a disappointment that the way to the Atroais had been closed, but just as Paul was redirected to the Macedonians from his plans to go to Asia, God was sending Don to answer the pleas of another group, the Sanumás. The Atroais would eventually receive the gospel, not through Don, but through the Wai Wais. "The heart of man plans his way, but the Lord establishes his steps." (Prov 16:9)

---

6. Don related to the editor a somewhat humorous particularity about this incident. When Don and the Maiongongs came up from under the water, Senhor Coutinho was nowhere to be seen. Don quickly and worriedly asked one of the others where he was. The man simply, and dispassionately, pointed down! Don quickly fished their missing partner out of the pool and things were set aright. Undoubtedly, the new missionary candidate never took his life preserver off again. And incidentally, he did not pursue being a missionary.

5

Transitions (1963 to 1968)

"For where you go I will go, and where you lodge I will lodge. Your people shall be my people, and your God my God." (Ruth 1:16b KJV)

FOLLOWING DON'S ATTEMPT TO contact the Atroais and the Samatali survey trip, significant transitions would now take place in both his life and mission.

Engagement and Marriage

Email from Don to editor, September 11, 2019

After a year at Mt. Surucucu, I left and went immediately to the States for my first furlough. Departing from Boa Vista in the last part of February 1962, I again went to the Summer Institute of Linguistics (S.I.L.) in Norman, Oklahoma, this time to get help on analyzing my data on the Waica language. I collaborated with coworker Sandy Cue, and we came up with a paper which was printed up in the *International Journal of American Linguistics*. The title was "Sentence and clause types in Central Waica (Shiriana)" published in 1963.

Much more significant to me that summer was the meeting of Barbara Hughes who was to become my wife. She had come to the S.I.L. course after quitting a teaching job in New Jersey and had wanted to prepare to engage in a literacy program among a tribal people. I took it upon myself to recruit her for the work in northern Brazil under the Unevangelized Fields Mission. The courses at S.I.L. started in June, and I hadn't noticed this girl until two weeks had passed. Because of a plane cancellation, Barbara arrived two weeks late and so it was that I noticed her for the first time at a prayer meeting held out on the lawn. (Heat was oppressive with no air conditioners in the buildings.) We "hit it off" right away and continued seeing each other after we left Oklahoma in late August. Conveniently, she lived just an hour and twenty minutes away from me, and during my furlough it was an easy trip from Bridgeport, CT to River Edge, NJ.

Newsletter from Don to support partners, August 1963

"The Lord is the Sun and Shield the Lord will give Grace and Glory. No good Thing will he withhold from them that walk uprightly." (Ps 84:11 KJV)

Hudson Taylor used to tell the single missionary candidates that we had no business anxiously seeking good things. Our part was to walk uprightly; God would give the good things.

I whole-heartedly believe this, although not always having obeyed its principle. I have found that God's ways are truly gracious and glorious, learning that what constitutes a "good thing" for others may not be God's good for me personally.

After giving me a joyful first term of service alone, God has seen fit to provide a prospective partner. Last summer, while studying at the Summer Institute of Linguistics in Oklahoma, I met Barbara Hughes, a grade-school teacher from New Jersey. She had come to the Institute to train for missionary work among primitive Indians. I, too, was interested in the Indians . . . and in Barbara. Our summer friendship flowered and flourished in the fall months. A semester at Moody Bible Institute for Barbara, and the commencement of a second term in Brazil, separated us in January.

Barbara is a member of the First Baptist Church in Hackensack, New Jersey, and is a graduate of Shelton College. During the past weeks she has attended the orientation period at mission headquarters and has been accepted as candidate for the Unevangelized Fields Mission. We now gratefully announce our engagement.

Barbara will be at Missionary Internship in Michigan from September to April. She will also be visiting friends and churches, presenting the Indian work by word and picture. Pray that God will direct in her contacts and travels, and that He will provide each need before coming to Brazil.
Sincerely in Christ,
Don Borgman

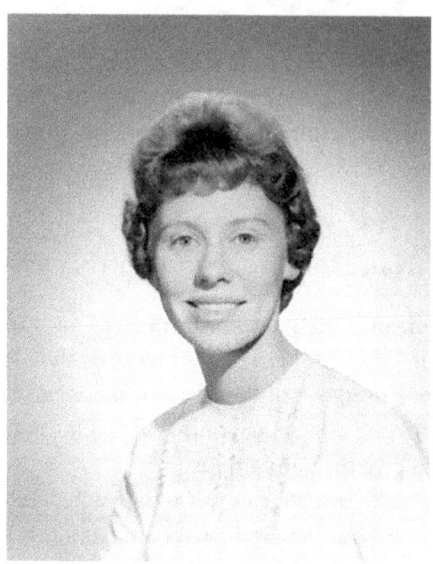

Barbara Hughes

The following provides background on Barb's early years leading up to her decision to go to the mission field.

Email from Barbara to editor, August 8, 2020

My grandmother figures greatly in my life. She was abandoned by her husband in a day when women were not trained for jobs. My dad, his two brothers, and their sister were only fifteen years old and younger. Grandma's faith in God and relationship to Jesus her Lord took her through that terrible time. She also raised me, you might say, on the weekends, giving my parents some free time. And so I went with her and my dear Aunt Kay to a fine Bible-teaching church in Hackensack, New Jersey. My dad and his brothers were not at all interested.

When I was about eight, I keenly realized my naughty nature (a child knows well). One Sunday morning, I reached up my hand to show I wanted to take the gift of forgiveness that Jesus offers, and I prayed for it, believing. How young I was! A few years later, when my grandma died, I was stunned. Aunt Kay assured me that she was with the Lord, but still it was painful. I continued to go to church with my aunt, but another blow fell when I was about thirteen. She married and moved to Texas. I felt very alone, for my parents still had no interest in seeking God.

Sunday School, church, and even youth group had become a big part of my life. Yet, I was very young in deeper understanding of the Bible and how to draw closer to God. This is why I feel that discipling one-on-one is so valuable when possible.

Once high school was over, I worked as a secretary in New York City at GE International. I had so wanted to go to college. At my church, which held a "Monday Night Bible Institute," I attended great classes. A year or so later, a rep from a small north New Jersey Christian college appeared at our church and explained how it might be financially possible for me to attend. After having worked for nearly two years, I happily took the step! There I went to Bible classes and formed close Christian friendships with students who modeled to me personal Bible study and prayer. Our small mission prayer groups were meaningful and inspiring. Those mission conferences were more intimate than when I'd been a young kid in a large church, and they touched my heart.

When college was over, one of my closest friends, who had trained at Wycliffe Bible Translators, left for Brazil. I taught after-school Bible clubs but began to feel I could use teaching in a setting where tribal people were getting the Word of God but needed to learn to read in their language. This concern grew and so I went to the course at Wycliffe in Oklahoma. There I met Don. It has been the greatest joy of my life to be united with a dedicated Christian man and to serve the Lord with him.

Letter from Don to support partners, June 1964[1]

Barbara Arrives!

It was a thrill for me to greet my fiancée after an absence of sixteen months. Just two weeks after she left Michigan, Barbara was in South America! Thank God for supplying funds, visa, and friends to help in the many preparations of getting off. We had two days together in Boa Vista before I left for Belem and Barbara for Rio de Janeiro. She will be studying Portuguese near Rio for the next six months.

Barbara gives glowing reports of the Missionary Internship program in Michigan, and both of us are grateful for the way in which the Lord has led, even though it was a long wait. God is ordering our steps and we "delight in his way."

---

1. Excerpt from previous June 1964 letter regarding the Samatali survey.

Don and Barb upon Barb's Arrival in Boa Vista

Personal letter from Barb, November 22, 1964

During the first five months, I have lived with a pastor's family in Nova Friburgo. The weather was rainy and cold. My wedding dress, which I had brought from home, hung covered on a hanger during all that time. The Thursday before the ceremony, I was aghast to see a large rust spot ruining the dress! What a blessing that in the church was a skilled, kind seamstress. Without a pattern she made an exact replica, a perfect fit, in just a day and a half!

Letter from Don to support partners, December 1964

"God be merciful unto us and bless us, that Thy way may be known upon the earth. Thy saving health among all nations." (Ps 67: 1,2 KJV)
Nova Friburgo
Rio de Janeiro
Dear praying friends,
    God has been merciful and blessed us bountifully. He has brought Barbara and me together as man and wife, has given us both good health, and has paved the way for us to open a new station among the Sanumá Indians. The wedding took place here in the town where Barbara studied Portuguese, and the ceremony was performed by the Brazilian pastor in whose home she lived for five months.

Beside the many Brazilian friends, several of our missionary friends from both UFM and Wycliffe attended the ceremony. Johnnie Peters came up from the Campinas Language School to be the best man. Barbara's closest girlfriend from college days is with Wycliffe Bible Translators in Brazil and was the matron of honor. And who should come down from America to represent our families and friends but my own dad who had combined business with pleasure to make the trip possible!!

We couldn't have asked for better weather and location for our honeymoon. After a few days in the tranquil, majestic mountains surrounding Nova Friburgo, we descended to spend the rest of the week in one of the most fascinating, naturally beautiful cities in the world—Rio de Janeiro.

Pray for our short ministry here in South Brazil. In January, we will be presenting to Brazilian young people the challenge of Indian work. As January is one of the vacation months, we will have the opportunity to speak in some of the camps such as Palavra da Vida (Word of Life, Brazil). The first two weeks of February we plan to participate in the program of a training camp for prospective workers among Indians.

Neill Hawkins has interviewed two Brazilian young ladies who have felt the call of God in their lives and who will be traveling north to spend a few months in an orientation period on our jungle stations. Remember these two as they continue to seek to know God's will. Pray that God will choose and prepare in his time just the ones who are to work with us.

In our next letter we'd like to tell you much more about the Sanumá Indians and the way we have been led to enter this tribe. We praise the Lord for raising me back to full strength after a long bout with malaria and bronchitis and for giving me about a month with the Sanumás before the wedding. While I was taking down text material on the tape recorder, Rod Lewis supervised the construction of our future home. We're eager to move in! But first, there will be a jungle training course for Barbara at Mucajaí station for at least a month.

Thank you all for thinking of us at this joyful time in our lives, and pray that our lives together might be blessed for the purpose of manifesting Christ to the ends of the world.

Article in the UFM Magazine

Borgman Wedding

North Amazon, Brazil

The wedding took place November 21 here in the town where Barbara studied Portuguese.

It was small, simple, and Brazilian. The pastor's family went all out to help. Dona Ieda and the girls worked on setting out the little sweet cakes that a missionary wife decided to make without my knowing it. There were scores of them! It poured incessantly the entire night before the wedding *and* that day. In the pavilion, half open, where the reception was to be held, there was the pastor, on his hands and knees, alone, mopping up the large puddles. I have never been so touched and hope God will enable me to show selflessness as I have seen it exhibited here. John and Lorraine Peters came and were terrific to us. Lorraine arranged most of the flowers. They sang beautifully at our wedding and reception. John was best man. The pastor gave a brief but touching evangelistic talk and challenge to us, and we gave brief testimonies at the reception.

Wedding Photo

Auarís—Living Among the Sanumás

Email from Don to editor, August 13, 2020

At the end of September 1964, Rod Lewis and his wife, Tommy, graciously went to supervise the building of the house (at Auarís Station) where I would bring my bride. This was a house with a dirt floor (except for the bedroom) and thatch roof. This was tough, especially on Barb (who by this time went by the name of Anita, which sounded a lot more Brazilian. This name was taken from her middle name, Ann.) Comfort level could only go up from then on as we immediately added an outhouse, then a mud stove, then an iron wood-burning stove, and finally a propane-fueled stove. A few years later, Rod again came up and built a house which was slightly elevated, with palm-slat flooring and an aluminum-sheet roof.

Auarís Station, where Don and Barb would live and work with the Sanumás

Barbara's journal, February 1965

Auarís, Entry 1

Neill Hawkins, field director, had to be away, and I was called in to Boa Vista to take the role of director while he was away.

Life in B.V. is quiet on the surface, but all kinds of "Mickey Mouse" things (as Don says) turn up until the day has whizzed by and little seems accomplished. Notes with requests come from the stations, from Bonfim, etc. and unless one is well-organized, it is easy to forget the many details: medicine for this one, plane reservations on FAB for that one, check on passports and tickets for visitors coming through, letters coming here for people in Bonfim or Boa Vista (people we often don't know) that have to be distributed, etc. Don has been carrying the burden since he is a little more familiar with mission business and drives the Jeep (I haven't gotten a license yet), but we're both seeing that it is no picnic to have the job of director.

Mary and Neill will be coming back on the round robin (I can't get it out of my head to call it the red robin!) this Wednesday. A few days after that, I guess we'll be going into the stations (Surucucu first, I think) by special flight. We'll spend a week at each, and I'll be getting an informal introduction to jungle life, observing and questioning and being taught several things by Don and John. Then there'll be a month at the Auaris before the field conference. We'll be taking barest necessities and living in the partly finished house. Don will continue working on the house and the language; I'll be adjusting and learning the language, i.e., getting a bare start. Following the field conference, there will be three weeks of formal jungle training with three other greenhorns—the Andersons (whom we knew at Wycliffe and who were in my candidate class), a Brazilian girl (whom Don and I met in the South), and me. That will complete jungle training, and we'll go up to the Auaris once more, indefinitely.

One highlight has been an outdoor evangelistic meeting in Boa Vista that Neill started some time ago. Don had charge of it, and we did some visiting. The second time he decided to take his guitar, and, besides the people we'd visited, many others came—drawn partly, I think, by the music, which Brazilians love. Five folks came to the Lord and have been progressing since their acceptance, as far as we can see.

Letter from Don to support partners, March 1965

Brazil, South America
Dear friends,

From time to time we ask you to pray that God will raise up Brazilian young people for Indian work, and we report thankfully that we are seeing him answer these prayers. Two young ladies came to the field in December for an orientation program of several months' duration. Another girl, a teacher-nurse, is expected to arrive from Sao Paulo any day.

During our short stay in a couple of the camps in South Brazil, we saw enthusiastic interest in Indian work. One young man, an ex-communist who was saved through the ministry of Word of Life, dedicated his life to the Lord's service while at camp, decided to enroll in Bible School this term, and told us he was preparing to enter Indian work as soon as possible. Pray that God will mature and direct young people like this who still have years of training ahead of them.

At last, Barbara and I are in Indian country! We are visiting all the stations before going to our own station among the Sanumás. Probably you would like to know a little more about this tribe and the open door that has been waiting for us . . .

Sanumá Indians have occasionally visited the Waicas and missionaries at Waica Station, and several times they have asked for a missionary to live among them. Their own dialect is unintelligible to other Waica dialects, and we have long felt that someone should go to them to give them the Word of God in their own language.

The choice of a site for the new station was obvious. A group of Maiongong Indian men had been contracted by the Brazilian Air Force to help make airstrips at Waica, Parima, and Surucucu Stations. These industrious, intelligent Maiongongs went back to their jungle village, made a beautiful landing field all on their own, and came down to invite us to come up and live there. They told us of a village of Sanumás who live right there at the new strip. The door was opened wide for us, and Barbara and I are happy for the privilege of moving in.

Personal letter by Don, April 1965

Auaris, Entry 2

It's been a busy first week here at the new Auaris Station. A malaria epidemic from Venezuela has hit here and was serious when we arrived. Five Sanumás had already died, and in this week, we treated more than fifty for malaria. I'm sure some, if not many, of these would have died if it were not for the Lord using the tablets we had. The Sanumá village nearest Waica was reduced from one hundred to about thirty because of this epidemic.

Fritz Harter and Wayne F. went up to that region with the Brazilian doctor from B.V., and since he is so near, we've radioed for him to come up here today, even though all thirty have pulled through all night. Some are still weak, and others have other ailments that really need a doctor's attention.

Barb and I are doing fine. Barbara is having to face the normal adjustment and having Indians looking at her most of the day. We've both been taking malaria suppressive so shouldn't be in danger.

Three more weeks and we'll be going to B.V. for our annual field conference. After that, Barb will have one month of jungle training with Andersons and two Brazilians. I might come back here and do some fixing up (stove, outhouse, etc.).

Keep praying for our physical and spiritual health these days.

Personal letter by Don, May 1965

Dr. Davis, Lethem, My healing

Both the alphabet and grammar are about set, and this is the year we'll be emphasizing translation. Of course, Barbara and I are just starting off in a new dialect, but with this background I think we should be able to catch up soon. I mean that the grammatical structure probably will be very similar to that of the other dialects.

As I mentioned on the tape (which you should receive with the letter of soon after—also mailed by Fran) that the Sanumá will be our next-door neighbors up there, and this has advantages for language learning, but it can by trying at times, so pray that we'll have profitable conversations with them each day—conversations in which we continue to learn new things.

We plan for the next couple of stints to stay in the tribe for three months each time with a month break in the middle. These breaks can be very profitable for language analysis as well as for a change of diet, etc. Our diet should steadily improve up there. I plan to bury a few seeds so that we can have some vegetables. We'll have enough protein, I think, with eggs and meat.

Anita and I both lost weight up there. The past week she was down with malaria, and I was kept too busy with sick patients, and often I didn't eat too well. Then out here in Boa Vista I came down with malaria, and then that, in turn, caused my resistance to go low and the old bronchial condition returned with its afternoon and night low fever. The plane was going over to Lethem last Friday, so I hopped on board to see Dr. Davis (medical wing of MAF) who had arrived in Lethem that very afternoon. We saw him and got attention between sprays—he was spraying to kill bed bugs that had accumulated. He was pretty busy, and Kitty was going back to B.V. the same afternoon, so I waited till Saturday for treatment. He gave me penicillin and sulfa and some stuff for a possible allergy, and the next day the fever was gone, and I picked right up. I'm well now with no cough or fever and ready to go back. (The bronchial cough never did come back!)

Personal letter by Don, May 1965

There have been some malaria patients, but just a few this time. The day I arrived, a woman came with news that a young lady was terribly sick upriver a day. I told the boys to paddle up and bring her down for treatment. They arrived with her about 9:00, and I quickly gave her penicillin and malaria medicine. She had had a fever for ten days. About 11:00 they came over and said that she was dying. They asked me to come over and also called for the Sanumá shaman. (This was a Maiongong woman that was sick.) The malaria medicine had broken the fever, but the woman was drooling some and eyes were half open and glassy. The Maiongong women were busily getting their pots and belongings out of the house, because of their belief of having to destroy the house and possessions where someone has died. I couldn't give more medicine, and I prayed that God would spare her life and give glory to his name. She seemed to breathe easier and start to sleep.

Then the Sanumá shaman showed up. They were going to take the lady to another house and "shamanize" over her. They asked me to untie one of the hammock ropes which was high for them, and I said that they could not trust in God and in the shaman at the same time. I reminded them that I had prayed, and that God could make her well. One of the boys untied the rope, and they stood discussing for about four minutes. Then I took leave and in about a minute the shaman came after saying that they didn't need him after all. I felt that a real battle was going on and prayed more that God would defeat Satan and his followers. The next morning I went over and felt something of what Darius the king must have felt. Was God able to deliver? Yes, she was still alive. I believe she's going to pull through. It's about a week later, and each day has seen some improvement. Praise the Lord.

Personal letter by Don, June 1965

Barb writes of her adjustment

I appreciate your prayers very much and realized the need of prayer for my own personal development more than ever that first month here. On more than one occasion, I gave in to impatience instead of accepting the phases that came with the situation in which God had placed me. The constant staring, cooking on the ground surrounded by our Indian friends (who were only curious), and disorganization since we were roughing it for just a month. At the end of the month, I admit I wanted to get out to Boa Vista so much!

I haven't mentioned those things for sympathy. They seem like little things now, but at the time I let them become big battles. When I left, I realized two things: I hadn't been content in "whatsoever state," and I, not the situation, would have to change.

Pastor Burtner's messages were a blessing. I remember the words that stood out to me: "We don't go into the conflict alone." One morning at jungle training I heard a message on tape; the theme was: "Whole Committal to the God in Me." I regretted the previous month, as we often regret failures, but took that opportunity for rededication.

I have a long way to go, that I know, but this month has been one of harmony and change. In answer to many prayers, I'm confident. Things that seemed pressures have become expected, natural things—the staring, poking into things, and other minor details that come with living among the Indians whose culture is so completely different than ours. Now, when I feel it becoming a bit wearing, I go into the bedroom and have a word of prayer. This makes such a difference. We are trying to do this together, too. If a difference or impatience comes up, we want to remind one another to leave and pray about it. Since we decided that, though, there seems to be a lessening of such moments. The Lord has been good in helping us to grow in love through many new adjustments for me. I say for me, because Don has been so used to all this, and I have had to make the most adjustments here.

Inroads with the Sanumás, Language Progress and Continued Adjustments

Personal letter from Barb, June 1965

Desire to read; Services with Sanumá

The other night we were excited when a teenage boy asked us if we would teach his people to read! This may be the influence of the Maiongong, but to have them ask is an exception. We said yes, and then he asked, "The women, too?" He was exulting, but no more than we were. We hope Don will have the phonemic statement ready by the end of the year (meaning we will then have decided on an alphabet), and we can start working on primers.

Last night we had our first simple service. We sang a little in Portuguese, and Don told the meaning of the words in Sanumá. Their interest surprised us. Don told the creation story, and they asked questions, clicked their tongues as they do when they're excited, and listened well. One man, a Maiongong, married to a Sanumá woman, told his kids to be quiet and stop fooling around! We ask for prayer for the growth of this little gathering. We'll be having it in late afternoon, as they told us this was the best time for them.

Personal letter from Don, June 1965

Brick stove with metal top

It feels great to be settled down at long last to a permanent station. We have no certain dwelling, it is true, and a few months from now we could be somewhere else, but we do want to stay here for as long as possible and see the Lord work in these lives.

At first, with just camping conditions and a lot of work to be done, and all the people to treat for malaria, life was a bit hectic to say the least. Living is much more enjoyable now that most of the people are better and the house is fixed up. Barb has a stove we made out of mud bricks and a metal (thick) top with three "burners." It works really well. We've made a partition for the kitchen so that the Indians aren't all over everything. It's a real cozy house.

Personal letter from Barb, July 1965

Birthday jungle flowers

This morning Don came to the kitchen early, and when I came out, there was a beautiful centerpiece of jungle flowers. He knows how I like them and did that for my birthday. A very nice guy, I'd say. He gets nicer every day.

Our quintal, a fenced-in yard, is finished. No more dogs and dirty fingers or banging on the stovepipe. Our garden and tools are a lot safer now, and the kids who loved crawling under our bedroom to look up through the floor have to find another occupation. I never thought I'd see Don excited about gardening (or clean dishes)!

Spouse beating

Recently I saw a Sanumá couple have a family fight. She jabbed him in the stomach with an oar, crying from the clout he'd given her with a heavy chunk of firewood. Soon all the women joined in yelling while the two were lunging at each other, crying and screaming. I was all goosepimples and almost crying myself. Don said that was nothing. Once at Waica, a husband became furious and branded his wife's back with a piece of flaming firewood. He is now a Christian. What a difference it must make!

Personal letter by Don, August 1965

Translation, Station lingo

I have the boys tell about an experience on the tape recorder. And then, I go over this phrase by phrase with an informant, writing it all down. In this way we get away from the "mission lingo," i.e., simplified speech. This transcribed text also will be good for translating—so that we will translate as they talk, not as we translate from our ingrained English patterns. I'm trying to spend most of my mornings in this procedure right now.

Personal letter from Barb, September 1965

Jungle training is over, and we are together again at the Auaris. Our neighbors, the Sanumá, have returned, too, from a hunting trip. So life is resuming at a lively pace.

Don is progressing enthusiastically on a tentative analysis of the language. Several good informants are still away hunting and visiting, but the young men and boys who are here give good language information and patiently repeat phrases. Even the children, who like to go swimming with us or "help" me wash clothes, patiently say words over and over. The women haven't quite caught on yet. When they repeat, they say it just as fast, only louder, thinking the loudness will make it register!

Since Don sprayed the houses, malaria has diminished and neither of us has been sick. However, when Don first returned after conference, he treated a young woman who had had fever for ten days. She was barely able to take the medicine and later appeared to be closer to death than ever. Don prayed before the Indians, but their fear was great, and they called in a shaman. They asked Don to help move her to another house where they would do shamanism over her. He refused, declaring he'd prayed, and God was in control; it would not be good to move her. This left a big decision to the Indians. As Don left, the shaman was dismissed and followed soon after. Deborah, as we named her, recovered, showing immediate improvement the following day.

In April, a young government doctor visited here. He appeared carefree and happy as he examined the Indians and joked with them. Now we receive news that he has just committed suicide in Boa Vista. Don told this to the Indians, curious to know if they ever take their own lives. They affirmed that Indians do commit suicide. Taking poison or a leap from a high tree are some means of doing it. It isn't merely "pressure of civilization" that drives men to desperation. We see even here that deep heart needs are universal.[2]

Personal letter from Barb, October 1965

Zeal flagging

God has been good to me, reminding me to keep on going on. Somehow the enthusiasm and eagerness to go deeper with the Lord of former years would tend to wane at times. Big decisions like life work and life partner are behind me instead of in front. Then settling down into a not-too glamorous spot, with many mundane duties—all this tends to make one, and me, less zealous and diligent in the things of the Lord. Added to all this, and maybe weighing most heavily, is the fact that we cannot speak the language, therefore we cannot preach or teach, or witness to any degree. So pray for patience as we are going through childhood days of our ministry.

Personal letter from Don, November 1965

Eugene Nida Workshop

Our next trip to Boa Vista will be in the middle of January. There will be a translation workshop with Dr. Nida and Dr. Loewen of the American Bible Society, and then our annual field conference right after that. To get the most out of the workshop, I should do what the others are doing, translating Luke 15, which will be the section used for basis of discussion. We're nowhere near ready for translation, but I'm going to make a stab at it. Pray for me in this.

Also in these next two months, I want to clear land and build a little guest house, where I can be secluded when I work with the recorder and with informants. Also it will be a place for guests! Once in a while the pilot will have to stay overnight. Neill comes through occasionally.

---

2. For further reflections by Barb in regard to her entry into the Sanumá world, see Appendix E.

Also I want to put up a simple shelter which will serve as a one-room schoolhouse and a place to have our services. So our work is cut out for us these next two months.

In B.V. we were able to type up a tentative alphabet. This entails quite a bit of chart making, and now that it is done it will require much more checking to verify or nullify our tentative conclusions.

A Child Is Born—David Andrew Borgman

Personal letter from Don, April 1966

David Delivery, Belem

This doctor had had one (or more) bad experiences with near fainting husbands in the delivery room so usually doesn't let them in. But I asked the nuns as they were preparing if I could attend, and they gladly let me in. I must have looked brave, cause the doc didn't kick me out and we all (except Barb) had a good time conversing with the doctor explaining a few things to me as he went along.

Personal letter by Don, May 1966

David born

With grateful and thrilled hearts, we send you the news of the arrival of our first-born, David Andrew. I always had the impression that newborn babies were tiny and ugly, so I was surprised at the size and cuteness of David as I saw him in the delivery room. Can it be that being a father has given me new eyes? All continues to go well, and our ever-hungry son is adding rapidly to his original seven pounds, thirteen ounces.

Personal letter from Don, June 1966

Sitiho steals

Our burglar proof storeroom was broken into while we were gone this last time. Someone crawled under the bedroom and then burrowed their way through the mud wall into the "dispensa" or pantry, carefully mixing mud and sand and filling up the hole after they had left. We had left Auaris on such short notice that we hadn't taken inventory and weren't quite sure just what was in the room, but Anita thought that a couple of her shirts were missing. Because of the uncertainty we said nothing, and just yesterday our famous friend Sitiho (whom we of course suspected) came up from washing clothes with an army shirt on, and under this I caught a glimpse of a yellow shirt with a girl's collar. Sitiho has had quite a history of stealing (including wives) from Waica Station to Surucucu (the time he took off during the night with a lot of the FAB stuff).

Fascination with David

There is a new attraction for the Indians. They are crazy about David and very solicitous. He cannot cry for a moment without them reminding me, "Anita, your child is crying. Tell him, 'Quiet, son,' and say 'ish-ish-ish-ish-ish.'" One day I was out in our yard hanging clothes and one of the other ladies was with me. Through the kitchen window I could watch David in the infant seat. He began to cry, and when I didn't run to him immediately, Sara (my name for her) couldn't stand it, ran into the house, and despite her wad of tobacco, got out a clear enough string in of "ish-ish-ish" to keep him happy until I was done! They are fascinated with every body part and exclaim over each one as if they'd never seen a baby before. They ask questions like, "Does he have a navel? Does he go to the bathroom? Does he sleep with Anita?" The last one is not surprising, because the Indian child sleeps with his mother in her hammock. They feel a baby would be frightened sleeping alone and can't get over his sleeping by himself in his own little hammock.

The Borgman family and Julieta, with neighbors at Auaris

UFM Responsibilities, Sanumá Ways, and a Fortuitous Breakthrough

Personal letter from Don, July 1966

Serving as Field Council chairman

Twice a year we have Field Council meetings; once at Field Conference and the other six months later. We had council meetings scheduled for this time, and then about a week or so ago Neill came down with bad pain and was sent to Lethem with Mary to the MAF doctor, who in turn examined him and sent him on to Georgetown for a probable gall bladder operation.

The MAF pilot told me this when he arrived to take me out of Auaris, and his report was that the members of council and others wanted to go ahead with council meetings anyway, and we did.

There was much business to take care of, and this was my first time for chairing meetings, so it was somewhat of a load, but the Lord gave real harmony throughout, and I felt no pressure except for the time involved.

Personal letter from Don, August 1966

Fight in group

The abundance of rain did give me a little discomfort the other day as I traveled about three or four hours away to the next village to treat a lady with fever, etc. For about an hour we waded through swamps up to our thighs. There's nothing more miserable than traveling in the rain. Especially miserable when you have to make a shelter and fire at night—which was not the case here.

I stayed only overnight. There was a visiting group at the village, and about 8:00 at night there was a rumpus and one of the Sanumá famous fights started. It is organized and nobody usually gets hurt too bad, but for the uninitiated it seems by the noise and gestures of knives and sticks that everybody is going to get cut. At this session, only one fellow got swatted on the back with the flat edge of a cutlass. These organized slug fests are the Shiriana way of settling their grievances. They sometimes slug each other on the chest, sometimes on the back with cutlasses, and sometimes on the head with clubs, all depending upon how deep the grievance is, I suppose.

Personal letter from Don, September 1966

Medical work; Bathing

I usually take care of the people who come for medicine after breakfast and before supper. If there is some kind of work program, I take that. I try to get in a full morning of study with or without an informant, and then visit the rest of the hours. Some days I'm gone all day for a hunt or for a visit to another village.

In the middle of the afternoon, Barb and Dave and I go for a swim. A "dunk" might be a better description. The water is frigid up here, and any thought of a bath after 5:00 in the afternoon is murder. We've dunked David's foot in for a split second a couple of times, but it scares the daylights out of him.

Recording, Abel, 1

One of the young men visitors has been on the outs with a couple of the fellows from here (they hit him on the head with an ax the last time he showed up) and came here, knowing that his enemies were away. The animosity is over a girl he took as wife without the proper legal procedures of petition, dowry, etc. He was badly wanting some cloth, so I asked him if he wanted to work as an informant. I was going to play an old tape of some men who had told me a few of their legends and history, and then with this boy's help transcribe it. He listened for a while and seemed pretty disgusted that they left out so much or told the stories wrong, so I changed procedures and put the mic in front of him. I told him to take his time and tell it slowly—the longer the tape, the longer the cloth.

That was one afternoon. He talked all afternoon till dark. The next morning he talked all day till dark with some time out for me to go to dinner. He filled up ten tapes, slow speed, on both sides—about twenty-five or thirty hours of talking. He'd literally talk without stopping for two hours straight, then ask to go out to the bathroom, or wait till I turned the tape over, then give it two more hours. Sometimes I'd leave to give medicine or something, and he'd keep going. It was amazing.

The Maiongongs and Lourenzo—
a Providential Friendship

Letter from Don and Barb to support partners, September 1966

Auaris River
Dear Friends,

Last month we were hosts to an anthropologist from Texas Tech. So we changed our emphasis from language study to the study of culture and personality for a couple of weeks. Once again it was underlined in our thinking the tremendous difference between our two sets of neighbors, the Sanumá and the Maiongong. Maybe the best way for you to see this difference is to list the basic characteristics of each group:

Maiongong	Sanumá
1. Stocky in build	1. Slight of build
2. Extremely intelligent—expert house and canoe builders. Confident traders with the outside world.	2. Admit that they just don't know how to build or weave well. Depend on Maiongongs for trading with outsiders.
3. Industrious	3. Make small, inadequate fields. Satisfied to steal extensively from Maiongong fields.
4. Reasonable sense of cleanliness	4. Hygiene, what's that?
5. Honest	5. Frequently steal
6. Courteous and considerate	6. Hard to live with
7. Quiet-mannered. Not easily excited.	7. Easily excited, boisterous, and rough in play or conversation.
8. Peace-loving	8. Fight and feud
9. Frequent and extensive travelers to the outside world. Welcome change.	9. Not very susceptible to change. Want trade goods but are wary of the outside world.

Personal letter from Don, September 1966

Lourenzo

Also, remember especially the name of one Maiongong who could be a key to reaching many Sanumá for Christ if he were converted. He is Lourenzo, who has a Sanumá wife. This is a rare situation, and Lourenzo is a rare

Maiongong who has many friends among the generally looked-down-upon Sanumá. He speaks their language and is respected.

Personal letter from Don, November 1966
Recording, Abel, 2

Just recently I obtained about twenty-five hours' worth of narrative text on Sanumá legends and history which will be invaluable for both linguistic and anthropological study. Anita and I try to spend about an hour a day on very simple texts, which is a good way to learn new vocabulary, etc. I learn a lot just by transcribing texts and asking questions.

Barb's journal, December 1966

Ilo ran up to the door panting, "Don, deer, deer, deer, deer . . . " Meat is one of the most important things in an Indian's life, and Don tore down to the port. Don felled it on the first shot, which zipped into his ear and ripped through his head. Of course, the deer was a sitting duck, but it was still a super shot. As we knew, some Maiongongs had gone off earlier with their dogs. The dogs find the deer and chase them into the river. Downstream other Maiongongs are waiting in a canoe waiting to shoot the game. When John (Maiongong) returned, he confirmed that it was one they'd shot at and missed. They took it but will probably give the Sanumá a piece for discovering it.

SURVEY TRIP OF THE SANUMÁS AND WAICAS, HELP AT AUARIS

Letter from Don and Barb to support partners, January 1967

Dear friends,

True to their word, the Maiongong boys returned from their long trip just before the big moon in December. We were eager to hear that some had turned to the Lord during the Indian Bible Conference they had attended in Venezuela, but there was no such report.

Was this lack of decision due to hardness of heart or lack of full understanding of the gospel? We feel it is mostly the latter with another big factor . . . the realization on their part of the tremendous implications of conversion to Christ. They know that their whole community and old way of life would undergo radical changes. Also, some have expressed their desire to be able to read before becoming Christians, presumably so that they could know how to follow on and read God's instructions for their everyday life.

Perhaps God wants us to pray in a new direction for the Maiongongs. We have heard of Maiongong Indian couples or families who have gone and stayed long periods in a village to teach the villagers to read, sing, pray, and to tell them God's Word. Pray with us for such an Indian missionary family to come to our village on the Auaris who will stay for a year or more. In the meantime, we will struggle along through Portuguese.

The language we are learning is Sanumá, and these last few months we've seen marked progress with willing informants spending morning after morning helping us transcribe and analyze tape recordings of their legends, narratives, and conversation.

For the next two months, I'll be leaving my little family and taking a break from the tapes and desk work. Steve Anderson and I plan to travel to the lower Auaris River. Steve is interested in contacting a Waica group who live at the mouth of the Auaris. Near them live a Sanumá group, the Tucushim people, who used to live nearer Waica Station, but moved nearer us after two of their group were killed by the Waicas.

A reportedly big Sanumá group, the Sikois, live inland from the river, and have never been contacted by the outside world. We plan to meet them and win their friendship.

Personal letter from Don, May 1967

Sikoi man, Julieta, 1

He yelled and "aaahed" for ten minutes straight. His bug eyes scanned us up and down from head to foot. His trembling hands rubbed our monkey-like hairy arms. In high, excited tones he kept exclaiming, "A 'civilizado,' a 'civilizado'!" Steve Anderson and I were the first specimens from the "civilized" world that this Sikoi Indian had ever seen.

We had hoped to meet all the Sikois, but a recent attack by an enemy group had dispersed them. Some were roaming the woods hunting for berries and fruit. Others were visiting another Sanumá village. A couple of families were at the spot where the future Sikoi village will be. It was here that our guides led us and where we met representatives of the last Sanumá group we know of in Brazil.

We had wondered if the Sikois belonged to the Sanumá dialect, and we kept wondering as these different looking Indians came up to us—skinny and not even wearing loin cloths. But after hearing just a few phrases, we knew that the Sikois were really Sanumá. Next year their fields will be producing, and we plan another visit at that time when all the Sikois expect to be settled in one spot.

How common is the report of attacks and reprisals! The Waicas who used to live at the mouth of the Auaris River have abandoned their houses and fields because of a recent killing and now live a day farther upriver.

The Tucushim people, who were attacked by Indians near Waica Station, now live way up the Auaris. Three years ago this group numbered about three hundred. We found only about sixty of them left after a malaria epidemic which hit two years ago.

Among this number we found some who still remembered songs and teaching they had acquired at Waica Station. Their hearts are open and seem to be waiting for more teaching. Pray especially for two Tucushim young men, Sebastião and Tiago. These two Sanumá brothers were especially close to us and might be potential leaders.

They were part of the party who took us from Sanumá territory on down the Auaris and then up the Parima River to Surucucu Station. On the way we passed through several Waica villages, one of which had never been contacted before.

After more than six weeks away, both Steve and I were anxious to see our families again, but we had no idea how soon after reaching Surucucu this would be possible. We emerged from the jungle trail at 11:30 a.m. and learned that our wives and children were on their way by plane and would land in less than half an hour! Not even time to shave or get into something that could be called "clothes." Barbara recognized me, but son David turned his head and clung for dear life to his mother.

Steve and family stayed on to work at Surucucu Station. We are back at our post at Auaris, clearing out the weeds, and building a house for a new worker.

Steve Anderson with son

For you who have prayed that God would send us Brazilian young people, we are especially happy to report that a Brazilian missionary, Julieta Souza, has joined us here at Auaris. Julieta grew up in very hard circumstances which perhaps have helped prepare her to "rough it" and to face the somewhat lonely life on a jungle post.

From the poorer state of Bahia, she moved to Rio de Janeiro where she studied and obtained her diploma from a Baptist seminary. She also attended a Summer Institute of Linguistic course at the University of Brasília. Julieta has had practical nursing experience and has lifted a big burden from our shoulders by taking over the medical program here. She plans to teach literacy soon. Co-laborers from different cultures and different mother tongues face some adjustments as they work together. So pray for us that we might experience the unity and love of the Holy Spirit as together we share this high calling of reaching Indians for Christ.

Julieta Souza with Sanumá children

First Joint Furlough for Don and Barb

Letter from Don and Barb to support partners, April 1968

Furlough Plans

We plan to arrive in New York on June 15th to spend at least nine months in the States. I plan to attend Wycliffe's Summer Institute of Linguistics in Oklahoma during the summer months to work on Sanumá grammar. From the last of September till March is open for visiting various churches and individual friends in the East and Midwest. We are looking forward to these times of being refreshed as we fellowship together once again.

Sanumá News

From the first of October till the middle of December, we had two Sanumá Indian informants in Boa Vista to help us in an intensive language learning course designed to build up the missionaries' fluency in the Sanumá language. Both students and informants weathered the heat well, and we thank

God for a successful course. Now we are back among the Sanumá and have started Sunday afternoon classes for them.

Field Developments

The medical evangelistic program in the more civilized regions nearer Boa Vista is having great effect and already is in need of more Brazilian workers. The doctor of the MAF Medical Wing has been a key in opening up eight centers which formerly had been unreached by Protestant missions.

The evangelist connected with this program is a zealous, dedicated Brazilian who is with our mission. In every clinic point there are now believers who want to form their local church. But there is just not enough time for one man to feed all these flocks, so we desperately need another Brazilian worker for this field.

Family Plans

In April, our son will be two years old, and the first part of the same month we will be in Boa Vista awaiting the arrival of a little companion for David. In June we plan to head to the States for a furlough of at least nine months. We expect to write again before that time, giving news of the addition to our family, and passing on any further report concerning the Wai Wai contact among the Atroais.

Family Report: Another Safe Arrival!

This one was sooner than expected. Born here in Boa Vista on March 20th . . . a boy, Stephen Hughes. All very well with both mother and son.

Letter from Barbara to support partners, May 1969

This is the last communique from our home away from home. April 18 will find us in South America again. How profitable, refreshing, and happy these ten months home have been. We've lived in Bridgeport, Connecticut, in Don's mother's home and have made frequent trips to New Jersey to visit my parents.

We returned to the United States the end of last June and, during the summer, Don typed the final draft of one hundred and fifty pages of Sanumá language material. He submitted it to a computer program at the University of Oklahoma, thanks to the kindness of a professor and friend there, Dr. Joe Grimes (of Wycliffe Bible Translators), who was co-publisher. The material is back, complete with a concordance of Sanumá text material. It is bound and ready as a tool for further study.

Don has attended two helpful seminars and has spoken in church services, missionary conferences, and colleges. We've traveled as a family to renew friendships and share the task we face with the churches here. Quality visits, when possible on these trips, have meant deepened relationships with you. Warm homes were opened to us and meaningful conversations and sharing in prayer informed us of your needs, too. We want to be together with you in prayer.

First Term Together in Retrospect

Thus completed Don and Barb's first term and furlough together. In looking back, one can only imagine the adjustment and culture shock experienced, especially by Barb. For both, however, the changes in life had been extreme, from singleness to married life, from Western ways of living to constant camping, from familiar social patterns to ones as foreign as could be conceived, and now as parents of two young children. Fortitude was certainly requisite, but despite obvious challenges, all were met with thankfulness and joy, as can only come through the Holy Spirit.

6

From Strength to Strength (1969 to 1973)

> "Blessed are those whose strength is in you, in whose heart are the highways to Zion. As they go through the Valley of Baca they make it a place of springs; the early rain also covers it with pools. They go from strength to strength; each one appears before God in Zion."
> (Ps 84:5–7)

Upon their return from *furlough, Don and Barb were ready to start in again with their work among the Sanumás. In some ways, life would be more settled. They knew the people and increasingly were coming to an understanding of their ways. Having completed a basic overview of the Sanumá language, Don could now get down to sustained translation work as his knowledge of the language grew. Along with this was the anticipation that life for Barb would become more routine as she and Don now had two sons to raise. New residents, both missionaries and non-missionaries, would come to reside at Auaris presenting a different dynamic to the community. Despite a sense of familiarity with Auaris and the Sanumás, there would be significant challenges, impediments, and sorrows.* [1]

---

1. As referred to in the Introduction, some of the entries below are out of order chronologically in order to maintain continuity of a particular topic or subject.

From Strength to Strength (1969 to 1973)

Getting Back to Life at Auaris

Personal letter from Don, May–June 1969

New house with Rod Lewis in charge of construction

The house is getting done, slowly but surely. This really is the lightest rain for May that I have ever seen, and this has helped us a lot in the construction of the house. Rod did not order enough aluminum sheeting for the completion of the roof, and there is none to be had just now in Boa Vista (another shortage), and we are waiting on that also. It's a nice house which will fit our needs very well. The aluminum roof will enable us to keep a good supply of water in barrels, both for drinking and washing.

Mundane schedule

Maybe even more than you know, we need to be refreshed by furlough, more so spiritually than physically. Most of the time as we are learning the Indian language, spending hours at the desk, writing letters, filling out financial reports, fixing a door or a water pump, washing diapers, taking care of kids, cooking, and washing dishes, we wonder if it all has to be this way—so "mundane." And with no speaking engagements and with hardly the facility to even witness personally to the Indians, we depend less and less upon God for our daily living, and the Word and prayer times take last place. So pray for us even during this last month on the field, that we might "seek first the kingdom of God and his righteousness."

New house

Our new house is really great. I have a little study. A big new feature, especially for Anita[2] is the bathroom. (I even rigged up a shower which even I will appreciate—a painted kerosene can with a shower head attached.) Instead of the half barrel we had for water supply in the kitchen, we now have two whole ones. Even with these added conveniences, Anita keeps busy all day long, and we could really use a maid.

---

2. "Anita" is a name that Barb adopted early on at Auaris since it sounded more Portuguese than Barbara.

Rod and Tommy Lewis with Julieta (second from right)

Immediate Challenges

Letter from Don to support partners, August 10, 1969

Boa Vista, Brazil
Dear faithful friends,

After a year of furlough, we met an abrupt change of environment as we landed at Auaris Station. Sickness and death were pressing in on the Sanumá Indians. One lady died just a couple of days after our arrival. She and others had contracted malaria which brought on pneumonia. In spite of our treatment day and night, three Sanumás died.

This whole ordeal has been an emotional and physical drain on us. I have sat and wept with those bereaved whose wailing usually reaches a peak as the body of the deceased is pulled out of the carrying basket and laid on the funeral pyre.

The heartbreak of these Indians is real. There are those who firmly believe that the jungle Indian lives an idyllic life of happiness, and that we missionaries should leave them alone. I wonder if these critics ever spent enough time in a tribe to know the deepest thoughts and needs that the tribal people express.

I have just returned from Brasília, having been called out of the jungle to represent our mission in a symposium sponsored by the National Indian Foundation.³ The purpose of this gathering was to discuss Indian problems and then to sign agreements between mission organizations and the National Indian Foundation. There are many anthropologists and other specialists within the National Indian Foundation who wanted to push through resolutions prohibiting missionaries from communicating the gospel or even from teaching isolated Indians to read and write.

But our God is over all and has shown us that He still works in governments and rules the hearts and deliberations of authorities. He put in the vice-presidency of the N. I. F. a Christian man who has been used of God to use his influence so that none of the programmed prohibitions came to fruition.

So at least for the present we can continue on our posts without restrictions as to religious activities.

As you pray for us, remember:

1. Dr. Benjamin Moraes, the Christian man in the N.I.F. who seems to be in a similar situation as was Daniel the prophet.
2. The need for permission for radio communications on all our jungle posts.
3. The need for physical, emotional, and spiritual strength day by day for us.
4. The answers to former prayer. We have had excellent attendance and attention during our Sunday afternoon services with the Sanumá. Also, in spite of sickness and other pressures, we have had many good hours of language study.

Personal letter from Don, June 1970

Flu

A very bad flu epidemic hit us here at Auaris. An epidemic is bad enough in civilization, but here among the Indians it is disastrous. Filthy living conditions and poor diet and little resistance. A Maiongong brought it in from Boa Vista. Fortunately, many of the Sanumás were away at the time, and the rest fled upstream and downstream and did not catch it.

---

3. The National Indian Foundation or FUNAI replaced the previous Indian Protection Service in 1967. The former had been riddled with scandal.

Julieta started treating the Maiongongs, but then she herself came down with fever and was out of commission for about three weeks. I took over treatment and within a couple of days every one of the sixty or so Maiongongs was in his hammock with high fever, aches, and vomiting some.

It was a nightmare. Everybody in one big longhouse. Smoke and semi-darkness. Phlegm all over the place. Some of the women with dysentery too weak to move from their hammocks; you can imagine the stench. It took me more than two hours maneuvering around in that house to take temperatures, give pills to some, and give shots to the more serious cases. I'd make the rounds in the morning, come back, and flop down and rest till the afternoon round. Soon I was feeling the flu with weakness, scratchy nasal passages, and low fever. I was in the guest house now to keep away from Anita and the kids. Julieta was still unable to walk around. Anita was just about able to handle things with me well to help some, but now with me away, it got to be too much for her. So we called for help.

A girl from Mucajaí and one from Surucucu came up to help with treatment of the Maiongongs and Julieta and me if we needed it. Anita was undecided up till the last minute but finally agreed to go out to Boa Vista with the kids. What a circus getting the three kids in the plane. Anita was in front with the pilot and Andrea. David in a seat behind with Stevie yelling and kicking like fury. We strapped in David and Stevie together, and I finally stuffed Stevie's legs inside and shut the door fast. Things were so hectic, and I was not feeling up to par, and I could have cried when they all took off.

I am thankful that my fever did not get worse, and with the girls helping out I was able to rest more, and within a few days I was feeling much better again. The Maiongongs were responding well and recuperating. Only one lady has not come out of it. She has continued with fever for over three weeks. Last night they thought she would die for sure. Only a miracle will save her life, but we are praying for this.

Aleuta

Yesterday, the sick lady, Aleuta, called for us to pray for her. She had done this a couple of times recently but was feeling that she wouldn't last long. We spent quite a while over there explaining the importance of the cure for the soul. We talked through a couple of Maiongongs who speak some Portuguese, one of whom has heard some of the gospel in his own tongue over in Venezuela. After a long while, Aleuta said she did want Christ to cleanse her soul. That she wanted his spirit to live in her, that she would obey his word. She prayed herself, and then we prayed for her spiritual and physical healing.

New Residents at Auaris

Personal letter from Don, May 1969
Anthropologists Ken Taylor and Alcida Ramos live next door

Ken Taylor and Alcida, a man and woman anthropologists, are here and have built a little house right next to the village, or right in it, and will be here for at least six more months. They have a completely different orientation than we do religiously and somewhat different orientation on the Indians and preserving their culture completely intact. But they are very friendly and understanding, and their stay here is a help to us.

Personal letter from Don, September 1970
Anthropologists

I finished typing up a translation of all the myths which went into my computer material. (There is still much to do on myths. I've translated only a tenth of the material I still have on tape). This translation was not only helpful for me, but the anthropologist, Ken Taylor, was enthused with the material, and I've given him a copy which he will probably use somewhere in his doctor's thesis.

We have had very friendly relations with the couple, and we had one evening in which we talked to them of spiritual matters before they left. They believe that even the idea of a supreme being is a cultural concept, and they themselves don't believe in God. Much of the discussion was in relation to the Sanumás, but I directed some comments directly to his own relationship with God and our concern, not only for the Sanumás, but for him and Alcida.[4] They are quite convinced of their position and naturally feel that we are "arrogant" in imposing another religion on anybody.

They are leaving for Rio tomorrow and then on to the States to the University of Wisconsin where he will teach and work on his doctorate. They plan to come back to work again among the Sanumá, maybe in about five years. They have been very friendly and cordial but admittedly very

---

4. Alcida Ramos would go on to write a book of their anthropological observations of the Sanumá called *Sanumá Memories - Yanomami Ethnography in Times of Crisis*.

much against our work. But they want to keep channels open for communication. He would like to work on the idea of some common denominator between us (as far as work among Sanumás) and try to come up with some kind of a message of "love your neighbor" without any mention of a vertical relationship with God. Better yet, I am sure as far as they are concerned, would be our exit from the Sanumá territory.

Getting to Know Sanumá Ways

Personal letter from Don, April 1970

On Having Babies

The Sanumá Comment:

- "All the way to Boa Vista just to have a baby? Much more convenient to stay at home or let it be born out in the forest while on a hunting trip."
- "Are your babies born in the same way as ours?"
- "Did it hurt?"
- "How in the world does the poor thing perform its natural functions all bundled up like that?"
- "They even knew that it would be born during this moon."
- "You've named her already?"
- "It's the jaguar milk (powdered cow's milk) that makes her grow so fast."
- "That's great. Two boys and a girl. But the family's not complete. You need another girl to even it off."

The Missionaries Reflect . . .

God gave us our desire, a healthy baby girl, Andrea, born February 15 in Boa Vista. We are thankful that the MAF doctor was on hand for the delivery.

In thinking about the Indian way of giving birth and bringing up children, we recognize many disadvantages of our own system. But we are victims of our culture and pray for loving patience in the midst of changing and washing dirty diapers and children's clothes, listening to screaming over toys, finding the kids into everything: the kitchen knife, the china cup presented by Aunt Tillie, our one good Pyrex, and the language notes. (Who left the study door open this time?!)

From Strength to Strength (1969 to 1973)

On Spirit Communication

The Sanumá Comment:

- "You mean that by talking into that thing you can make your voice heard right away in Boa Vista?"
- "You must really be able to manipulate the spirits to do that!"
- "Well, if it's not by the spirits, then how do they hear your voice so far away?"

The Missionaries Reflect...

We don't know much more than the Indians as to how a radio works, and we, too, marvel at being able to talk with those in Boa Vista.

For a long time we were without radio contact. Thank you for your prayers in this regard. The governor of the territory recently set up a new communications system and graciously included all our mission stations, allocating to each one a radio transmitter and a generator. The operator in the government office is most helpful in giving and receiving important messages during the two daily contacts.

We praise God for excellent relations with the territorial government. On the national level, indications are that missionaries will be able to continue unrestricted in their work as long as the conservative military regime is in power.

On the Apollo Program

The Sanumá Comment:

- "People actually landed on the moon! They must be Christians; only people with God's Spirit could ever perform a feat like that."
- "The top of the sky isn't hard? If I kept on walking, I'd never come to the bottom of the sky?"
- "He's saying that the earth is like a ball—round like the moon—and that the people underneath us don't fall off!"

The Missionaries Reflect...

God, airplanes, Christ, knives, the Holy Spirit, cooking pots: these merge together to make up the Indian's idea of the universe. He does not compartmentalize religion, crop yield, medicine, and material wealth. The distinction between the natural and supernatural all but vanishes for the man in primitive society. Not that he is a materialist. He is more a "supernaturalist" than most Americans, interpreting much that we would call material or natural in terms of God and the spirits.

So we as missionaries must change lenses, trying to see and reason like a Sanumá in order to be able to present and apply the gospel message in all its clarity and force. This certainly means contradicting their ideas at times, but it also involves surgery on us, cutting out some deep-seated views injected into us by a largely materialistic society.

Personal letter from Don, January 1971

Indian Raids

In our more than ten years among Indians, we had never witnessed anything like it. The stillness of the late afternoon was shattered by the shrieks of twenty-five charging men who let go with a barrage of arrows. The helpless victims looked like gigantic pin cushions as they reeled and fell to the earth. Hardly an arrow had missed its mark. And then the "choppers" came in, not to rescue but to finish them off by hacking away at the prostrate forms with cutlasses.

This was merely a practice session, and the victims were only dummies made of twigs and leaves, but the real thing had taken place just a month before. Now these men, dressed in their raid uniforms (bodies smeared with black paint) were practicing for a surprise attack against enemies reported to be coming for a reprisal.

Last November the men from a nearby village joined other allies in a raid on a distant village. Several were killed and some were wounded. One woman's ear was purposely sliced off. Why the raid? Here are two of the grievances mentioned: 1) The distant group had killed the wife of a leader of this nearby village by blowing the powder of a magic root on her. 2) Another leader died because the big hawk which possessed his "alter-ego" spirit had been shot by the enemy group.

The killers and families have all taken refuge in the Sanumá village where we live. Everyone is on edge expecting a revenge attack any day. Many families have fled to other locations. Others, including the actual killers, are staying here near the gardens.

How does this all affect us? For one thing, it is possible that a segment of the Sanumás who live in this village will move to a new location. This would include Lourenzo and Saula, and such a move would mean that we would travel more in order to instruct these young converts.

From Strength to Strength (1969 to 1973)

For those who stay and who are interested in the gospel, we must instruct on what the Bible says about warfare. Here it is not even a question of defending family, possessions, and land. Among the Sanumás it is a matter of retaliation and revenge, and so we will be presenting the instructions of Paul regarding the words of the Lord: "Vengeance is mine, I will repay." (Rom 12:17–21) We know from cases at Surucucu Station that it is exceedingly hard on young Christians who do not want to take part in the raids, and yet who, especially because of their closely-knit social organization, feel obligated to participate when pressure is put on them by their elders.

We are thankful that, in spite of the turmoil, I have had the help of informants and have completed a rough translation of four chapters of the book of Mark. We are praying that all sixteen chapters will be ready for checking when the consultant of Wycliffe Bible Translators arrives the second week of April.

Lourenzo—a Providential Relationship

Personal letter from Don, October 1970

Conversation with Lourenzo; Pays a "deer" price for confab

It was the unmistakable splash of a deer jumping into the stream escaping from the pursuing hunting dogs. Lourenzo leaped up and dashed over to verify the tracks. As he was crossing back over the wobbly pole that served as bridge, his grin showed both amusement and remorse as he chided, "We were carrying on like a couple of little kids!" If we hadn't been "yakking" so much, the deer would have jumped in upstream from where we were waiting in ambush, and we would have shot it as it swam past. But upon hearing our animated conversation, the deer had quickly changed its route.

Frankly, this time neither Lourenzo nor I cared that much, for we both felt that our uninterrupted conversation was worth even more than the deer. Possibly for the first time, Lourenzo realized that Christianity was not a "package deal" as so many Indian societies assume: a package including such items as trade goods, education, medicine... and Christ!

I sat there on the bank answering Lourenzo's questions about life in America, what being a Christian involves, and what it does not involve. Questions like: "Are all Americans Christians?" "Can a Christian have two wives like David?" "Does a Christian really have to throw away his chewing tobacco, like I've heard from my people in Venezuela?" "Are you going to make us wear clothes to church?"

Flees the flu

That was the last good conversation I had with Lourenzo for over two months. Another Indian traveler brought in some vicious type of Asian flu. As various members of his communal house came down with high fever, we encouraged Lourenzo and those of other houses to take off. They did so in the one hour it takes an Indian household to wrap up its belongings and move on out. Some went to other villages. Most went to nearby fields or into the forest. None of those who evacuated came down with the flu.

For more than a month we let all other types of work go and battled the flu which had assaulted the big communal house. Seventy people all down with fever, nausea, and other internal upsets. Some with pneumonia. (Julieta, the nurse, came down with a bad case herself. I caught a light case. Barbara and the kids flew out to Boa Vista, and two girls from other stations came in to help us out.)

We praise God that there were no fatalities. One notable case was that of an elderly lady who accepted Christ and came back from death's door in answer to sessions of prayer with her.

This lady deeply impressed Lourenzo as she later recounted to him the whole experience. She was Lourenzo's sister.

Lourenzo

From Strength to Strength (1969 to 1973)

Ongoing Language Work and Literacy Classes with the Sanumás

Personal letter from Don, September 1970

Wycliffe consultant at Auaris

A consultant from Wycliffe is coming up in April to work with Sandy especially and anybody else on translation. So I'm revising my work for the next months and will start a first draft of Mark. I feel that this is early for me, but the consultant's help will be invaluable, and the consultant speaks of getting to the translators early in their work. We plan to meet at Auaris, inviting others working with Waicas (some from New Tribes and Merrill Seely[5] from Venezuela).

Translation work with Abel[6]

Personal letter from Don, December 1971

Literacy

How like home: that familiar race against the relentless clock. Here it is squeezing in housework, a time with the children, heating of the wood-burning stove in time to make supper, cooking, baths, dishes and, just at dark, a call at the door, "Anita," from the class of three Sanumá men.

---

5. Merrill Seely worked with the Sanumás in Venezuela and would become a close collaborator in translation work with Don in the years to come.

6. Abel was the Sanumá man who made recordings for Don in exchange for red cloth.

With a homemade blackboard hanging on our dining nook wall and the simple primers, the students begin to discover reading. Five evenings a week they come faithfully. The length of the "semesters" is determined by the frequency of hunting, visiting, or trading trips, a common feature of these semi-nomadic people (who gather palm fruits, caterpillars, grubs, etc.), for weeks at a time. Two fellows were able to continue for two weeks, and Saula did for about three weeks. As they passed by our house on their way to the port, among the possessions slung over their shoulders were the plastic sacks containing their study materials. They are well-motivated and will be studying again when they return. Other classes, of two and three, are taught by Julieta and Paulo Silas.

Literacy lessons, Barb and Abel

Don worked up each primer and is still working on the series and on the more advanced readers. However, if it weren't for the meticulous artwork and mimeographing by Kitty Pierce, we would not have a program under way so soon. None of us would have had the ability or time to produce such fine work. When she leaves us in March, she will leave behind a good quantity of excellent material for which we are very grateful.

How not like home: the hygiene. We struggle to know how to cause food preparation and eating habits, among other things, to become cleaner without imposing the necessities of stoves, tables, and chairs upon a people not ready for them economically nor socially. What are simple ways of raising the standard of cleanliness which would not complicate their already laborious struggle to keep their stomachs full from day to day? The Sanumá housewife often goes fishing before it is light, must descend a slippery path a good distance from home to get water, must go to her field in drizzle or heat to bring back heavy loads of food which must be prepared upon return for the late afternoon main meal. Before dark, she is in charge of getting a huge basket of firewood for the night. Should sweeping, washing all the kids' hands, and other practices in which she is equally disinterested be added? Merely dispensing medicine is not improving the local people's resistance, but then how do we convince the people these ideas are good and necessary? Suggestions often bring chuckles but no results.

How is God related to the giving of medicines? Is the Sanumá impression that we depend on medicine most of the time and God only in serious cases? Is that what a Sanumá Christian will do in practice while the shaman calls consistently upon the spirits? Will it present a struggle to him if the missionary someday has to leave with all his medicines? These are questions we ask ourselves in relation to the medical program.

Family Life

Personal letter from Don, July 1970

Daily schedule

I'll get back to your letter later but will continue commenting on the health situation. The medical load hasn't been too heavy since Julieta left, partly because a big group of Sanumás and also the household of Lourenzo are away hunting for about a month. Those that need treatment need it at least once every twelve hours, so I get up and treat them before breakfast. We have changed our supper hour from sunset to 5:30 p.m. (theoretically) so that gives me about a half hour or more after supper to treat the sick again. (The first and last activity of the daylight day is opening and closing the chicken house. We have two roosters, four hens, and six chicks. On average, two eggs a day.

I might as well go through the rest of the day now. After breakfast we have a short devotional time together with Cleonice, the maid. We memorize verses, sing a hymn, and pray. The outside work program has been minimal, but it is after devotions that I get any workers orientated. Then, about 8:30 or 9:00 a.m. I go over to the guest house where I study. I spend the morning on the language, either in making Bible story lessons or translating Sanumá myths, a project I am working hard on these days.

After lunch, Anita keeps going, but if I don't get a shut eye, I drag for the rest of the day. The best hour for quiet time is right after that. That is the time of the day that virtually all Indians are off doing something, when I, too, am at my most awake time. Then I spend two more hours on the language. After that come little odd jobs, a jog up and down the airstrip, maybe a walk with the kids, a bath, and then supper. After dark, I come and help get the kids to bed. By then it is 8:00 p.m. and sometimes I work more on the language, sometimes read, rarely type letters, or listen to a tape with Anita (we have an excellent series of messages given by Howard Ball at Campus Crusade Layman's conference).

Bible memory; Steve

David and Stevie play well together these days, perhaps it's because most of the Indians are away right now, so Stevie is the only playmate. They "read" books together, wrestle, and go for short walks. David is learning Bible verses from a blackboard in his room, and I'm getting him acquainted—very informally—with letters and sounds. I'm very thankful for the "Good Children" devotional books.

(I remember him standing in our living room quoting part of 2 Cor 5:8 (TLB): "We are not afraid . . . for then we will be at home with the Lord.")

David and Stephen Borgman

From Strength to Strength (1969 to 1973)

Personal letter from Barb, February 1971

Walks with David and Steve

For about a year we have wanted another couple to work at Auaris. Don needs another man around to handle some of the maintenance, work program and pay, and to do some of the visiting to outlying villages he can't fit in and do a thorough job on language work too. When we were in Boa Vista, we got to know one of our Brazilian missionaries better. He is Paulo Silas,[7] a personable young fellow about twenty-three years old, who has acted as an evangelist this past year in another area of the mission's work—semi-civilized Indian folk who speak Portuguese in the interior but not jungle areas. He's wanted to change over to Indian work in the jungle as soon as the other evangelist returned from furlough, and Paulo has requested to come to Auaris. There is still a lot to think through, but he will probably join us sometime this spring.

The single girl who is literacy coordinator for the field needs a place to hang her hat temporarily, so she will be with us from March through July, and this will give Julieta some companionship.

Getting back to the walk the boys took this morning, they were just as thrilled when they came back. They were gone for three hours. On the way back Stevie was so tired he kept falling, Don said, and David fell on purpose to show Stevie he was clumsy, too, so Stevie wouldn't feel bad! They got to a creek and stopped for a picnic lunch. They mixed water with milk powder and cocoa in a can and drank it with the plastic straws you sent, Dad. Then they took off their clothes and went swimming in the creek. They picked me some flowers and noticed all the things around—a tiny hummingbird the size of Andrea's toy bird and lots of things Stevie told me afterward. Are they exhausted! David is snoring like an old bear.

Tragedy

Personal letter from Don, July 1971

David's death

Across the clearing from our house lived Pedro, brother of Lourenzo. He had a teenage daughter whom we thought was a responsible girl, so when

---

7. This man married Iveli Alt, daughter of the pastor who married Don and Barb. The two would eventually work at Auaris.

she asked if David could go over to her house to play, we thought it would be safe for him to do so. Sadly this was not so, as the following account shows:

One morning on the jungle post an Indian girl gave David what she and everybody else thought was a harmless snake. By way of general precaution, we ordered the snake to be thrown away, but it was too late.

Evidently the snake was a coral. That afternoon David began complaining of a sore throat and later developed swelling around the eyes. During the night the respiratory tract was hit hard, and shortly after daybreak our boy was suddenly gone.

We were able to call for the MAF plane on the morning contact, and the burial took place in Boa Vista early the next morning. Through a ham radio operator we were able to talk with our parents in the States, and it was decided that we would go to the States to spend a couple of weeks with loved ones there.

Now we are back in South America planning to go back to our jungle post shortly. It is going to be hard, especially for Barbara, to face that environment with its vivid memories, and we really count on your prayers and God's special undertaking. "Here I raise mine Ebenezer; Hither by Thy help I'm come . . . "

God has been helping in these past months since our last letter. The war scare has abated with the Indians not fearing a mass attack with bows and arrows but rather a reprisal by magic performed by the enemy group.

The translation workshop meant a tremendous push forward, as we not only were able to translate and check out the first draft of Mark, but learned foundational principles which will mean a big difference in how we go about translating the rest of the New Testament.

The written Word without readers is useless, of course, and now we plan to launch a literacy program. This means making up primers and reading material and holding classes to teach the Sanumás to read.

We might add that the MAF pilot, Bill Born, did a wonderful job of coming around some clouds, bringing with him Kitty Pierce, in order that he might get David out to Boa Vista for burial.[8] This was June 11, 1971.[9]

---

8. For Bill Born's account of bringing the family out of Auaris, refer to Appendix F.

9. The family returned to the States for a brief time following David's death and then went back to take up their work once again. The editor once asked Don if, following this terrible loss, they had contemplated leaving the field. His reply was that that was never a consideration.

Aftermath

Ps 84 speaks of Israel's experience in the Valley of Baca. Don and Barb had truly walked through this valley. Yet, as Don would reflect in later years, God gave them spiritual comfort, even in the midst of ongoing sorrow. Springs of living water were there in that valley from which they would drink and continue on. These same springs would provide refreshment and strength in the years to come as they continued their journey toward Zion. Life would go on with the rest of their family. In addition, both Don and Barb remained committed to the work to bring others to those springs of living water in this sin-parched world.

7

Location Change, New Contacts, and First Fruit (1973 to 1978)

"I believe that I shall look upon the goodness of the
Lord in the land of the living!" (Ps 27:13)

Settling into their third term together on the field, Don and Barb made significant changes to their living situation. They would now reside in Boa Vista at the mission compound instead of at Auaris. The plan was for Don to make several trips a year out to the station to keep in contact with the Sanumás as well as to continue language study and translation work. Barb would take up new responsibilities for the mission headquarters in Boa Vista while beginning to focus on education for their children.[1] In addition to such things, Don would continue to find a way to make contact with a Sanumá subgroup known as the Sikoi, which was a desire that he had held for some time.[2]

---

1. For Barb's thoughts on educating their children, see Appendix G.

2. As referred to in the Introduction, some of the entries below are out of order chronologically in order to maintain continuity of a particular topic or subject. As noted in the "Format" section of the Introduction, some of the entries in this chapter do not doggedly follow a strict chronology, as will be noted. The purpose behind this was to provide continuity to certain topics.

Rebasing in Boa Vista and Trips Out to Auaris

Letter from Don to support partners, June 1973

Plans for next term

What do we plan to do this next term? (Departure date is July 11.) I plan to continue on in the translation of the New Testament into the Sanumá language. Also, a new role for me will be that of translation consultant, working with other translators and checking through books they have translated.

We will base in Boa Vista. About four times a year I plan to make visits of three to four weeks into the Sanumá tribe. Indian helpers will be coming out to Boa Vista to help in translation work.

Barbara will be in charge of the hospitality department at the mission base in Boa Vista. With our being in the city, Stevie and Andrea will be attending a Brazilian elementary school as well as receiving instruction in English from their mother at home in the afternoon.

Family photo, June 1973

Letters from Don to support partners, March to April 1974

Sikoi plans: Trips to Auaris

Wednesday, March 20

Flew over Sikoi settlements on the way to Auaris. For ten years I have wanted to visit this group, and now I am planning to finally make the trips overland in four or five days of travel from Auaris Station. Kalihoko said that Sikois would kill me, and when I laughed this off, he and Lourenzo reminded me of the time the Parahuris had almost killed me on the trip Steve A. and I made from Auaris to Surucucu. It must have been over a matter of not doling out all the trade goods they wanted. Kalepo, a Sanumá from the lower Auaris River, was the one who reported this. He went with us to Surucucu and claimed he was the one who talked the Parahuris out of the killing. However, I'm sure that neither Kalihoko nor anyone else thinks there is any danger in my going to the Sikois.

Sikoi plans canceled because of sickness

Wednesday. March 27

This was a very black Wednesday for me. Down with a bad cold, alone, one baby cremated, and the other buried on this day. And will it stop at this? Nothing so depressing as an epidemic that you are in the middle of, and you are the one responsible for treatment.

Worms

Monday, April 8

Went before breakfast to check up on Helena one more time. She's doing a lot better.

The single men were eating breakfast in the middle room and invited me to join. Started with beiju (cassava bread) and pepper sauce. Each course got better. Next came the roasted earthworms which were in their broth. Then I got a hunk of tapir. Finally, a couple of small gourds full of banana drink—hot. This was the best of all.

After radio contact, I watch some kids having the last course of their breakfast. They were out in the grass digging with one hand and holding their cassava bread or banana in the other. They were collecting huge fat "sauva" ants and eating them raw.

Getting back to worms but a different kind. I had given out roundworm medicine to all the kids ages one to six yesterday, and the results were unbelievable. You wouldn't think that so many and such big worms could fit in one small body.

One serious case I haven't mentioned was a Maiongong boy about one year old who was just about delirious when I got here this time. He stopped eating and would lie on the ground, not focusing eyes. A worm treatment slowly brought him out of it. The Maiongongs thought he was a goner.

Personal letter from Don, April 13, 1973

David, "saved others"

We never know what a day will bring forth. I was just starting to prepare lunch, feeling somewhat relieved that the flu epidemic had passed, and things were pretty much under control health wise. At this moment Pedro, Ilo's father-in-law, came and said his "child" had been bitten by a poisonous snake. One of my first thoughts was "at least it wasn't of Ilo's family. This would have been a blow after all he's been through these days and after he had prayed especially for protection the night before." As I talked more with Pedro, I learned it was his oldest daughter— Ilo's wife.

Iwoto (or Kasusoma = capibara), Ilo's wife was sitting down leaning against her mother, weak and in pain, in the middle of the field where they had been weeding. The snake was poisonous (Jararaca) but a small one. Gave three vials of serum by injection. Once again, I relived the day David was bitten by the coral. The Lord knows how many patients we have treated so as to save their lives. And yet our own son died. I have thought so often of the verse, "He saved others. Himself he cannot save." We did not treat David properly . . . our eyes were blind or blinded. But we lift up our tear-soaked faces to God, our God of mercy and all comfort, and believe—believe that in spite of our mistakes and failures, He is right there. And that David's death is working for our good, his good, and God's glory.

Personal letter from Don, May 5, 1974

David, sensitive

In mentioning Stevie and his adjusting, I meant to put in just this word, that he is so much different than David was in this respect. David probably couldn't have taken the harassment and the fact of being different. We have thought that he is being spared a rough life and that possibly this is some part of God taking him when He did. The Poulsons, who lost their eleven-year-old boy lately, wrote to this same effect regarding their son who was having a tremendously tough time in school and with other kids. More next week.

Personal letter from Don, June 1974

Doctor team

Yesterday we spent time with the young people of the church at a picnic and beach party where I brought a word during the devotional time. Anita and I have been asked to serve with some other couples as "friends" of the young people and to help out from time to time and be open for any counsel, etc. that the young people might want. We went yesterday as a family, and it was good for us to get out of the rut. Anita mentioned this especially. (I haven't had too much time to get into a rut with all the trips up to Auaris.)

A team of doctors has been here studying a type of filaria disease, and so I went with them to the Sanumás this past week, spending four days as their interpreter and helping out in general. You can't believe the disorganization of the team. They got to the hangar with tons more stuff than would fit in the plane, so they had to leave back food and hammocks, which meant that they ate off the Auaris station supplies and slept on the mattresses that I had to dig out of the barrels.

This government team has been a burden and has been anything but understanding wherever they have gone among the missionaries—even complaining about non-cooperation, etc. Well, I have thought again on Matt 5:38 and following verses, of walking the second mile, giving cheerfully without thought of getting back, etc.

BIRTH OF DARLENE

Personal letter from Don, June 26, 1974

Darlene born

Baby girl born last night at 6:30 p.m., seven pounds, eleven ounces, and doing fine. So is Anita, although labor was hard on her. We've named our daughter Darlene.

Personal letter from Barb, June 27, 1974

Darlene born

Everything (except labor without anesthesia, which I detest—I am not a romantic who *adores* natural childbirth. That's good enough for the Sanumá ladies. Is agony for me!) was wonderful, and I thought the verses in Ps 42:8

expressed the feeling of my spirit during the birth of our second little girl. "By day the Lord will confirm his loving kindness and in the night his song shall be with me." Though I cried to him in the labor, I felt full of praise for little but dear things:

- An air-conditioned room. I've been so hot during this pregnancy. The day before Darlene's birth, the rainy season had come with some cool days, but it was terribly humid and hot. Only two rooms at the hospital here have air conditioning, and even that is recent. Am so thankful it was unoccupied (this room)—affords coolness and privacy.
- At the time baby was due, according to our calculations, both doctors (mine and a substitute) were out of town. By this past Saturday a third was gone too. So, God had the baby wait, and my doctor was back in town "on time."
- The head nurse on duty, as I went into induced labor, was as sweet as can be—spent as much time with me (as I moaned and carried on) as if she'd been my relative.
- A friend from our church, who works in one of the offices here, came in frequently to see me, and we talked a lot as sisters in Christ, and again, it was like having a member of the family here.
- I am having an excellent recuperation; I feel wonderful! You know how hard it is for me to be still if I'm at home (though I've had a wonderful peaceful time here at the maternity ward). Also, after Andrea's birth, I was exhausted and terribly on edge (for another of God's purposes that time). I expect to be going home today.
- I did have a dear gal from our mission come with me for a while the first night. She's new, only been here two weeks, has a five-year-old, and one and a half-year-old and a four-week-old, but here she popped in at 3:00 a.m. after nursing the baby! She is Dianne Butler, and she and Joe will be taking over hospitality and purchasing, and I'll be giving her help whenever she needs it. She is the kind of person I've missed having to share with. We are all delighted with their arrival.

Personal letter from Don, June 30, 1974

Darlene born, kitchen repair

Anita came home from the hospital Thursday evening and felt so good that she went right to work on Friday. Then yesterday and today her stitches have been hurting her quite a bit, and she has not been able to sit down. I fixed her up with a hammock in the living room as some girls from her Sunday School class plan to make a "surprise" visit this afternoon.

I wrote you a short note Wednesday announcing the birth of Darlene. Just in case you didn't receive it, here are the details, the ones I gave in the note. A baby girl, Darlene, born 6:30 p.m. Tuesday evening, June 25th.

It was about 6 p.m. on Monday when the sac evidently broke. Even though there were nothing like labor pains, the doctor advised her to go the hospital and have an exam. He examined her about 11:00 p.m. and advised that she stay interned.

This hospital is really called a Maternity Hospital and is the same one where Stevie and Andrea were born (same room in fact). Things are somewhat different there now. The Catholic nuns are no longer in charge. Also, Dr. Patton of MAF wasn't on hand, so that Anita had been consulting with another man here in town and a competent gynecologist. Another added feature was that in the hospital they had two air-conditioned apartments, and knowing how Anita feels the heat, I put her in one of those. She had a good night's sleep.

Labor pains must have started about 2:00 p.m. on Tuesday. I dropped in about 5:00 p.m., and she was having hard pains then. It was a very difficult time for her from then on. They don't give the anesthesia here that they do in the States or elsewhere in Brazil possibly. Even Dr. Patton had nothing more effective for her. I went back at 7:00 p.m. and was surprised to see her tummy deflated, and it was all over. She felt great. I stayed only for a couple of minutes and came back at 10:00 p.m., and then we asked for the baby to be brought in, so we got the first look at her. To us she is darling, though she's a typical newborn.

I worked like crazy while Anita was away. She had been asking that I put a ceiling in the kitchen for many months. So Lourenzo and I worked hard and got it all finished before she came home. And then there was "cooking" for the kids—it was a time of simple meals. At noon I got some food from a restaurant to take out, and the Lewises had us for one meal. The Butlers took the kids for supper the night Darlene was born.

Personal letter from Don, July 1974

Andrea's itch

I spoke in church this morning. It was kind of hard because Anita had to be at the hospital for a change of dressing, so I was alone with Andrea and

Stevie. All went well until the end of the message when Andrea walked up to me and said she had an itch "on the bottom of her foot."

Stirrings of Faith among the Sanumás

Personal Letter from Don, April 14, 1974

Abel's dream[3]

Ilo said he was too tired to attend the get-together tonight. Abel, who attended for first time last night came alone, and we had a good talk together. He told me that he had dreamed that there were two paths. On one path, the people were happy. On the other, they were suffering, without food, burned up, and wandering around lost. I wondered how much of this was conditioned and precipitated by what he had heard from us. I asked him when it was that he had this dream and where he was at the time. His answer, "It was before you came, the first time I was living over the boundary in Venezuela, at the time, when I woke from this dream, I wondered to myself. 'Is this the way it really is maybe?' Then I came over to the Brazil side and heard your teaching. I knew then that my dream was true. And what you were teaching was true."

This was more than ten years ago. Abel had never mentioned anything like this before, nor expressed verbally an interest in our message. But as I look back, I realize that he always came to our meetings, and it was he, along with Saula, who helped me translate the book of Mark—my first effort.

Saula

3. Abel was the young man, mentioned earlier, who had made the deal with Don to trade tape recordings of Sanumá ways in exchange for red cloth.

Abel is one of the two most gifted shamans in our area. Many a night we have heard his booming bass voice chanting on into the wee hours of the morning. I am sure he is undergoing an intense inner struggle.

Personal letter from Don, June 26, 1974

Darlene, birth pangs

The headline from the Borgman family is that we have another girl, Darlene, born last night here in Boa Vista. All of us are excited and thankful for this seven-pound, eleven-ounce addition.

Homilies on the awesomeness of childbirth and newborn babies usually appear only in circular letters announcing the firstborn. I won't break with this tradition, but I do want to relate a fact of physical childbirth to reproducing in a spiritual sense. The apostle Paul wrote to young, vacillating Christians at Galatia, "O my dear children, I am suffering a mother's birth pangs for you again, until Christ is formed in you." (Gal 4:19 Wms)

Have you ever experienced birth pangs with no anesthesia to diminish the pain? I haven't either, but I have held Barbara as she went through that excruciating experience. This is the kind of pain the apostle refers to in illustrating what he went through as he was involved first in the spiritual rebirth of the Galatians and then again in crucial steps in their spiritual development.

My last visit to the Sanumás taught me more of this principle of travail before triumph, frustration before fruit-bearing. The purpose of the trip was to contact a Sanumá group that never before had been contacted by anyone from the outside world. For ten years I have wanted to meet this group called the Sikois, but each time plans were frustrated. This time an influenza epidemic hit Auaris just about the same time I arrived. For two weeks I did nothing but treat the sick. Never in my life had I felt so beaten down, homesick, wanting to be anywhere but in the middle of these who were near death. But God meant it for good at least in two lives, Ilo's and mine.

No sooner had I gotten off the plane than Ilo sat me down and proceeded to rant and rave, "Being a Christian just doesn't work. Everybody's against me. Nobody listens to me. And even you think I'm bad. I'm moving to Venezuela, and I'll get another wife over there."

I had heard that Ilo had initiated all night "sing-ins" which included a civilized-style dancing with mixed couples. (This was their worship service.) My response was that this was not conducive to worshiping God . . . and everyone, including Ilo, knew this was true. After this initial explosion Ilo quickly calmed down and invited me to hang my hammock in his house, and that's where I stayed for the next twenty-eight nights. It was a great experience of being close to this Sanumá, praying with him, instructing him, encouraging him, and yet bringing out his (and my) faults.

Paulo Ilo

He certainly needed all of this. Two days later his father-in-law and others arrived from a ten-month stay from out near Boa Vista. It took them fifty hard days by canoe to get from Boa Vista to Auaris. Three of them greeted Ilo by swatting him on the back with the flat end of their cutlasses. The father-in-law drew blood because Ilo had told the tribe that he had another wife (this was a lie). Another lashed out with his cutlass on behalf of his sister with whom Ilo had reportedly had an affair. The third had heard that Ilo was being too friendly with his wife during the "sing-ins."

Two more days passed before the next traumatic experience for Ilo. His wife gave birth to a rather ugly, somewhat deformed baby girl. Everyone agreed that the cause was Ilo, who had broken a taboo by eating fish while his wife was pregnant. As the newborn infant lay on the ground, the tearful mother-in-law picked up a huge hunk of firewood and only some fast talking and pleading saved Ilo's head from some mean gashes. (Two days later the baby died suddenly, probably from pneumonia.)

Ilo hit a low point somewhere during this time, but the Lord somehow picked him up and gave him a new level of comprehension and spiritual growth. Just before I left, he did something unheard of for a Sanumá. He openly confessed his past sins before a group of fellows and prayed God's forgiveness and then was bold enough to rebuke another buddy of his who was secretly going off with a young girl who was not his wife. There still will be many falls and failings, but I believe that as we labor in prayer, God will work so that Christ will be formed in the life of this and other young, struggling Sanumá Christians.

Personal letter from Don, October 10, 1974

In Paulo Ilo's house

I had another very good visit to Auaris. This time there was good dry weather and no colds or sickness among the Indians. There are always the minor things to treat like sore eyes, cuts, and diarrhea, but there was nothing serious or of epidemic proportions.

Paulo Ilo was his own up-and-down self. I had appointed him to watch the houses against termites and robbery and promised to pay him for this. He himself dug a hole in one of the walls and took out all the cans of meat and some other things. He is a very good talker and can talk his way out of things well—something that the Lord (and we) are going to have to keep dealing with. I talked sternly but quietly with him alone and he seemed to be repentant. But even so, I can never really trust him completely again, at least for a long time. (He always has been this way.) It all showed me that we must reach out and move out to seek more disciples.

It was very encouraging to see other young men very interested in receiving Christ this time. There were about four of them, one from another village. They seemed very sincere and there was no pressure on my part. With all Ilo's faults, he still gets excited about getting together and praying and helping others to come to Christ. He was more a positive factor than a negative one as far as the other young men were concerned by encouraging them to become Christians.

Much of my time was spent in fixing up the place—cutting the grass (the Indians do this with cutlasses), mending a fence, building a new outhouse, etc. Again I slept in Ilo's house, really the house of his in-laws, and endured the smoke and enjoyed the stay very much. I had counted on those dozen cans of meat so existed on soups much of the time. Also some of the Indians from another village brought in meat a couple of times, so that I didn't suffer at all. I even got to taste some flying ants, caterpillars, and earthworms, all of which tasted good.

Personal letter from Don, December 8, 1974

Pleasantness

I'm sure you understand that I don't mean to say that this place is only for God's special people or anything like that. Just that we better be sure He wants us here before we embark.

It has not been all unpleasantness. There are many occasions that could be called a picnic. We have enjoyed God's creation, times of real peace and quietness as to outward circumstances, good times together as family and workers, etc. Often, as I have glided down a little jungle river in a dugout, with the soft noise of the river and an occasional call of a parrot, I have thought of how many businessmen would give their right arm to be in my position. But these have been some enjoyable byproducts of following God into what is, by and large, a terrific battle.

Personal letter from Don, December 13, 1974

Demon possession

The man who went crazy up at Auaris never did show up at the post again. The Maiongongs said they were going to try to get him back to where he lives in Venezuela. We as missionaries have a lot to learn about confronting cases like this and believingly praying that God would rebuke Satan. With all our Bible school training, etc., I find myself still not confident in the realm of prayer and/or medicine. Is there such a thing as mental illness which is not a work of spirits? If so, how do we discern? And even if it isn't a direct work of demon activity, do we not have the prerogative to pray for healing? In any event, I believe that having the man go back to Venezuela was the best solution as Paulo was bringing in Iveli for her first experience of jungle living.

Letter from Don to support partners, July 24, 1976

Our basing in Boa Vista and making extended trips to the Sanumás has been working out well. Our whole family was able to spend two months in the tribe during the school vacation period. (Stevie and Andrea go to Brazilian schools here, and they have their summer vacation in January and February.) The rest of the year I leave the family to make three-week trips to the Sanumás. My time in Boa Vista is taken up with language analysis and

Bible translation for the Sanumás and also with checking translations of other dialects in this area. Next week, for example, Bob Hawkins and a Wai Wai Indian will come to Boa Vista, and together we will check through their translation of Philippians.

During the time in the tribe, I try to immerse myself in the language, spending as much time as possible with the Indians. Being alone, I can sleep right in the communal house and feel free to travel with them for visits to other villages or for food gathering in the forest. The most memorable of these occasions recently was a caterpillar-gathering party in the pouring rain. (You who have sunk your teeth into a roasted caterpillar know that it was worth it all.) During my last visit, we met early each morning with a few of the fellows for teaching and prayer. Ilo's brother, "Big Bird," made a commitment to Christ, and it was encouraging to hear him pray something I'd never heard from another Sanumá, "Father, the spirits didn't make us; You did. And now I am calling only on You." Pray that Ilo (also called Paulo), Luis, Big Bird, and Saula will continue to grow in love to God and to one another.

FAMILY LIFE AND RESPONSIBILITIES IN BOA VISTA

Personal letter from Don, March 1, 1975

Kids play in B.V.

Stevie and Andrea liked Auaris but were glad to get back to their bicycles and friends in Boa Vista. But it was definitely a plus or positive experience for them in Auaris. They got along well with the few Indian children who were around there, and also did play together well at times, or for short periods (Andrea and Stevie), outside. Stevie commented on how "smart" the Sanumás are in doing things, and this is a good attitude that I've tried to instill in the kids—appreciating the way the Indians can survive on the little they have in the way of technology and toys. Instead of spending fortunes on plastic junk in the way of toys, the following are some of the things I think of that the kids make:

- A little raft made out of the pithy heart of a palm tree.
- Toy guns that really pop, made out of a stalk that can be hollowed out. They have another pithy stalk that they bite off into little plugs that act as the bullets. With a twig used as a ramrod they poke one plug down to the end of the gun, then poke another plug through. The

air pressure builds up and the first plug goes popping out—enough to scare dogs and delight children.
- Little bows and arrows, of course. They shot a rat out on the branches of a tree by the swimming hole where we were one day.
- No junky bubble blowing sets. They can blow bubbles just by getting the right kind of bath soap lather in their hands, cupping their hands in the right way and blowing.
- "Army" helmets made from the cardboard-like wasps' nests (without the wasps).
- Substitute for gas model planes. They catch bees down by the beach, take out the stingers, tie thread around the body of the bee and set it loose, holding on to the thread.

Then we had some good science lessons out in the open. How many kids in the States see an animal cut up? The one our kids saw was pregnant, and besides identifying the liver, heart, kidneys, lungs, and intestines, they saw the womb cut open and a little fetus pop out.

March 30, 1975, Andrea, dogs

Today's chuckle from Andrea—I took her out in the van with me to get bread, and just as we were starting from our driveway a couple of cute small dogs crossed in front of us. Andrea said, "Don't kill the doggies. I hate the smell of dead dogs."

Borgman family, circa 1975

Personal letter from Don, April 1975

FUNAI meeting in Manaus

Back home after a full week of meetings in Manaus. They were well planned, and for the most part there was lively discussion. One afternoon was especially lively as we discussed whether or not missions could continue with freedom to preach the gospel. The atheistic anthropologists declared their desire to suppress any "interference" in the religious life of the Indian. Catholics and Protestants were united in their insistence that the Indian has the right to choose his religion and the right of the missionary to propagate. The intellectual strain within the FUNAI wants to limit severely religious activity of the missionary, but I believe that the president is fairly neutral on this point and that we can continue on with liberty as long as the present general is in the presidency of the FUNAI. (FUNAI stands for Fundação Nacional do Indio, or National Indian Foundation.)

Personal letter from Don, May 20, 1975

Field leadership

I keep busy with odds and ends these days. The field leader's position is no picnic. It's a combination of a lot of "Mickey Mouse" jobs combined with the bigger and knottier personnel or personality problems.

Personal letter from Don, July 1975

Reading Stories

We've been reading *Great Stories for Boys and Girls*, or some such title, composed of four stories, among them: "Treasures of the Snow," "Happy Acres," and I'm reading them "Lost on the Trail" now by Ken Taylor. It might be a little corny for adults, but I still enjoy reading the story, and the kids are thrilled with it. They loved the other stories, too. Remember you trying to get me to read the classics? If I had had something like this book, I know I would have gone more for reading. My whole literary experience was negative as I grew up. Imagine, they threw *Ivanhoe* at us in 9th grade, to say nothing of trying to read Cicero and the like in Latin. Come to think of it, my college lit course was no better—terrible, in fact. Or maybe it was that I just wasn't cut out to enjoy the classics. Anyway, changing the subject a bit, Stevie loves to read and is about two grades ahead of his age group in this area.

Personal letter from Don, August 20, 1975

Devotional guide

For some time I had felt that Anita and I needed some simple devotional plan or guide, and I thought of Scripture Union. I wondered how to get in touch with them. (While still in college, I had a little talk with Alan Redpath, and he mentioned he used these Scripture Union notes on the Bible readings.) Well, in the mail just recently came a free copy of their reading schedule and a booklet of notes called "Encounter with God." Each day there is a Bible reading of about twelve verses. Then good comments in the notes. Anita and I have tried all times to get together. At night we're tired, and I fall asleep. Early in the morning it takes us a while to get going. Our prime time and the time that has worked out best is right after breakfast when the two kids go to school.

Personal letter from Don, September 1975

Steve's profession

Stevie has a battle with temper and teasing but realizes it and works somewhat on these traits. He loves reading and is enjoying reading the *Children's Living Bible*. Only a word here and there that he has trouble with. In the front of the Bible there is a blank page entitled, "My Important Events." He asked about this, and Anita told him that becoming a Christian was the most important event in one's life. So on his own he wrote out the following, "I became a Christian when I was six years old in 1975. Ever since then I have been very happy because I have received him as my Savior. Now I am eight and the Lord's son." He says that he remembers my kneeling with him by the bunkbed up at Auaris and that he had prayed "various times," but this was when he made it certain.

Personal letter from Barb, December 1, 1975

Base duties

It was a wearying and frustrating day for Don. He is the only man on the base; consequently he is a jack-of-all trades, with field leader duties thrown in. He changes flats, directs maintenance, takes workers home (some live way out in the boonies), and is doing the buying for flights this month, which includes meeting all flights, bringing people into town, etc. He even had to stop and help a Macushi Indian with some of the painting on the guesthouse, after giving him quite a bit of instruction, because so much paint was being used. The electric company was cutting off our lights with no warning, so he had to race out to the company to show our receipt to prove we'd paid. Things like this pop up all the time, and he will be glad when the year of being field leader is over.

Personal letter from Don, May 3, 1976

Andrea's profession

Last night I stayed home with the girls while Anita went to church with Stevie. I had a good talk with Andrea. Earlier in the day Anita had been talking with Stevie about communism, the situation in Guyana, etc. Andrea is at the age of questions of all kinds. Some are senseless, but others are well thought out. She asked all sorts of questions about war, communist takeovers, would we stop worshiping God if they told us to, what would be the consequences of not obeying if they forbid us from practicing religion, etc. I could have brushed it off but feel that American kids are overprotected from world reality, and I told her some of the consequences some families have had to face in holding to their faith. She had big tears dropping down on her legs as she thought that this could happen to her someday, like going to prison or being separated from family. I told her of the Christian's comfort and asked if she were a Christian. She said no, that she didn't know if she knew enough, so I explained how to become a Christian, and she prayed with me for Jesus to forgive her sins and come into her heart. Before she dropped off to sleep, I asked her if she was glad she was a Christian now, and she said, "Yes, but I'm a weak one." I think we had prayed for some weak Indian Christians. Granted she was shook up, but I felt it was the time to ask her if she didn't want to become a Christian—probably past time. We underrate the intelligence and spiritual capacity of kids. As a family we meet in the mornings to memorize verses and learn some hymns. I thought last night of the importance of preparing them for any of the tragedies of war, separation, and Satan's attacks in general.

Back to Andrea. The other night she prayed for the Browns back there in Connecticut, that they would be happy in their cuddly little house, and that they would remember Eccl 3:11! I was a little curious about this and asked her what she meant. She commented that if they realized that God made everything beautiful that they would find it easier to be happy and added that it was talking more about our hearts being beautiful than trees and things like that.

Personal letter from Don, May 23, 1976

Driving in Boa Vista

It is now Wednesday, May 26. Monday, I went to a place called Maracanã and had a good day. Yesterday a lot of running around on various matters. Stevie started his new school yesterday, and he loves it. He told me, "I have an easy time making friends." This is true and a gift from the Lord. The discipline is good at that school. He'll be taking his bike as it is kind of far to walk. I believe he's old enough for this, but we continually pray for his safety as he crosses these streets. There's not much traffic in B.V., but what there is crazy. People don't even slow down for stop signs. No exaggeration. I had one guy in back of me get mad because I slowed down and put my car in second.

Personal letter from Don, June 14, 1976

Boa Vista—"The Battle Is Not Done"

How can the sun shine so brightly when the darkness of death encloses us? The night is past . . . a loved one lies silent and stiff. More fitting a storm than the sun right now.

Among the Sanumás, how often I have felt the incongruity of man's suffering, pain, and death mingled simultaneously with nature's excitement, pleasure, and life? While our hearts are breaking, the birds continue to sing, the stream keeps on running and tumbling, and billowy white clouds slowly do their kaleidoscoping against a clear blue backdrop.

This stark contrast between nature's calm and man's calamity stung me again this morning as I drove into town from the pilot's house. Flo had just called in reporting that lives were in danger because of presence of the fearless, demanding Atroais. With this dark picture in my mind, my eyes were looking at the sun forcing its way through the clouds to reflect in the serene little lake by the side of the road.

Then like lightning, the word "battle" flashed into my mind. This world is a battleground. Diabolical forces against the Heavenly hosts. The turbulent against the peaceful, the deceitful against the sincere, the destructive against the enriching—Satan against God.

Then again, there welled up in me the song we had sung in Friday night's prayer meeting:

> This is my Father's world,
> Oh! Let me ne'er forget,
> That though the wrong seems oft so strong,
> God is the Ruler yet.
> This is my Father's world,
> The battle is not done,
> Jesus who died shall be satisfied,
> And earth and Heaven be one.

We sometimes ask with Habakkuk, "How long? Why?" And God's answer to us is the same! "The just shall live by faith . . . For the earth shall be filled with the knowledge of the glory of the Lord, as the waters cover the sea." The battle is not done!

Newsletter from Don and Barb to supporters, July 1976

"For it is from the Head that the whole body as a harmonious structure knit together by the joints with which it is provided, grows by the proper functioning of individual parts to its full maturity in love." (Eph 4:16)

It takes a tremendous team effort to reach even one little Indian group with the gospel. You, with your prayers, encouragement, and gifts, are part of the team. Then there are those in the home office, those working on the base in Boa Vista, the MAF pilots and all who support them, those of the Wycliffe Bible Translators who have given days and weeks of linguistic and translation help to us, and many others, like the faithful woman who sends out these letters.

This year the Head has seen fit to change my function from translation to that of taking over the responsibilities of our field leader who is on furlough. Probably most in this position, including me, have rebelled inwardly as they wade into a myriad of activities, including field correspondence, public relations, and personnel problems. But, when seen in the light of "the proper functioning of individual parts," rebellion is replaced with rejoicing.

It has been a joyous experience getting to know and feel what is going on in other tribes beside the Sanumá. The medical-evangelistic team invited me to speak for the dedication of clinics in four different Macushi Indian villages. Macushi fellows have been trained by the nurse to administer medicine and shots, and it is they who are responsible for the clinic in between the monthly visits from the team. It was a joy, too, seeing the local churches which are under native leadership.

Recently I was called upon to go into the Wai Wai village because of trouble with the visiting Atroai Indians, who are noted killers. On June 6, eleven Atroai men entered the Wai Wai village and for three days demanded not only trade goods, but also Wai Wai women to take back with them. Finally, they left, but instead of heading home, they secretly camped out in the forest near the village.

One night the Wai Wai's heard the "killer call" as Atroais encircled the village. But something scared them off. Fearing an attack, the Wai Wais asked Flo Riedle, the only missionary living with them, to call for the plane so that she could be evacuated. Also, they wanted counsel and possibly some kind of outside help in this harrowing situation. I flew in with the pilots and, together with Flo, we talked with the Wai Wais about the best course of action. Then, in spite of a very muddy airstrip, we took off for Boa Vista and had Flo with us.

Since then the Atroais have left for home, and the Wai Wais have calmed down. But they expect the Atroais back in August or September when the rains subside. Pray that God will give clear direction to the Wai Wais concerning their role in reaching the Atroais. They're pretty discouraged right now and about to give up the project.

Even out here in Boa Vista, I have small contact with the Sanumás through letters. Paulo Silas carries on literacy classes, and writing letters is a stimulus to the handful of students. It takes some deciphering to read the letters of these beginners, but it is well worth the effort. Yesterday, I received a letter from a boy who says he wants to receive Christ into his life. (The content of most letters are requests for me to send in items like puppies, cats, or fruit from our backyard.)

For this year of filling in as field leader, pray that I will "function properly" so that the body of Christ will grow to maturity in love. Barbara needs daily grace and patience as she deals with two noisy, teasing kids (Stevie and Andrea) on vacation from their Brazilian schools, and one two-year-old (Darlene) who also has been blessed with a powerful set of lungs. For about half of the day, Barbara teaches the two older ones in English. We both count on your prayers.

Personal letter from Don, January 3, 1976

Back to Uraricoera

Another more real cause for unsettledness is what happened at Surucucu with the Indians going into the houses and demanding ammunition. Bob has sent the guns and ammunition out to Boa Vista along with trade goods. They have made a big decision to move their base of operations back over to the Uraricoera River among the Parimitheli Indians (which was sort of an outstation) and make Surucucu the outstation now. For the past few years there has not been good contact with the Indians at Surucucu, and the work of teaching has been paralyzed. Pray for the missionaries in this move, as in many ways it is a sad time and frustrating.

PROGRESS AND HELP WITH THE SANUMÁ LANGUAGE

Personal letter from Don, December 23, 1974

Eunice (Burgess),[4] prayer

Anita mentioned this morning that she appreciated Eunice more than anyone else who has been in our house. She, Eunice, has been through some real spiritual battles in the past and came to a point of desperation when the Spirit really worked in her life. She is quiet, understanding, filled always with praise, and one who really believes God. Praying is not perfunctory with her. At one point when we hit a hard problem, she suggested taking a day off for prayer, which we both did separately and with outstanding results. We finished up the work Saturday noon.

Pedagogical Grammar

At this point I am champing at the bit, wanting to take the skeleton of the grammar we worked on and round it out into a written paper, but this might have to wait for a while. I was mentioning to Anita this morning how great

---

4. Eunice Burgess was a linguist consultant with SIL who came to Boa Vista in October of the year to work with Don in regard to ongoing language study, particularly as he worked on a pedagogical grammar.

it is to have a job which I am excited about. The big project I see as most important now is putting all this into pedagogical grammar, which is quite different from a descriptive grammar. The pedagogical grammar is to get the student not to understand the grammar but to speak the language, and so it consists of interestingly laid out and varied drills, conversations, etc. I plan to work on this during the two months we're up at Auaris. I'm thinking of the need to get Paulo's wife, Iveli, into something of this nature. Then there will be Kitty and, we trust, a nurse before too long.

Personal letter from Don, August 10, 1975

Sanumá grammar

This next week I plan to finish a rough draft of another big section of Sanumá grammar (really rough—untyped) which will describe the very complicated and extensive verb phrase. Then I want to get into some translation of Sanumá again before going back and doing a write-up on the nouns and sentences. I'm happy in translation work. A relatively small segment of the Earth's population, but from time to time I reflect on the many opportunities English speakers have. In front of me on the shelf I have fifteen different English translations and another volume which has excerpts from twenty-six translations! And I'm pressing on to give the Sanumás one.

Personal letter from Don, November 9, 1975

Orthography workshop

Our schedule has been especially full these days. We've just finished up an orthography workshop with a consultant from SIL heading it up with a Brazilian linguist present from Rio and also a representative from their education department down in Brasília. Also present were two New Tribers and the Seelys from Venezuela. The purpose of the workshop was to agree on the symbols we're going to use for all the Yanomami languages: Ninam or Shirishana dialect at Mucajaí; Yanomam (Waica) at Surucucu; and Sanumá (Auaris). The Yanomam also includes the New Tribes station and also a Catholic mission station. The priest there was also present at the workshop.

Personal letter from Don, November 11, 1975

Pedagogical grammar

Did I tell you I'm making up a new language course for new missionaries learning Sanumá? It is going along well, and both Kitty and Iveli appreciate this and have started to dig in. There are two improvements over the old system we had of going through a lot of (seven hundred sixty) slips with just drill. I've set this course up on the basis of short dialogues and useful expressions for everyday conversation. Also, I've set the thing up with units: one unit a week with a test at the end (oral, with another member of the station who is more proficient in the language) and with twenty-four units in all (six months). This gives the student something to aim at.

Personal letter from Don, July 1977

Seelys, Venezuela

Got a good letter from Merrill Seely[5] in Venezuela. They pray for us often and we appreciate them a lot. We keep in touch quite often. He says there is a group of Sanumás there, about one hundred of them, meeting for worship and prayer four times a week. A Venezuelan missionary is there among them. I have been sending my grammar material and translations, too, over there and they have been able to use it, so I'm glad for this.

---

5. Merrill Seely was a missionary from a different mission society working with the Sanumá in Venezuela.

Reaching the Sikoi[6]

The pastor of Don's church, Rev. Stanley Allaby, had written Don about the possibility of his son, Norman, visiting Don and the Sanumás work.

Personal letter from Barb, March 1977

Sikoi Trip

One other word, Norman and his friend Tom Sorkness arrived early today in Manaus. Their flight was slated for April 8, and I hope they'll be able to make it to Auaris. When Don gets back from Manaus, he still has to do food buying and get together blankets, hammocks, and hammock nets for the boys. It is a bit of a rushed time for Don to drop responsibilities here and go to the jungle, and I pray that the time spent here will be genuinely profitable for Norman. Would also like you to pray concerning their health, as malaria is rampant, and it is a cerebral type, very serious. They'll be taking preventative medicine, but this is no guarantee.

Letter from Don to support partners, May 1977

God really answered prayer in a wonderful way during our trip. I guess I've never made a trip in which in the natural world I was so apprehensive, mainly regarding the malaria, both for us and for our guides. But I felt definitely that God was leading in this direction and thus could trust him day by day to carry us through. And He did much more abundantly than I would have thought.

I had about decided not to go in the direction of the Sikois, but Lourenzo was genuinely keyed up to go. I asked him several times whether he was strong enough, and he said yes. He himself had been wanting to go see and talk to the Sikois about some matters. I think a few days earlier and he wouldn't have been strong enough. And any later the rains would have hit us hard.

The weather was unbelievable. It rained hard the two days before we left on the trip. But not once did we get wet on the trail. A couple of times it

---

6. In April of 1977, the editor along with Norman Allaby, mentioned in the text, were able to join Don in a successful expedition to finally reach the Sikoi. Lourenzo and his son Komak (Alberto) guided us along the way. For the editor's record of the expedition, in part, see Appendix H.

rained during the night. We did get wet in the canoe from the Maiongong house to Auaris during the last twenty minutes of the trip.

The whole last day we came upriver by motorboat, and the gas ran out just as we were pulling into the Maiongong port. There another Indian took us in his boat (or motor) up to the station.

Either the terrain was a lot more rugged, or twenty years make a difference. I remember the days back in jungle training when Claude Leavitt would start us going at daybreak, and we'd go till 4:00 p.m. and then have to help with house building. And with packs on our backs. We carried packs for two days on this trip, but not full days really, and we moved fairly slowly. Lourenzo and I both decided that it was imperative to pick up carriers at the last village before heading out into the wilds. The carriers were out on a hunt but did come in the next day after being called by their father. Even going without packs was hard because of the steep hills. But God gave us sufficient strength for each day. And we watched while the Indians built our shelter each night.

We learned that the Sikoi village men, women, and children, were not at home, but were moving slowly toward us. Good thing, or we wouldn't have gotten to see them, Time and energy were running short. We had a good rest for two days at a beautiful little river while we waited for the Sikois. This after over two real hard days of trekking. Contact was good with the Sikois.

Good talks with Lourenzo along the way. Finally back at Auaris, we had a time of prayer together and he received Christ as his own Savior. The high point of the trip.

**On the trail to the Sikois, with Lourenzo and Komak (Alberto)
(Photo by Thomas J. Sorkness)**

Rebasing at Auaris (Short Term)

Late in 1977, Don and Barb, along with Darlene, relocated to Auaris for a period of time. The older children remained behind to return to school at Puraquequara[7] along the Amazon. In addition, a nurse by the name of Lois Cunningham would now reside at Auaris. She would play a prominent role in ministering to the physical/medical needs of the Sanumás and the Maiongongs.

Personal letter from Don, September 1977

Family and Lois at Auaris

It has been hard on Darlene, having her siblings going away, and then coming up here. She adapts well and would do a lot better if we let her run wild with the Indian kids with whom she gets along fine and loves to play. But we keep a close watch on her as we must, and this is hard on her and on us. But she is doing well. Just now I had to get up to light the pressure lamp. It's kind of dark in here, but the Indians are still wanting to look on, so I'll continue and try to finish up.

Paulo has the house fixed up nicely here. He's tremendous at improvising. He'd have made a good inventor. He's put in an inside flush toilet. Eight drums outside catch the rain so we haven't run out of water yet. We have a stove run by bottled gas (but we've been using a little pressure kerosene burner because we're low on gas.) There's a telephone between our house and Lois'. There's a pail on a pulley for a shower, and Darlene has just burned her hand by putting her hand in the way as Barb was pouring in boiling hot water.

The time thus far in Auaris (a month and a half now) has been most valuable, and we have seen the Lord answer prayer in many aspects of our lives and work here. Adjustment was surprisingly easy for Barb and me. It was hardest the first few days for Darlene, but now she is enjoying each day. She is content to stay in the house with Barb for long periods of time and plays well with the little kids who are around the house, usually in the afternoon. I take her down to the tiny beach across from us once a day just before dinner. I've rearranged my schedule to get in a run on the airstrip and bath in the river. Late in the afternoon the river's too cold.

---

7. Puraquequara was/is a school for missionary children. It was/is located along the Amazon River to the east of Manaus. All three of Don and Barb's children would attend there in the following years and it would also play prominently in Don and Barb's lives as well.

Barb and Lois each have literacy classes from about 4:00 to 5:00. I have the more advanced students. (I have no patience for beginners. It takes maybe a week to teach "a, i, o." Then another two for "ka, ki, ko." And by that time they get "a, i, o" wrong.) There are about five who can read about anything and who are eager to get a copy of the Old Testament Bible stories which I am revising at present.

Also, my main project is an abridgement of Acts—maybe about a third of the entire book. Also selected verses elsewhere for memory. And with the trauma of Honai's death I've translated 1 Thess 4:13.

We are grateful that the malaria epidemic is over. Now in comparison, a bad flu bug seems mild. Everyone here has had bad colds, most with fever and earaches. We white ones have gotten off easy with Lois escaping completely, me with bad cough and nose for a few days, Anita a slight cough, and Darlene with cough and fever for a couple of days (the fever subsided but the cough hung on.)

Paulo Ilo has been severely shaken by the death of his boy. He especially has been crying each day and each night. They had a feast just a couple of days ago in which they ground up the bones, drank some of the ashes, and put the rest in a gourd for a later feast or feasts.

Father-in-law Pedro had some strong drink made from sugarcane, and quite a few got drunk. Paulo didn't take any. He came in and really lectured the Christian fellows one morning against drinking. About five of the Christian fellows come each morning before breakfast for a short time of singing, Bible, and prayer.

Big fight at Solosama's house last night—one of the most vicious I've seen. Paulo was in the middle of it defending his brother and really getting clobbered. As if all this were not enough, this morning he came saying that his wife wants him to go back to his parents; she doesn't want him. I don't know how true this is.

We'd appreciate your prayers this next week. I plan to visit Lourenzo's group for several days—not more than a week. Lord willing, I plan to teach as much as possible—both of the gospel and reading and writing. Barb and Darlene will be staying here.

Personal letter from Don, November 1977

Feast for the Dead

A radio news report reminds us that it is Thanksgiving season there in the States. (Christmas and New Year's will have passed by the time you get this.

One year we would have missed Christmas had we not heard a report that "Lady Bird" was opening her presents "this Christmas Eve"). In the colder climes the leaves have dried up; here, the season is marked by the trails drying up and the rivers going down. It is "dry season" and with it, a lot of Indian travel, chiefly to attend feast in memory of the dead. These can go on for as long as a month, with plenty to eat, dancing, and singing, climaxed with a banana drink, mixed with the bone ashes of the deceased loved one.

I have just spent eight days at such a feast. Lourenzo had invited me down to teach him and his family the message of the Bible, and the only feasible time was during this feast. Things were pretty dead in the mornings, so we were able to meet for about an hour and a half each day with visitors also listening in.

The feast got wild at times. One night, José, Lourenzo's son, came in from a fight and had a long talk with me (starting at 1:00 a.m.). He firmly stated that he wanted to follow Christ, learn to read God's Word, and live a different kind of life. José and his father are leaders among the Sanumás in their area. They plan to make a new village and airstrip three days down the river from our present station. I'm excited about this and plan to do a lot of visiting there after furlough. From there we can easily reach the rest of the Sanumá villages in Brazil. José is eager to learn and to teach others. Pray that he'll carry through on this.

José

Personal letter from Don, December 12, 1977

Lourenzo's Plan to Relocate

We've had a great three months in Auaris. And my time at Lourenzo's was very good. After talking with him, he has decided to relocate, make new fields, and build an airstrip three days down the Auaris from the present station. Another village would move there with him. I plan to make visits there on a regular basis after furlough.

Personal letter from Don, December 27, 1977

Don, Malaria

Two weeks after I had that bout of malaria, I came down with it again. Don't know exactly why—whether it was still in my blood and popped out or whether I could have gotten reinfected by a mosquito that had bitten me while I had the first attack. (We hadn't heard nor seen any mosquitoes around.) Fever lasted only one day this time, but the medicine always leaves me weak for a few days. I'm back on my feet again taking a 14-day treatment that is supposed to get your blood cleared of the stuff. (I got over it just before kids came home.)

Personal letter from Don, January 10, 1978

Don, Malaria Again

I had one more relapse of malaria, and it really knocked me down for about a week. Malaria acts funny at different times. There are different types which act differently, and even within one type there can be variations. I had a resistant strain which evidently was just suppressed by the medicine I took the first two times (two times down with it separated by two weeks). Then I felt good again but came down a third time a week later. So I changed medicine and think I've finally knocked it out. This last time both the malaria and medicine were working on my liver, and I was nauseous quite a bit. I feel back to normal now.

Personal letter from Barb, January 31, 1978

Treating Malaria

Our return to the Indians on January 24 was as we had suspected. Malaria hit hard, as it hit Don during the Christmas break. He was quite ill. Here, several adults and children died, though not from this immediate village. Lois walked forty minutes away to treat sixty-seven people who had moved to temporary shacks in their fields to be near their food supply while weak. Don went to another village where a number of people were sick, some in serious condition. This month will be given to treating the sick, traveling to spray Indian houses for mosquitoes, and Bible teaching. Illness among Indians is constant, time-consuming, and depressing.

Personal letter from Don, February 1978

Malaria Epidemic

We went into Auaris January 25 as planned, and as planned we spent the whole time treating the sick, spraying for mosquitoes, visiting other villages, and there was some time left over to do a few minor repairs around the station—enough to keep the place from falling apart till Paulo gets back. One of the Maiongongs who is a "medical attendant" (can give out medicine and administer shots) treated his own people and some of the Sanumás. But they had run out of medicine and were very grateful for our arrival. The medicine we needed I was able to obtain in Manaus on our visit there.

The day we arrived, or rather the next day, Lois treated seventy Maiongongs. I went upstream to a village there and returned for two more days to treat the sick. Then I went downstream to a village where Saula was suffering from bad asthma attacks. Then about six days later I went in another direction to treat another village. These trips gave me more of a feel for the Sanumás, their life, and their sorrows. Several had died in these places. Others were skeletons and yellow from malfunctioning livers. Wailing was every night and often during the day. The headman of one village had died, and I was there for his cremation. Over in Venezuela, news came of a whole village just about wiped out from malaria. Not one kid under ten survived.

Personal letter from Don, July 1979

Ron and Robin Brown

Our plan is to do much of the Bible translation here in town with the help of Indians who will come out from the tribe. About every six weeks I plan to spend two or three weeks back in the Indian villages, teaching and reaching out to new areas.

The needs of personnel on the field are being met. Several are back from furlough. Three new Brazilian candidates have joined the Mission. Ron and Robin Brown, new workers for the Sanumás who had to come to the field on tourist visas, have completed their application for permanent ones, and this means they will be able to stay on till a decision comes back from the Immigration Department. Continue to pray that permanent visas for them and others will be granted.

Personal letter from Lois Cunningham, November 1979

God is doing his work here in these days in spite of everything (malaria and severe family fights.) Paulo Ilo (one of the Christians who has passed through much sorrow) was talking with two fellows from the Katimani village and spent forty-five minutes talking with them about the Lord. They said they wanted to accept. He prayed with them to receive Christ. Also, on Sunday, I had Kakali give a presentation of the broad way and the narrow way which Paulo Silas had already taught here. He was very nervous but did it. I asked them afterward if anyone wanted to pray and choose God's way. Soon as we closed our eyes, Satali (14-year-old son of one of the most mocking shamans) prayed without any hesitation, saying he wanted to receive Jesus.

Tsopi's wife feebly started to pray but was too afraid, so afterward I talked with her, and she said that she really wanted to receive Christ. Napa (mother of the above-mentioned shaman) was there, and I asked her if she wanted to accept. She said she did but was too afraid to pray and told me to pray for her.

Satali borrowed the poster showing the two paths for three days and said that he wanted to show it to his father.

Only God knows the hearts (and perception) of these, and I just pray they would be real decisions for him.

Reflections on a Third Term among the Sanumás

Despite the battles with bouts of malaria, much progress had been made in regard to the Sanumás. Don had finally been able to make contact with the Sikoi, paving the way for future opportunities for the gospel. Not only was there significant evidence of the stirring of faith amongst some Sanumás, but also Lourenzo, which would prove important for the future. Of great delight was the profession of faith by Steve and Andrea and of course, the birth of Darlene. God seemed to be blessing his servants' efforts as Don and Barb headed into their next furlough.

8

Olomai, Part I, The Sprouting of Seeds Sown (1979 to 1986)

"Therefore let it be known to you that this salvation of God has been sent to the Gentiles; they will listen." (Acts 28:28)

A SIGNIFICANT COMMUNITY SHIFT *occurred in 1979 and 1980 with the establishment of a new Sanumá village downriver about three days from Auaris. This new village would be called Olomai, named for the creek which runs into the Auaris River at this location. Lourenzo, along with his son, José, were the instigators of the move. The primary reason given was because of lack of game (meat) in the area of Auaris. One wonders, however, if part of the thinking was to get away from the bad influences of some Sanumás who lived at Auaris. At one point, Lourenzo, in expressing his desire to move downriver, stated, "We would only do it if Don promised to come and teach us about God and continue to treat us," referencing medical help, no doubt. Although Auaris would continue to be the primary focus of the Sanumá mission work, Olomai, over the next decade, would increasingly become the location of Don's interest.*

Despite ongoing difficulties with regular bouts of malaria and the flu, the coming years would witness tremendous spiritual growth among the Sanumás, both at Auaris and Olomai. Family life for Don and Barb back in Boa Vista would continue on routinely with greater involvement in the local church. Changes would come, however, as their children were now off to a missionary boarding school far to the south along the Amazon. [1]

---

1. Note entries out of chronological order designed to maintain a particular topic or subject.

Lourenzo and Developments with the Sanumás at Olomai

Personal letter from Don, November 1979

Lourenzo, Sikoi trail

Lourenzo came up Monday, and there was a long conference with him. Paulo hadn't told me what had happened, for he promised Lourenzo that he wouldn't. Lourenzo told the whole story (in front of other Sanumás present) of how he and José went over to Venezuela and took by force a couple of wives, one for José and one for himself. He confessed that this was bad, and that the girl he took had left and gone back. He reaffirmed that he didn't want to continue this way and that he very much wanted me to come down and teach him and his family (village) as well as other villages that can be reached from there. Already there is close contact with the Koima or Lalau people. The Sikois have already made a trail to the new strip. And a village over in Venezuela will be doing so shortly.

The presence of the Browns and Lois here has been tremendous, both in the physical help of the station and in the spiritual encouragement of the rest of us. I keep praying that they can stay. Things are functioning really well at present.

Social gospel

Our trip of two weeks was good. No accidents or sickness, and for this we are grateful. Lourenzo and his group are wide open to receive the gospel message. They want a new way of life. This includes every part of their life. They want to learn the gospel, and they want to learn how to read and write. They want also full assistance materially and medically. These three things have taken up our time here these years: trade goods (involving work program, payment, etc.), medicine, and the gospel. At times I have wanted to divorce these three things from each other, and while they are not the same and very much different, still they make up the total life of the people here, and I am no longer as disturbed as I used to be about the Indians talking about God in one breath and trade goods in the next. This is what most evangelicals are saying these days, that while the social dimension is not equal nor as primary as the spiritual dimension, yet still the social aspect is an integral part of our mission. It is too bad that many have taken the social dimension as primary and see (our church's) mission as primarily social.

Visas denied

Our problem now is insufficient personnel. I am committed to Lourenzo and his group at the new village and airstrip. The Browns have been denied permanent visas from their original request from the States, and I don't see how they will be staying on. The reason given was that the FUNAI has no agreement with our mission to let us give religious instruction. This is true, and they let us stay on here on the basis of our medical assistance, no doubt.

Personal letter from Don, January 1980

Genesis with Lourenzo

Lourenzo comes and says he wants to hear about God's son, Jesus, from the beginning (Adam). He ties his hammock next to mine (true Maiongong style). One-on-one he is free to ask many questions. We went from Adam through to Joseph in Genesis! He said he learned for the first time that in those days God was not seen and was not a man like us. I emphasize God's providence for those who trust him, even though there might be suffering and scorn for a time.

Personal letter from Don, March 1980

Hepatitis, Barb

Things are quiet now, a little too quiet, for Barb is in the hospital with hepatitis. Last Monday she came down with a high fever, and Wednesday we decided (with the nurses) to start her on a treatment for malaria, especially since there is malaria going around Boa Vista now. This was a three-day treatment, and she felt miserable all the time, especially in the stomach. She ate nothing all week, and worse yet, drank very little. At the end of the treatment her fever was down considerably, but not gone, and still she felt nauseous. Saturday night we took her to a doctor, and the doctor recommended the hospital, so I put her right in. She had a blood test done this morning, and the doctor gave her the verdict early this afternoon. I believe it is viral hepatitis, not toxic. This means that it is contagious, and I'll be looking into any precautions we should be taking for Darlene and myself and others. Barb probably will come home from the hospital by the end of the week but will be in bed for at least ten days, or more. Barb does feel quite a bit better already after taking liquid (glucose and salts) intravenously.

Letter from Don to support partners, June 1980

Olomai Report
Auaris Station, Brazil
Dear friends,

The year before our last furlough, as we lived among and ministered to the Indians at Auaris Station, our hearts became increasingly burdened for the totally unreached Sanumás living far from the station, as well as for those living closer, who received only sporadic teaching. Of this latter group, we thought especially of Lourenzo and his group, who lived three hours downstream. Lourenzo, the headman of the village, had received Christ into his life but badly needed spiritual nourishment.

As we were asking God just how it would be possible to effectively reach these other villages, the answer came from Lourenzo himself as we were paddling downstream, slowly wending our way to his village. "I'd like to move our village way downriver to better fishing and hunting grounds," he said, "but only if you can come down to teach and treat us. If you can do that, we'll make an airstrip." I thought of the ideal location he mentioned, at the mouth of the Olomai Creek. From there we would have contact with the unreached villages at the eastern half of Sanumá territory in Brazil.

The logistics of making an airstrip, planting new fields, and moving a whole village to a place more than four days travel away from home were fantastic, but they did it. And this with no machinery and with no direction from the missionaries.

But it took more than brains and brawn on the part of Lourenzo and his group. It took belief—faith that God would protect them in this new location and faith that we would keep our word and come to help them once the airstrip was made. Lourenzo could identify with Noah, who received scoffing and jeers while building the ark, Lourenzo told me how others had jibed, "You're out of your mind. The missionary will never land his plane here." More serious still, he told how another chief had warned him not to settle at Olomai because of the spirits of the dead former enemies who were still roaming that area and who would be out to bring illness and calamity. This unsettling admonition was met with Lourenzo's firm conviction, "God will protect us."

I learned all this one morning after having taught a two-hour lesson on Genesis, explaining how God had protected his people, as seen in the stories of Noah, Abraham, Jacob, and Joseph. This bolstered Lourenzo's faith, for he related how that while making the airstrip, they had dug up evidence that they were settling right top of the former village and burial ground of their old enemies!

Pray for Lourenzo, that his faith will not fail. Pray for his three sons, who recently have turned to Christ for salvation. One of them is José, a gifted hunter, worker, and talker, and a wild man by nature. (In a fit of rage, he killed his companion a few years ago, and even now lashes out at his wife and others.) Pray that the Spirit of God will help him control his own spirit.

The other two sons are Dino (married with a family of five) and Alberto, a teenager. These two are peace-loving but do not have much love for their brother, José. Pray that others will come to Christ. One whole village (a group called the Halaikana people) has already moved to the new airstrip.

This term, while a Brazilian couple and a Canadian nurse continue at Auaris Station, we have turned most of our attention to the new village at Olomai (pronounced Oh-low-MY). Ask God to give me wisdom in preparing meaningful lessons to these jungle Indians and to make me effective in discipling the new Christians.

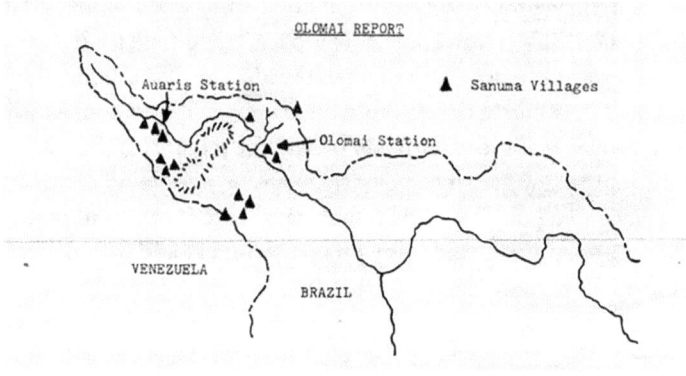

Sanumá Villages along the Auaris River and Interior (Don Borgman)

Personal letter from Don, August 1980

Cockroaches, stations, and personnel

They are building me a house at Olomai. It consists of a little room with dirt floor which serves as entrance and will serve as a place of prayer in the morning where we can light a fire because of the cold. Then the rest of the house is slightly elevated with palm slat floor, with room for school and clinic. A room for slinging my hammock and keeping my stuff and a little porch for eating and studying. I will miss the "coziness" of the Indian house at night with the people and fires, but I will not miss the dense smoke (day and night), multitudes of cockroaches, and burrowing fleas.

We sprayed and got rid of crickets, but cockroaches seem to thrive on the insecticide. Every time I opened the food box there would be literally (can be taken "litter-ally") scores and scores of cockroaches. Each morning I would empty everything out and feed the critters to the chickens and pet bush turkeys that continually stalked my compartment. They would eat the roaches but also leave their messy droppings all over the dirt floor for me to step in if I weren't very alert. Getting back to the roaches. At night they would crawl up my legs and over my face, leaving their little droppings in my hair (these are not messy—very small and hard and easy to deal with—the droppings that is). I could have used a mosquito net, but with no mosquitoes there, the net is a real bother during the day when you want to sit in hammock, so I opted to leave it off—preferring the roaches, believe it or not, to the net. (That's why they give us furloughs, so that we—some of us—won't go completely berserk. "Berserk," that is what this typewriter ribbon was just now. I get impatient with stuff that doesn't work. Machines . . . I don't like them. Nor do I like plumbing that doesn't work. I got home and found that the drain in one sink was busted and that one of the toilets didn't flush right.)

It's probably good that lunch was ready at this point so that I wouldn't go on and on complaining about the annoyances that come with this technological age.

You mentioned being confused about names of stations and people. Here's a rundown:

- Auaris (Sanumá and Maiongong)—Sanumá: Paulo and Iveli Diniz, Lois Cunningham, Dianne Voth. Maiongong: Dave and Joanne Feltz.
- Palimi-U: (Waicas or Yanomam) Bob and Gay Cable, Sandy Cue, Edith Moreira, and soon another Brazilian couple.[2]
- Mucajaí (Shirishanas): Steve and Dawn Anderson, Carole Swain, Carol James, and a Brazilian couple, Milton and Marcia.

---

2. According to Don Borgman and Gay Cable, the original Waica Station was abandoned when the Waicas there moved downriver. The missionaries then moved over to Opo-U on the side of Mount Surucucu. Eventually, because of warfare among the Yanomams, those Yanomams living at Opo-U moved away as well. Also, problems between the missionaries and the Yanomams there led to the missionaries relocating once again, this time to Palimi-U, downriver from the original Waica Station. Gay states that the Yanomams living at Palimi-U were the same as those who had lived at Waica Station. Having moved there, they had no access to medical help from missionaries, so their return was welcomed. Palimi-U Station was established by the late 1970s. (Emails to editor from Don Borgman, October 23, 2023 and Gay Cable, October 30, 2023.)

- Kashmi (pronounced KashMEE) (Wai Wais led by Yakutá, about one hundred and fifty in number) Enoque and Eliane, who are about to work with the Atroais, Flo, Ruth Langer, a Brazilian. Also Joe and Tamara Hill of World Team on loan to UFM.

- Mapuera (Wai Wais led by Elká numbering about six hundred) Graça ("Grace" in English) and at the moment (for a few months till Irene Benson gets back) Flo.

Map referencing the tribes and UFM mission works (Don Borgman)

Personal letter from Don, January 1981

Vaccinations

While our professed theology here among the Indians might have been a bit lacking and lopsided on the side of the spoken word through the years, in practice we have (just about by necessity) majored on the people's physical needs. I think we have needed to see that this part is a part of our mission, and this would have alleviated some of our frustration in being "sidetracked" by so much time spent on the "material." On February 3 I am going up to Olomai with a medical team to spend some time in a vaccination program and treating general health needs. Because Auaris will not have another flight for over a month, I probably will spend just a few days there and come back, saving a longer trip for later.

Personal letter from Don, February 1981

Dino and José

The translation of the epistle of John has just been checked, and now as I plunge into Philippians, I stop to reflect and write to you who are "partners in the gospel." (Phil 1:5) You have helped by prayer, and some of the answers to your prayers are given below. We want to thank each one for your participation in a material way for the ongoing work here. This has meant a lot to us as inflation hit us so hard this last year. Thank you, too, for the special gifts that came at Christmas. On our whole field we have some special causes for joy and giving thanks, as we are seeing that "he who has begun a good work ... will carry it on to completion." (Phil 1:6)

The group of Sanumás at Auaris Station is back together in fellowship after a "down" period which dipped to a new low after a break-in and theft which took place during the missionaries' absence. Paulo Ilo, a Christian fellow who was paid to watch the houses, turned out to be one of the accomplices. But latest word is that he has confessed, shown a good attitude, and has even offered to work off the money he received for his less than adequate services as watchman.

At Olomai, our place of ministry, two young Sanumás give us encouragement. In our absence, Dino led his wife to the Lord. He had been praying for her daily and couldn't wait to tell us of her decision. Before I left the village this time, Dino made sure I left a carbon copy of 1 John so that he could read and share, especially with his family. Somewhat temperamental Alberto, a 17-year-old boy, is growing in stability. (Maybe his recent marriage is a contributing factor! Yes, they do marry young.) He was the one who lovingly reprimanded another of his peers, a Christian, who under pressure one day, had taken dope and called on the spirits. (José is another one who is having a hard time conquering the pull toward shamanism ... and women.)

A SANUMÁ CHILD IS BORN: "BILL"

Personal letter from Don, February 9, 1981

Indian baby "Bill"

As I was dashing out to the plane, Lourenzo came up and said that there was a Sanumá woman of the Halaikana people who was having trouble with a baby to be born but crosswise in the womb. (Just that morning the wife of Lourenzo talked about how she went through the same thing thirteen years ago. We were on a trip and halfway between Auaris and Surucucu she had this trouble. Lourenzo, who was not a Christian then, asked me to pray, and that I did, going over to his wife and asking the Lord to undertake. Within ten minutes the baby was born. Lourenzo's wife reminded me that I was the one responsible for this girl's, and possibly her own, life.)

Then started the big discussion of whether the mother would survive or not and whether we should take her out to Boa Vista. This was on the part of Lourenzo's group and others. They decided yes. Bill[3] and I had decided yes, too. So they ran and got the brother of the lady (her husband was off on a trip). Some more heated discussion and the brother consented. Then they ran off to get the poor lady—really a girl, probably 18 years old or less—this was to be her first baby. Propped up by two people, one on each side, they came walking toward the plane, she more hobbling than walking.

As she was about to step onto the plane, she started yelling that more labor pains were beginning. So the ladies escorted her to the other side of the plane. She squatted, and Lourenzo's wife held her and assisted. The other ladies gave the customary yells of support, sort of like a cheering section: "Push! Push!" "Come on, you can do it." "A little more." "Push!" The women had the box seats (along with me and the photographer, Bill Born). The men discreetly were on the other side of the airstrip in the grandstand and bleachers. Well, praise the Lord, within ten minutes the baby came out. He was in pretty bad shape, but we had to move on because of time and soared down the airstrip, passing by about fifteen feet the woman still squatting (awaiting afterbirth) along with those assisting her, and the box seaters. So we took off between them and the gang on the other side of the strip thirty feet away. Wow! It wasn't until we were in the air again that we realized how good the Lord was in seeing to it that the baby was born at that instant instead of five minutes later in the plane with just Bill and I and the woman aboard. (They named the baby "Bill.")[4]

---

3. Bill Born was the same MAF pilot who had flown the Borgman family out of Auaris upon the death of David.

4. The editor had opportunity to speak on the phone with Mr. Born and his recollection of the incident was exactly as Don recorded. We both found it amusing that somewhere, among all those people with Portuguese and Sanumá names, was an individual by the name "Bill"—certainly an honor and gesture of thankfulness to Mr. Bill Born, nonetheless.

Family Life at Boa Vista

Personal letter from Don, February 18, 1981

Grammar for HAL (Handbook on Amazonian Languages)

I have my work cut out for me for the next eight months or so. I have consented to do a Sanumá grammar write-up for Des Derbyshire.[5] He is co-ordinating a project for Amazonian languages, and the descriptions will go into a handbook published in England. Then I have the regular translation work (we have a workshop on Philippians coming up immediately following conference) and the regular trips to Olomai. And right now I will try to get caught up on correspondence before conference.

Lunch on beach

In the dry season (which it is now until the end of April), every once in a while we go swimming at a little river which empties into the larger Rio Branco. Nice beach and not many people. Last Sunday after church we decided to pack a "Brazilian" lunch and eat it out there. The Brazilian style is *not* sandwiches. Barb warmed up some macaroni and some rice, put in some lettuce and tomatoes, and fried up a little meat. This we put into little pans which stack up and are carried like a big lunch box.

Picnic site

Personal letter from Barb, April 1981

Barb's testimony

Referring to the poem, "A Solitary Way,"[6] it is hard to explain to anyone who just cannot know what we are feeling exactly what our experience is,

---

5. Desmond C. Derbyshire was a linguist with SIL who had spent quite a number of years working with Hixkaryána people in northern Brazil.

6. Author unknown, based on Ps 107:4.

such as certain shades or aspects of loneliness or weariness. Knowing the Lord desires our love in all of these things, or through it all, I can see it is for us to want what he wants, above all. The old flesh rationalizes, sees others going a different path (but you are left), desires what it thinks is "normal." All of these hit. It makes the mistake, I know, of thinking satisfaction will come through a change. He wants to be our satisfaction. Please pray that the Holy Spirit will impress this firmly upon my heart.

Personal letter from Don, May 1981

Baptist church ministry

Pastor from Baptist church is gone, and we are a little more involved there now. Barb has been teaching the adult ladies, and I have spoken now and then. Tomorrow and next week I'll be taking Pat's place teaching adults out at the mission church.

Kids' trio

Steve and Andrea are home, and we are all a big, united, happy family once again. We were all missing each other a lot. There at school they give awards at the end of the school year, grouping 5th and 6th and 7th and 8th together. We were surprised that Steve got the scholarship award for 7th and 8th. Andrea actually had better marks than he, but there is a very smart girl in the 6th grade who beat her out for the award. They seem to work hard academically but have time for a lot of other activities, too. They both like music. As of now, Darlene doesn't show much gift in the line of music (having a hard time holding on the right pitch sometimes in a song), but she might improve. This morning I went by the window and the three of them on their own were singing a three-part trio in Portuguese. It sounded good.

Personal letter from Don, June 1981

Steve scared

We've had a real great time as a family together. Darlene, really for the first time in her life, seems to have grown to the point of fitting in with the other two. They all play well together. It sure is good to have this time to get to know our kids better. Steve has been having some problems waking up at night and being scared of a break-in. When we first moved here, there were some weird goings on across the street with supposed break-ins, and one time a cutlass was left on the bed with a note that the intruder would be back. That might have started it off for Steve.

Lordship salvation

Am reading Charles Ryrie's *Balancing the Christian Life*. (Kind of an old book, but which I hadn't read through before.) He has a lot of good stuff here, but once again, I realize that we cannot take any human teacher blindly, but "search the Scriptures" whether these things be true. I disagree with him in his chapter on "must Christ be Lord as well as Savior" (in order for a person to become a Christian). This had some pertinent observations as I have been thinking about the Sanumá and their reticence to give up shamanism. Ryrie cites Acts 19:18,19 and later on in the discussion says, "Their salvation did not depend on faith plus willingness to submit to the lordship of Christ in the matter of magical arts." I believe that saving faith is such that includes this willingness to submit to the Lordship of Christ.

Steve at Olomai

By the way, Steve loved his time at Olomai and playing with the kids quite a bit. First soccer on the airstrip, then jumping in the river upstream and floating down to the base of the airstrip, then more soccer and another swim. Then a walk through the fields and woods. Then some reading, etc.

Steve at Olomai (continued)

One thought led to another at this point, and I thought of J. Vernon McGee and his "Through the Bible" broadcast which comes over the radio. This is one more thing that Steve really liked up at Olomai. He would listen to McGee's half-hour message and really drink it in. One report was thrilling, of how Arabs were writing in and telling of their conversion through his expounding of the Word. He mentioned that in Cairo there is a group, as many as two thousand, that meet together for prayer (this latter is not in connection with his ministry).

Personal letter from Don, July 1981

Steve nervous

Steve still has problems with being nervous (or scared) at night; this really surprised us as he used to be so spunky. He and I have had a lot of long talks together, and I haven't heard anything from him which shows any deep problem. The only thing he mentioned in connection with his nervousness is the fear of robbers breaking in. I mentioned the robberies that took place here about a year ago, right across the street. We have slung up a hammock in our room, and if he awakes during the night and can't get back to sleep, we have told him to feel free to come in the hammock, which he does frequently. In other respects he is a normal adolescent acting like a nut a lot of times during the day, and then talking so seriously at other times, especially when I am with him for prayer at night. He tends to feel guilty a lot for his failures, and I try to encourage him at these times. He looked through my library (bookcase) and picked out *They Found the Secret* and loved reading that. He really wants God's best and had a lot of questions about a crisis experience a lot of the men talked about. Together we went over the last chapter in Ryrie's *Balancing the Christian Life*, which I think is Biblical.

At Baptist church

This is the last week the Baptist Church here will be without a pastor, and once again I spoke this morning, more a lesson, really, with blackboard to help up on the platform. With the pastor coming, the tendency will be for the members to sit back and to let the pastor do all. Partly with this in mind I emphasized what a church really is, the relationship that members have one to another, and duties, and attitudes, based on the injunctions ending with "one another": "Love one another," "preferring one another," "submitting to one another," "forbearing one another," "forgiving one another," "admonishing one another," and "comforting one another."

Personal letter from Don, August 1981

Darlene, doll, and Bible

When she opened that doll up, the package that is, her expression was amazed, and she was speechless. Finally, she said, "I *never* expected it, I *never* expected it!" and was so very happy. She repeated that comment throughout the rest of the vacation! A week or so after her birthday, she said that before her party she had dreamed that Sarah and Lisa each received the same doll, but she didn't; however, they let her hold theirs, but that was as close as I guess she expected to come to the doll! She was also thrilled because she received her first Bible. Sarah and Lisa had each received their NIV for Christmas, and I waited, but it was worth it. She can now read it well and took part in family Bible reading each morning during vacation. She had wondered and wondered what she'd do without a Bible at PQQ and was most moved to have her own. Darlene was delighted, too (going back again), with the dear little doll clothes and understood they and the doll were also a gift from you.

Measles at Olomai

Personal letter from Don, September 1981

Measles

Two or three times a year those of us from this field who are involved in translating the New Testament get together for a two-week workshop. During this time we take a book, carefully go through the exegesis verse by verse, discuss special translation problems, and come up with a first draft in our individual Indian dialects. Early this month we were working on the book of James, but an emergency called Barb and me away, right in the middle of the workshop. As we hurriedly left Boa Vista, we took with us this exhortation from James, "Count it pure joy, my brothers, whenever you face trials of many kinds." (Jas 1:2)

A Sanumá had broken out with measles at Olomai village. Runners had been sent to Auaris Station, two days away, and we received the news by radio late in the afternoon of September 9.

When we were kids, measles meant a few uneventful days in bed with the shades drawn and plenty of juice. Among Indians, measles means death on a large scale. A few years ago about one-half the population died off where the epidemic hit. In August we heard of two villages near here being wiped out by this disease. In the same month, several of our missionaries worked night and day trying to save people of a distant village who had not been vaccinated.

So it was with fear and trembling that we flew into Olomai. Most of the village had been vaccinated, but there were at least thirty new arrivals who weren't, and strangely enough, the fellow who brought the measles in from the outside was himself vaccinated. Probably because of this, his was a light case, and fortunately the chief of the village had the intelligence to isolate him and his two wives right away. But one of the wives (not so intelligent) broke out of isolation one day and entered her house where five non-vaccinated visitors were staying. That very day she came down with a high fever and measle marks, so now we have isolated those with whom she came in contact. We must wait to see if they come down with measles after the fourteen-day incubation period.

In the midst of this, we are treating one of the worst flu epidemics we have seen. News came today of four who have died from it in villages downriver. We started giving injections of penicillin the day we arrived and are still at it, two weeks later. (Because of the high fevers, we could not vaccinate the visitors against measles.) No one has died, and most are on the mend, but you wouldn't think so if you could hear the chorus of coughing during the night hours. Barb escaped this, and while I got off with a light case, I join in with the hackers each evening.

We ask, "Why this, Lord? We didn't come to do medical work." Well, if there are no doctors or nurses available, we had better acquire the right attitudes and aptitudes to save these people's lives at a time like this, or the translation and teaching ministries won't mean much!

We also ask why this should come at a time when we are unprepared to take care of the extra flights and medicines involved. We hesitate mentioning this but believe that some of you would appreciate knowing about this particular emergency and need.

There is one other of the "trials of many kinds" that we are experiencing. As of last month, all of our three children are away from home. The last to flutter away to boarding school was our 7-year-old, Darlene. It was imperative that she go, and she loves school, as do Steve and Andrea, but the empty bedrooms and silent house have been hard, especially for Barb. Included is a picture of us all together during the kids' vacation.

Borgman family, 1981

Bus Accident on Manaus Trip and Olomai Concerns

Personal letter from Don, November 12, 1981

Bus accident

We are writing to all of you at once, telling you about our trip home from Manaus to Boa Vista. Barb and I had decided to take the bus trip to Manaus to see the kids. The bus trip down went pretty well, with one mishap that could have been really bad. The steering mechanism broke, but fortunately it was at a place where the road was level, and the bus came to a stop without any misfortune. In a couple of hours the drivers had it fixed.

On the way back all went well from Manaus to Caracarai. Because there was a fair in Caracarai, there were many people along the road who wanted a ride, and there must have been about thirty-five or more people standing in the aisle for the last part of that stretch. About all of them got off at Caracarai.

Barb and I had the seat right in back of the driver: nice if you want to see the scenery, but not too safe in case of an accident. About fifteen kilometers outside of Caracarai, as we came over a hill, we saw a very disconcerting sight. The army engineers were making repairs on the road. There must have been about thirty truckloads of dirt piled up on the left-hand lane along a stretch of about two-hundred yards, blocking that whole lane, of course. Then, blocking the other narrow lane was a big army truck. We came barreling down the hill with no chance at all to stop before the truck. The driver did the only thing he could. He swerved off the road to avoid the truck, and as he did, we turned completely over and landed about eight feet below. I was in the aisle seat and had a ringside seat to see the whole thing. The bus was upside down, and Barb and I climbed out of a window and up onto the road. Fortunately nobody died or was even critically hurt. Because we were in that front seat with no seat in front of us, Barb and I probably got it worse than anybody else—a good whack in the rib cage, Barb in the lower right side and me on the upper right in the chest. We were conscious the whole time and did get a couple of cuts on the head that required stitches. We were taken to the hospital in Caracarai. Barb got stitches there, and my cut wasn't so bad and was hurting a lot in the chest and feeling rather faint, so they didn't get to stitch me. We came on to Boa Vista by taxi. Two other ladies were in a hurry to get back, and as it was uncertain when another bus would arrive, Barb and I agreed to go with them.

The doctors in Caracarai recommended X-rays in Boa Vista, although they did say that they were pretty sure there were no broken ribs. We went in for X-rays today and will get results maybe tomorrow. X-ray machine in Caracarai was not working, neither is the one in the government hospital in Boa Vista, so we had to go to a private place, and the doctor that reads the X-rays lives in Manaus! He comes up here every weekend. Unbelievable. I guess that in an emergency there would be other doctors here who could read the thing but maybe at extra cost. So here we are, at our home sweet home, with probably some bad muscle bruises which really hurt when we move the wrong way, breathe too deeply, etc. I didn't mention above that there were absolutely no signs whatsoever saying that men were working over the hill. And of course no seatbelts on the bus. Round trip the bus is a saving of about $200.00 for two adults, but this experience has decided it for us; never go by bus again or until conditions improve on road.

Personal letter from Don, November 23, 1981

Indian dies from anesthesia

After I last wrote, we felt a little worse than better. I was having a low fever every day, so I started on some sulfa that Dr. Frame had given me a couple of years ago, and it seemed to do the trick. Maybe we were trying to do too much those first few days, lifted up by the pain killers. I took some time to accompany a wounded Sanumá to the hospital who was sent in after he had been cut open with an ax in a fight. It was a sad case, because they sewed him up all right, but something went wrong with the anesthesia. He went into a coma and never did wake up after the operation. He died about three days later. You can't imagine the trauma this was for the people at Auaris, for the Indians, beside their grief, were angry and thinking of taking revenge right away. So Dianne Voth asked that I go up to Auaris with the body and talk with the people there. I knew I wouldn't be able to do too much, but just my being there took a tremendous load off of Dianne, and she appreciated it very much. We stayed overnight. Edson and Myriam are back there but just starting in on the language.

Personal letter from Don, December 1981

Pain

Barb and I are feeling a little better every day. I would say that I am just about back to normal. But I had some trouble with my tooth, or gums, the day before yesterday. It hurt a lot, and I spent most of yesterday in the hammock, so I guess I'll finally get to go to the dentist this week. I had constantly had a little trouble, with a little pus coming out, but with no pain. But now with this abscess, I'll have to do something, maybe have the tooth out, I don't know. It's the back tooth on left side on bottom, with the top tooth also in really bad shape. The teeth themselves are okay, but there is a disintegration of the bone, etc. In the midst of this I had to prepare for a message to give at church this morning since the pastor was away and had asked me to speak. I chose an appropriate subject, at least for me, "Why Pain?" I got some ideas from Philip Yancey's book, *Where is God When it Hurts?* He discussed quite a bit the work of Dr. Paul Brand among lepers and the fact that the trouble with lepers is the very fact that they do not feel pain, and therefore burn themselves, cut themselves without feeling, and then infection sets in. So there is a protective purpose in pain. I went further and mentioned the pain and suffering in the world at large, showing that God wants to tell us through this that all is not well, that we can't go on with the desire to "eat, drink, and be merry." That God wants us to turn to him in complete dependence and in complete devotion (Matt 6:33, Col 3:1–2, Ps 119:67, 71). Today I feel somewhat better.

CONTINUED WORK AT BOA VISTA AND FURTHER DEVELOPMENTS AT OLOMAI

Personal letter from Barb, February 1982

Church retreat

I think Don told you that we are leaving for a retreat this weekend, since this is Carnival time. A national orgy, as I see it, like Mardi Gras but held in every city and town. Don has been asked by one of the church groups to teach Bible to the young people each morning. I think I get to help in the kitchen (insert disappointed emoji.) Those also serve who only stir the beans.

Personal letter from Don, February 1982

Intravenous shots given

One of Lourenzo's Maiongong daughters had a bad attack of asthma when I was there, and she had run out of her pills which she usually keeps on hand. I had inadvertently left a box of the pills back in Boa Vista, so had to give her intravenous shots—something I haven't done till recently and don't especially like to do. But it seemed to do the trick, and I give the Lord the praise for this.

Personal letter from Don, April 1982

Cantata

My stamina isn't too great these days with old age creeping up on me. Workshop, then Field Council meetings, then Field Conference meetings, and added committee meetings; all filled up the time and more so. Added to this they got me to *lead* a cantata at church, and this has taken time. The raw material is lamentable. I couldn't believe that most of them have just the words printed, not the music. But then I learned that nobody reads music anyway. They get the regular scale okay but aren't too used to sharps and flats. Can you imagine trying to learn one of John Peterson's cantatas? Well, this is what we are doing. I have decided to do my part and not get uptight over lack of perfection (to put it mildly). Added to this, I have never led any kind of a choral group, nor hardly even sung in one. Oh well.

Baptism, when to administer

Both Barb and I are glad for this extra week out here in Boa Vista. She is in charge of hospitality, the housing part anyway, and she needs this time to break in a new maid before traveling. And I have been grateful for time in the office again. I'm translating portions having to do with baptism and the Lord's Supper. I feel that biblically we have put too little emphasis on baptism, and I believe we need to teach this right away to those who have made decisions. In the future, I believe that we should do more teaching before we bring a person to a decision, so that baptism will not take place so long after a person receives Christ. The more I read Scripture, the more I feel that baptism should come right away.

Letter from Barb to support partners, July 1982

Dear Friends,

All is well at Olomai. We are happy to report that no one died during the measle scare. God was gracious to all of us. Lourenzo, the father of the first case, stood outside the isolation hut and prayed with Dino, his other son. God honored their trust and their faithfulness, because Lourenzo would have no shamanism during what were very dark hours to him.

Don visited Olomai again in the following months. The April visit was a bright encouragement. Lourenzo, of his own initiative, called together leading Sanumá men of the village to air some community affairs. And, for the first time, as far as Don knows, he gave a clear witness of his faith in Jesus to them all.

As you may recall, Lourenzo is a Maiongong married to a Sanumá wife, and he has much influence among the Sanumás. Of course, he speaks Sanumá with an accent, so after he was finished, José, his son, got up and asked, "Did you understand that?" José decided to repeat it all in his own excellent Sanumá. Lourenzo later told Don some of the Sanumá men appear interested in these truths. For years, these Sanumás, who live so far from the original Auaris station, heard little or nothing of the gospel, and they need more background for fully understanding these new concepts. They need your prayers for their understanding and receptiveness.

Lourenzo told Don he and several others are enthusiastic about building a place for worship and tables and benches for studying. How great, because this month the two nurses from Auaris station are visiting Olomai to teach reading, while Don is at Auaris teaching the Christians in Paulo Silas's absence (furlough). Don will be speaking personally to men he has known for years who have resisted the gospel: Soloxama and Abel among them. Pray for these hard and stony hearts; nice men, but they are involved in spirits and closed thus far to God's Word.

I'm here in Boa Vista with the children, as they are still on vacation. Steve plays lots of basketball with our Brazilian pastor's son and is glad to have a missionary pal back from furlough, too. They spend hours playing soccer (kicking goals), still basking in the glow of the exciting World Cup games. (Andrea still insists that Brazil's Best!) Andrea sticks close to home reading, helping, cooking, and practicing music. She was baptized in May, to our joy. Darlene is thrilled to have her two best pals back from furlough and is between the two houses constantly.

There are opportunities here in the city for service, too. Don has preached several times and ministers to Indians from Olomai or Auaris who come here for medical treatment. Soon I will have a chance to teach English, and include simple Bible study, to two small groups of women.

Slowly, slowly, the gospel penetrates some Indian hearts.

Personal letter from Don, August 1982

Leishmaniasis

The sore on my leg is slowly getting better. It was an open sore about an inch in diameter with the raw meat showing and oozing. Also a little swelling in the leg. This could have been one of two things, and the doctor just took a chance and started treating for the more serious of the two (leishmaniasis). And yesterday when I saw him, he was happy that the thing was starting to clear up, which meant the diagnosis was right. Barb had to give me a shot of 10 cc every morning, and from this I would get fever and general malaise every afternoon and evening. Now I am off the medicine for ten days and should be perking up getting ready for the next series of ten shots. (Normally there are four series of ten days of shots.) I probably picked this up at Olomai; it is transmitted by a bug, something like a big gnat.

Barb is teaching four women twice a week and is grateful for this opportunity to reach women. This came about from a woman herself (Barb's sewing lady) who asked if she knew someone who could help her and some others with English. And right now Barb is with the girls of her S.S. class, going out for ice cream cones. (Not too much sacrifice on Barb's part.)

Schedule till Christmas

We are thankful that Pat Foster fixed our typewriter. He is a whiz at anything mechanical. (The top professional typewriter repair man said he couldn't fix it, then Pat, with no experience, looked at it, cleaned up a few points, and it is running fine.) This means that Barb is continuing on with the Sanumá dictionary, and then after that will be the life of Christ, mostly from Mark. I am working on the grammar write-up. I think I told you my schedule: We have a big meeting with the FUNAI early this next week, then Field Council meetings for three or four days. They have begged me to help direct the choir, so from now till Christmas, I'll be involved with that on Tues. evenings and Sat. afternoons. First two weeks in October I plan to be in Olomai, and then the last two weeks is translation workshop here in Boa Vista.

Personal letter from Don, September 1982

Leishmaniasis

Dianne Voth thinks she, too, has this leishmaniasis or forest yaws, as it is also called. Looks like Olomai is the place we're picking this up, although some at Auaris also have it. It is transmitted by a type of sand fly. I'm on a series of ten days of shots and not doing too much better as far as the reaction is concerned. I thought that taking the shots in the late afternoon instead of the morning might help, but not so. But today I'm feeling okay.

Personal letter from Don, November 1982

Basing in B.V. workable

I came out of Olomai on Friday the 15th, and it is always good to get home. I have often weighed the advantages and disadvantages of living in the city, but in our particular case, this has been far better, and I don't think the Indians have suffered that much as far as teaching is concerned. They plan their trips around our going there. They are now scattered, having gone upriver and downriver and plan to stay about three weeks, fishing, hunting, etc., and then come back in time for the girls' visit. I certainly can produce a lot more here on the language and translation.

Traffic in B.V.

The lack of traffic control here makes us angry. The *only* infraction that one gets a fine for is parking a few centimeters too far from the curb on the main street. No fines for speeding, going through stop signs, etc. About two years ago they put up stop signs all over the city, but nobody obeyed them. Solution: They took down most of the stop signs. The ones they left in the really strategic areas are not enforced. Stop really means yield, and I would be for this if they would really yield. In many ways we are safer in the jungle. Pray for our safety here in the city.

First Baptisms among the Sanumás and Furlough

Newsletter from Don and Barb, January 1984

Field News

In May we had the *first Sanumá baptism* ever to take place in Brazil. To us this was a thrill and a glorious reward after many years of working among the Sanumá Indians. The service took place at Olomai, the village where *Lourenzo is headman*. He, two of his sons, a grandson, and a daughter-in-law were five of the seven whom we baptized.

Baptism of Alberto at Olomai (Don officiating)

One of these sons, Dino, has recently attended an intensive course so that he can more effectively work in the role of medical attendant at Olomai. Pray for Dino as there are no permanent missionaries at this station, and he has all the medical responsibility on his shoulders as well as much of the spiritual leadership of the group.

From Auaris Station, there were *twenty-eight Sanumás who attended a Christmas Conference* over in Venezuela, two weeks travel by land and river. Probably about ten of these who went were Christians. Pray for lasting results of this conference. We praise God that Sanumás are responding to the gospel on the Venezuela side as well as in Brazil. There are two stations there manned by two Venezuelan couples.

Furlough News

This furlough time has been super. It's just great to have the whole family together for a year. Steve (sophomore), Andrea (8th), and Darlene (4th) are attending the same Christian school and enjoying it immensely (but are still homesick for their school and friends in Brazil). Barbara helps out at the school for a couple of hours each day and has participated in missionary conferences and Bible studies.

Along with speaking at various churches and church groups, I am engaged in producing a full grammar write-up for the Sanumá language. This could take three full months. To speed up the translation process, we are planning to buy a computer for word processing. Those specializing in Bible translation have told us that without a word processor, 50% of the translator's time is taken up in just editing and typing. By the end of this month, I should decide which computer will suit our needs the best.

Newsletter from Don and Barb, August 1984

Back to Brazil

Within a week we plan to be on our way back to Brazil again, traveling the 8th, overnighting in the airport in Georgetown, Guyana, and then on to Boa Vista early in the morning. We go with the promise of Christ to those who follow him, "And surely I will be with you always, to the very end of the age." (Matt 28:20) Once again, we leave many dear friends and relatives along with rich, supportive fellowship that we have so appreciated this year. But we are eager to get back to the ministry among the Sanumás and to the translation job that awaits us. After about three days in Boa Vista, our kids will be traveling off to school, more than four hundred and fifty miles away. The house is going to seem mighty empty, especially after this year that we have had together as a family. Steve will be a junior, Andrea a freshman, and Darlene will be a 5th grader. All three are excited about going back, even though they have had a great year at an excellent Christian school and have made some lasting friendships here.

We go back equipped with a computer for word processing and with a printer, a system which was provided through some generous gifts from God's people. This is going to help tremendously in the whole translation process. Pray that the computer will enter safely into Brazil, and that it will keep functioning well. We've heard that computers don't like heat, humidity, and dust, and we have a super-abundance of all three there in north Brazil.

Pray, too, about what might turn out to be an annual conference for Sanumás. Last year the Sanumás from Brazil went over to Venezuela and met with Christians there for the first time. There is talk of another conference to be held on our Brazil side sometime this fall. Pray that if this is God's will, that no obstacle Satan puts in the way will hinder, and that the work of the Holy Spirit will be evident.

Spiritual Growth among the Sanumás and Medical Concerns

Newsletter from Don and Barb, February 1985

Conference at Auaris

It was nearing Christmas as I sat watching the Sanumás gather for their Christmas conference at Auaris. They came from various villages, about two hundred and fifty people in all. One group from Venezuela had traveled eight hard days in order to attend.

For this occasion, the Sanumás of Auaris had decided months before to build a church building, and here I was sitting on one of the huge poles that served as a pew. I thought back twenty years when we had built our first mud-walled, thatched-roof home on this very site and how the gospel had seemed painfully slow in taking root.

But now, here were the Sanumás singing heartily. Here was Paulo Ilo giving his testimony and exhorting his people to receive Christ and to follow the Lord in baptism. Another night it was Ari, confessing how he had stolen and how much this weighed on his conscience. Stealing can include stealing through adultery, and as Ari went on and on, someone from the audience asked what or who he had stolen. Then came the short reply which surprised us all, "A bar of soap." Others of the Sanumá Christians gave messages throughout the conference, along with the missionaries. On the last day of the conference, I had the joy of baptizing twenty-three Sanumá believers. Among them was Pedro, a man over 50 years old, whose testimony has had a great impact. Now all in his household are Christians: his wife, six children, two sons-in-law, and a daughter-in-law.

During those days of conference, I repeated Simeon's words of adoration, "My eyes have seen Your salvation . . . a light for revelation to the

Gentiles." (Luke 2:30–32) *Thank you* for praying. Now we ask you to pray for a health problem that has come up.

Newsletter from Don and Barb, September 1985

Embolism, Kwaiam

Our last letter was started here in Brazil and finished from a hospital bed in the States. What was diagnosed in South America as TB was really a pulmonary embolism (a blood clot which got lodged in the lung). It was the second attack that sent me to the hospital in Connecticut more than a month after the first one. The doctor said I was a "very fortunate man" to have come through okay, and we know that God's protecting hand was upon us. Thank you for praying during that time. How thankful I am for my present good health and strength. I have put in long hours trying to finish up a complete analysis and write-up of the Sanumá grammar, a necessity for good translation work. The next translation projects will probably be Paul's letters to Timothy, to the Thessalonians, and to the Philippians. Also there have been good visits to Olomai. On the last trip, another young man, Kwaiam, put his faith in Christ. He said he was hesitant to make this step because his wife was adamantly against the gospel, and he was afraid he "couldn't hold out." So we had good opportunity to emphasize some basic truths of the Christian life.

Lourenzo is visibly getting older and seems to be in the process of handing over the leadership of the village to his son, José. Please pray for the salvation of this young man. He has expressed a desire to become a Christian, but his pride is evident, and we pray for a deep working of the Holy Spirit in his heart. Dino continues with his work as a medical attendant.

NEWSLETTER FROM DON AND BARB, NOVEMBER 1985

Alberto

Alberto,[7] Lourenzo's son, spent three days helping Don check the translation of 1–2 Timothy, 1–2 Thessalonians, and Philippians just before this trip. Don was joyful to hear Alberto's questions and sense his interest. After they discussed one particular passage, Alberto thought on it during the

---

7. Alberto (his Indigenous name was Komak) accompanied his father, Don, Norman Allaby, and the editor on their expedition to contact the Sikoi in 1977.

night. The next morning he told Don he hadn't slept. He realized yet another mistake related to a fight with his former father-in-law (fourteen years ago or more) he knows he must make right. He commented, "If I weren't a Christian, I know I wouldn't feel this way."

Alberto with Don—Bible translation

Newsletter from Don and Barb, February 1986

Second conference

In mid-January the 2nd Sanumá Bible Conference was coming up. The ladies were baking extra *beiju* (round, flat manioc "bread"), and the hunters were bringing in meat for the extra guests who would be arriving. One could feel their enthusiasm, but the missionaries struggled with uneasy feelings over a recent battle royale in which one of last year's leaders had been involved, and rumors of another having taken a second wife.

The Olomai people (downriver two to three days) arrived late, giving extra time for missionaries, Christian Sanumá men of Auaris, Kakali (Brazilian name: Carlos), and Ilo (Brazilian name: Paulo) to meet. Where did these two men stand spiritually? Should they participate as leaders in the conference this year?

Kakali poured out his desperation, loneliness, and sadness at having been branded a hypocrite by everyone. As he explained, missionaries learned he had not been responsible for smashing and breaking a woman's arm with a gun barrel, and they learned more about the culture. When a man's mother or her honor is under attack, it is his obligation to defend.

Kakali, as the oldest, was considered responsible for whatever occurred during a recent fight over his mother's honor. We outsiders realized once again that this is their age-old way of administering justice: a (usually) planned event in which offenders and defenders hit with sticks and poles. Unfortunately, Kakali's younger brother broke a woman's arm in uncontrollable anger. Kakali was considered as the one who did it by his peers.

The title of a well-known Christian book asks, "What shall this man do?" If Kakali decided to stop any participation in family feuds, he'd leave his mother vulnerable and would be a social outcast. The group heard him confess his problem, his anger at his brother, and his repentance for that anger. He expressed his joyful relief, because God had washed him again. It made me think of our home pastor's frequent prayer: "We thank you, O God, that you are a God of new beginnings." Ilo was at least honest, saying he still wanted to take a second wife and was struggling with it. There was no spirit of repentance.

Ongoing Problems with the Brazilian Government

Newsletter from Don and Barb, November 1985

Accusations

For years, recurring waves of accusations against Yankees have surged throughout Brazil. Not only do Third World people resent and suspect Americans, but they cannot even faintly comprehend that anyone would serve Indians from spiritual motives. The question, "What are they really doing?" beats on their thinking as it is constantly asked also by reporters and politicians in newspapers, magazines, on radio, and on TV. The ire is growing.

Newsletter from Don and Barb, November 1985

Flights stopped

Flights stopped, radio contact with jungle posts ended, missionary personnel couldn't move (some were off stations for medical reasons or mission council meetings; others returned from furlough), Indians could not have left for medical emergencies had there been any (God kept everyone well), and the vaccination program hung in mid-air. Finally we received 30-day permission to use the services of MAF as long as each flight is accompanied by a FUNAI (National Indian Foundation) person. Shortly this permission will run out, and renewal is questionable. *Don has been able to go to Olomai and will remain there for two weeks. Pray that this will be a time of growth in the understanding of Biblical truths for the Christians there, especially Kwaiam, a new brother in Christ* (letter of September 1985).

There have been two men in power in the FUNAI who are violently anti-missionary. One was its president and the other an influential man known as the defender of Brazil's Indians to international organizations such as Survival Int'l. Organizations such as that want to keep the Indian cultures "pure."

Newsletter from Don and Barb, February 1986

Alukusima, Flight permission

And then, the conference began. For three mornings Don taught. Two of these mornings Lourenzo (chief at Olomai), respected by many, shared from his Christian experience and exhorted the Sanumá Christians. Suddenly he said, "We have depended greatly on the missionaries, but what if they ever have to leave? Let's practice singing without them." He called Kakali to come and lead. The voices rang out, moving each missionary heart deeply. Lourenzo brought his 20-year-old daughter, Alukusima, to the front to give her testimony. (She recently prayed to receive Christ at our home in Boa Vista; she and her father were here for three weeks, while she was treated for filaria). That morning Don baptized Alukusima and three children (ages 12, 9, and 9).

A word about MAF: Your prayers have been most effective. How encouraging to receive letters from some of you saying you would be praying specifically. *Thank you!* MAF has had verbal permission to fly for about two months now. A contract will be made up by the government dictating what MAF can and cannot (or must) do to serve here in the future. All of us pray that the conditions specified in the contract will not hinder or demand to the point that MAF can't carry on its ministry effectively here.

GOD'S SPIRIT AT WORK

After nearly twenty years of missionary activity among the Sanumás, the Spirit of God was beginning to show its work. Not only were key individuals evidencing faith, but with the conferences taking place, it was obvious that a powerful work of conversion was occurring. Of course, it was difficult to know how much was understood by the people, but the seeds had been planted and were beginning to sprout. Much more work needed to be done and would be done, but the faithfulness of the sowers and waterers was pointing to a harvest yet to come. Phil 1:6 must have echoed in the hearts of those who had been ministering to the Sanumá for so long: "And I am certain of this, that he who began a good work in you will bring it to completion at the day of Jesus Christ."

9

Olomai, Part II, Spiritual Growth and Challenges (1986 to 1991)

> "I have said these things to you, that in me you may have peace.
> In the world you will have tribulation. But take heart;
> I have overcome the world." (John 16:33)

FOLLOWING THEIR SIXTH TERM with the Sanumás, significant changes were to take place for Don and Barb, particularly in terms of where they would reside in order to be most effective in Don's translation work. Spiritual growth among the Sanumás would be ongoing, although there would be considerable challenges ahead.

Transitions, Deepening Relationships, and New Opportunities

Newsletter from Don and Barb, May 1986

Move to Florida

We have prayed about this move for a couple of years and for various reasons. One is ministry: Don's main objective at this point is the translation, which will serve not only the Sanumás in Brazil, but also those in Venezuela, who are more than twice in number than those in this country. For many years he has been in contact with a missionary among the Sanumás in Venezuela, Merrill Seely, and they have tried to make the alphabet as uniform as possible and have shared materials. He and his wife are now semi-retired, living in Bradenton, and working on various Sanumá projects. Don believes that collaborating with Merrill will greatly speed up the translation. This will be his full-time work and "GOAL." He will travel back to Brazil once or twice a year for translation checking and teaching. Don has often chuckled at himself for being different and not having gone through a mid-life crisis. Analyzing it, he decided it is because he is still in the midst of his life's work . . .

During his first term he helped to open new strips and stations. It wasn't until 1965, when we were married, that he settled down to one dialect. First comes the trying to grasp and communicate in an unwritten language; then analyzing; then writing of a tentative grammar to be written formally later on; then messages, lessons (verbal and written), primers to teach reading, a chorus book, a dictionary, and a Sanumá language course for new missionaries, etc. Interspersed have been translation, epidemics, and medical treatment, trips to other groups, teaching sessions, some years of administration when the field leader was away, and furloughs.

Family is another reason—our children have lived and studied far from us since they were 9 and 7. Now, as Steve enters a new culture and college, we will be closer to him. And health. Though Don is doing well since being ill last year with an embolism, he does not feel completely up to par. We will appreciate being near much better medical facilities. There is a "TEAM" remaining at Auaris and making trips to Olomai. Our Brazilian coworkers, Paulo Silas, Iveli Diniz, and Edson and Myriam Silva are at the U. of Brasilia (the course adapted for missionaries). Then there are two special and lovely women: Canadian nurses Lois Cunningham and Dianne Voth.

Lois Cunningham   Dianne Voth

Newsletter from Don and Barb, July 1987

Lourenzo's family

In our last form letter you read about two of Lourenzo's daughters, Tieto and Kaki, coming to Christ: they joined their sister, Alukusima, who had already made this decision. These girls grew in their faith as a result of the Sanumá Conference. Their brother, Alberto, was the leader of the group who traveled upriver four days to attend the conference. All visitors arrived safe and sound in health.

While Carlos and others continued firm in their choice to turn from Christ to follow the spirits, another son of Lourenzo, José, showed full attention to what he was hearing. On Saturday afternoon of the conference, he knocked at my door, came in, and told me how God had been working in his heart during the past year. He felt that God was working to drive the spirits away from him and that shamanism just wasn't working for him anymore. That afternoon José repented, turned to Christ, and gave clear testimony to this fact before all the Sanumás gathered the next morning.

Lourenzo's family and ours

I believe God will use José's leadership abilities as we keep praying for him. He, his brothers, and father all expressed their desire to encourage one another, to grow in the Lord, and to win others to Christ. Lourenzo and the group at Olomai are very eager to receive more teaching, and we feel that this is an important time to make more frequent trips to them and ground them in Scriptural truth.

As for our family, we have written most of the following to some of you personally and would like to repeat it for you who have not heard from us in a while. Before my trip to Brazil in April, Barbara and I had been feeling that God might be leading us back to Brazil for another term of service. We evaluated carefully both the needs of the field and our own family situation. Steve did very well in his freshman year at Wheaton and is excited about getting back. Andrea has one more year of high school and would like to go to either Wheaton or Cedarville in the fall of 1988. Darlene will be going into 8th grade this year. The girls have done fairly well in a Christian school here but sorely miss their friends and life at the boarding school in Brazil.

So after a few months of thinking, praying, and discussing, Barb and I have made the decision to return to Brazil for another term. Our plans are to be together as a family this summer, let the girls go ahead of us to Brazil in August to start their school semester (which begins August 13), and say goodbye to Steve as he leaves about a week later.

Newsletter from Don and Barb, August 1988

Old Testament selections translated

For the past six months I have been living with the patriarchs and the Israelites, day after day following God's dealing with them in their pilgrimage. Translating this for the Sanumás has been a somewhat tiring but very rewarding experience. This has been in abridged form, and what we have is most of Genesis and Exodus, a few chapters in Leviticus, and several from Numbers and Deuteronomy.

A missionary working with a tribe in the Philippines has developed what he calls a "chronological approach" for teaching Indigenous peoples. His contention is that we must lay the foundation of the Old Testament, especially the Pentateuch, before going on to present the gospel as given us in the New Testament. Several of us here have agreed that we need to give more background so that such concepts such as sin, sacrifice, faith, and obedience can be more readily understood. In the Old Testament these concepts come to us couched in flesh and blood experiences of people needing the power and grace of God. Primitive peoples relate well to such experiences and learn in a vivid manner what God is like and what He expects of us.

For the last two months I have had the help of a sharp-minded Sanumá, Moises (Portuguese for Moses). He came to Boa Vista of his own accord by hopping a ride on the back flight of a non-mission plane. He is working about an hour away from here, but each week he has come in to work with me for about three days, checking over the translation and putting it into good Sanumá.

Moises

Working with Moises has been a great encouragement these days in which we continue to feel the temptation toward discouragement. At this point it looks like our computer printer will never be released. Gold miners continue to flood Indian areas, anti-American sentiments are strong, and there is general displeasure in our teaching anything of a religious nature to the Indians. Just recently the local administrator of the National Indian Foundation, quoting a law giving him such authority, sent out an announcement that in the Indian villages there could be no religious activity promoted by any non-Indian.

Newsletter from Don and Barb, January 1989

Computer freed from customs, Tepequem purchase

It is evident that many of you have been praying these last months. One big answer to prayer is that the computer and printer have been released from customs and are in hand. It has been over a year of frustration and disappointment working on this, with three long expensive trips to Manaus, running here and there, with hours of sitting and waiting to talk to officials. Finally, two days before Christmas, we received the computer and printer along with documents authorizing their importation. On the documents it was expressly stated that this was an "exceptional case." We praise our God who is the God of the impossible and who has lovingly taught us more of faith, patience, and perseverance this last year.

Our last visit to Olomai was a time of encouragement, both for the Sanumá Christians and for us. José is doing well in treating the sick. While many have died in an ongoing malaria epidemic both upriver and downriver from Olomai, all at Olomai have survived thanks to prayer and medicine. Reports from Olomai inform us that Indians downriver attributed the malaria to miners who have flooded into their region, and because of the deaths of their people, they took revenge and killed two miners.

Recently we have had to send two emergency flights to Olomai to bring out Indians who had severe internal infections. One of them is here in Boa Vista now, and we visit several times a day at the hospital, trying to give a little nursing care which the hospital does not provide.

Alberto, during our last visit, sat me down and had a long talk about his wanting a more intensive period of training. He wants to learn to read and write better, to learn the Scriptures, and to be able to be the leader he feels he should be there at Olomai. Pray that he will continue to feel this desire and that we might know how and where to best train him.

Another big answer to prayer is that special gifts have made it possible to purchase the land at Tepequem. Plans are underway to start building there so that soon we can have fellows like Alberto come out and study for three or four months at a time. We need guidance and funds as this project gets underway, and we know that God is going to meet these needs just as he has so abundantly provided till now.

Newsletter from Don and Barb, June 1989

Conference at Olomai

Thank you for praying for us during the days of the Sanumá Indian Conference held at the Olomai village. Because of flu (which hit us, too) and the subsequent lack of preparation on the part of the Indians, we started off rather discouraged but ended up very much encouraged as we saw the Lord take over and work in many hearts.

Another encouragement was the unexpected last-minute arrival of Paulo Silas, our Brazilian coworker from Auaris. He helped tremendously, presenting filmstrips of Bible stories each night, teaching new Sanumá songs, and organizing the afternoon of games.

Visitors from a village four days away arrived first and these followed the established custom for feasts, with the men going out for a five-to-ten-day hunting trip and the women preparing stacks of cassava bread. Some from two other closer villages arrived just in time for the beginning of the conference and feasting time.

The visitors who arrived first were all from the village whose headman is Pedro, brother of Lourenzo. Pedro's whole family are believers and each Sunday, they walk the trail for one and a half hours one way in order to attend the services at Auaris. Dianne Voth, a nurse from Auaris, came down for a day just before activities started to give vaccinations and to pull a few teeth.

Alberto, one of the two Indian "conference speakers," was especially thankful to get relief from the constant pain he had felt.

We met for four days, with Bible lessons in the morning, followed by the big communal meal at noon (smoked tapir, curassow, peccary, and armadillo with cassava bread). In the afternoon, in between rain showers, they played soccer and had one afternoon of contests. At night there were testimonies, lots of singing, and filmstrips.

These testimonies were part personal experience and part exhortation. Dino, one of the first at Olomai to become a Christian, recently had started practicing shamanism. He confessed this and other sins before the whole group, asking the Christians to help him instead of shunning him.

Kuaiamo, whose child died a few days before, got up to say that though grief-stricken, he was not going to doubt God nor depart from following him.

Mitia asked if he could give "a word." He spoke for about twenty minutes, mentioning his past failures but also his repentance and God's forgiveness. To our surprise, he then asked if there were any who wanted to become Christians and to give this confession publicly. There were three who did so.

Pedro

Pedro is the leader of his little village which is located an hour and a half by foot from Auaris Station. He is Lourenzo's brother, and while much more reserved by nature, he has proved to be a solid Christian and gave effective exhortation at conference time.

It was Pedro who questioned and gave counsel to the three who made a profession of faith and who wanted to be baptized. He baptized the young man from his village, while his brother, Lourenzo, baptized his own daughter and another young woman, both from Olomai.

Newsletter from Don and Barb, October 1989

José in clinic, prayer

Along with victories, we have suffered some losses in the battle to make Christ king among the Sanumás. In this letter, I'd like to tell you more about José and Dino, about the depletion of our staff at Auaris, and give you an update of our activities as well as the effect of gold miners on the Indians.

José continues to be an encouragement to us. He has done a great job taking over the small clinic and treating the sick, looking to the Lord in prayer for wisdom and for healing.

Each morning before daybreak he would come for prayer, waking me up at exactly 5:45 a.m. (Not once did I hear my watch-alarm which must have lost itself along with my arm in one of the folds of my sleeping bag.) Here is a sampling of what he shared with God in prayer:

"You are greater than all the spirits, and our eyes are fixed on you each day."

"We have come short of what you demanded, but thank you for sending your son, Jesus, to die in payment for the bad that we have done."

"As Satan deceived Adam and Eve, so he deceives us. Protect us from him."

"We cannot see you like the shamans see the spirits, but we know that you are here."

"Thank you for healing my wife, who was bitten by that snake. Thank you for answering our prayer and bringing Kuaiamo out of the faint he experienced." (He had been "out" for an hour and a half, and the women were all mourning and wailing.)

We are concerned for Dino, the first to have made a profession of faith in Christ at Olomai. Once again, he seems to have grown cold spiritually, and his brothers feel that he still dabbles in shamanism. Please keep praying for him as well as for Kuaiamo, mentioned above. Even after we prayed for him and he snapped out of the faint he was in, he continued feeling bad and allowed the shamans to chant over him. He is a professing Christian, but not too knowledgeable, and very discouraged that God has not answered his prayer for healing.

Three different groups of gold miners have made Olomai their base of operations, even though the actual prospecting is taking place upriver. The Indians are taking advantage of their presence to beg a few things from them and to learn how to pan for gold. But everyone will be glad when they are gone. They make demands on the Indians' time and food supply. More seriously, the Sanumás feel that the miners could turn on them and even kill if they are crossed. One Sanumá came back and told of a miner who had been hacked to death with an ax by his "buddies" in an early morning sneak attack.

During our last two visits to Olomai, each evening as darkness fell, we would meet together for singing and teaching from Genesis and Exodus. Just recently we received a small projector and slides which illustrate the Bible stories we used, and this visual aid has helped tremendously in holding attention. Each slide is labeled as to the verses it illustrates, and we just read from Scripture in Sanumá as we showed the slides.

And now we are into a house building project at Olomai. Our present camp house has only one room which serves as kitchen and place to hang hammocks at night with a small porch which serves as dining and study area. Aside from the fact that these quarters are cramped, the roof leaks badly. Dan and Dave Brown, two college age fellows from our home church in Connecticut, spent a month in Olomai and were the impetus for beginning the construction of a new house. The Indians have cut wood shingles for the roof and are now bringing in palm slats for the floor and walls.

Dan and Dave then moved on to help for a few months in the development of the training center at Tepequem. There have been a couple of work teams which have come from North America, and we are happy to report that two houses have been built.

As we think of the future of Tepequem, and for all our Indian posts, we see the desperate need for new workers, both Americans and Brazilians. One of our couples, Edson and Myriam, has decided to leave Auaris (our other Sanumá post) by the end of this year. The other couple working there also plans to leave at the end of this school year, so that they can be with their children going to school in Boa Vista. So we are facing the *possible closing of Auaris Station* as far as permanent missionary personnel is concerned, even though the ministry will continue through periodic visits.

"Smoke" by Don Borgman, Brazil
(UFM article published January 1990)

When food and fowl are abundant, two routines signal the approaching dawn in a typical Sanumá Indian village. The first is the crowing of roosters. This no doubt alerts the women to the fact that if they do not get the daily cassava bread baked before daybreak, the hungry men will start "crowing" too! It was this latter routine that woke me up—the sound of flat, round cassava cakes being slapped on to the grills.

Lourenzo had just established this new village at a creek called Olomai. His group had quickly put up this temporary shelter, completely covered, roof and sides, by leaves. This gave warmth and protection from the rain and cold, but also prevented fresh air from entering or smoke from exiting. Smoke by night as fires were stoked for warmth; smoke by day as the women cooked. It was in this long, very low shelter that I hung my hammock: low enough to get under the thickest layer of smoke, but careful not to get too close to the cockroaches which carpeted the earthen floor. This would be my "accommodations" for the next three weeks.

The next morning I awoke with a craving for fresh air! I relished the thought of getting outside to clean out my lungs. Just then, Lourenzo arrived with his hammock over his shoulder. Hanging it parallel to mine, he sat down and said, "Don, it has been a long time since you first told me about God as we sat on the banks of Deer Creek, waiting for the boys to scare a deer our way. Now tell me in detail just how everything began and what it was like in the beginning."

I must confess that I had mixed emotions! Sitting there in that smoky shelter was not on my agenda that morning, but of course I had waited for such an opportunity and was grateful that Lourenzo had this desire and free time to listen.

I started telling how God created the spirits. The good ones we call angels, but others became proud and rebellious, turning into evil spirits. I described God's creation of the world, animals, and man. I kept going, describing man's fall, Babel, and the flood. By now my throat was parched and my eyes burning; time to pronounce the benediction and get out! As I paused to contemplate this move, Lourenzo came back with, "Is that all?"

So on we went through Abraham, Isaac, and Jacob . . . and the life of Joseph (that's a whole narrative in itself). But this true account of God's working gripped both Lourenzo and me, and at the end, Lourenzo showed that he had understood. "How great God is! Look how he protected his people," he marveled and then added, "God has protected us, too, in our move to Olomai. I know He will keep on protecting us from the evil spirits of our former enemies who are buried here."

It is at times like these, when God opens up the understanding of an Indian, and when He makes me finally forget smoke and surroundings, that I realize that people far away are visualizing our situation and praying. That morning I was keenly aware that God was listening and answering those earnest requests—that his Spirit was with us there among the hammocks and the smoke of that remote Indian hut.

Newsletter from Don and Barb, March 1990

Dino

In our last letter, we asked prayer for Dino, who had grown cold spiritually and even was experimenting contact with the spirits by means of a hallucinogenic drug many of the Sanumá men use for this purpose. Also, although he had been trained as a medical attendant, he had refused to help his brother, José, in the medical work. On our next visit to Olomai, Dino came to me smiling, relating that he had come back into fellowship with the Lord and with his brother. José told me how this happened. The Christians and some others had gotten together for singing and prayer, after which he (José) got up and talked forcefully to Dino, reprimanding him right there in public. (Although not the Biblical pattern, the Sanumás, Christians included, find confrontation much easier in public than in private!) I believe that it was through your prayers that Dino responded positively.

Dino told me he wanted to take two of his sons out of the village for a special time of Bible instruction. So this week the three of them will be coming out to Boa Vista, and we will then go to our new property at Tepequem for a time of Bible teaching, manual work, and learning more in the line of dispensing medicine. Dianne Voth will be there with a couple of Sanumás from Auaris station and will be training them, too. Barb and I go up this week with Dino and his sons to help get ready for a work team coming down the first of April to put up an all-purpose building for housing and feeding Indians. Looking ahead, there will be some changes and some traveling for us.

Our move to Puraquequara boarding school

For the next two years, we will be living at the school for missionary children where Darlene is right now. Barb will be using her gifts and training by serving as teacher. I will have no responsibilities there and expect to continue on in Bible translation, doing the first drafts at the school, and then traveling quite a bit into the tribe, checking out the translation and teaching the Bible material translated.

Tragedy—Loss of a Dear Friend and Leader

Newsletter from Don and Barb, October 1990

Lourenzo murdered

Lourenzo, my closest Indian friend and my dear brother in Christ, was murdered by gold miners on the morning of September 6.[1] It so happened that just three hours later I arrived by plane, ready to spend three weeks with the group at Olomai, the village and region where Lourenzo was chief.

As the plane rolled to a stop, I knew someone had died. Men and women were grief-stricken, stamping back and forth at the side of the airstrip, wailing, and crying in full voice. As soon as I stepped outside, some came and embraced me (a spontaneous act I had never before experienced). They cried out that their chief was dead and that two others were badly wounded: Lourenzo's son, Alberto, and Wasi, a visitor from Auaris.

Quickly the pilot and I verified that Lourenzo indeed was dead, and then we got the other two, badly bleeding, into the plane. Wasi made it to Boa Vista and his life was spared; Alberto died during the stop at Auaris.

According to the Indians, five miners had appeared that morning with maybe that many lurking close by. The five approached Lourenzo's house in a normal manner, but when Lourenzo and Alberto came out to greet them, two of the miners, one with a revolver and the other with a shotgun, opened up at close range. Lourenzo died immediately with a bullet through his head. Bedlam broke out with the Olomai people killing two miners and probably fatally wounding another who escaped into the woods but who has not been seen since.

No one could tell how many more miners might be in the area nor what their mood and actions might be in the next few days, so I felt it was best to go back to Auaris Station, but I did stay one night at Olomai. I wanted to comfort the bereaved, hear more about just what had happened, and be present if the Federal Police came in to take out the bodies of the two miners. That night I felt like I was in a stockade. There were about six Indians with me, some of whom stayed awake all night with their guns ready to shoot through the cracks in the palm slats.

---

1. The editor was particularly struck by this when he learned of this tragic occurrence only a few years ago, for it had been Lourenzo and Alberto (Komak) who had guided our expedition to make contact with the Sikoi many years before. This crime was only one more example of the ongoing brutality against the Indigenous people of Brazil as avaricious men sought to make their fortunes in gold, whatever the cost to others.

That night I had time to sit down with the family, mourn with them, remind them of Lourenzo's life and exhortations, and that the lifeless form in the hammock we encircled was not Lourenzo anymore, but only his body which soon would be burned. Lourenzo was now with the Lord he so often talked about.

The next day during radio contact with Boa Vista, I learned that the Federal Police would not be in, and so I asked for a flight back to Auaris (the station Barbara and I had started when we were first married). There, for three weeks, at least six hours a day I worked on checking the translation of Old Testament selected portions with an excellent helper, Hona. This young man was a close friend and relative of Ari, who had died of a snake bite three months before. Ari was the most fervent Christian at Auaris, and it was evident through Hona's prayers that he felt responsible to carry the torch that Ari had left.

Each night the villagers gathered for a short time of singing and teaching from Genesis and Exodus with help of slides. On the last night I gave opportunity for any of them to share. The first fellow, Moises, got carried away and went on for more than half an hour. Paulo Ilo then got up and confessed that he had been "swept away downstream" (a new idiom for me, meaning either "over the hill" or "down the tube"). But this confession and following words were very effective.

Satali was the last to get up. He had been publicly resisting the gospel for the last three years. His father, Solosama, is the chief shaman of the village, and together they practiced the inhaling of dope and invoking the spirits. Satali spoke in a very subdued manner for a Sanumá, but even the little kids quieted down as he started. He told of his past and then about the impact that Ari's death had had on him and his father. Now they had witnessed Alberto dying. Ari's father had said, "Son, I'm not going to ask you to do shamanism with me anymore. Follow God and teach the other kids to do the same." Satali now was publicly affirming his faith in Christ and then ending by praying.

My heart, throat, and eyes are full as I write this, so grateful for God's power and faithfulness in crushing Satan's head after this evil serpent had bruised our heel. Also I am reflecting on you who have been and who will be praying in an urgent manner during these days. For myself, I need to be shaken up from time to time and realize that God really does respond when we pray.

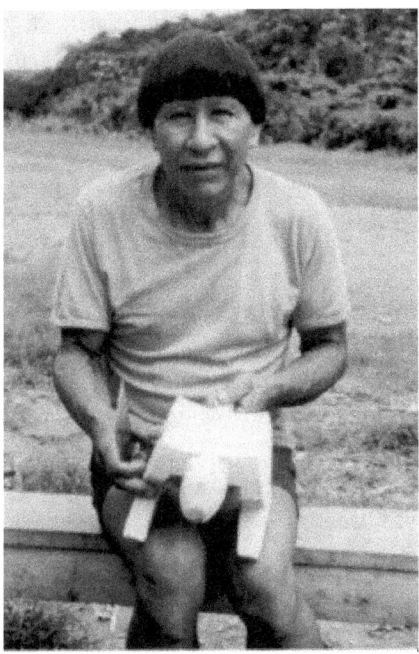

Lourenzo

Newsletter from Don and Barb, October 1991

Lourenzo murdered, the timing of my arrival

I had a flight scheduled for September 4 to go into Olomai, planning to stay there three weeks. That morning I woke up with the worst case of dizziness I had ever had. The room was spinning around, and I was terribly nauseous, so much so that I had to call the pilot and postpone the flight. I was better by September 6 and flew to Olomai on that date, about an hour after Lourenzo had been shot.

The reason for the shooting was the fact that many months previous, some of the men at Olomai had roughed up some of the miners, had taken their knapsacks, and had stolen the gold inside. Of course, the miners were furious, and this was the day for their payback. Even though Lourenzo was not one of those who accosted the miners, he was considered to blame because of his leadership position. The miners also considered us Americans as leaders of the Indians and hated our presence there. I reasoned that if I had been there the morning of the killing that I could very well have been a victim; so I was thankful for that bout of tinnitus which meant that my arrival at Olomai was delayed. A few months later, we received the prayer bulletin from our mission, and the request for September 6 was for the Borgmans!

Newsletter from Don and Barb, March 1991

End of Olomai

Flu, and especially a highly resistant strain of malaria, have taken many Yanomami lives in recent months. Some of these were close to us. During my last stay at Auaris Station in October, Paulo Ilo, on his own initiative, would come over every morning before dawn to pray with me. Almost every day he would thank God for the gift of his three children who were given after the tragic death some years ago of his only child, a seven-year-old boy. Paulo especially prized his little girl, and it was she, and only she, who died during a flu epidemic before Christmas. Devastated, Paulo burned his house (an Indian custom when a loved one dies), moved to a small hut on the outskirts of the village, and there all but hibernated, mourning day and night for his only daughter.

On our trip to Auaris and Olomai in February, I sought him out and he bared his confused, angry, grief-stricken heart to me. After a long talk and prayer together, he expressed thanks for this help. Pray for Paulo and his wife, Ilda, that their faith might not fail.

On the way to Auaris, when the pilot had buzzed low over the Olomai village, we saw that the Indians had not finished cutting the grass and the encroaching jungle growth along the sides of the airstrip. Not being able to land there, my travel companion, an attorney from Florida, and I prepared for a four-day river trip to Olomai, the village where Lourenzo and Alberto had been shot.

Halfway there, we stopped at another Sanumá village and heard a confirmation of the report we had gotten that Lourenzo's adult daughter, Koki, had died and that others were dying of malaria. Hearing this, Pedro, Lourenzo's brother and our guide for the trip, decided not to go on any further, fearing to take his family into such a dangerous situation. So we turned back upriver (a good thing, for that very afternoon Pedro came down with a high malarial fever and the cold I was harboring decided to break out into a bad sore throat and fever).

A day and a half after arriving back at Auaris, the plane came in, and by this time the Indians had completed cutting the strip at Olomai (generously leaving at least a couple of feet clearance for each of the airplane wings). Our pilot deftly maneuvered the landing, and we were able to bring medicines to this suffering group. Just that morning they had buried Lourenzo's bones in the middle of the dirt floor of the house where we were received. Within the last couple of weeks Koki had died of malaria right after giving birth to a stillborn child. Following her, both her husband and her mother (Lourenzo's wife) died, along with two of Alberto's children.

It looks like this is the end of Olomai as we have known it. Because of all the deaths, many of the Indians have already cut fields closer to Auaris and will be moving there as soon as food gives out at Olomai. As for us missionaries, we are extremely short-handed. Paulo Silas and family have moved out to Boa Vista because of educational needs for their children. During school vacations, they do go back to Auaris for ministry, but many months of the year there is no missionary to help the Sanumá there. With the constant demands of the Sanumá, and with continued influx of miners passing through the station, the two nurses have felt they cannot continue living at Auaris without a man on the station. So one of them is in town serving in the finance department while the other is in charge of guest facilities, making trips to Auaris when possible, treating the sick and continuing to train the medical attendants.

Newsletter from Don and Barb, September 1991

Dear friends,

We have just spent three months in Boa Vista checking over Bible translation with four Sanumá young men. After the first six weeks, the first two went back to Auaris and two more came out, one of which was Hona, the best informant I've had. The selections from Genesis through Deuteronomy have already been printed up, and now we've completed a second check on the rest of the Old Testament selections. We should check through these sections one more time before printing and hope to have this done by March of 1992.

Overcoming

With this tragic and devastating set of events, it would seem as if there was little to no future for Olomai as well as Christian leadership among the Sanumás. But God was not finished with either Olomai or the Sanumá people, as the years to come would prove. God was preparing to raise up others to lead this fledgling Christian community. Satan had thrown up many impediments in regard to the Sanumá work over the years. This was perhaps the greatest threat yet. Nevertheless, the missionaries and Sanumá Christians continued their faithful work, believing the words of Matt 16:17-19: "I will build my church, and the gates of hell shall not prevail against it."

10

My Word Will Not Return Void
(1992 to 1999)

> "... so shall my word be that goes out from my mouth; it shall not return to me empty, but it shall accomplish that which I purpose, and shall succeed in the thing for which I sent it." (Isa 55:11)

GOD STATES IN ISA 55:11 *that his word will not return to him void. In the previous decade, despite trials and setbacks, the Holy Spirit evidenced his mark on the Sanumá people. Groups of believers in families and from different villages were now showing the indicators of a future church. Leaders had been identified, and despite the loss of Lourenzo and Alberto, able followers of Christ were being set apart by God to encourage and challenge this group of believers. It had now been well over thirty years since initial contact had been made with the Sanumás. The fruit of true faith was now evidencing itself.*

Finishing their time at Puraquequara, Don and Barb would now return to Bradenton permanently. The plan now was for Don to spend time at Tepequem from time to time in order to continue translation work, as well as to simply spend time with Sanumá friends, deepen relationships, and disciple young believers.

BACK TO BRADENTON AND CONTINUED WORK AT TEPEQUEM

Newsletter from Don and Barb, April 1992

End of time at Puraquequara

Barbara and I are finishing two years here at Puraquequara: a Brazilian named locality here on the banks of the huge Amazon river, just below the "meeting of the waters," a tourist attraction where the black water of the Rio Negro meets the muddy colored water of the Rio Salomões to form the Amazon. Although one river, the two waters go along side by side for miles with a sharp line between the light- and dark-colored waters before finally starting to merge.

Dino and boys at Tepequem

Just yesterday I returned from a five-week trip, spending most of the time discipling Dino and his two sons at the mission property at Tepequem. We spent time going through Genesis, Exodus, and the life of Christ—a most rewarding time. Dino is one of the sons of chief Lourenzo who was killed by miners a year and a half ago. He said he was devastated by the death of his father and drifted far from the Lord, but recently resolved to follow Christ and teach the Word to his family. He appreciated so much this time of instruction and also the fact that we were able to get him reading glasses in Boa Vista.

Newsletter from Don and Barb, August 1992

Bradenton, FL again

Six years ago we based in Bradenton, Florida, so that we could collaborate with Merrill and Louise Seely, veteran missionaries who had worked with the Sanumás on the Venezuelan side. We had thought this might be a permanent move, but after a year and a half went back to Brazil for another four-and-a-half-year term. But now we feel that Bradenton is the place to be for the most effective use of our time in Bible translating ministry, and UFM is fully behind us in this move. Two or three months of the year we plan to return to Brazil to work with Sanumás, checking over and teaching the material translated.

Merrill and Louise Seely

Newsletter from Don and Barb, April 1993

Government official consults medium

This same department head told a friend of ours face to face in a lengthy conversation that he would accept the promotion of drugs, prostitution, alcohol, homosexuality, adultery, and pornography, but that he would openly resist the teachings of Jesus with all his might and would do everything in his power to keep missionaries out.

Between the writing of the last sentence and this one, we received word that a bill to prohibit the teaching of Christianity among Indigenous peoples as prepared by the above-described person has been signed by the Minister of Justice (even though it is clearly unconstitutional, and he knows it).

The leaders of several mission organizations are now meeting to discuss next steps. Perhaps the best would be if it were to be taken to the Supreme Court, where it would hopefully be forthrightly declared illegal and dealt with openly.

Newsletter from Don and Barb, October 1993

Tepequem, four men

This past summer was the most productive and gratifying two months I have ever spent with any of the Sanumás. Four of them came to join me at Tepequem, a piece of property our mission bought near the top of Tepequem Mountain, located just outside the tightly restricted Yanomami area in North Brazil, about five hours by dirt road from Boa Vista. This property is being developed to serve as a training center for Indian leaders. I was alone with these four Sanumá young men, and together we were able to check over the first drafts of the books of John, Acts, Galatians, and 1 Peter—much more material than I thought we could cover.

Tepequem

Each fellow would work alone with me for about two hours at a stretch. They would take turns coming in from outside manual work to work on the translation. I had left the States with a sore back and swollen leg; thus using the pillow, rocking chair, and footstool (a propane gas tank). This was our position for about seven hours a day.

Two of the boys can read and write well and spent their mornings poring over my translation and putting it into better Sanumá. Carlos cut his hand and couldn't handle a machete for a while, but he was able to wield a pencil. Besides going through Galatians, he made more minor corrections on our translation of "The Life of Christ," selections from the four gospels which we had already printed up and distributed.

Various work teams from North America have helped in the development of Tepequem. You can see a duplex, each side big enough for at least four Indians. I stayed in one of the vacant missionary houses, and you get a glimpse of the dining hall (behind which is the kitchen and storeroom.)

No one complained about the food. An alligator from a nearby stream is one of the delicacies we enjoyed. Rezende had been out near Boa Vista for several years and somewhere learned how to cook. It was he who prepared our noon meal each day. He told me to get to the dining hall at "12:00 sharp," and sure enough, every day he had the meal on the table at that time.

Besides a good diet, we enjoyed good health the whole time. This was an answer to prayer, because malaria and flu are so prevalent, and usually in a two-month period like this, one, or all of us, would have come down with something.

The dining hall serves also as a room for instruction and meetings. We go over the various symbols used in Sanumá punctuation. It was here, too, that we would sing and pray together. One prayer time was especially meaningful for me as, after a discussion of God's standards for us, each one prayed a sincere and specific prayer of confession. Confession has been rare among the Sanumás.

Sanumá Translators with Don. Left to right: Sapá (Sopai), Uriel (Honai), Carlos (Kakali), and Rezende (Masiba)

The four men:

Sapá (Sopai) an older fellow who was deep into shamanism and who made a profession of faith in Christ this summer.

Uriel (Honai), one of the more faithful Christians, but who had slipped into "shamanizing" at the insistence of his father, a strong shaman.

Carlos (Kakali), the brightest Sanumá in terms of reading and comprehension. At one time he was even teaching the Bible to his people, but he had grown cold toward spiritual things and had dropped out of services altogether. He confessed this to God, and we trust that he will go forward with Christ as he goes back to his village.

Rezende (Masiba), who had been living a life of drinking out in "civilization." This summer was a time of coming back to the Lord and of rehabilitation for him. Let's pray that he will continue on as he goes back to his village for the first time in six years.

Newsletter from Don and Barb, October 1993

Barb at home, family update

Barbara is working part-time in the church office and will be helping out in the program for preschoolers three mornings a week at the church. She stayed home this summer, partly to be with Darlene, who was working before going back to school.

Newsletter from Don and Barb, March 1994

Translation checking, alphabet, current activities and plans

It is getting close to the time when I plan to go again to Brazil for two months to check Bible translation. I am currently working on 1–2 Corinthians. Also this trip I'd like to do another final check on the books which received extensive correction last summer: John, Acts, Galatians, and 1 Peter. I am counting on Paulo Silas, our coworker there in Brazil, to arrange for language helpers to come out from the jungle to work with me. Please pray that these arrangements will go well.

Computer Course at Wycliffe

This past January I spent two weeks at a workshop put on by Wycliffe Bible Translators. They were introducing us to a computer software program, Microsoft Word for Windows, with special emphasis on applications for Bible translators. One of the very helpful features of the workshop was helping us to produce on the computer screen and on a laser printer the special characters in the language in which we are working.

"What letters do you use for the Sanumá alphabet?" This section needs help with Portuguese lettering!

We've been asked the above question many times. As is true for those working in Indigenous languages around the world, we try to conform the Indian language as much as possible to the alphabet of the national language. In our case, it is the Brazilian alphabet (which like English has the a, e, i, o, and u).

In addition to these letters, Sanumá has a letter which sounds similar to the English "i" as in the word "bit" and another letter which sounds like the "u" in "but." These we write as ö and ä. Also, each vowel can be nasalized (for example, like the letter "e" in the English word "bent"). These vowels are symbolized as they are in the Brazilian alphabet, with a tilde over the vowel. So here you see what letters we use in the Sanumá alphabet. (It took many, many hours of work to set up a program on the computer so that we'd be able to type these out with ease and speed.)

aeiouöäãẽĩõũõ̃ã̃
AEIOUÖÄÃÕ̃

Sanumá alphabet

Ongoing Spiritual Growth among the Sanumás and Leaps Forward with Translation

Newsletter from Don and Barb, March 1994

Mateus, nine baptisms at Auaris

Pedro, like his brother, Lourenzo, who was killed three and a half years ago, is a Christian and also headman of a small village located an hour and a half by trail from Auaris Station. For years, Pedro and his family have been faithful in walking that distance in order to attend the services at Auaris.

Now Pedro's son, Mateus, has initiated services at their own village. Mateus is a young man who spent three years among Christian Macushi Indians out near Boa Vista. While falling into bad habits after leaving the fellowship of Christians and working for Brazilian ranchers, he finally realized his condition and returned to the Lord and to his own people. He has a desire to teach them to read and write. Paulo Silas says that he shows "positive qualities of leadership." He came to Paulo and said that there were nine in his village who wanted to be baptized. They were baptized by Paulo's father-in-law, Iveli's father, at Christmas. (This man is the pastor who married Barbara and me in south Brazil. Paulo wrote that he prays daily for us and the translation work.)

Newsletter from Don and Barb, September 1994

Translation checking, Rezende and Mateus

In Brazil, Paulo Silas, our Brazilian coworker among the Sanumás, had arranged for two Christian Indians to come and help me with translation checking. This was one of the answers to prayer, for I can think of no other two fellows I would rather have had come out of the jungle to be with me for the summer.

Rezende is probably the best translation checker we have. He is a very willing worker and exceptionally bright. He seems to grasp the idea of what I read to him, stops to reflect, and then changes it into good Sanumá. As a result, the corrections are extensive and the work goes slowly, but this is just the way I would have it. I am very suspicious when a checker lets too much of my Sanumá go by without revision. Rezende also was our chief cook and each noon put on a first-class meal.

Mateus is one of the sons of Pedro and lives with his father at a village about an hour and a half by foot from Auaris Station. There is a good group of Christians in this village, and just this last Christmas nine young people who had made professions of faith through their contact with Pedro's group were baptized. Mateus has taken it upon himself to lead the Christians as much as he can. He related to me how they meet twice a week for singing, prayer, and reflecting on God's Word, mostly without a missionary present. Mateus is making an attempt, too, at teaching, reading, and writing. For all this, he and others need a lot of instruction, and we still pray for missionaries who will learn the language and be able to train leaders.

Mateus and Rezende

I believe this summer was a "shot in the arm" for both the boys. They both talked of getting together back at Auaris to plan a time of festivity and Christian celebration at Christmas. Mateus took back a set of pictures illustrating Bible stories which I gave him, and he plans to use these in teaching.

Every workday, each of the boys would spend two hours with me in the morning, and many times one of them would come again in the afternoon. When not with me they would read Bible portions on their own and pencil in corrections. And each afternoon they would spend at least a couple of hours in manual work around the grounds. Then as I wearily went to bed, often they would be out in the woods hunting. (We had some fine delicacies such as agouti, paca, curassow, and alligator.)

Right now I am busy at the computer typing in all the corrections made during the summer. Almost half the time was spent on 1 Corinthians, as this was a first draft and included some difficult material. We were also able to complete a second check on the Gospel of John, John's epistles, Philippians, 1–2 Thessalonians, 1–2 Timothy, Titus, and James. I figure that we've now gone through fifty percent of the New Testament, along with most of the Old Testament selections we plan to do.

Here is an update on the situation between the FUNAI and the evangelical missions working with tribes in Brazil. I preface this by explaining that the FUNAI (National Indian Foundation) is a federal agency under the Ministry of Justice, and all missions working in Indigenous areas are under the jurisdiction of the FUNAI.

The FUNAI has made a ruling which, among other things, prohibits the teaching and the translation of the Bible. In August, representatives of about twelve evangelical missions sent a letter of protest to the FUNAI, but to no avail. The representatives then obtained a hearing with the Minister of Justice. At first, he voiced the opinion of the FUNAI, that the Gospel destroyed the Indian culture. But after the group of evangelicals meeting with him showed how the FUNAI ruling was really at odds with the Brazilian constitution, the Minister visibly changed, and in the end gave the men legal advice as to how to proceed in order to challenge the ruling.

Borgman Family, September 1994

Newsletter from Don and Barb, March 1995

Brazilian young people temporarily "holding the fort" at Auaris: Ademir ("Mimica") with little formal training but who has an ear for language learning. He is encouraging and teaching Sanumá Christians. Debora is involved in the medical side of the ministry. Others, Walter, Rosana, and Rosangela, help with both medicine and literacy.

Government people stationed at Auaris: Paulo Silas and Iveli ask for prayer that there will be good relationship between the missionaries and the new National Indian Foundation couple living on the station. Missionary work among the Sanumás in Brazil is carried out only under the authorization of the N.I.F.

In July, a detachment of soldiers and their families will move to Auaris. Houses have already been built, as well as a small hydro-electric facility. Pray that their contact with the Sanumás will be positive. There could be many negative influences such as satellite TV.

These Brazilian young people belonged to the mission "Youth With A Mission" (YWAM), which in Brazil has the name of "Jovens Com Uma Missão" (JOCUM). They came to Auaris and were "on loan" to our Brazilian mission "Missão Evangelica da Amazônia" (MEVA). One by one they dropped out, but Mimica stayed on, ministering by himself. It is evident that he had a gift for language learning and soon became very fluent in the Sanumá language. He spent many days and nights right with the Sanumás, whether going barefoot and hunting trips or hanging his hammock with a Sanumá family.

Newsletter from Don and Barb, July 1995

Ron and Robin Brown

Back in the 1970s, Ron quit his job in the telephone company, and together with Robin and their three boys, went to Brazil to work among the Sanumá Indians where Barb and I were serving. Very disappointingly, this was one of those times when the government was not issuing permanent visas, and the Browns, after over a year of serving there, had to come back to the States. Ron got his job back, and the family continued with keen missionary interest as they poured their lives into helping Cambodian refugees there in Connecticut while still praying for the Sanumá Indians of Brazil.

Newsletter from Don and Barb, October 1995

Dear friends,

Back in early July we headed south through Venezuela and on to Brazil. After a five-hour ride by pickup from Boa Vista, we arrived at Tepequem ready to spend two months in Bible translation checking and maintenance work. Ron Brown and his son, Jon, were a tremendous help, not only in the great Christian fellowship they provided, but in all the repairs they made on the buildings. Jon got in some time hunting and fishing, most times with the Indians.

Two of the three Sanumá fellows I mentioned in our last letter didn't come out to help in the translation project. I was glad that Rezende made it, for he is our best translation helper. Two others, Kanawati and Cláudio, joined him and arrived in Boa Vista excited to get on to Tepequem. A couple of days before we were to leave, Cláudio said he wasn't feeling well, and he must have felt pretty bad, for he opted to stay in Boa Vista to get checked out as the rest of us moved on to Tepequem. It turned out that he had Hepatitis

B! We were sorry he had to spend time recuperating in the heat of Boa Vista but thankful that he hadn't gone with us. I'd like to add that Paulo and Iveli Diniz, along with other Brazilian coworkers, have helped greatly not only to providing transportation to and from Tepequem, but also in taking care of sick Sanumás like Cláudio who need treatment in the city.

Rezende worked on the book of Romans with me, and Kanawati helped with 2 Corinthians. We went through the book of Ephesians twice, once with Rezende and once with Kanawati. So there are three more New Testament books which have gone through the first checking verse by verse. I am thankful for health and motivation which God gave, enabling us to see the job through to completion. I'd like to have Hebrews, Luke, and Colossians ready for next summer.

Along with Mateus, who was with us last year, Kanawati leads those of his village in Sunday services. He is probably the strongest Sanumá Christian in Brazil, and his life before his tribesmen has been exemplary. He told me how he has witnessed to his father, a shaman, and other elders of the village where he grew up. (He now lives in his wife's village.) Kanawati told how he spends a lot of time discussing the Sanumá creation stories with them and relating them to the Biblical account. His question to the elders is, "Why don't you have any dealing with your creator, especially now that you have the true account which has been written down since time of old?"

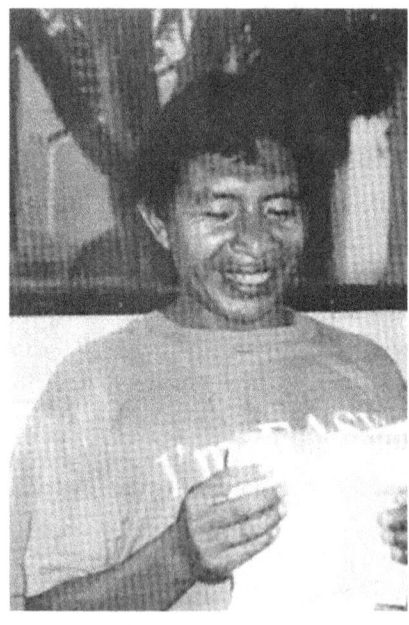

Kanawati sings a new song

Newsletter from Don and Barb, January 1996

Mimica, book of Luke, and the Jesus film

We'd like to introduce to you Ademir (called "Mimica"). He is the leader of the young Brazilian missionaries at Auaris Station. He admits he is short on education, but God has very evidently gifted him for Indian work, having given an extraordinary ability to pick up the language. He spends much time with the Sanumás in their houses and out on the trail, usually going barefoot as they do. The Indians love him for his friendliness, humor, and willingness to help them in their many health needs. Pray for him as he dispenses medicine and shares the Word of God individually and in the regular Sunday services.

Mimica

Our priority in translation these days is the book of Luke. Missionaries working in the three Yanomami languages of Brazil, including Sanumá, are eager to produce a video of the "Life of Christ," based on the text of Luke. Please pray for this project.

Newsletter from Don and Barb, September 1996

Pedro's three sons

Pedro's village is an hour and a half down river from Auaris Station. One of his sons, Mateus, has taken over the leadership of the village and is also the spiritual leader there. He gets the villagers together about three times a week for a time of singing, prayer, and exhortation from the Word of God. He, along with two of his brothers, Enoki, and Jakó, were the ones who went with us to Tepequem. We checked out the entire book of Luke and also taped portions of Scripture. Ron Brown has spearheaded this tape ministry and has procured solar powered tape recorders the Indians can use in their villages.

One of the highlights of the trip was listening to Enoki telling me of answered prayer in his life. One time, far down river and away from medical help, his wife was on the brink of death. He told how he, along with his father and brothers, prayed all night for her while the children, thinking that their mother was about to leave them, wept and wailed. As morning broke, so did her fever and sickness. Suddenly she was well. To all those present, this was evidence of God's power. Another time Enoki's wife and young daughter were spared from a falling tree. Enoki went on to tell how he himself escaped from a jaguar. In each case he and his family believed that it was God who intervened in answer to prayer.

Enoki

Another high point of the trip was getting together with various members of the mission family down there, especially with Paulo Silas and Iveli Diniz, our coworkers in the Sanumá work. Also I got to room with Mimica (Ademir) there in Boa Vista. He is doing a great job at Auaris Station.

After Mateus, Enoki, and Jakó had returned to Auaris, I was able to spend some time with Dan and Krista Brown, who have their heart set on working among the Sanumá Indians. We went over some of the main points of pronunciation and grammar. Along with continuing with Portuguese language learning, they also have in hand the Sanumá language learning course along with tapes made by the Sanumás.

Sanumá translation helpers along with missionary family

Newsletter from Don and Barb, March 1997

Back-translations

This month I am preparing for a translation workshop being held in Boa Vista, Brazil, during April. This will be sponsored by a Wycliffe couple who live in Boa Vista, and there will be Wycliffe translation consultants there to check various books that we have translated. Those of us attending represent the three major languages of the Yanomami Language Family (Sanumá being one of them), as well as a Carib language, Macushi.

To prepare for this workshop I must prepare a back-translation in English for all the material I want checked. After having checked over my first draft with more than one Sanumá Indian, I take the Sanumá translation and translate it back into English pretty literally. (As you might imagine, this does not and should not look like the King James or the New International Versions.) The consultant studies this back-translation and can pick up various errors and short-comings. It might be a verse that was inadvertently omitted. It might be a figure of speech which was translated too literally. For example, in Luke 13 Jesus says, "Go tell that fox..." referring to Herod. The consultant probably would ask if the Indian thinks Christ was referring to a literal animal. If the Sanumá realizes that Jesus is speaking figuratively, then what quality or characteristic is meant? I might have to change the translation to something like, "Go tell that sly, destructive man..." On the other hand, my Sanumá translation might be too "free" in places, with material that might better go into footnotes or even a commentary.

Newsletter from Don and Barb, June 1997

Consultants

The purpose of the workshop was to get together those translating in the Yanomami languages so that we could exchange our ideas of how to translate key terms, to have some of our material checked by Wycliffe consultants, and then learn from them to sharpen up on translation principles. Besides having our material checked, the consultants trained three of us to be future consultants, so that we could check each other's translations. Before the Bible societies will print a New Testament, it must have been checked by an authorized consultant, and this is what we were being trained to be.

Newsletter from Don and Barb, October 1997

Robbed at gunpoint

This last trip to Brazil was by far the most profitable and productive thus far, even though the beginning of the trip was rather "bumpy." Many of you know that I was robbed at gunpoint in a Miami airport motel. It was a three-story building with entrance to rooms only from inside corridors. The motel was fenced in and had a security officer, and each guest had a key to the entrance of the building. So it was quite a shock to be sitting on the side of my bed and to look up and see a gun in my face. He took everything: all my money, credit cards, driver's license, passport, permanent visa for Brazil, the language work to be checked, camera, and other items. I felt devastated!

Praise God that in two and a half days of alternate dashing and waiting, all I needed to continue travel was replaced, including the money which my home church in Connecticut graciously wired to me. I am also thankful that no one else in our party was harmed or robbed (except for a couple of items lying next to my carry-on bag, one of which was a video camera). Ron Brown was rooming with me while his wife and a young teenage girl were in the next room.

Ron and Robin were a vital part of the translation checking time for those two months of August and September. Robin cheerfully took on the cooking for us, most of the time providing also for the four hungry Indians who were with us. Ron took care of repairs and maintenance of buildings and the vehicle we had.

My wife Barbara was able to get onto our computer and make a copy of all the language work to be checked. She sent this to me in Miami by FedEx, and I was able to travel on to Brazil with all that I needed.

Newsletter from Don and Barb, April 1, 1998

The Venezuelan Connection

As you pray for the Sanumá Indians, we would remind you that the Sanumás are not limited to Brazil. There might be as many as four times as many Sanumás in Venezuela than there are in Brazil. To avoid any overlap in translation work and to promote cooperation, from the beginning of our work among the Sanumás at Auaris Station in Brazil, we have sought to maintain contact with Merrill and Louise Seely, who established a station which was named Simaraña. Because of the national boundaries, we could not visit by going overland, but we have corresponded, and now we have moved to Bradenton, Florida, so as to be in close contact with the Seelys who live here.

The Seelys are now retired, but at Simaraña there is a functioning station with two single girls, one of whom is Maira, who has been there for many years and who teaches the Bible. Recently a girl who is a Brazilian joined her and is now learning the language. Also there is a family there:

Ray and Gloria Mills with their six young boys. Ray is an American who married a Venezuelan.

A Venezuelan couple, Hernan and Elizabeth Ragas, who worked with the Seelys in Simarafla in the early days of the work there, wanted to reach the Sanumás far to the northwest, and established a station there which came to be called Majawaña [Mah-ha-WAH-nya]. Hernan started some Bible translation for that dialect of Sanumá, and then a couple of years ago was tragically killed along with an MAF pilot as they were trying to take off from the jungle station. God has blessed the work under the couple, and now Hernan's wife, Elizabeth, carries on there, along with other workers, among them Maribel, a lady wanting to work toward providing a New Testament for the Indians there, many of whom are believers.

This last January a man from New Tribes Mission wrote and asked about what we would think about them starting a work among the Kobalis, an unreached group whose dialect is very close to one we have been translating for. We are excited about this possibility and sending them language material that we have already developed as well as Bible translation.

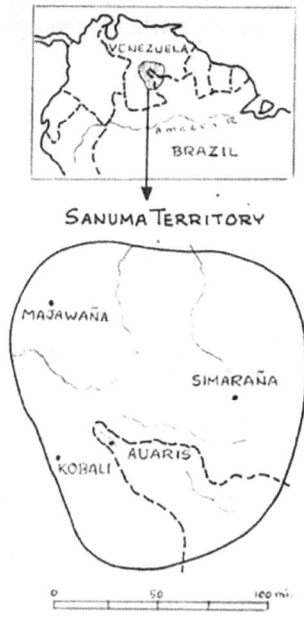

Map of Kobalis in Venezuela

So the translation we are working on will serve not only the Sanumás of Brazil but hopefully also the larger population of Sanumás in Venezuela.

To maximize the quality and usefulness of the translation I am working on, I feel the need to meet with missionaries from the Venezuelan side to discuss such items as differences of dialect, key terms, and the alphabet we use. I believe this would be of great mutual help and encouragement.

There has entered upon the scene a translation consultant, Bruce Moore, of the Wycliffe Bible Translators. He has had occasion to meet with the missionaries of Majawaña and contacted me. On the first of April, I plan to be out in Dallas, spending a few days with Bruce Moore with a dual purpose. One is to discuss getting together with some of the Venezuelan missionaries. Bruce would be ideal for this inasmuch as he speaks Spanish and has had wide experience in both Bible translating and consulting with other Bible translators.

Another purpose of my meeting with Bruce is to go over some of the translations I have done. Already I have sent him a back-translation into English of my Sanumá translation of a couple of chapters of Luke plus the books of 1 Thessalonians and 1 John. Bruce has carefully gone over most of this material and has made many valuable corrections and suggestions by mail and e-mail.

Newsletter from Don and Barb, August 1998

Army, FUNAI, Mimica

A brief report on Auaris, our former post: We'd like to remind you of how different the Sanumá village called Auaris (being on the Auaris River) now is. Years ago we had a dirt strip for the MAF plane. There is now a large Army post with a huge asphalt strip. We used to do the medical work, but that has been taken over by the National Indian Foundation. One Brazilian missionary remains in this new ambience, a young single man, Mimica.

He does much traveling to distant villages not only to witness, but to accompany the medical personnel and interpret for them. Mimica has been very ill with malaria, at least five times recently. He faces loneliness and, naturally, desires a wife someday.

This dedicated young man has been discipling a group of Sanumá fellows. There are times when he sees weaknesses in them, and his heart sinks, but the verse he wrote in his letter, and which fortifies him, is Gal 6:9, "Let us not become weary in doing good . . . "

Elizabeth Ragas and Bruce Moore

The Venezuelan trip is going to happen. Don and Bruce Moore, the consultant from Wycliffe who will also be the Spanish interpreter, will be leaving on September 25th for this long-awaited opportunity to meet with Elizabeth Ragas (whose husband headed their Sanumá post until his sudden death by plane crash several years ago) and her coworkers. They will discuss the Sanumá New Testament and ways in which they can help each other. As Don mentioned last time, we are excited about sending them language material that is already developed, as well as Bible translation.

Newsletter from Don and Barb, January 1999

Kobalis

"Do not be afraid or discouraged. For the Lord your God is with you wherever you go." (Josh 1:9) These words encouraged me as I boarded the bus in Boa Vista, Brazil, and started the long trip to Venezuela, where eventually I would meet up with a New Tribes missionary and contact a very primitive, isolated tribe, the Kobalis. I wasn't feeling well, was fearing the possibility of getting malaria, and wondering if my heart could take climbing the hills.

As it turned out, the situation was much easier than I had anticipated. In charge of the trip was Simun Tuni, a rugged missionary from the Faroese Islands who works with New Tribes Mission among the Yanomamis on a base called Parima. (Thirty-seven years ago the Brazilian Air Force, thinking this was Brazil, opened an airstrip there, and I had been a part of that operation! Today in that spot there is a thriving Indigenous church.) Years before Simun had visited the Kobalis, had found a natural clearing in the jungle, and had made an airstrip. Six months ago the grass was cut again in preparation for our coming. So in twentieth century style, we strapped ourselves into the small Cessna plane, flew high above the jungle, circled the Kobali village (three hours by foot from the airstrip), and then landed on the three-hundred-yard, bumpy strip. Fortunately the Indians ran to the strip and met us there where a little hut already had been built. So we didn't have to labor walking over the hills. And there were no mosquitoes or malaria. Just the kind of life I remembered from my early days among the Yanomami—living with people in an environment of dirt, smoke, and smells. There were no mosquitoes but millions of pesky gnats which were curious to find out the inner workings of our ears, eyes, and noses.

My Word Will Not Return Void (1992 to 1999)

Kobali children and Don

The purpose for the trip was to find out what the Kobali language was like, whether or not it was close to the Sanumá dialect of Yanomami. We concluded that while there were many similarities, that there was enough difference to warrant a missionary team going in to learn the language and minister to this group.

Newsletter from Don and Barb, May 1999

Translation checking at Tepequem with Ron and Robin Brown

It was evident that God was with us in the planning and carrying out of another Sanumá Bible translation session held at Tepequem during the last part of January, all of February, and the first part of March. The three Sanumás, Shileno, Cláudio, and Manu, all received authorization to come out of the tribe to help us in this project. Ron and Robin Brown again were an invaluable part of our team, as Robin took over the kitchen and Ron, the maintenance.

Sanumá translation checkers (left to right: Shileno, Cláudio, and Manu)

Ron and Robin Brown

Each of the Sanumá men are Christians, from three different villages, and each has shown himself to be a steadfast follower of Christ. Shileno is definitely the leader of the believers and is respected by all. He was both enthusiastic and conscientious as a language helper, giving me pointers that I had never received before. And he spurred the other two on. I heard him telling them, "Put all you have into this work; it's not going to benefit Don, it is going to benefit *us*." This was the first time these men have worked with me, and they proved to be excellent.

We checked over the books of Acts, Philippians, Colossians, as well as 1–2 Timothy. I have put all these corrections into the computer and printed out the revised copies, photocopied them, and bound them so that there are sixteen sets to be sent to Brazil and one to Venezuela. We are trusting that they will be well used and that there will be further feedback before the final printing of the New Testament.

Consultants still need to go over the other books of the New Testament, and I still have Matthew and Revelation to translate in first draft form.

Retrospection—God's Faithfulness

God had proved his faithfulness to his people among the Sanumás. After the tragic loss of Lourenzo and Alberto, as well as the possible failure of Olomai as a viable Sanumá village, new leaders appeared and Olomai was reestablished. With Don's ongoing visits to work with Sanumá volunteers at Tepequem, the translation of God's word in Sanumá would continue toward the goal of publishing a Sanumá Bible.

11

The Fruit of Their Labor
(2000 to 2018)

"You shall eat the fruit of the labor of your hands; you shall be blessed, and it shall be well with you." (Ps 128:2)

Don's primary focus from the beginning of his work at Auaris was to put the Word of God into Sanumá. With ongoing efforts at both Olomai and Tepequem over the years, that goal was being realized, despite attempts within the Brazilian government and others to thwart that objective. By 2006 and 2007 the translation was accomplished, with the help of Sanumá individuals who were eager to participate. It had been over forty years since Don and Barb first settled down at Auaris. What a wonderful milestone that must have been to observe and commemorate!

Ongoing Translation Work
and Changes Reflected Upon

Newsletter from Don and Barb, April 2000

Since the Mission sold the property at Tepequem,[1] we had to think about another venue, and we ended up at Serra Grande, a little farm owned by the

---

1. "Tepequem had been purchased with the purpose of having a place to set up a school for Brazilian missionary kids and also for a place to work with native language helpers. It turned out that the Brazilians did not want to set up this school and also the property was no longer used for translators to work with language helpers. The Mission was just paying to maintain the property, so it was decided to sell it." Don Borgman in email to editor, April 18, 2022.

Mission and used as a Bible school for a small number of Macushi Indians. It is only forty-five minutes by road from Boa Vista and located near the base of the mountain which is named Serra Grande. The Bible school is headed up by two nurses, so we were in good hands, medically. The Macushi students were on vacation, so there was plenty of room for us. A resident Macushi older couple helped us tremendously as the man oversaw the Sanumá men as they worked cutting down high growth in the pasture, and his wife worked hard with her two daughters putting on great meals for us in the dining hall. Every day we had rice, beans, lettuce, tomatoes, fresh milk, and clabber. The Sanumá men hunted and brought in two big peccaries, an alligator, a paca, several agoutis, and three types of monkeys. However, there were some times when we had to resort to plain old beef!

Each day I would work with the men individually, having a two-hour session with each of them. We finished checking the first drafts of Matthew and Revelation and revised Ephesians, James, Philemon, and Jude.

When not working with me, the fellows worked outside and also spent a couple of hours doing some editorial work on their own, reading and checking over a volume of Old Testament selections. At night, after supper, we would go over their corrections for about an hour. We all felt a lot better about some of the key terms of Scripture that we changed or modified, terms like "Holy Spirit," "priest," "angel," and "believe." Some of these terms cannot be translated by one or two words but have to be described by a phrase as in the word "priest." What is the function of a priest? Here are some phrases we thought about:

1. One who talks to God for others
2. One who causes people to come to God
3. One who works in the temple
4. One who presents people's offerings/debts to God
5. One who causes people to be friends with God

Well, we chose number 4 and, in some instances, have used number 3.

The Fruit of Their Labor (2000 to 2018)

Newsletter from Don and Barb, August 2000

Shileno,[2] Genesis brought new life

"I dreamed that one of my friends asked to borrow my Bible. I was reluctant to do so, but when he promised to give it back, I gave it to him. He took it away, and to my dismay, my Bible disappeared even though I searched for it. On another night I dreamed that I was carrying my Scripture booklets in a backpack when someone from behind shot and ruined them. When I woke, I pondered the meaning of the dreams and thought that maybe this is what is going to happen to me. Because I am holding on to God's Word, Satan wants to cause me to suffer. And this is just what came to pass. Some of my tribespeople, one in particular, nailed me and just about convinced me that God's Word was not true and that what I was doing was wrong and futile. Besides, I felt I was the only one up there at Auaris really following the Lord. Why go on this way? I was at the point of giving it all up when I received word that Don wanted me to come out and help in translation work. I didn't want to, but I went. Part of our work was to read through Genesis on our own and make corrections. As I read the story of Adam and Eve, I realized that Satan was the same right from the beginning. He deceived the first couple, and he wants to deceive us today. It was through reading this account that I got turned around in my thinking and was strengthened in my heart to follow the Lord against all opposition."

Shileno

2. Shileno is one of the Sanumá men who would come to help with translation work at Serra Grande. This is his testimony as to why he wanted to help with the work.

Ademir (Mimica) and Lucelene (Lene) are married

Christian Indians, along with many of us, had been praying that Mimica would find a wife to join him and who might share in his burning desire to serve among the Sanumá Indians. After almost ten years of Mimica's serving as a single man, God answered that prayer, and in January we had the privilege of attending the wedding of Mimica and Lene. They are living in Boa Vista where Mimica is taking a one-year nursing course and where Lene is finishing up her last year at the university. They visit the twenty-one Sanumás who are in the city for six months being treated for tuberculosis. After this year, the couple will go for a one-year training course in anthropology and Bible before entering the Sanumá work again.

Mimica and Lene

Newsletter from Don and Barb, March 2001

On this last trip to Brazil (end of January till the beginning of March) it hit me what drastic changes had taken place since Barb and I started ministry together among the Sanumá Indians in a way-off corner of North Brazil. In this letter I'd like to share just some of those changes.

Changes in Boa Vista

The base of operations for our jungle stations is Boa Vista, a town of under five thousand people when we first arrived there in the early 1960s. You could count on one hand the number of cars that traveled the dirt streets.

Water came in a truck, and the town generators churned out electricity about four hours a day. Once a week, meat would arrive, and we would have to get up at 4:00 a.m. to go to the open market to get it. Then there were the bread lines each day. Vegetables were grown by a few Japanese immigrants out past the edge of town, and that's where we went to get them. Today, Boa Vista is home to over a quarter of a million people. The roads are paved, and traffic can be wild. There is running water which passes through a purifying plant and electricity is around-the-clock. Supermarkets compare favorably to the ones in the States.

Changes in our Mission

We started out with about twenty North American missionaries, and now we are more than twice that size with well over half being Brazilians. The president, vice-president, and first treasurer are all Brazilians.

Changes in Auaris Mission Station

The Indians had hacked out a small jungle airstrip in preparation for our arrival in the four-seater Missionary Aviation Fellowship plane. We were isolated from the outside world, with three hundred miles separating us from the nearest town, Boa Vista. Now at Auaris there is a detachment of soldiers and their wives living by the side of an asphalted airstrip twelve football fields in length. At the other end of the strip are headquarters for National Indian Foundation personnel. And in the middle are twenty health workers from a non-governmental organization called "Urihi," which in Yanomami means "Forest" or "Region." These workers fan out over most of the Sanumá territory in Brazil.

Changes in the Sanumá Indians of Brazil

The population has increased from five hundred to one thousand four hundred, and there are roughly twice this number in Venezuela. The acquisition of goods from the outside world has been notable: aluminum pots, machetes, axes, fishhooks, cloth, and clothes, along with some new customs such as haircutting for the men. Spiritually, while we have desired more rapid change, we have seen many lives transformed. I think of the four men who were with us for Bible translation checking in February. All of them can read and write and have an earnest desire to have the Word of God in their own language. Each one of them grew up from infancy hearing the incessant chanting of their fathers who were shamans. Now these sons are saying that their "eyes are fixed on Christ" and not on the spirits. Moises told me that when he would wake up at various hours during the night, he could hear Paulo Ilo praying in the next room. This inner change has shown itself in social behavior. Rezende was telling us that because of Christ, they don't get into brawls in which heads would be cut open and arms would be broken with blows of clubs. "Look at us," he said, "We don't have deep scars on our scalps and go around with crooked arms like those without Christ!"

Changes in the Sanumá Bible Translation

It wasn't too long ago that I reported having completed all the New Testament books in rough draft form. Sanumás have gone over all these at least one time to improve the way the Sanumá language is expressed in the translation. But there are other steps in the translation process which take up a lot of time and effort. One of these steps is to produce a translation of Sanumá back into English, so that a translation consultant can carefully check each verse to look for items like omissions, inconsistencies, a translation which might be too "free," and so on. In producing what we call this back-translation, I myself go carefully through each verse, often making revisions before the translation goes to the consultant. After the consultant sends back corrections and suggestions, I redo the necessary sections and then take the new draft down to Brazil to be checked again by Sanumás. This is what I did this last trip, making a (near) final check on the Corinthian letters, Hebrews, Galatians, and James. Now I am putting them into the form of booklets and will send them to Brazil for use among the Indians and missionaries.

Another change had to do with a tricky vowel in Sanumá. There were many words which we were writing with an "e" which the newer generation of Sanumás were insisting should be written with what is symbolized in Sanumá as "ä," a vowel very close to the sound of "e." So after a long council meeting with the four language helpers we had with us (and at first there was disagreement among them), we decided to write many common words with this different vowel. Now the Bible material we have formerly sent out must be reprinted.

The Unchanging Christ

In the midst of a myriad of changes, we run the race with patience and endurance, keeping our eyes fixed on Jesus who (in the Sanumá translation) "is the same now as he always was, and who will forever be the same as he is now." (Heb 13:8)

Newsletter from Don and Barb, February 2004

In one sense my whole year here at the desk and computer is a preparation for the month or so I spend with the Sanumá Indians who check over the work done here at home. My last trip to Brazil started the end of December and ended the first part of March with many people, missionaries and Indians alike, cooperating to make the trip a success.

Meeting with (left to right) Carlos, Rezende, Paulo Ilo, and Moises

Long hours each day were spent going over the books of Matthew, Romans, and Revelation, verse by verse, and we were able to complete the checking of these three books. You have seen pictures of me working with a Sanumá across the table from me, so in this letter I'd like to share not only the main translation phase of the work but also a brief account of some of the other activities that were a part of an action-packed month at Serra Grande.

Missionary Paulo Silas contacted the three Sanumá men who agreed to come out of the tribe to check out the translation. Our mission director in Boa Vista obtained the permission from the National Indian Foundation for the men to come out. Another missionary arranged for a Macushi Indian Christian couple to travel to Serra Grande to be responsible for maintenance and cooking. Serra Grande is a farm an hour's drive away from Boa Vista. This farm is used during most of the year for a training school for

Macushi Indians, and January is vacation time for them, so we were able to take advantage of this beautiful spot with its dormitory and kitchen facilities. All the students and staff from this training center were on vacation, and we had the full use of the farm.

Debrão and Leonízia graduated from the training school at Serra Grande and now are studying at a seminary in Manaus (four hundred and fifty miles from Boa Vista) in further preparation to serve in the pastorate among their own people. They agreed to use their vacation time to help us with the translation workshop. Upon arrival at Serra Grande, Debrão biked a whole day to get his eleven-year-old brother to be a babysitter for their infant boy.

I ate three meals a day with these Macushi and Sanumá Indians; it was quite a change from the nearly non-fat diet Barb and I are used to. And as you can imagine it was rice and beans twice a day, plus meat that Rezende, the hunter, brought in. Cláudio grilled some fish. Cows were milked every morning, so we had plenty of milk and clabber (look that one up).

Speaking of cows, one of them went through a medical crisis and Debrão and the third Sanumá, Carlos prepared for an IV. While one of the Sanumás was with me for a two-hour checking session, the other two would work clearing away land for pasture with an implement which is a cross between a sickle and a scythe. They would take turns between doing this and working with me. One afternoon right after lunch, in the heat of the day and when the wind was gusting, the young boy living with us threw away a match which he thought had burned out, but the result was almost disastrous. The grass of one of the pastures caught on fire. Everyone jumped into action! One hooked up a small hose to the water tower. The rest filled up buckets and ran furiously to the edge of the fire. Fortunately the fire was contained before it hit any of our buildings or spread to neighboring farms. It was a wild two hours, and only after it was over did we realize what a disaster it could have been, and that God had intervened.

Midway through our time in Serra Grande we were given the use of a Volkswagen station wagon, and right away Debrão lined up evangelistic home meetings on some of the weeknights. So my Portuguese, as well as my Sanumá, was put to the test that month. Sundays we traveled an hour away to a Macushi Indian village for morning worship.

Thank you for your prayers which had a big part in working out all the details and in guarding us from any mishaps. (One day out in the field, a very poisonous snake attacked Cláudio, but fortunately he was wearing rubber boots which took the bite and the venom.) Now I look forward to heavily revising Mark, Luke, and John along with 2 Thessalonians. Luke is already in the hands of Bruce Moore (the SIL translation consultant in Dallas).

Newsletter from Don and Barb, November 2002

In October, I traveled out to Dallas, Texas, and spent two weeks at the Wycliffe Bible Translators' linguistic center. Each day I sat at the opposite end of the table from Bruce Moore, my translation consultant.

Elisabeth Elliot, in her book *These Strange Ashes*, tells of her days among the Colorado Indians of Ecuador before she married Jim. On her way out of the tribe, all her language analysis she had worked on for almost a year was stolen from the back of the truck she was traveling in. In her epilogue, she tells of the couple from the Summer Institute of Linguistics (Wycliffe Bible Translators), Bruce Moore and his wife (Joyce), who followed her in working among the Colorado Indians and who translated the New Testament into their language. Since then, both Bruce and Joyce have had wide experience in serving as Bible translation consultants. Bruce has graciously taken on the task of helping to see the Sanumá New Testament to completion.

During those two weeks in Dallas, we went over all the comments Bruce had made by mail on the books of Matthew, Luke, Romans, 1–2 Corinthians, Galatians, Hebrews, and Revelation. Now it's time for checking the revision of these books with the Sanumá Indians. Paulo Silas and his wife, Iveli, have spent quite a bit of time among the Sanumás recently and have been in contact with me by e-mail. They have agreed to take care of most of the logistics for this time of translation checking which will be held at the Mission's property at Serra Grande, one hour by road from Boa Vista. We're aiming for the month of February 2003. Paulo is with the Sanumás right now and will be inviting the three best translation helpers I have worked with: Carlos, Rezende, and Shileno. Carlos will be bringing out his wife, and there is a teenager, Laércio, who wrote me a personal letter, pleading with me to let him come out and help.

Mimica and Lene are now in Boa Vista with their newborn boy, and Mimica has already spent some time up at Auaris Station. He wrote to me saying that Shileno had said that when he spent time at Serra Grande helping in the translation work, he "learned much of God's Word" and that he would like to come out again this year and be part of the team. He also said (and this is a first), "Tell Don that I'll be willing to work free if he doesn't want to pay me. But if Don wants to, he could give a few fishhooks for my kids."

Newsletter from Don and Barb, May 2003

Once again, we praise the Lord that the translation session in February and March was a huge success. As in the past few years, we gathered the participants together at a small farm owned by the mission and situated an hour by truck outside the city of Boa Vista.

How grateful we were that again this year the Macushi Indian couple, Debrão and Leonízia cheerfully agreed to use their vacation time from Bible school to come and take care of outside maintenance and the ever-important kitchen responsibilities.

Brazilian missionary Paulo Silas, who ministers to the Sanumá Indians and who is very fluent in the language, came and spent the whole time with us. He arranged for the four Sanumá Christians to come out of the jungle, purchased the food, helped with transportation, fixed generators so that we could have water and lights, and helped in many of the translation checking sessions. Sabá, a friend of ours since the inception of our work in Auaris, Laércio, a sixteen-year-old, and Moises all were eager to come and work. Young Laércio, whom I had never met, the son of a fine Christian friend of ours who died of a snake bite, wrote me a letter from the jungle asking if he could please take part in the translation work. Paulo Silas scanned the letter and sent it by e-mail to me in the States!

Of special note is Shileno. He has stood firm in his Christian walk and testimony since his conversion eight years ago. A non-governmental organization in charge of health in our area has trained him (along with eight others) to use a microscope and examine blood slides. These are taken to determine the existence of malaria and, if present, to classify the type of malaria. Because of his employment, Shileno has not been able to help with translation work for three years, but this year he had a vacation coming and was excited to use this time to come and be with us. One night he got Paulo, the other Sanumás and me together and asked, "When are we going to have a church in our village with a pastor?" This encouraged us greatly, and we are praying that Shileno will be an elder someday soon and that there will be others qualified to join him. Pray that an organized church among the Sanumás at Auaris will soon become a reality.

The Fruit of Their Labor (2000 to 2018)

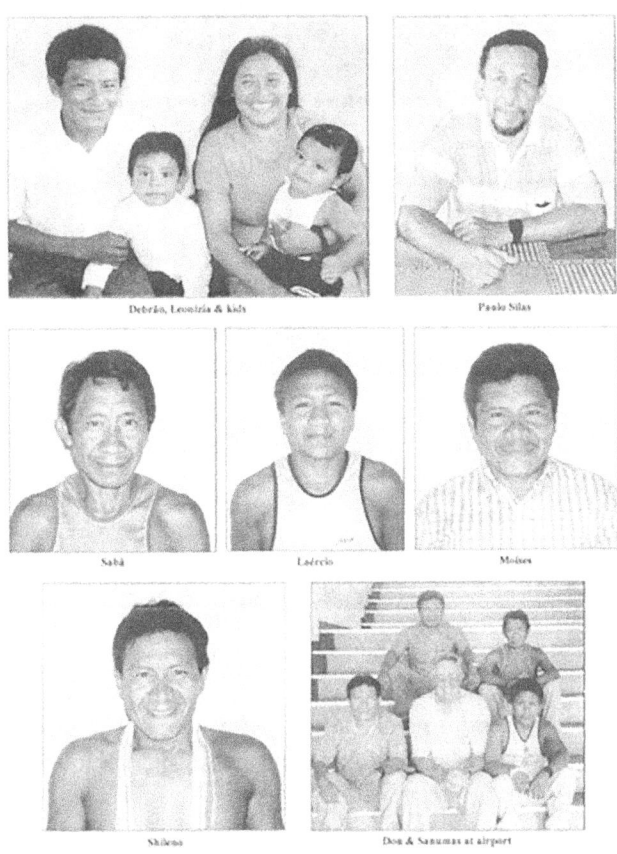

Our translation team at Serra Grande this year

Newsletter from Don and Barb, April 2004

Sanumá Indians are deft at cupping a flashlight between their neck and shoulder, freeing their hands for the task at hand (much as we do with the telephone). Imagine my emotion as one pitch-black night I came upon Holeto reading and underlining his Scripture booklet by using his flashlight in this way. He and three other Sanumás manifested enthusiasm as they spent January and part of February working with Paulo Silas and me in the job of revising books of the Sanumá New Testament.

Holeto reading Scripture in the dark

We were able to check over the gospels of Mark and John and did further revisions in Paul's epistles to the Thessalonians, to Timothy and Titus, and in 1 Peter. We also spent profitable time teaching, answering their questions, and praying together. The Sanumás initiated a discussion in which they expressed their desire to build a church building when they returned to their village. They do realize that the real "church" is a body of believers and that this body needs leaders. This is an urgent prayer request: that there would be Sanumá Christians who meet the Biblical qualifications for church leadership.

God has answered your prayers in leading back to Auaris Station Mimica, Lene, and their small son, Thalles. They have recently built a house next to the Sanumá village and just this last weekend have slept in it for the first time. Paulo Silas and his wife, Iveli, also go to Auaris and minister there for periods of a month or two at a time. While Paulo and I were out near Boa Vista engaged in translation checking, Mimica and his wife were hosting four prospective new workers for our mission. One couple showed keen interest in working permanently among the Sanumás at Auaris Station, and we do pray that this might become a reality.

Paulo and Iveli

This latest trip to Brazil was not without its adventures. The stretch from interior Venezuela to Boa Vista, Brazil was a thirteen-hour bus trip, or it should have been. On the way down there was political unrest in the northern state of Brazil, and the protesting group had set up three barricades at different points with the barricades made up of piles of tires and semi-trucks parked crossways. Starting at the border of Brazil, no vehicles could get through, but pedestrians could. So those of us intent on going on dragged our baggage through the barricades and took taxis and hitchhiked our way to our destination, paying our drivers, of course. And then there was an unusual episode on the way back. All of us got off the bus to stamp our passports at the Venezuela border, leaving our baggage on the bus for this short stop. Imagine my dismay when I came out of the police station (I was the last one in line) and found that the bus had gone on without me, leaving me without my baggage, including a month's worth of translation work. The good news was that the passing taxi I quickly hopped into overtook the bus in twenty minutes at the point where the bus had to stop for fuel.

Newsletter from Don and Barb, September 2004

Couples at Auaris

Two Brazilian couples presently are at Auaris Station serving the Sanumás (part of the Yanomami language family.) Mimica, Lene, and their young boy Thalles are now living in the house they have just built, and Paulo and Iveli are also there on one of their many extended stays during the year. Their main concern is that of making disciples and training leaders who will lead the Sanumá church in that area.

During this trip, Paulo will be arranging for two Sanumá men to come out to Boa Vista to spend three weeks in another Bible translation checking session with me. I'll be leaving October 22 and coming back November 19. Since April of this year, I have done a back-translation into English of the Sanumá translation of the Gospel of John, 2 Thessalonians, Titus, 1–2 Peter, and the last two epistles of John. These have been checked over by my translation consultant with Wycliffe Bible Translators, and now I'll be taking them to Brazil for a final checking with the Sanumás.

Newsletter from Don and Barb, January 2005

Contact with Sanumás in B. V.

The new name of our mission, Crossworld, formerly UFM International, reflects more clearly to the public the same purpose we have always had, that of working together to take the message of the cross of Christ to the world.

Once again God gave us an excellent time of Bible translation checking with Sanumás in Brazil in October and November of 2004. The two best language helpers, Carlos and Rezende, were able to come out from the tribe to Boa Vista where the work sessions were held. Also our Brazilian colleague, Paulo Silas, participated every day and all day, giving many valuable suggestions. We went through the remaining books of the New Testament that needed review: John, 2 Thessalonians, Titus, 1–2 Peter, and two epistles of John. The two Sanumás also read through Acts on their own, penciling in corrections and improvements.

While working in the city, I had the surprise opportunity of getting together with two other Sanumá Christian men, Mateus and Shileno, who had been flown out to Boa Vista on a government plane so that they could take a refresher course in reading slides under a microscope. These fellows are paid by the government to do this work back in their villages, with the main purpose of reading blood slides to detect the possible presence of malaria. I was thrilled as I listened to Mateus, leader of a village an hour and a half downstream from the main Auaris Station. He and his brothers had spent three months with me a few years ago, helping in the translation of New Testament books. Mateus told of a two-year period of drifting away from fellowship with the Lord, and how that recently he had repented and decided to become a faithful follower of Christ. His brothers and other villagers had

The Fruit of Their Labor (2000 to 2018)

made the same decision and were now meeting together a couple of times a week for times of worship. One of the brothers, Renato, has composed eight songs on his own, something we had long desired to see happen. For the last months, Brazilian missionary Mimica has been going down from the post at Auaris to teach and counsel them.

The Christians at Mateus' village asked to have a baptismal service, and this took place the last part of November. Mimica phoned me all the way from Brazil and excitedly related what had happened. Ten Sanumás were baptized, and as meaningful as this event was, the focal point of the day turned out to be the celebration of the Lord's Supper, in which a Sanumá, Renato, took the lead in distributing the elements and explaining carefully and powerfully what it means to "eat his flesh and drink his blood."

Newsletter from Don and Barb, July 2005

What made me look up the phrase "give up" in the NIV Bible this morning? Maybe I needed encouragement to keep plugging on in the project of getting God's Word into the Sanumá language. "Jesus told his disciples . . . that they should always pray and not give up." (Luke 18:1) The Apostle Paul exhorts us: "Let us not become weary in doing good, for at the proper time we will reap a harvest if we do not give up." Perhaps now, more than ever before, we feel the need of your prayers; we are told by many Bible translators that the last stretch is the most difficult of all and a time at which Satan's attacks are most felt.

Here is some good news to encourage us all: during my recent trip to Dallas, my Bible translation consultant, Bruce Moore, checked over the last books of the Sanumá New Testament. But this isn't the end; I'll still need to get together with Sanumás to check over the corrections made at that checking time in Dallas. Also, I've been strongly advised to compose an introduction for each book, which is more work that will need to be checked over by both consultant and Sanumás.

Then there is a myriad of checks to be made before publication can take place, and I've obtained special software put out by the United Bible Societies to make this process both easier and more thorough. There is lots of mechanical work, such as checking chapter and verse numbers, spelling, and punctuation (for example, quotation marks and quotations within quotations which are abundant in Sanumá). Another area for verification is that of "key terms." Have I been consistent in translating terms like "believe," "repent," and "priest"?

Another item of good news is that the Jesus Film Project is underway. The manuscript for this took over three months to translate, with the material coming mainly from the book of Luke. Care had to be taken to fit each translation in the time slot allotted. I've sent this manuscript to Mimica in Brazil, and he will be working with various Sanumás who will be doing the narration which will be dubbed into the film. Two professionals will be coming up from South Brazil to work on this. This is going to be a huge effort on Mimica's part, so please pray for him.

The Word of God in Sanumá!

Newsletter from Don and Barb, October 2006

The Jesus Film

We praise God for the successful production of the Jesus film in the Sanumá language. Missionary Mimica went with two Wycliffe technicians into Auaris village and worked with twelve Sanumás whose voices will be heard in the film.

Final New Testament Checking Session in Brazil

After having proofread the whole Sanumá New Testament, I went to Brazil last May to make a final check with the Sanumás. I worked with three of them, Moises, Renato, and Shileno, going over the questions I had, and then copying down the corrections each of them made as they read over the N.T. on their own. Also we spent a lot of time discussing some changes that Sanumás wanted made as they worked on the Jesus film. One big change was our name for the Devil. We had transliterated the Portuguese word "Satanás," but that term, they said, sounded too foreign to them, and so we followed their suggestion and are using: "The evil spirit above all others."

Publishing the Sanumá New Testament

Even though we had thought of having the Brazilian Bible Society publish the New Testament, there were some obstacles that led the administration of our mission in Brazil to suggest that I look elsewhere. Wycliffe International graciously took on this project and invited me to come to their International Publishing Department in Dallas to work with Darrel Eppler, the one who would do the typesetting, more properly called "compositing." This process is mostly computerized, and we made use of two software programs, one which had a series of checks for things like punctuation and other mechanical errors, and another which Darrel used in composing the actual layout of print and illustrations (sixty of them). Because of these new programs, what took three months or more just a few years ago now can be done in about a month.

Day of Celebration

September 8 was my last day in Dallas, and on this day, members of the Publishing Department met together to hear more about the Sanumás and to present me with a prepublication copy of the Sanumá New Testament, which had come off their press just the day before. This was a paperback with thick paper. The final printing of the five hundred New Testaments with thin, termite-resistant paper and a beautiful, tough vinyl cover will be done in South Korea and shipped from there to Boa Vista, Brazil. This is by far the most economical way to do it. (Please pray for the printing process in South Korea and that there will be no hassles in connection with importation into Brazil.) After the presentation, those present gathered around me and prayed for all of us Sanumá workers and for the Sanumás themselves as they receive the Scriptures in their language.

Newsletter from Don and Barb, March 2007

Jesus film, O.T. selections

We have just received an update from Wycliffe, the publisher. The five hundred New Testaments will be printed in South Korea on March 30, will be shipped on April 11, and are scheduled to arrive in Brazil on May 11. For various reasons, the date for the "dedication feast" has been postponed till November of this year. At that time Barbara and I plan to travel to Brazil and fly into the jungle village and celebrate together with missionaries and Indians. The importation process often meets with technical hassles, so keep praying that the shipment will go through customs without difficulty.

The Scriptures "make wise for salvation"

In his last newsletter, Mimica, a Brazilian working among the Sanumás, told a most interesting story of the truth of the Apostle Paul's statement to

Timothy written in the heading above. Over fifteen years ago, just before leaving Auaris, missionary nurse Lois (Cunningham) gave printed copies of some Scripture passages to a Sanumá village leader, Passarao ("Big Bird"). He put them into his suitcase (the Sanumá depository of all valuables) but never read them. When his young son, Enagio, learned to read, his father, who has never made a public confession of faith, counseled him, "Son, this is the Word of God. When you are despondent or depressed, read it and it will give you help."

At the end of this last year Enagio, now 20 years of age, gave this testimony, "I got involved in everything that was bad, but I always read the Word of God and discovered that indeed this was the Way."

More Sanumá baptisms

One week later, Enagio, along with his wife and two nieces, were baptized at the annual Sanumá Christmas celebration. In a joyful atmosphere with much singing, twenty-five Sanumás from five different villages were baptized by their own Christian leaders.

Mimica writes that the church has grown and that daily there are those who are coming to the Lord. He laments that he does not have enough time for a more thorough discipleship and asks your prayer for more Sanumá workers.

The Jesus film

During the Christmas activities, more than three hundred crowded around a twenty-inch television screen to see this film and many were moved to tears as they heard Jesus speaking in their own language. Barb and I plan to buy a projector and take it down to Brazil in November so that Mimica can travel to surrounding villages and show this powerful film which has been put on a DVD.

Revision of Old Testament Selections Complete

We've just completed revising, printing, and putting a spiral binding on ten copies of *Selections of the Old Testament* in Sanumá. These went to Boa Vista, Brazil via generous missionaries who were headed that way. Along with the ten copies went a master copy which can be used to produce many more right there in Boa Vista. Each copy has about three hundred pages of text plus twenty-eight full-page colored illustrations. The books include about one half of Genesis and go on to include the history, main themes, and characters of the Old Testament.

Newsletter from Don and Barb, August 2007

Sanumá New Testaments out of customs

After a few hassles and delays, the shipment of Sanumá New Testaments has cleared customs in the inland port city of Manaus in Brazil and will soon be taken by truck to Boa Vista. From there the New Testaments will be taken into the jungle village of Auaris in time to be distributed on the day of dedication in latter November.

Sanumás in Venezuela without the Scriptures

About a year ago the Venezuelan government expelled from Indian territories all New Tribes missionaries and the pilots with Missionary Aviation Fellowship. But there is a young man who is seeking ways to regain entrance into the Sanumá area in that country. To this end he has resigned from New Tribes Mission of Venezuela and has aligned himself with local national churches who in turn have a burden to reach the Indians of their nation. Along with a team of Venezuelan Christians from these churches, this man and his family plan to engage in a project which includes improving the health of the Sanumás along with Bible teaching. There are other means of air support that they are thinking about. Please pray that nothing will thwart these efforts.

Newsletter from Don and Barb, January 2008

Dedication of N.T.

"Now, our God, we give you thanks, and praise your glorious name." (1 Chr 29:13)
 While you were recounting blessings during Thanksgiving weekend in the States, Barb and I were with the Sanumá Indians of North Brazil giving thanks to God for the completion of the Sanumá New Testament and for its arrival into the jungle village. Sanumás from seven villages had arrived for the two days of festivities. Paulo Silas and Mimica, two Brazilians working among the Sanumás, had planned and worked for this for months. These

two men labored together with the villagers to repair the houses which would house the non-Indian visitors as well makeshift, plastic covered shelters which would keep dry the almost five hundred Indians who would come from other villages.

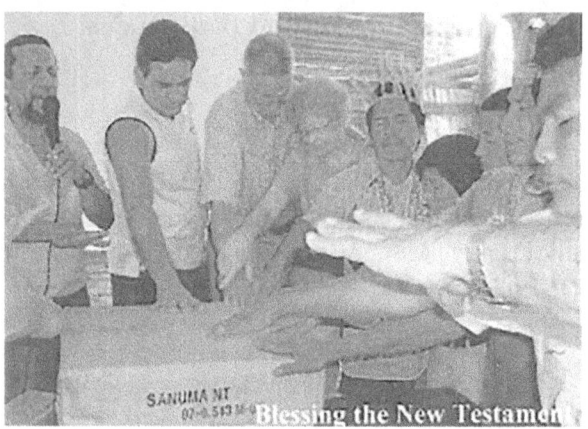

Blessing the New Testament

What a joy to reunite with former coworkers as well as to meet a pastor and friends of the two Brazilian families working with the Sanumás. Then there was the thrill of greeting so many of the Sanumás, many of whom remembered us well from the days when Barb and I established the post which we named Auaris. This photo shows us together with Paulo Silas and his wife and grown son, with Mimica and his wife and two kids, and with our former coworker and nurse, Lois Cunningham. The festivities started Friday with soccer and other competitions. The crowd gathered at night to sing and give words of greeting and praise to God after which came the showing of the Jesus film. About a dozen of them had taken part in producing the Sanumá version of the film which has had a tremendous impact on those who have seen it.

Dedication Gathering with key missionary team members

Early the next morning thirteen believers gave their testimonies and were baptized in the Auaris River which flows by the village. Then we gathered for the dedication of the New Testament. After more singing and words from the eight Christian leaders from their respective villages, I stood and thanked those Sanumás who worked with me on the translation of the New Testament and encouraged everyone who would receive copies of this part of the Word of God to realize the importance of reading, getting understanding, and obeying God's message to us.

Sanumá Crowd for N.T. Dedication and Don thanking Sanumá Translators

How gratifying to see the joy with which they received their copies—particularly to see Moises, one of the most diligent translation helpers, hugging his New Testament after receiving it. Another young man worthy of mention is Kashi, a fervent believer who could not attend the dedication ceremony. He was lying in a hospital bed in Boa Vista and had already been given a New Testament which he avidly started reading. He had finished three of the gospels when I visited him after getting back from Auaris. The doctors don't give him much chance to live because of his defective heart, but we are thankful that he has been sent to South Brazil for further medical help.

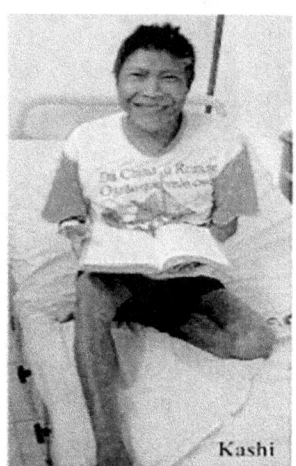

Moises and Kashi

We have moved from Florida to Fishers, Indiana. The motivation for this move was to live near our daughter Andrea and her family, who had moved here from Michigan, and to be nearer to our son Steve and his family who live in Des Plaines, IL. (Darlene and family plan to join New Tribes Mission and probably will be serving overseas.)

Newsletter from Don and Barb, September 2008

Kashi, CONPLEI conference

"A great door for effective work has opened . . . and there are many who oppose." (1 Cor 16:9)

Last week concluded an intensive two-week training course for the Christian Sanumá leaders. American missionary Dan Teeter, along with

Mimica, administered the course which was held in the town of Boa Vista. The Sanumás demonstrated keen interest in learning and showed spiritual growth and perception.

Midway through the course, Mimica and these Sanumá leaders traveled four hundred and fifty miles away to the city of Manaus on the Amazon River to participate in a huge conference (CONPLEI: Congress for Indigenous Evangelical Pastors and Leaders) in which over one thousand two hundred Indigenous people from all over Brazil came together for a time of learning and inspiration. Actually, a whole bus load of Indians piled aboard a rented bus in Boa Vista with representatives of various tribes: Yanomami (of which Sanumá is a dialect), Macushi, Wapishana, and Wai Wai. Just the encouragement through the camaraderie on the bus trip was worth the whole trip.

Praise God for Kashi's recovery—You may recall from our last letter that doctors in the Boa Vista hospital had about given up on saving Kashi's life, but then sent him to São Paulo in South Brazil where he underwent a long, delicate, but successful operation. Today he is back to health and strength, evidenced in part by his one and a half hour walk one way from his home to worship with other believers at Auaris Station. Kashi is one of those who went to Boa Vista for the Leadership Training Course.

I continue to produce Bible study lessons in Sanumá, starting with Creation and going through the Old Testament, giving highlights and background necessary for understanding of the gospel and teaching of the New Testament. This requires wisdom as to the selection of material, full recollection of the Sanumá language, and guidance in making relevant applications. I'd like to acknowledge my wife, Barb, who has kept me going and has done so much in the home and in the office to free me up for the actual job of translating.

A Sanumá Church is Established

Newsletter from Don and Barb, April 2009

Elders appointed

There is exciting news to report—the beginning of an "organized" Sanumá church! We have been envisioning this for a long time and this is how it finally became a reality:

There had already been two special courses for Christian Sanumá leaders. Now Edson, Mimica, and I boarded the small plane in Boa Vista and headed for the jungle village of Auaris to join Paulo to hold a third course. This one would cover the subjects of "The Church" (What is the church?) and "Church Leadership" (What are the qualifications of elders/pastors? What are their functions? How are they appointed?). The twenty-four Sanumás present studied hard for five and a half days, in and out of class.

Bible teaching for the Sanumás

Sanumás in class

Saturday morning one of the Sanumá leaders stood up and said, "We believe that before the three of you leave for Boa Vista you should suggest to us the names of those whom we should consider in choosing our elders or pastors." So that night we missionaries met, and after prayer and much discussion, we agreed that, if possible, there should be more than one leader from each village. We also agreed that at present there were five men whom we felt met the qualifications. The next morning, after a three-hour worship service led by the Sanumás, we gave the group our decisions, and the

Sanumás heartily agreed, saying they had been thinking along the same lines. So, we ended our week together with a joyful ordination service.

The five ordained Sanumás for three villages were Enoki (Olomai Village), Tishawa and Kashi (Maushinya Village), and Piauí and Renato (Auaris Village). The four missionaries leading the discussion were Mimica, Don, Edson, and Paulo. Edson and I were former residents among the Sanumás, while Mimica and Paulo and his wife, Iveli, have lived in Auaris and continue to make extended visits there. Praise the Lord with us for this important step in the life of the Sanumá church and pray earnestly for these five leaders, that they will be faithful, fervent, humble, and loving ministers of the gospel, more often than not in the absence of missionaries.

Ordination of Sanumá Elders

Newsletter from Don and Barb, February 2011

N.T. on Audio

"Faith comes by hearing, and hearing by the word of God." (Rom 10:17 NKJV)

I've just returned from Brazil, where I spent one of the most productive months of my missionary career. I was part of a team whose goal was to put the Sanumá New Testament into an audio format, playable on a device the size of a small radio.

The team was headed up by three young Brazilian ladies who belong to an organization called "Hosanna" in Brazil and "Faith Comes by Hearing" in the States. The Sanumás did the actual reading, the three ladies did the technical work of recording using computers, and Mimica, Paulo, Iveli, and I helped with listening and correcting. At times we missionaries would have to help those Sanumás who could not read well; they would repeat phrase by phrase what we missionaries read to them. There were at least twelve

Sanumás who did the recording. Women read the parts of people like Mary and Martha while the words of personages such as God, Satan, Pilate, and Herod were spoken by different Sanumá men. The more fluent readers took the parts of Jesus and Paul.

There were some tough obstacles to overcome, but we were able to record eighty-five% of the New Testament there in the tribal area. Mimica plans to take a Sanumá man back to his base in Porto Velho, Brazil, also the base of the recording group "Hosanna," where they plan to complete the project. What a thrilling prospect, to get these listening devices called "Proclaimers" into every Sanumá village in Brazil and even to some villages in Venezuela! There are many who cannot read but who will be eager to listen to the reading of the Word of God.

A "Proclaimer" is an audio player containing the New Testament on an embedded microchip. It has just one purpose: to proclaim the Good News of Jesus Christ to the nations. The "Proclaimer" is practically indestructible. It can be played by solar panel, rechargeable batteries, hand crank, or AC adapter. A specially engineered speaker system allows groups of three hundred or more people to hear God's Word anytime, anywhere!

Don with Sanumás working on "Proclaimer" recording

Newsletter from Don and Barb, July 2011

Encouraging news of the Sanumá Bible courses

This last course, in June, was attended by fifty-seven people who came from seven villages. Many of them had come from a distance of one or two days away, climbing mountains, traversing swamps, and even having to swim at times. They said that they "never would have come if it were not to learn more of the Word of God." (In the old days, it would have been only to get medicine or trade goods.) One illiterate man from a distant village told of how he had heard the plane overhead and had come running to attend the course, eager to go back and tell his people all he had learned.

Our mission (in Brazil called "The Evangelical Mission of the Amazon") has come up with Bible study material which is written out in Portuguese and sent to the translators of the different language groups among which our mission works. My role right now is to adapt and translate this material and send it by e-mail down to Brazil. There it is made up into syllabuses and distributed to the Sanumás attending the course. These courses take place three times a year when the students gather from various villages to give five days of their time for concentrated study using their Bible and their syllabus.

The method of teaching is unique in that a Brazilian missionary who does not speak Sanumá gives the course in Portuguese with Mimica translating into Sanumá. The Sanumás have been used to this kind of teaching (and like it, maybe in part because they learn more Portuguese, the national language of Brazil).

This time the course covered the second half of the life of Christ. At night one hundred and fifty came for singing, testimonies, and video clips of the Holy Land that Paulo and Iveli, Brazilian missionaries, had taken during their recent trip to Israel. As they had filmed, they narrated into the Sanumá language. Many of the Sanumás had possibly thought that the Bible story places were all "mythical."

For us, another highlight was getting the following report about Renato: "Wanting to share how his sin had affected so many others, he got up in front with the other fifteen people from his village. Then he shared how he had backslidden from the Lord, and how that along with him those with him had also fallen away. Then he had a vision in which God told him to quit backsliding and remain faithful to him and that He would use him in the lives of others. He did come back to the Lord and went to each one of those people to restore them also. And there they were standing with him up front!"

Newsletter from Don and Barb, July 2012

Trimester Bible Courses

We are grateful for each one of you who has prayed for and contributed to our ministry to the Sanumás, a ministry we now carry on from the States. As we have written in previous letters, three times a year the Sanumá Christians meet together all day for six days for an intensive study of the Bible. They have prepared for this ahead of time by getting enough food and meat to last them for the whole week. We prepare the Sanumá Bible study material here and then send it to Brazil where the material is put into syllabuses for the students. The next course of study at the village of Auaris is scheduled for August 13–20, and it will cover the last third of the book of Acts. The administrator of the course, Brazilian missionary Mimica, will then fly to Olomai and spend August 21–27 teaching from the Old Testament.

New Missionary Couple

Mimica has spent much time encouraging the church at Olomai, a village ten minutes away from Auaris by air (three days by trail). You and we have been praying for new missionaries for a long time, and recently Mimica recruited a couple in their early sixties, Valdir and Vanderly. They plan to live at Olomai and set up a school there. They are in the process of raising financial and prayer support from churches in South Brazil, and this August they plan to go to Olomai to build their house. Please pray for this couple.

Newsletter from Don and Barb, January 2013

Renato, Enoki, Valdir, Vanderly

Our Brazilian coworkers and I had planned to get together in Boa Vista the end of January for a couple of weeks of planning and mutual encouragement, but evidently God had other plans. Just after the turn of the year I found out that I needed a pacemaker, and less than a week after its implantation I developed some blood clots, so the trip was canceled. I am thankful for God's care and for the prayers of many. Right now I am feeling fine and ready to get back to work on Sanumá Bible study material.

Yesterday I had the great joy of talking face to face with Mimica, one of our coworkers. This was by means of Skype which we used for the first time in contact with Brazil. We talked for over an hour, and Mimica had lots to report.

The two spiritual leaders are firm and growing

The two main Sanumá villages which have airstrips are Auaris and Olomai. These are three days apart by trail and ten minutes from each other by plane. Renato is the spiritual leader of Auaris. He has been faithful in guiding the church group, and in the last two years there have been ninety-seven baptisms in his village. Enoki has taken on the leadership of the Christians at Olomai.

The village of Olomai has tripled in population

This recently established village has had a strong Christian influence, and mostly because of its peace and stability, other groups have abandoned their villages and have moved to Olomai. This has the potential of a couple of problems: One might be the shortage of food supply. The other is the influx of many, including shamans, who are still following animistic practices. The shamans are not antagonistic to the Christian way of life and have shown themselves most friendly toward believers. Their idea is to live together in peace, each following their own beliefs, hence the danger of mixing of beliefs (syncretism) on the part of the Christians.

Valdir and Vanderly starting well

The "new" Brazilian couple, in their early sixties, have begun ministry at Olomai. Earlier this month they flew in with a small team of helpers to build a small house and school, as well as to dig a well with a solar powered pump. They will be teaching in Portuguese as well as overseeing two Sanumá teachers who will be helping students to read and write in their own Sanumá language.

Newsletter from Don and Barb, April 2013

Report on Sanumá Bible Conference at the Auaris Village (from a Skype contact with Mimica, the Brazilian missionary)

The first day of the conference started off on a sad note, as an eighteen-year-old girl went missing. Three days later it was learned that she had hanged herself in the woods not far from the village. There have been more than this one instance of suicide, usually because of a love affair gone awry.

Aside from this, it was evident that God was blessing, and had been blessing, in an unusual way. People from many different villages have been converting to Christ through the witness and teaching of their own people, some of them children who have been leading their parents to the Lord. These Christians traveled from as far as four hours away to attend the week-long conference (based on the material I have translated and sent down to the missionaries). These people are poor in this world's goods, but rich in faith. One elderly, very frail lady led in a prayer of thanksgiving at the last meeting and then was observed packing up and trudging off for a two-hour walk back home with all her worldly possessions: a hammock, machete, and a cooking pot with a newly acquired puppy inside.

Saturday night was a high point as thirty-six Sanumás rose and gave their testimonies in preparation for their being baptized the next morning. Among them was a group from the village where a young man Kudumuni lives. Three years ago, I remember sitting next to this small, not-too-attractive man as publicly he bemoaned the fact that he was the only believer in his village. Since then, he has led several of his villagers to the Lord, and he brought them to this conference and had the privilege of baptizing them. He was just beaming with happiness.

Newsletter from Don and Barb, May 2014

May we join the psalmist David, who said, "In the morning, Lord, you hear my voice; in the morning I lay my requests before you and wait expectantly." (Ps 5:3) We share with you two requests which God has answered recently, requests which had to do with the Sanumá village named Olomai [Oh-low-MY]:

New workers move into the Olomai village

We have already introduced Valdir and Vanderly, an older couple who are in their sixties. He is gifted in maintenance work, and she is teaching in the small school. Now a younger couple, Sergio and Nathaly (Natalie in English) have just built their house and have moved in along with their little daughter, Julia. Sergio will be teaching Bible and discipling believers. He also has had training in dentistry and already has been called upon for pulling teeth.

Daniel, a shaman, determines to follow Christ

In 1996 a young Sanumá man who took the Portuguese name of Daniel, along with another Sanumá, worked with me for two months as we translated some books of the New Testament. At that time Daniel professed faith in Jesus, and he was delighted in reading material that spoke of the Savior. Sadly, little by little he strayed from the Lord and eventually became a shaman. He moved to the village of Olomai, and even though the majority there were Christians, he continued in his role as shaman. Now, eighteen years later, at the end of a one-week Bible Study Conference, Daniel asked to have a talk with Mimica (Brazilian missionary to the Sanumás), Sergio, and Sergio's father, also a full-time worker with our mission. For over an hour Daniel related his testimony of how God had been speaking to his heart, of how, in the midst of his sadness and sense of hopelessness, he had a dream in which he saw the nail-pierced hand of Jesus reaching out to him. Also, in the dream he saw God's "Book of Life" in which he saw his own name written. "God has chosen this time for me to come back again to follow Christ," Daniel said, and then told the group that he wanted to kneel in repentance and tell God that he was turning to Christ, determined to follow him.

Newsletter from Don and Barb, May 2015

"... a time to weep and a time to laugh, a time to mourn and a time to dance ..." (Eccl 3:4)

At the very beginning of the week-long Bible study conference in Auaris, a Sanumá man named Piaui got up and said they all needed to have a serious talk. He reminded the group what it is like when a son or daughter dies and how sad everyone is. Instead of singing, they just cry. Well, that is what they felt like with a fallen church leader. He also likened the situation to an old machine that has broken down and needs fixing.

The church leader who had fallen was Renato, the pastor at the village of Maushinya. Recently his child broke a bone, so Renato accompanied him to the hospital in Boa Vista. After surgery, they spent about a month in the government "Indian House," and while there someone put strong alcoholic drink in front of him. Renato succumbed and also became involved with a woman.

Because of this, the Christians decided to appoint four more people to help with church leadership. Also, a woman was appointed to get the women together and disciple them.

After Piaui told the group that they needed their leadership fixed, he continued by saying that they were sad, but he affirmed that they were going to deal with Renato, bringing him back into fellowship, and that their church was going to "rise again." Roque, another leader from upriver, got up and assured the missionaries that they were going to take care of all these problems, restore Renato, and restore enthusiasm for the Bible study conferences. Nadema, the head church leader there now, also got up and told the people that "Renato isn't God; the missionaries are not God. They are mere men who need God!"

This is a cause for sadness, but also a cause for joy and praise that the Sanumá Christians are determined to engage in restoration and to go on "growing in the grace and knowledge of our Lord and Savior Jesus Christ." (2 Pet 3:18)

Newsletter from Don and Barb, April 2016

Kulapoi is the name recently given to a village two hours by foot upstream from Auaris Station. This village has never had a resident missionary, but there are many new believers there who had been reached by Sanumá Christians who live downriver. The end of last year Mimica spent six days there teaching from a Bible study course on Acts that I had translated into the Sanumá language. God used the course to attract even the ten shamans living in that area, some of whom had never even attended a "Christian" meeting. According to Mimica's report, "three of them turned to the Lord, and at the end of the course these three shamans, along with twenty-nine others, were baptized."

In the last year God has been notably working in hearts at Kulapoi. Of the one hundred and fifty people there, about one hundred have become Christians. There is no resident missionary among them, but there are native Sanumás who have taken on the spiritual leadership and direct worship and Bible teaching. One of these leaders, Piaui (pronounced pee-ow-E) sent me a letter recently in which he expressed his gratitude for the Bible studies I have sent down by e-mail. From these Bible studies he has prepared messages for those who meet weekly for worship and learning God's Word.

Three or four times a year a Brazilian missionary, Mimica, travels to Kulapoi and holds a one-week Bible conference in which he and the Sanumás spend each day, all day, studying God's Word.

I stay in contact with Mimica by a free cell phone application called WhatsApp. We had tried Skype, which turned out to be problematical.

Mimica urged me to use WhatsApp, and that has proved to be a tremendous blessing.

Recent Years and Ongoing Work with the Sanumá Church

The following newsletter excerpts relate God's ongoing work in the Sanumá church in more recent years. Sanumá church leaders have continued to emerge. Despite ongoing battles with the darkness of the old ways, as well as personal struggles by Sanumá believers, God continues to be faithful to his people. Mimica, who has committed his life ministry to the Sanumá people, has been key to much of the work in recent years. His love for the Sanumás has demonstrated the love of Christ for his church.

Newsletter from Don and Barb, March 2017

Renato was by far the most knowledgeable and capable Sanumá church leader, but very sadly he fell victim to alcohol and dropped out of leadership and even attendance at the Bible Study Conferences. We believe that God is answering prayer on his behalf. Here's part of the report we have just received from the field: "Renato has been walking far from the Lord for quite a while now. His own people confronted him on his lifestyle and told him to get his life straightened out with God so he could teach them the Bible again. It was good to see Renato once again at the Bible Conference. He seems repentant." And he told missionary Mimica that he hadn't been drinking since last November.

God is also answering your prayers for me here at the desk, that the Holy Spirit would give energy and wisdom as I work on Sanumá Bible study materials. Currently I'm writing up a course on the book of Revelation. Brazilian missionary Mimica continues to administer these courses both at Olomai and Kulapoi. We are grateful for his faithfulness and enthusiasm as he spends weeks at a time at both these villages teaching and encouraging the Christians.

Newsletter from Don and Barb, September 2017

The Kulapoi villagers are in the process of building a schoolhouse which will also serve as a meeting place for Bible instruction and worship. There are no resident missionaries living in this village, but Piaui is faithful as leader of the believers.

Kulapoi villager studying the Bible

Brazilian missionary Mimica tells of a heart-warming experience on his last visit. During the night, instead of hearing the constant chanting of one or more shamans (which has been so common), he listened to various Christians singing songs of praise or praying out loud in their hammocks.

Pictured are two couples who have made Olomai village their permanent residence. Sergio and Natalie are doing well in language learning and Bible teaching. The older couple, Valdemir and Vanderly, are engaged in maintenance and in teaching literacy. Recently they have had their flooding problems with the river overflowing and coming to within 10 centimeters of their house.

Brazilian missionaries at Olomai

The leaders: Enoki, pictured with glasses, does a good job in leading the Christians, who comprise over half the village. Mimica, on Enoki's right, continues to hold one-week long Bible teaching conferences at both Olomai and Kulapoi.

Leaders, Enoki and Mimica, with others

Newsletter from Don and Barb, October 2017

I quote from a letter we just received from Brazil: "We were encouraged with a testimony shared during the course at Olomai. Kashi, a church leader, had been selected to attend a school for Indigenous people in South Brazil. After three years there, he returned home arrogant and rebellious. Now, at this course, he was a completely different person. He shared how he had let his sin grow until he became miserable and couldn't stand his life anymore. He went out into the jungle one day and cried out to God to break him and cleanse him. He was now encouraging others to clean up the first dirty spot as soon as it appeared and not let the filth of sin accumulate."

Kashi recording parts of the Sanumá New Testament

And from the same letter: "Renato, from Auaris, is going strong spiritually again. [He had become addicted to drink.] The Sanumás were singing a song that he wrote about God's protection in every way . . . The song includes how God brought him back from the depths of sin and placed him back into God's ultimate protection again."

Renato and Family

Mission Complete or Just Beginning?

At the time of this writing, it will have been over sixty years since the Maiongongs first built the airstrip at Auaris, facilitating the entrance of Don and the gospel to the Sanumás. And it was closer to sixty-five years since Don first went to South America to answer God's call to place the Scriptures in native hands.[3] *Over those years, souls were saved, the Word of God was firmly established in native hands, and churches were founded with strong leadership identified, ordained, and installed. Yet, the work among the Sanumás, as well as others, was really just beginning. It must be remembered that from beginning to end, the work accomplished was of the Holy Spirit who is fulfilling Christ's great commission through his servants, as He has always done. Don, Barb and the other missionaries and Indigenous believers have been the means through which this chapter of the expanding church has been realized. Yet, the work of the Holy Spirit in Christ's church is ongoing and will remain so until all God's people appear in Zion.*

---

3. For a complete overview of Don and Barb's terms of service, including Don's initial years on the field, refer to Appendix J.

Barb and Don Borgman at their home in Fishers, Indiana, 2018

Afterword

The Sovereignty of God and the Propagation of the Gospel

God is sovereign over the affairs of man and in the expansion of his kingdom. I was struck by two major themes in contemplating this truth in relation to the gospel work among the Yanomami people and particularly the Sanumás: the perseverance of God's workers in bringing the Word of God to unreached people, and the providence of God to make that happen.

The commitment of Don and Barb to their missional calling is a striking example of this perseverance. Impediments to fulfilling that call were unceasing and at times appeared insurmountable: from primitive living conditions to health concerns (both for themselves and the Sanumás), and including resistance of the native people to the gospel, constant distractions of administrative work, the Brazilian government seeking to thwart the work along the way, dealing with and ministering to different and at times very difficult personality types among the people with whom they were working, and the list could go on. It is amazing, considering everything with which they had to contend, that the Sanumá language was learned, and the Bible translated and distributed. It took forty years! Many would have simply given up, yet Don and Barb were unwavering in their commitment to the work. Of course, none of the above can compare with the devastating loss of their son, David. As mentioned earlier in the account, giving up, even in the face of this tragedy, was never a consideration. All of this, as I'm sure both Don and Barb would testify, was not accomplished in their own strength but through the prayers and support of others and ultimately, through the power of the Holy Spirit who gave them the desire and ability to continue on. And all of this by and through faith. They persevered and saw the fruit of their labor—fruit which continues to grow today.

At the same time, this account underscores the work of God's providential and superintending hand. Had it not been for Rader Hawkins marrying a member of Black Rock Congregational Church, Don would not have heard of work among the Indigenous people of South America. Had it not been for Don finishing up his work at Wheaton Grad School as Neill Hawkins was looking for missionaries for UFM, it is doubtful that he would have considered going to work with the Yanomami people.

It had been Neill's vision and tenacity to open up the Yanomami territory that led to the establishment of new mission stations along the Uraricoera, Mucajaí, Parima, and Auaris Rivers. Yet had it not been for God placing a desire in the hearts of the Wai Wais to take the good news of Jesus Christ to other tribes, it is doubtful that the UFM missionaries would have had much success in ascending those rivers and making contact with the various Yanomami groups.

All would have been thwarted had God not brought Colonel João Camarão into the picture to counter efforts within the Brazilian government to throw the missionaries out. And even though the Colonel had different motives for putting in those airfields, God used that motivation, in the end, to disseminate the gospel.

Had God not placed the Maiongongs strategically next to the Sanumás, their former enemies, at Auaris, and had the Maiongongs not taken the initiative to carve out an airstrip for their own purposes, it is unlikely that a mission would have been established among the Sanumás, at least at that time.

Had God not closed the "back door" to Don and the others in their attempt to contact the Atroais, focus on Auaris and the Sanumás may have been averted. Had a young Sanumá man not come to Don with an offer to make recordings of the Sanumá language in order to receive red cloth, so he could gain a wife, it is difficult to say how long it would have taken Don to begin learning the language.

And in reference to the Maiongongs, had the Maiongong man, Lourenzo, not married into the Sanumás, it is doubtful that significant leadership in regard to accepting the gospel among the Sanumás would have taken place. In many ways, Lourenzo became the linchpin for reaching the Sanumá people.

The evidences of God's providential work in this episode of his unfolding kingdom are too numerous to provide a full account. They all bear testimony to God's sovereign control in the expansion of his kingdom, which never has been and never will be thwarted. All of this should not be seen as out of the ordinary in the way God has worked through the ages. From the inception of the church, these two themes are apparent concerning the propagation of the gospel. Luke's account of the early church shows this pattern. Paul's persevering efforts to bring the good news to the Gentiles reads very similarly to that of Don and Barb. As they sought to carry out their mission, their lives were filled with hardship. Yet, they persevered by God's grace. And they experienced joy! At the same time, we see God's providential hand at work through the early years of the church with Paul's circumstances in his missionary journeys, his mission to the Macedonians, and ultimately his journey to Rome itself. All occurred by the superintending work of God, even to placing the right people in the right places at the right time. The history of Christian missions has witnessed the same. Luck? Coincidence? Hardly! All these circumstances and occurrences—both in the time of the early church as well as proclamation of the gospel to the Yanomamis and the Sanumás—are placed against the backdrop of two thousand years of missionary effort over which God has reigned.

The gospel has been challenged at every turn along the way, yet the kingdom of God has continued to expand. This has been the work of God. No other force in the history of the world has had the efficacy and staying power of the gospel message. The story of Don and Barb Borgman, and the Sanumás, is but one more chapter of that glorious story—a story of God's redemptive work of calling in the nations so that one day, as stated in the Book of Revelation, the Apostle John's vision will be fulfilled: "a great multitude that no one could number, from every nation, from all tribes and peoples and languages, standing before the throne and before the Lamb, clothed in white robes, with palm branches in their hands, and crying out with a loud voice, 'Salvation belongs to our God who sits on the throne, and to the Lamb!'" (Rev 7:9–10)

Soli Deo Gloria!

Appendix A

Yanomami Terms and Denominations, by Donald Borgman

There have been a lot of different terms, both for the language family and for the subgroups. I have before me a very helpful volume: *Yanomama Grammar and Intelligibility*, a Ph.D. thesis by Ernest Migliazza,[1] who served for a time under Baptist Mid-Missions. He and his wife worked with a group closely related to the Ninam of Mucajaí and were located off the Uraricaá River north of Mucajaí and north of the Uraricoera River. For the language family name, Migliazza gave the name *Yanomama* for the family name. His criterion was to give a name which was not the self-designated name for any subgroup. Anthropologists and journalists in Brazil settled on the name *Yanomami*, and this has stuck.

Yanomamö has been given as the family name by anthropologists like Chagnon. Actually he was writing about one subgroup in Venezuela but gave the impression that what he wrote applied to the whole language family. My own conjecture about the term *Yanomamo* is that it was easier for publishers to print the term *Yanomamö* without the umlaut over the "o." *Yanoama* has also been given as the family name.

---

1. Migliazza, *Yanomama Grammar*, 1972.

Appendix A

Subgroups of *Yanomami* (four main ones, self-denomination). These are names that the subgroup would call themselves, or "auto-denomination" terms:

1. *Yanomamö* (also called *Shamatari* or *Xamatari*) on the western side, mostly in Venezuela.
2. *Sanöma* (*Sanumá*, *Sanema*) on Auaris River in Brazil and on upper Padamo, Venturari, and Caura Rivers in Venezuela.
3. *Yanomam* (*Waica*).
4. *Ninam* on Mucajaí River and *Yanam* on Uraricaá River.

Terms given by outside groups (outside Indian groups as well as non-Indians):

1. *Shamatari*, given by groups west of themselves. For example, the *Yanomam* would call the *Sanöma* by *Shamataris*.
2. *Shirishana*, name given by the *Maiongongs* to the *Yanomamis*. (Note that the term *maiongong* was given by outsiders in Brazil. In Venezuela, outsiders use the term *maquiritare*, not *maiongong*. These terms have been changed to "*yekuana*" as an auto-denomination term.
3. *Shiriana*, name given to the *Yanam*.
4. *Parahuri* (*Padahudi*), large group of *Yanomam* living in the region of Mt. Surucucu. A distinguishing feature for them is that they use the sound "f" for "h." So, for example, they pronounce "nohi" (friendly) as "nofi."
5. *Maitas*, groups living between the *Palimithelis* on the Uraricoera and the *Parahuris* of Surucucu. (Today the mission has posts with the two *Maita* groups: Budu-U and Halikato-U.)
6. *Waica* (*Uaika*), a term used by *Yanomami* (at least in Brazil) for the people who speak the *Yanomam* dialect.
7. *Jawari*, a denomination for the *Yanomami* living on the upper Ajarani River, a tributary of the lower Rio Branco River. As far as I know, there has not been constant contact with this small group.

Term for people living in a particular village:

1. "-teri/-theri" is an affix ("-tili" in Sanumá). This affix may occur on place, people, or animal names.
2. The "-th" is not pronounced as the English "-th," but rather indicates aspiration.
3. *Palimitheri*, those living in a village or group of small villages on the Palimi-U and Palimi River. (Brazilians call this the Uraricoera River).
4. Some small groups of people of the Surucucu region include: *Aicamteri*, *Rokoteri*, *Hakomateri*, *Wutahaiteri*, and *Mayubteri*.

Appendix B

"Trail Song," by Donald Borgman

THIS IS A SONG I composed while walking with a heavy pack on my back, hour by hour, mile after mile, on our way back from the Apiaú River to Mucajaí Station. This was in May 1959. (The pictured accompaniment was composed by Don's mother, Mrs. Winifred Borgman.)

Trail Song

Lord Jesus, I ask Thee for guidance today;
The course of my going is Thine to impart;
To Thee I am looking to show me the way;
To some soul who is needy of heart.

When strength starts to fail and the burdens increase;
For help I would ask Thee a blessing to be;
For fruits of Thy Spirit, for love, joy, and peace;
That the life of my Lord all shall see.

While trav'ling below in a world full of sin;
My thoughts often turn to the things that are vain;
May self be dispelled, may Thy Word dwell within;
That eternity's values might reign.

For others who need a fresh touch from above;
In prayer cause my heart to ascend to Thy throne;
In heaven we'll praise Thy great mercy and love;
Where all answers to prayer shall be known.

Appendix B

"Trail Song" Music Arrangement by Don Borgman

Appendix B

337

"Trail Song" Accompaniment by Winifred Borgman

Appendix C

Letter, by Arnold C. Borgman

Arnold C. Borgman
Hilltop Road
Bridgeport 5, Connecticut
May 8, 1959

Dear friends:

Through unusual circumstances Don is "marooned" at the Mucajaí station with no plane service, therefore, no way to get mail in or out. We felt you would like an up-to-date report, and this is particularly important as the Indian work is facing some great problems. The entire work is threatened with curtailment.

Don's last general letter was written just before the expedition to the Apiaú River villages. The party consisted of Claude Leavitt, John Peters, Don, two Wai Wai Christians and several Shirishanas. Don had stated that they anticipated some possible hardships, particularly a scarcity of water, as they took this 50-mile overland trek, cutting their way through the jungle. The hardships were there, thirst was intense, but God's deliverances and provisions were also there—just when needed. When some of the Indians felt they could go no further, the party stopped for prayer. Fifteen minutes later they reached the river, or what was left of it in this dry season. Don says they jumped in and drank up half of it. An airdrop of food was made to them a couple of days later, some mail was let down by bucket, but the bucket caught in the trees on the way up and no mail came out.

At the first village contacted, some Indian kiddies took one look and scampered for cover. Later some women appeared on the scene, and after some wild gesticulation and jabbering by the Shirishanas, the women were convinced the party was friendly. All of the village men were evidently off for an extended hunting expedition. Before they appeared, the Shirishanas decided they would rather not meet them. They were also short of food and decided to go back to their own village. This left our fellows and the Wai Wais a little low. However, prayer was answered when the men finally did appear, and there was no trouble. Happily also, there was a man among them from another village who the fellows wanted to contact, and he acted as a guide.

These Indians along the Apiaú were quite different from the Shirishanas. The Shirishanas wear loincloths or aprons, are industrious, have good fields, and are very friendly. The Apiaú people are naked, have poor fields, and are probably not as friendly. The language was unlike the Shirishana, but something like the Waica.

The whole trek took about five weeks. Don said when they got back within a mile of the Mucajaí station they yelled, and the Shirishanas ran to meet them with a wonderful welcome back "home."

Soon after their return, Claude and Don were flown to Bonfim for a conference of all the UFM missionaries of that field. This was a good time of reunion as well as meeting new missionaries who had arrived since Don's departure. As one missionary had to remain at the station, Don took in only half the conference and then was flown back to the Mucajaí to replace John Peters who had been left behind.

A few days later, without prior notice, the new governor of the state appeared at Bonfim with word that he had been asked by the National Defense to investigate the work, particularly the building of airstrips. No one knows all that is behind this as it is very involved and confusing. The governor himself was friendly, but because of political intrigue and red tape, he had a job to do. Without going into too much detail, the end result was that another official suddenly decided to hold the MAF plane at Boa Vista, so it is out of service, probably for several weeks. The mission got permission to hire a commercial plane to drop three- or four-week's food supply to Don's station and two others, but it could not land, and this will probably be the last contact for these weeks.

Don is the only missionary at this station, although he has two Christian Wai Wais with him. He has been picking up some of the Shirishana language since January, and knows just a little Wai Wai, but communication with them must still be quite difficult. We feel sure, however, that he would rather be in there with them, even with the difficulties, than outside, as he will be able to continue the language study with them while using this to tell them of God's love. We should pray that he will soon be able to give them more of the message of the glorious gospel. Somehow, we feel that we can confidently claim these friendly Shirishanas for him.

Neill Hawkins, the field director, and Harold Berk, the pilot, are now in Rio, contacting officials and trying to straighten out this whole situation. We must face the fact that there are those who would like to see this whole work abandoned. They use the argument that the airstrips are within 150 km of the border and could be used for alien infiltration. They have arguments against the use of the MAF plane in Brazil. There are false stories given about the nature of the work.

Specifically we should pray that all officials and departments involved will grant proper clearance for the present work and its expansion. (This had been previously cleared, but some local officials had started trouble.) We should pray also for the free use of the plane and for two-way radio. Let us remind ourselves that "The heart of the king is in the hands of the Lord, as the rivers of water: he turned it whithersoever he will."

Appendix D

Subsequent Contacts with the Atroais by the Wai Wais, by Donald Borgman

Letters from Don to support partners (1968 to 1981)

DESPITE THE EARLY FAILED attempts to reach the Atroais, contact was finally made by the Wai Wais in 1968. Early contacts were filled with tension, and the murderous ways of the tribe would continue for quite some time. A couple of these are mentioned in the excerpts below. In addition to the desire of both the Wai Wais and UFM to make contact with this tribe, the Brazilian government was now increasingly interested in contacting the group. This was not for the sake of the gospel, however, but for pacifying them. Plans were underway to construct a highway linking Manaus to Boa Vista and communities even further north. The layout of this road would go right through traditional Atroai territory. If the road were to be constructed, issues with the tribe would need to be resolved, one way or another.

In addition, and quite significantly, the Guyanese government was now interested in creating a trail from its territory to Manaus. This would lead right into Atroai territory as well. Since the Guyanese government would use Wai Wai workers to accomplish this task, a door would now be opened for them to finally make contact with the tribe. The following records the subsequent efforts and ultimate contacts by the Wai Wais with the Atroais, which were fraught with frustration and danger.[1]

---

1. For a full account of subsequent contacts with the Atroais, one should read *Christ's Jungle*, by Homer Dowdy.

Appendix D

Contact 1: Indian Protection Service Changeover (February 1968)

Because of inefficiency and corruption, the Indian Protection Service (IPS) has been replaced by the National Indian Foundation (NIF). This radical changeover necessitated another trip to Brasilia recently. Policies of the new organization are still being formulated, but it seems evident that Protestant missions will be affected in two major ways: more open doors and more direct responsibility and accountability to the government.

Some missions which have been waiting for years for permissions to enter some tribes are now being given the "go-ahead." But with these wider opportunities will come greater involvement on the part of missions in the programs of the former IPS: economics, education, medicine, and the protection of Indian rights.

Pray for mission representatives and for the head of the NIF as they together work out policies. There is some fear that some missionaries will be called upon to take over duties which the government could perform . . . duties which could divert personnel from the tasks of evangelism and church planting.

Atroai Report

The one big opened door which concerns our mission is that of the Atroais. We have verbal permission to do what we can to pacify these Indians who have inflicted and suffered many attacks during the past few decades.

It is urgent that something be done this year. The government is putting through a road from Manaus to Boa Vista which will cut right through three of the Atroai villages. Last week in Manaus I talked to the Colonel in charge of the road, and he said that his three teams of surveyors are armed and that they should be in Atroai territory within a month.

Not only we missionaries, but Wai Wai Indian Christians as well, have been praying and planning as to how and when to reach the Atroais. Just as we were thinking of cutting a long trail from Wai Wai country to the headwaters of the river of the Atroais, the Guyanese government has come along to ask the help of Wai Wais to cut a 400-mile trail from Guyana to Manaus. Very remarkable that the trail will follow the exact same route which we had mapped out to reach the Atroais!

Missionary Claude Leavitt will accompany the government expedition down to Manaus. At the Alalau River, ten Christian Wai Wais headed by

Yakutá will break off from the expedition and will go alone down river to seek out a friendly contact.

As you read this letter, Yakutá and his men should be among the long-feared Atroais. Pray for safety and wisdom as the Wai Wais try to lay the groundwork for future contacts, and that in the meantime there will be no bloodshed as the road builders push through.

Atroai Contact Report: Sweet and Bitter (April 1968)

The last time that Yakutá and his men had been seen was at a big Atroai round-house. By means of a signal sheet, the Wai Wais relayed the following message to the MAF plane overhead: "Round-house empty; no contact with Atroais as yet."

The next overflight was set for the following week. Even though the plane circled over all ten of the Atroai villages, there was not a sign of the presence of the group of seven Wai Wais. Concern mounted as the days and weeks went by. Then, toward the end of March, the plane took off for one more search, following the approximate route of the path the Wai Wais had cut down below. Far out of Atroai country, near the border of Brazil and Guyana, the pilot and passenger noticed a smoke signal. The Wai Wais were on their way home, heard the plane, and quickly built a fire!

Just more than a week later the fuller story came from Kanashen, the Wai Wai mission station. The Wai Wais had made contact with the Atroais. Yakutá and all his men were safe and sound, but it had been a somewhat harrowing experience.

Soon after the last contact with the plane, the Wai Wais had gone to another village where they were met by a large group of completely naked men and boys. The Wai Wai men were halted two hundred yards from the house. The wild looking Atroai men yanked the beads from the Wai Wais' necks and frisked their pockets.

The Wai Wais could speak five languages between them, but all attempts at verbal communication were hopeless. Yakutá said that they sounded like a band of parrots yakking excitedly. We had hoped that there would be some similarity between Atroai and Wai Wai and, also, that there would be a friendly reception because of the fact that the Wai Wais are Indians, too. So this report was disappointing.

After three hours of frustration, Yakutá felt that it was definitely time to leave. Ten Atroais accompanied the Wai Wais down the trail. When they came to the canoe, the Atroais demanded to see the rest of the goods, but at this point Yakutá refused, not wanting to part with their hammocks. The

Atroais were also adamant, refusing to let their visitors leave, holding securely on to the canoe.

But, somehow, the Wai Wais got away and paddled up to where they had left two of their group (left behind in case of an unsuccessful contact by the other five Wai Wais). The group decided not even to overnight in that spot, fearing that the Atroais might kill just to get their hammocks.

We have asked you constantly to pray that we might receive an answer from God as to "Where do we go from here?" Praise the Lord that the Wai Wais returned safely and pray for guidance as to next steps.

Atroai Massacre (January 1975)

Heard yesterday that there had been another massacre by the Atroais. Last month they killed six Brazilians. The 29th of December they killed three, among them the big man with the FUNAI in Manaus who has been in charge of the Atroai pacification.[2] I knew this man. It is quite a shock. We feel that this is the last straw as far as the Brazilian Government patience is concerned and that now they'll send in the army to see that the road construction goes through without further trouble from the Atroais. This is only our conjecture.

Sanumás, Atroais, Personnel (July 24, 1975)

The Atroais

In time past we have written about the hostile Atroais who have constantly warded off attempts by outsiders to enter their territory. Six months ago they murdered the top man in the government pacification team based in Manaus—a climax to a series of killings over the years.

The Wai Wais have made about five contacts with the Atroais, but each visit has been for only a day or two. In March, a group of five Atroais followed the Wai Wais back within two days of the Wai Wai village (two hundred miles from the Atroais villages) and then suddenly turned back.

We are watching to see if the Atroais will want to move away from the new highway being built right through their territory and settle nearer the Wai Wai village.

---

2. This man was Gilberto Pinto Figueiredo. As reported in the New York Times on January 4, 1975, he, along with two other employees of the Brazil Department of Indian Affairs, were killed for no apparent reason after a seemingly friendly contact.

The Wai Wais plan another trip this August. Pray for continued safety and for wisdom on the part of the Wai Wais who are looking to the Lord as to the best way to establish permanent contact and an effective ministry among these suspicious, demanding, and aggressive tribespeople.

Personnel

What if the Atroais do reach the point of accepting outsiders and want a literacy and teaching program? We will need additional personnel. What about the work that already is in progress in other tribes? There are four jungle stations, each in desperate need of another couple, and three of them are without nurses. I used to think that with more than two thousand tribes to be reached, we should not place more than one couple in each tribe.

Atroai Visit (December 1, 1975)

The Wai Wais just had another visit from the Atroais; there were eight of them. It was a good visit this time, and five of the Wai Wais went back to the Atroai village with the visitors. This was just at the beginning of this week. No missionaries were on station at the time.

Trouble with the Atroais (July 1976)

Recently I was called upon to go into the Wai Wai village because of trouble with the visiting Atroai Indians, who are noted killers. On June 6, eleven Atroai men entered the Wai Wai village and for three days demanded not only trade goods, but Wai Wai women to take back with them. Finally, they left; but instead of heading home, they secretly camped out in the forest near the village.

One night the Wai Wais heard the "killer call" as Atroais encircled the village. But something scared them off. Fearing an attack, the Wai Wais asked Flo Riedle, the only missionary living with them, to call for the plane so that she could be evacuated. Also, they wanted counsel and possibly some kind of outside help in this harrowing situation. I flew in with the pilots and, together with Flo, we talked with the Wai Wais about the best course of action. Then, in spite of a very muddy airstrip, we took off for Boa Vista taking Flo with us.

Since then the Atroais have left for home, and the Wai Wais have calmed down. But they expect the Atroais to be back in August or September when the rains subside. Pray that God will give clear direction to the Wai Wais concerning their role in reaching the Atroais. They're pretty discouraged right now and about to give up the project.

Atroais, Kashmi, Joe Hill (October 1980)

There are nine Atroais at Kashmi right now, and you might pray that all might go well there during this visit. Only the Hills are there with the Wai Wais. Joe Hill is getting excellent cooperation with the Atroais on the language; this is the first time in history that anything like this has happened.

Atroais Arrive, 92 of them (January 1981)

P.S. I almost forgot some big news from over Wai Wai way where ninety-two Atroais showed up: men, women, children, cooking pots, etc. A whole village apparently has come to stay. This is what we have been praying for years now. I am sure it is going to work hardship on the Wai Wais for a while till the new fields start producing. Motivation for the move might have been sickness and death in the village. Who knows other reasons? Joe Hill has already gotten more language material than he can assimilate. I am sure that the Hills need health and stamina to keep up with things there.

Map showing the relative locations of various tribes worked with by UFM, including the Atrowaris (Atroais)

Appendix D

Atroais (February 1981)

In a sense, the most spectacular happening of recent weeks is the appearance at the Wai Wai village of ninety-two men, women, and children of the noted tribe of killers, the Atroais. This has been our dream and prayer for nearly twenty years. It was that long ago that I took part in the initial aerial survey of the isolated Atroai tribe. It was at that time that two of us, along with Wai Wai chief Elká and two other Indians, made a long trip in the endeavor of contacting this wild group. The attempt was unsuccessful, and the ensuing years saw more killings and then finally successful contacts by the Wai Wais. But contacts were all too brief, with no basis for solid friendship and language learning. The first breakthrough came when a group of Atroai men followed the Wai Wais back home, a full two and a half weeks by trail. And now this, several Atroai families who are right now building houses and fields right next door to the Wai Wais! This is going to work a hardship on the food supply, but the Wai Wais have sacrificed before in their desire to reach the Atroais with the gospel, and they are trusting God to supply this material need they are feeling now. (This might mean that farinha will have to be shipped in from town here until the new fields start producing.)

Atroais Go Back (March 1981)

Conference starts the middle of next week. The Hills will be living with us during that time. Right now, they are at Puraquequara, vacationing and visiting their oldest boy. They were pretty beat when they came out. Word from there is that most of the Atroais have returned, with only about twelve staying. At this stage, this is good news, because of the food problem.

Appendix D

Resolution and Further Problems with the Atroais

By the mid-1970s, a relative peace had been established between the Brazilian government and the Atroai tribe. Completion of the road was inevitable and accomplished during this time period, but not without cost to both sides. In recent years, members of the tribe have brought allegations of genocide against the Brazilian government from the period of the road building during the 1960s to the 1970s. The government disputes these claims.[3] The editor traveled this road from Manaus to Boa Vista in the spring of 1977.[4]

---

3. As reported in the *New York Post*, March 8, 2019.

4. Along the route, there were checkpoints on both sides of the Atroai territory. Because of the danger traveling through the region, all vehicles had to go through in convoy in case of breakdown. As it turned out, a passenger bus broke down along the way. When we came to it and got out of the van in which we were driving, a Brazilian Army truck showed up and in the back bed were two Atroai warriors, armed with their bows and arrows and completely naked except for a string around the waist to tie up their private parts. Don approached them and tried to communicate with them, presumably in Wai Wai, but neither responded to him. Don later said that he recognized one of the men—a known killer. No explanation was given as to why the two Atroai men were in the back of the truck.

Appendix E

Reflections on Adjusting at Auaris,
by Barbara Borgman

BRAZIL! AFTER FIVE MONTHS of Portuguese study, during which I lived in a Brazilian home, Don and I were married by the pastor whose family had hosted me. (It was a marvelous experience living with that family of five children!) Our honeymoon was a week on a Rio de Janeiro beach, one night in Brasília, and a flight to Boa Vista, a simple rural town where the mission was based. It was a rural town of 4000 but a metropolis compared to the dusty airstrip in the jungle where we first landed!

We walked to the village clearing. Open, thatch-roofed dwellings but no people! Such isolation! Oh, there was an older lady with a young toddler and a wide, welcoming smile. A few days before, after a malaria epidemic and deaths, the people had fled.

Slowly they returned. After all, some huge contraption had appeared, and also a strange woman! Don had spent time there building a mud-walled home on the ground, so they knew him, but my skin, light sprinkling of blond hairs on my arms which the women pulled, funny light hair, and clothes were fascinating. The women smiled and commented, pointed to my clothes, and waved their upturned palms meaning, "How about sharing some of your clothes with us?"

Though we lived very simply, we did have riches in their eyes. That bothered me. But the Sanumás were more than happy to be able to get fishhooks, pots, decorative beads, cloth, soap, and machetes in exchange for food, firewood, and maintenance work, especially on the airstrip. I came to see that among themselves they traded, and if a visitor who had come to trade didn't want to give something up, that was stinginess (which to them is a cardinal sin).

Our mud-walled house plan was half-walled in the front with a "reception" area and benches for visitors who were always crowding around. On the other side of that half wall was a "kitchen" area (no stove yet but a fire on the ground, no sink with running water—a wash basin sufficed, and no refrigerator). Across from that area, a table and benches. The wall behind that living area was a solid wall with a door leading to a narrow storeroom which had palm-slat shelves and three steps which led to our bedroom.

I was really a city girl who had only done camping with Girl Scouts! Soon, though, we had piped-in water from the roof for dishwashing, a mud brick stove which Don and some of the men helped him make, and blessing of blessings, an outhouse! A little privacy at last (I shivered going there at night because of the bats)! A few years later I had a kerosene refrigerator and wood-burning stove. Even a Maytag wringer washer run by a gasoline motor. I felt rich!

Don was the linguist and had done some work in a language from a related dialect, but I had so much to learn. "Say it again," I'd request in order to write down the sounds. With the wad of tobacco in their lower lips, the women would get annoyed and repeat it very loudly instead of more slowly. One day, while visiting, one of the women said something, and they cracked up. I asked Don, "What was it they said?" and he truthfully told me, "You have a crooked tongue." Tears.

There were years of learning ahead, not just to speak a language beyond Level One and saying, "Yes, I'll buy your bananas," to a very deep level when you might be able to explain new biblical spiritual concepts strange to them. It's vital to learn what they think and believe. We have heard American people wonder why telling The Message doesn't cause a culture to change much sooner. And I think: "Why do they even wonder that?"

There were nights of the men sniffing a hallucinogenic drug to get in touch with their spirits and the accompanying loud chanting of the shaman. Spirits are genuinely real to the Sanumás, and their lives are controlled by them and taboos. I have come to realize that Satan is more real and powerful than I had ever perceived. I became puzzled that never was spiritism ever mentioned in any Bible school, college, or churches that I attended in America. Spiritism in various forms exists here, too.

There would be fierce fights. From my perspective, it was shocking. In time I accepted that their justice is carried out differently. A wronged person faces the perpetrator, and both grasp their machetes. This is arranged. The victim gives a powerful blow to the chest or back with the flat edge of the machete. Or it might be a blow to the head with a wooden pole. This is returned by the perpetrator. It's horrible. But then, Don was told, the anger runs out with the blood, and it is over. This is one type of their justice system.

After a few years later, Julieta, a Brazilian practical nurse, joined us. Up until then we did simple health treatments for worms, flu, and malaria.

Malaria was a serious threat through the years as well as outsiders visiting if they had the flu. Julieta's arrival was a blessing.

It would be a while before reading classes started, but in the early days we tried to have *National Geographic* and other magazines for them to get used to reading pictures and the idea of printing. Another new single coworker joined us, Paulo Silas, a fine teacher. Besides reading and writing, the folks slowly learned about money by buying trade goods from us. Introduction to these things was vital because civilization would eventually invade the jungle. It did, in the form of an Army post with a new asphalt airstrip, a contingent of soldiers, TV, and a telephone. (The reason for this post is that Auaris is on the Venezuelan border.)

A pair of anthropologists stayed at Auaris for a year or two gathering material for their theses. We were on friendly terms even though we knew that it angered them that we were introducing new spiritual concepts that would change the culture they wanted to preserve for history. Surreptitiously they tried to have us removed, but it was God's plan for us to stay.

To me, the wonder of a growing church of Indigenous native Sanumás who can write their language and read the Scriptures makes my small part worth it all. Another thrilling happening for me is that educated and dedicated Brazilian Christians joined us. It is they who now carry on the growing ministry.

Appendix F

"God Parts the Clouds," by William G. Born

> "Do not boast about tomorrow, for you do not know what a day may bring forth." (Prov 27:1)

OUT OF BED, MY feet just recently hit the floor, as the room fills with the dawn of a brand-new day. All of Boa Vista was beginning to buzz with life in this new and fresh day. This is where the airplane was based that served the people interior in the very remote places far from the noise of Boa Vista, a small hustling and bustling city in the territory of Roraima, Brazil. I am a pilot who flew a single-engine Cessna 206 airplane over the lush, green Amazon jungles. A quick glance outside reports the sky heavy with almost all the signs of poor weather, not the weather a pilot enjoys seeing as he ponders the flight schedule before him.

The date was June 11, 1971. My wife, Betty Jane, and I were greatly enjoying our son, Billy, who was almost 6 months old and a huge blessing our Lord brought into our lives. Brazil had been our home for almost two years, as we used our education, preparation, and skills to provide communication and transportation to the missionaries who lived and worked with Indigenous people in the jungle. These were folks we had come to love. We were participants in something much bigger than just flying and serving. Much bigger than ourselves—something with eternal value. We were part of a team involved in the spread of the Gospel, the Good News of Jesus Christ to the people of Brazil. Those sharing the Good News realized the airplane saved them endless hours of time and energy in their work. Without the need to spend weeks traveling by canoe, more time was economized in relating to the peoples to whom they ministered. Because of regular contact for assistance and physical care available by air support, the physical condition of the missionaries was also enhanced with reduced sickness.

Appendix F

So far it was somewhat a "normal" morning, whatever that means. "Normal" is a very relative term, especially when it comes to the life and events of a missionary pilot. Each day begins with routine chores to prepare for the known and unknown events of his day. Very shortly my wife and I would be standing by the short-wave radio preparing to say "Bom Dia" (Portuguese for "Good Morning") to all the folks in the interior locations of the vast northern jungles of this huge country of Brazil. Betty Jane was preparing breakfast as we waited for 7:00 a.m. to initiate the scheduled morning contact. Time was fast approaching to call the respective mission stations. The short-wave radio was fired up and ready. There was some static on the radio today, but not nearly as much as other days.

Early mornings are always the best time of day in the tropics. It is cooler. In the tropics one rarely says it is cool but rather, it is cooler than the hotter time in the day, which inevitably comes. It was always a good time for me. Still is. Most days, then and even now, one favorite thought from Scripture pops into my mind almost automatically at the dawn of a fresh, new day. As I look ahead to the busy hours of this day, these words scroll across the screen of my mind, "Yet there is one ray of hope: his compassion never ends. It is only the Lord's mercies that have kept us from complete destruction. Great is his faithfulness; his loving-kindness begins afresh each day." (Lam 3:21–23) At that moment, and for that day, little did I realize how much these words would once again ring true when I reflected later on all that took place.

With breakfast complete, it was time to make radio contact. The volume on the high frequency radio had been lowered to squelch the annoying static; not the most pleasant sound to go along with breakfast. Billy was already wide awake, sporting a clean diaper and a tummy full of fresh milk, contentedly kicking and wiggling on a blanket on the floor. It was always fun to watch stretching movements and listen to his baby sounds. I believe he too enjoyed the newness and freshness of the morning hours.

The time finally arrived. Turning up the volume, Betty Jane picked up the microphone and began her daily radio call. "Muinto Bom dia, hoje e onze de Junho mil novencentos setenta e um." ("Good morning, today is June 11, 1971.") She then proceeded to call the various posts in their usual order. There was Mucajaí, Surucucu, Toototobi, Marari, and Auaris, each responding with a responsive "good morning," a brief weather report, any short messages or requests, and indicating whether they had more they would like to communicate after the initial contact. One message came very early in the contact that caused all other messages and requests to be minimized and placed on hold, if not completely forgotten.

The message came from Auaris and could be described as the kind that makes its hearers immediately stop what they were doing and listen intently. While the message was difficult to receive, it had to be difficult for the missionary to convey. Heart-gripping words came out of the radio's speaker bringing immediate pain, grief, and for those listening, great shock. Oh, how hard it was to hear! It took us all by surprise—leaving us dumbfounded and stunned. Don reported that his son had died that morning. His son David, age 5, had apparently been bitten by a snake the previous day, just 24 hours earlier. Now, dear David was with the Lord. The same Lord his parents had come to Brazil to serve. The same Lord and Savior they came to reveal to those primitive Brazilian Indians. The words spoken that morning were far from routine. Actually, both the spoken words as well as those unspoken in the hearts of everyone listening. There was a heaviness so thick it was as if one could cut it. Throughout the day there were many thoughts and prayers ascending to our Heavenly Father. At that given moment there was no way for me to know all that would shortly be required of me, the pilot. Little did I realize how greatly I too would benefit from those very same prayers.

The family requested a flight, although it was not on the schedule that day. However, by the nature of it, their request took precedence over any other. It was on the schedule now. Their request and expressed desire were to bring the body of their son out of the tribal station of Auaris to bury him in the city of Boa Vista. You will recall that the weather in Boa Vista was not good. I was informed by the mission stations that they had completely overcast skies, and it was raining at the destination. This poor weather report added stress for me relating to planning, navigation, and wise judgment and decision making. The added stress also caused me to seek increased wisdom from the Lord.

Auaris reported it had rained all night and was still raining. I wondered what the condition of the dirt airstrip was. What would it be upon arrival? Soft? Too soft? Muddy? Too muddy? What about the enroute weather? How broken would the clouds be? Would they be broken at all; would it be a completely clouded sky? How high might the clouds ascend? More importantly, how close to the ground would they be? With zero electronic navigation, visual navigation is essential.

In the jungle there was no weather bureau or flight service station providing weather reports. Rather, any weather reports were just the words of missionary observers going outside, looking up and around to see how much blue sky they could see, if any. They would report the percentage of cloud coverage and possible visibility from their vantage point. Better weather had a higher percentage of blue and a lower percentage of clouds. Eight-eighths of clouds was not a good report, worse when the report included the word "rain." A fraction of eights is used to report cloud coverage. For example, five-eighths of clouds indicate a remaining three-eighths of blue sky. One of my frequent passengers always had a saying that he shared on almost every jungle run. In a spiritual sense he said, "The blue of the sky is always greater than the clouds." He was right. As Christ-followers we are told that in this world we will have tribulation. Yet, we are to be of good cheer, for our Savior has overcome the world. I believe it for certain. No doubt. However, I have to fly a Cessna 206 for about 560 miles. In known bad weather. With a lot of clouds and very little blue sky. I still like and believe my friend's regular reminder. But I was looking at reality in the face on this specific day—bad weather and a very difficult situation. It promised to be stressful in many ways. Yet, one like all others when "the wisdom that comes from above" is required.

After some planning and discussion over the radio, a new twist emerged. Since the entire family would be coming out to Boa Vista, they requested that someone come from another post to be in Auaris to watch over things while they were away. Who would that be? What individual was available to fly into Auaris with me and remain there while the Borgman family flew out? It was determined that Kitty Pierce, a veteran missionary, would do that. Where was Kitty? She was presently at Surucucu about 205 miles directly West. Auaris was about 280 miles West-northwest from Boa Vista. From Surucucu to Auaris was North-northwest, about 100 miles. This increased the total flight mileage by an additional 25 miles, as well as the exposure to the very poor flying weather. A plan for the day was agreed upon by everyone involved.

It was time to head out to the hangar and prepare the airplane for the flight. Time to gather up whatever cargo may be in the hangar for the destination stations where the flight would land. As always, a complete pre-flight inspection of the airplane was in order. Many a pilot has had occasion to wish there were in-flight repair stations. To date, there has never been one. This then demands a rigorous full check of the airworthiness of the "apparatus" while it was still on the ground.

"Apparatus," do you like that word? I really didn't. Another of my regular missionary flyers always used that word when I requested that he pray for our flight prior to departure. I suppose it is a good word. Yet, for whatever reason I found myself cringing as he used it to describe my airplane in his prayers. My airplane and I were very good partners, and I felt like that word hurt its dignity, if an airplane can have such. I always appreciated his prayers, tolerating the use of that word, but secretly and caringly telling my airplane that it was much more than an "apparatus" to me.

In light of the very possible weather detours or airborne flight delays, this flight would require a full load of fuel. I made sure the fuel tanks were completely full. For safety purposes, I would need to return to Boa Vista with a minimum of 1 hour reserve fuel, in compliance with MAF regulations. Normally, quite possible. That is, if further consumption of fuel was not required due to detours and landing delays because of poor weather.

In the hangar we rounded up everything that would be helpful in making good economical use of the unscheduled emergency flight. Don't forget the mail. Oh my, yes, we had to remember any mail that might be ready to take to Surucucu and Auaris. It only takes one time forgetting the mail that a pilot quickly learns to never forget the mail again. Knowing we would have a full plane of passengers and cargo upon return, we had to be certain all necessary seats and seatbelts were also on board.

With an eye in the western sky I walked to the airport administration building to file my flight plan. How would I classify the weather I saw? Well, it would not be classified as CAVU, "Ceiling and Visibility Unlimited." Far from that. At this moment in time it would not be classified as "formidable" because it was not. Yet, the sky gave this pilot no comfort that the flight was going to be a "piece of cake." Both the weather evaluation and the purpose of the flight created a tighter throat as well as a recognizable knot in my stomach.

Lifting off I was on the way to Surucucu, a flight of 205 miles or about an hour and 40 minutes to the first stop. I was able to see the checkpoints along the route. "Delta" was well seen as the clouds were still well above me. When flying over the vast jungles of Brazil, positions are chosen that are on the flight course and distinctive enough to positively identify. Position "Delta" is a distinctive D-shaped bend in the river that is readily identifiable and confirms the accuracy of the desired flight path. Approaching the next position I looked down to see the jungle station Mucajaí. Now, 105 miles were behind me, with a hundred to go to arrive at Surucucu.

It was comforting to know that Mucajaí had several believing Indians and missionaries who were in prayer for Don, Barb, and family. Also comforting was the awareness that they were praying for the flight. I am sure overflying the airstrip the sound of the airplane was an auditory reminder that prompted additional prayers for this flight and this pilot. What a comfort. Prayer, something we know a lot about. Something we all need to participate in much more often. Something we often take for granted until life's circumstances grab our attention and point out our helplessness. Prayer, that comes out of our needs to be in touch with our Maker. Hallesby says that the foundation of prayer is helplessness, "for it is only when we are helpless that we open our hearts to Jesus and let him help us in our distress, according to his grace and mercy."[1] Yes indeed, the thought of those praying people below me was very powerful, helpful, and comforting. Being fully aware that others, almost all the others on the morning radio contact, were also praying added palpable power for me during this flight.

Below was a familiar landmark assuring me that I was still on course. Surucucu should be about 20 minutes ahead. Looking out over the nose of the airplane, it was easy to see both the darkness and thickness of the ever-increasing clouds.

The arrival over the station and landing was significantly normal. Surucucu sits in a bowl, surrounded by hills. Often on days like this it is surrounded by clouds. Sometimes it was particularly difficult to locate the runway and land at the station. Today, opening the door and stepping out of the airplane there was a significant difference; there was deep heaviness. What was different was the entire aura of the folks. The missionaries were all hurting for what had happened to their colleagues in Auaris. Tears were shed for the family and the loss of their son. On all their faces and in the words spoken were the telltale signs of the pain we all were bearing. Kitty was quite ready with a few things she needed to "hold down things" at Auaris while the family was away in Boa Vista. It was unknown just when, or perhaps even, if the family would return.

Before take-off there was a brief time of prayer. Several prayed. I asked that those who remained at Surucucu also pray for the flight as well as adequate weather to get there safely. Auaris was 100 miles away with one position-reporting location about halfway. Would I ever see that position? Would the weather and related clouds cooperate for a safe and successfully completed flight?

I was flying in a mountainous area and therefore above the clouds and believed it was raining below me. Thankfully, I was able to catch a quick glimpse of Position "Alpha" at the halfway point enroute to Auaris. It was very important to see this position point since I needed to affirm my location, particularly in weather like this. Little did I know at that moment this was the last time I would see the ground for the next 50 miles, plus several additional minutes circling over what I hoped was my destination. Thinking ahead, I wondered, would it even be possible to make a safe landing at Auaris? With the clouds ever-increasing in quantity, density, and darkness would it be possible to even see the runway below? Would it still be raining there? What would be the condition of the airstrip? Arriving near or over Auaris, would it be possible to peer through the clouds to even see the destination or would I need to divert course? How many layers of clouds

---

1. Hallesby, *Prayer*, 9.

might there be? Usually flights were made with high clouds above and better visibility below. Not today... not this day.

Most of the clouds were now forming a lower and lower obstruction to any clear tracking along a ground path. The closer we came to our destination the less we could see the ground. I had to use the old fundamental and primary form of navigation, that is, using only a firmly held heading and the clock called "dead reckoning." This method is subject to cumulative errors. On a day like today, instead of the commonly called "dead" reckoning, replace it with the word "deduced" reckoning. A pilot deduces from previous information where he is. Oh, how a more modern form of satellite navigation, provided by today's GPS (Global Positioning System) would have calmed my nerves. Yet it is important to say that the more I flew over these vast green carpets the more I became a strong believer in the navigation method of the compass heading and the clock. It works. Dead reckoning still works but has become less used on a routine basis. However, it is all we had that day to estimate if we were near Auaris or not.

Now, flying above the clouds with zero ground visibility, the feeling of increased concern drove me to turn to my God with my helplessness. A familiar verse emerged in my thoughts. One about passing through waters. "When you go through deep waters and great trouble, I will be with you. When you go through rivers of difficulty, you will not drown! When you walk through the fire of oppression, you will not be burned up—the flames will not consume you. For I am the Lord your God, your Savior, the Holy One of Israel." (Isa 43:2-3 TLB)

Turning to Kitty, I commented that we should be very close. Over 15 minutes had passed since we last saw a hint of the ground. Clouds were all that was visibly below us. There was one other aid that came in very "handy" at times such as this: the short-wave radio. Auaris had already told me by radio that it was raining there. In and of itself that information was not an encouragement. Squeezing the button on the microphone I called to see what additional information I could get from those on the ground. "I know I am very close and should be almost over your station. Can you hear the sound of the airplane?" "Give me a moment, I'll go outside and listen carefully," came the reply. About 30 seconds later came the news, "No, we cannot hear the engine." The primitive people often were very adept at hearing the airplane even a far distance off. Not this time. At the moment, I was flying in clear skies above any clouds and knew I was well above any mountainous terrain harmful to this "aluminum bird" and its contents. By the results of my well-held heading and the minutes in flight, I knew it was time to start some large, gradual turns. Actually, large circles, to be more precise. It was my hope and experience that possibly, just possibly, one of the missionaries or nationals would hear me if indeed I was as close as I suspected and calculated.

The speaker in the airplane jumped to life with a report that the rain had lessened and may be stopping. To say the end of the rain was a good sign would be an understatement. Now if only they could hear the airplane. Still, all we could see were clouds. Kitty, an experienced missionary flyer, was my helper peering into the clouds, searching for a sighting of something more than clouds, which was all we could see below us. In my neediness I reflected on a familiar verse to jungle pilots, "I will instruct you and teach you in the way you should go; I will counsel you and watch over you." (Ps 32:8 NIV)

It was about then that something happened which I had never experienced before and never since. Thousands of feet above the ground, in the location I believed to be my destination, God seemed to open a small hole in the clouds. It was spectacular! There, out my pilot-side window, while making a very large and gradual circle to the left I spotted a small piece of ground. That ground was a welcome sight, to be sure. But this was not just any old spot of ground. It was only a small consecutive hole in what appeared to be layers of clouds. At this sighting I was not aware how many layers of clouds there were. And what did I see through that small cloud-layered hole? I saw only one thing. I recognized something I had seen before: one end of the Auaris runway. One tiny, tiny piece of real estate, familiar real estate. A piece I had seen before. It was the first ground-sighting in well over 20 minutes. Not even a big enough hole to see the entire airstrip. Another decision was required. Would I dare descend through that hole? Would I be able to maneuver, circling down through such a small hole? Would the clouds roll back in again and block my vision and cause me to have to abandon the descent? All questions that required a quick judgment call. And an even quicker decision. I pulled the power back and informed Kitty we would be executing a tight, spiraling descent.

Just as I began the descent, the radio speaker once again came to life with the call, "Bill, we can hear the airplane!" I confirmed their report and told them I was descending through a hole in the clouds. First, we passed through one layer of clouds only to be followed by another. I looked to see if there were any other larger holes around and found none. Quickly peering back down I could still see that small part of the airstrip. Thankfully, there was still that small miraculous hole in the clouds, making only a part of the runway visible to me. His fresh mercy was evident and was very good; actually, it was miraculous. Now, through the second layer of clouds. Made it. More thanks to the Master Pilot. Still unable to find any larger holes, I continued, with eyes fixed on both the hole in a third layer of cloud and the small piece of the airstrip that remained visible. Through the third hole we passed. Finally, no more cloud layers, I could see the entire airstrip. One small hole in three consecutive layers of cloud; one hole over the exact spot that made my location identifiable! I wanted to shout. I actually did. That was okay with Kitty. She said a hearty praise to the Lord too. He not only opened a small hole, but He did it through three layers of cloud. He not only did it through three layers of cloud, but He did it over the specific piece of real estate I needed in order to land. What a great God of wonders! His mercies indeed are new and fresh every morning. Great is his faithfulness. How many people were praying by then? We will never know for sure. Yet, at a very minimum, I knew beyond a shadow of doubt that it was our great, ever-present God who did it. What a relief that particular part of the "sweaty palms" was over.

My next observation was a very shiny airstrip. Shiny, as in water soaked. I knew it was not paved with glass or mirrors. A highly polished car or airplane looks good when shiny. Not airstrips. This was my next point of evaluation and another critical decision point. The Auaris airstrip had pretty good drainage, but there was still a lot of shiny reflection on the surface. The radio report from the missionaries indicated it was wet, but had no large standing water, more commonly called large puddles. An overfly to evaluate was helpful. I had just seen the God of all creation open a small hole. The same God impressed on me that He wanted me to land. However, keeping the airstrip in sight at all times, I circled it several times, giving more opportunity for the rain to drain. Then, with less and less shine, I landed. Water and some mud were spraying from the wheels, but no danger. Sweet terra firma! Finally! I turned to Kitty as I pulled the mixture to idle-cut-off and again gave praise and thanks to our Lord. Kitty was not rattled. I told you she was an experienced missionary flyer. I never told her what was going on in my own nervous stomach. Perhaps she knew. Probably not. At least she didn't acknowledge anything to me.

Landings at jungle posts are a fun time for both the pilot as well as the residents. For them the arrival of the airplane is like prime-time television; nobody wants to miss the all-star performance of the landing. The missionaries are very happy to see whoever is aboard the airplane. One good reason is that they get some new mail from friends and loved ones from all over the world. Most of these folks are global Christians by the very nature of what they have chosen to do with their lives. There are friendly and warm handshakes or "abraços" ("hugs"). It is generally a time of fun, celebration, and warmth of relationships. Not so this time. This time everything was different. The aura was heavy. Emotions were reeling at the loss of a child, the precious child of a missionary family. All the expressions, both spoken

Appendix F

and facial, were ones of grief, sorrow, and sadness. Missionaries tend to live in the real world, and nothing screams out with the greatest degree of reality like loss and death. All death is heavy, but the death of a child is truly weighty for everyone involved. Yes indeed, this landing was different. The purpose of the flight, the weather, the arrival over Auaris, the landing, and the somber reunion all made this flight and landing remarkably different.

After an hour or so it was time to fulfill the family's request to bring their son to the city for burial. Though planning to return, the sudden death motivated the couple to leave the jungle, bury their son in Boa Vista, and receive encouragement from the mission family there. Essentially, that was the purpose for this flight. Throughout the entire day my awareness of this purpose remained clear in my thinking and influential in each prayerful decision. Flight conditions, weather decisions, landing decisions and, yes, shortly you will see how it even affected a very important takeoff decision. The family had given years of their lives to see that this particular tribe hears the Good News of Jesus Christ.

As each of the family members made final preparations to fly out, I too began making my preparations for takeoff. I installed the seats I had tied down with the cargo when I departed Boa Vista, leaving room for the child's body. I climbed onto the wings to confirm my fuel quantity was adequate to get to my destination with the required fuel reserves. The oil was checked, and a walk-around inspection of the airplane was completed. All was almost ready to go, except one very important part, the evaluation of the wet airstrip and a calculation of the distance required for liftoff with the necessary payload of passengers. Not just a successful liftoff, but also a safe climb out over the trees at the end of the runway. It was clear the airstrip was still quite wet. Fortunately, there were no large bodies of standing water which would make a takeoff and climb out almost impossible. Safety has always been and still is the top priority. This takeoff was no exception. Yet, the airstrip was not in ideal condition. I had landed well under aircraft gross weight, but we would be near or at gross takeoff weight for departure. All of my calculations indicated the takeoff was possible, with little margin to spare. There is a difference between the calculation and the experience gained in actually operating in such environments. My calculation was accurate. My "gut level" said it should work, but I did not completely like the airstrip condition, yet.

I walked the strip several times. I argued and debated with myself. Would the condition of the runway allow a successful and safe takeoff? Was it now dry enough? Was it now firm enough? Would I have the required aircraft takeoff performance with a much heavier airplane than when I landed? Sometimes I felt certain it was good enough. Other times I felt it still may be too soft. There was the back-and-forth battle within me. It was a real battle. A battle of experience versus narrow calculation. Such decisions often fall into subjectivity and would seem far less difficult if they could be more objective. Operations in this environment are not completely objective. Subjectivity enters into many decisions based on past experience.

I was influenced by the apparent urgency to depart to Boa Vista. Burials are quick in countries where bodies are not embalmed, especially tropical countries, because of the heat. It was with great sincerity that I prayed, asking the Lord that I make the decision He wanted. Out of my helplessness, I cried out to God for his wisdom; the wisdom that comes from above was what I really wanted, and desperately needed. "If you don't know what you're doing, pray to the Father. He loves to help. You'll get his help, and won't be condescended to when you ask for it. Ask boldly, believingly, without a second thought. People who 'worry their prayers' are like wind-whipped waves. Don't think you're going to get anything from the Master that way, adrift at sea, keeping all your options open." (Jas 1:5 THE MESSAGE) I knew what I was doing. Yet I really needed the help of my heavenly Father. Certainly there was comfort from remembering this truth of his word. After all my walking the airstrip, calculating, evaluating, and praying for wisdom, I had an answer I firmly believed was from the Lord. It was a go. I had an "ok, go" confirmation from everything that was within me. I fully sensed I had that same "go" from my heavenly Father.

With that internal battle behind me, I looked to see the folks heading toward the runway. I could see Don carrying the body of his precious son wrapped in a blanket. The time to load passengers and cargo for departure had come. There were many people heading toward the airstrip from the village. Many of the villagers were walking along with the family. The people had come to know and care for "their" missionaries. The tribal children had run and played with the missionary children. My emotions were on edge as we placed David's body in the airplane. We know and often speak that God is good all the time. Yet, how does He intend to use this? Naturally, I wondered what I would be thinking and feeling if I had to suffer the loss of my own son. These thoughts ran deep. And, I could sense them coming to the surface, close to spilling out for all to see. The realization of how much God loved this family and his thoughts of their loss of a precious son almost overwhelmed me. Yet I knew that David was even more precious in the sight of his Creator, the God this family was living to serve and honor. So much strong emotion was bubbling up within me. The reality that I was moments away from a takeoff I had planned and wrestled with had already extracted a lot of my emotional energy. "Lord, keep me focused as I safely make this takeoff and complete this flight."

The rest of the passengers were seated now in the airplane, secured in their seatbelts and shoulder harnesses. Don, the father, was seated to my right in the front seat. Barb, the mother, was seated just behind me, with the two siblings, Andrea and Stephen, in the center seat alongside her. On one seat in the rear sat the Borgmans' house helper who was from another village near Boa Vista. Alongside her was David's body. We prayed together for wisdom, safety, and the ability of each one to sense the presence and comfort of the Lord in the flight and in all that lies ahead.

It was time to close all doors, start the engine, and taxi to the end of the runway. All the precious cargo was now inside. Taxiing to the takeoff end of the runway, I looked with great frequency out my pilot-side window at the tire to see how little or how much of an impression it was making in the soft spots on the surface. In aviation we call that the "footprint." At times it looked very good, not too deep, and sometimes not overly encouraging. There had been no rain since landing. That was good. An old pilot saying, "You cannot use the airstrip left behind you," is very true, so I made a clear decision to taxi to the very extreme end of the usable surface. I even planned to have the tail of the airplane overhang the unprepared surface at the very end.

Turning around to check each passenger, I confirmed they were all ready for takeoff, and they all confirmed their readiness. Looking forward once again, I strongly focused on this takeoff. How would I manage the airplane for best acceleration and good liftoff to climb over the trees? I knew I would use a soft-field takeoff procedure. Would I use the normal 20 degrees flaps for takeoff? Or would I add a little more to get off the soft runway? My mind was full of all these unforgiving technical requirements. I thought about flap configuration for a soft-field takeoff. How long would I hold the brakes prior to release? I would confirm that I had full power; both the manifold pressure and the RPM were where I wanted them. If I wasn't satisfied with the takeoff performance what was my plan? When and where, at what point on the airstrip would I pull the power off and begin heavy braking? Once again, I turned to the One in Whom I placed my trust and in Whom I had experienced confidence. Just prior to applying full power I closed my eyes and asked the Lord again for wisdom. I did not have Hallesby's quote then. Later I read where he said, "Listen, my friend! Your helplessness is your best prayer. It calls from your heart to the heart of God with greater effect than all your uttered pleas. He hears it from the very moment that you are seized with helplessness, and He becomes actively engaged at once in hearing and answering the prayer of your helplessness."[2] Of course I had

---

2. Hallesby, *Prayer*, 7.

prayer as my powerful resource and made good use of praying to the Father all day. This prayer also contained a small but important question, "Is it still a 'go,' Lord?" His answer was clearly a "yes." I had peace. Until . . .

Until I felt a small, light but persistent tap on my shoulder. At first, I thought it was the pull of the shoulder harness as I moved in my seat. It was not; it came from the passenger behind me. It was David's mother, Barb. I paused and turned around to hear why she tapped me. What was it? Why, at that moment? What she said shook me to my core, but not for very long. She said, "Bill, if you don't think we can make it, it's OK, we'll stay and bury David here." What a flood of emotions came over me. It was very momentary but felt like an eternity. I had wrestled so much with this decision but felt for certain all was in order; all was "good to go." Yet that question at that particular moment seemed to take my breath away.

Remembering the primary reason for this flight and the one upon which almost all of my decisions were made, I was thankful for the powerful prayers of God's people and my persistence in asking the Lord for his wisdom. With an authentic smile that demonstrated my clear and real understanding of her question and yet communicating the practical consequences of my decision, I turned to Barbara and affirmed to her the assurance I had from the Lord. "Barb, thank you. I am firmly convinced that all will be well. Here we go." God was so good to me. When is He not? He always is. Even in my questions, perhaps doubts, He confirmed it was a "go" for takeoff. Even when it was challenged by external circumstances, it was still a "go." All doubt was consistently overruled by the firm, clear conviction that I knew my God spoke clearly to me, "It's a go."

The airplane rolled on the runway surface a little bit longer than normal for this takeoff. But not too much. When I reached my previously chosen location to abort the takeoff, I was fully aware that acceleration was good enough to continue and successfully liftoff. Accelerating in what is called the "ground affect" I knew we were gaining good airspeed, and that the climb would also be more than adequate to clear all obstacles. It is when liftoff occurs, and the climb is well established that a pilot experiences a type of "relaxation" or "sigh of relief." That relaxation is only more complete when a good, safe cruising altitude is reached. With a good climb established, I turned to look at each of my passengers. They each appeared to be doing well. Over the years I observed during my flights that regardless of the surrounding difficulties of any given flight, most often the passengers were pretty relaxed and often slept. As a young pilot, the apparent complete confidence the passenger had in me and the flight was a bit unsettling. Then it became much more acceptable when I realized even though their confidence may have seemed to be in me, perhaps it was more in the Lord. After all, I was confiding in the Lord. But then again, I was the sole manipulator of the aircraft. Or was I? I guess I still wonder . . . especially on that day.

To some degree the Lord was not finished showing me his active hand in the events of that day in June. It was no longer raining when we departed Auaris. The weather was just adequate, but in no way reassuring, because the blue sky was still obscured with dark, gray clouds. However, the very dark, black clouds were less and less. As we arrived at cruising altitude I began to see a very strange weather pattern. The distance to Boa Vista was 280 miles. Before me were the clouds. But instead of more clouds, a clearing was forming just in front and ahead of our flight path. The poor weather was succumbing to slowly diminishing clouds that continued to give way to fewer and fewer clouds and more and more blue skies.

You have certainly seen what happens behind a motorboat as it moves through the water. Behind it a "V" shape is formed that becomes larger and larger as the boat moves ahead and away. This time the airplane was the vortex of the "V," and the clouds were widening before me instead of behind me. I saw the very same thing happening with the clouds before me. The "V" was opening up as I went toward it. Yes, it seemed that our Lord was clearing the way by continuously parting the clouds before the path of the airplane. My sense was again that we have a great God. One who cares. One who perhaps knew I was a bit exhausted and needed a more relaxed flight condition for this final leg of the day. For all the poor weather we had experienced on the flight into the jungle station, we had quite the opposite on the return. By the time we arrived in Boa Vista it was all blue sky—which is always greater than the clouds.

Don and I talked some during the flight as he opened the mail I had just brought to him. It was an uneventful flight that was clearly a time for some degree of relaxation for all involved. Soon we would be arriving at the hangar in Boa Vista. The thought ran quickly through my mind: What will the arrival be like? Who all might be at the hangar? How many people? What would they say? What do you say to brothers and sisters in Christ who are deep in raw, fresh grief, surrounding great loss?

Betty Jane and many others had followed every word of the entire flight. A non-scheduled, emergency flight that involved missionary colleagues is always a huge event and followed by anyone throughout the jungle who has a short-wave radio. It was the "breaking news" that day. Yet, for those there to give the "Good News" to others, it is far more than just a busy news day. It is a day when they rally together to pray for their colleagues. I am so thankful for the radio as well as those who were upholding the family and this flight in their prayers. They knew every time a microphone button was pressed exactly what was going on. They all knew exactly when we would arrive with all the precious cargo from Auaris. "Boa Vista tower, this is PT- BJY, ten miles to the west, estimating Boa Vista." Now the government control tower also knew my time of arrival. I wondered if even the tower operators knew why this flight was made. In a small town, news spreads rapidly.

On our final approach to landing I could see there were quite a few cars at my house and hangar, more than I expected. Part of me didn't like to see that many people. Leave this poor family alone, I thought to myself. The group was made up of colleagues, fellow workers with other missions, and friends, both Brazilian and expatriate. It didn't take long after landing to realize that all these people loved Don, Barbara, and family. I decided that no, it actually was very good that so many were there to show loving support for the Borgman family. "Boa Vista tower, PT-BJY on the ground." We had landed safely and in good condition. I had developed the habit of saying, "Thank You, Lord" after every trip. Regardless of the type of transport, I still take a moment to say thank you to my Lord.

There were so many verbal and visual expressions of support. So many expressions of sorrow in the depths of their souls for what had happened. So many expressed their hearts and promised continued prayer for the family. A goodly amount of time passed while one by one people wept, embraced, and expressed their love and continued support.

The leadership of the mission had asked their own mission doctor to have a look at David's body and make a medical and legal pronouncement. At that particular time we had the great joy of having Dr. Dankwart as part of the mission. He was a Brazilian doctor of German descent from southern Brazil, serving with the mission. More than being a doctor he was a man of God, and he and his wife, Inge, were very good friends to Betty Jane and me. David's body was taken over to our house and placed in one of our bedrooms. There I watched and wept as Dr. Dankwart examined him.

Sunset began to settle down upon the city of Boa Vista. All the people had returned to their homes and "routine" responsibilities. We knew there would now be a lot of planning to care for Don, Barb, and family. Additionally, there would be much preparation for David's burial. There would be the best of plans and the effort required to make it a time of authentic grieving that would also honor the family and the God they had come to Brazil to represent. There was awareness that the town's people would be watching to see how these Christians, these guests of Brazil, would respond to this most difficult loss.

With the house where just Betty Jane, Billy, and I lived now quieted, we sat and reflected on the eventful day. The airplane was in the hangar and the doors were closed. The Kubota diesel generator was quietly purring in the distance, supplying power for the lights. There was little noise other than that of Billy playing and exercising, as babies do. I recall looking at him lying on a blanket on the surface of the hard concrete floor in the house. Quietly, I thanked God for him and asked that our good, always good God would protect and preserve him. Watching Billy wiggle, Betty Jane and I reflected about the day and all the ways in which I had seen up close and personal the very hand of God. Some days, sadly, we do what we do in such a routine manner that we can almost do it without regard to our God who is in the details of our lives. This was not that kind of day. I would not choose each day to be eventful like this one, but it was such a beautiful and powerful reminder of Who our Great God is. He is our God of details.

Together Betty Jane and I reflected on all the ways we felt, observed and experienced the Lord throughout that long day:

- Good radio reception on the regular morning contact
- The airplane in ready flight status, no maintenance pending
- The airplane and all of its systems functioned perfectly all day
- The guidance of our great God: weather enroute, upon arrival and take off, no GPS, just very dependable time and heading
- The navigation that was guided by him
- The opening of the hole in the clouds: three cloud layers and three aligned holes
- The rain that stopped as we arrived over Auaris
- Adequate airstrip conditions after a lot of rain
- Weather conditions from bad to poor to adequate to beautiful late in the day
- Flight to Boa Vista with ever-improved weather as God continued to part the clouds
- The great grace of God given to the Borgman family
- The contrast between the wicked and those who trust in the Lord, seeing as "the LORD'S unfailing love surrounds the man who trusts in him. Rejoice in the LORD and be glad, you righteous; sing, all you who are upright in heart!" (Ps 32:10–11 NIV)

Each day begins like a blank sheet of paper upon which the events of our life are inscribed. We know not what that particular day will bring. "The heart of man plans his way, but the Lord establishes his steps." (Prov 16:9) Yet, we can and must confidently trust our God of unfailing love. So often

I hear him say, "Trust Me!" Throughout this day, many before, and many since, I have heard his voice saying those same words. He is fully trustworthy. As his precious children, we are held in the palm of his hand. We who know him and belong to him because of our Savior, Jesus Christ, can trust our own Abba, Father completely. I trust this account renews you as you fully trust our heavenly "Dear Daddy."

Kitty Pierce

Bill Born Fueling PT-BJY in Boa Vista

Appendix G

Reflections on Their Children's Education, by Barbara Borgman

WHEN OUR FIRST CHILD was four years old, I began simple education for him using homeschool materials I got through the mail. It was very hard to keep his attention because he, like any kid, wanted to be outside. He had a little brother, too! Nevertheless, we began. As he was drawing near the age of 5, all was stunningly interrupted by his death. Brother Steve would not need school for another two years.

When I returned to Auaris, truthfully my heart was still deeply wounded. When Steve was almost 5, he started his studies at home. I was expecting another child. It was at that point, with agreement from our mission, that Don and I moved to the mission base in the town for my sake. Some of us mothers grieve longer than others. As a missionary friend, who lost three boys in a terrible drowning, said, "We missionaries have clay feet. Our grief is no different."

During these years, Don would make extensive trips of several weeks to two months up to the tribe to work on translation work with Sanumá helpers.

Our son Steve did American studies at home in the morning and went to Brazilian school in the afternoon. Finally, I realized, when he was about 7, that these double curriculums were a burden. All the other missionary kids in our area were going to a top-notch mission school on the Amazon River, with a truly firm but loving staff. Steve was excited at the prospect. And so it was.

Later, when Andrea went, it was with a group of kids who were like family. It breaks our hearts as parents, but we knew they were socially fulfilled. It was very odd, yet the thing to do for the children's sakes. Surprisingly, even today, there are still missionaries whose children study away from home, though it is not the norm. Their parents live in very isolated places such as in Africa.

The kids would come home for Christmas break and for the entire summer break. None of our children, nor many of their "brother and sister" missionary kids, are bitter, and they remain close to these friends for life. For the parents, it is very tough and lonely, but honestly God does comfort us through it all.

Appendix H

Sikoi Encounter, by Thomas J. Sorkness

IN THE SPRING OF 1977, I traveled to Brazil with Norman (Norm) Allaby with the express purpose of accompanying Don Borgman on an expedition to make contact with the Sikois. The expedition was almost scratched due to a virulent outbreak of malaria in the Auaris area. By the time Norm and I flew into Auaris with Don, however, the outbreak had abated. Don prevailed upon Lourenzo and his son, Komak (Alberto) to guide us to the Sikoi. We traveled by canoe for a couple of days before striking a trail to our destination. After two more days, we arrived at a Sanumá village whose headman was referred to as "Hairy Chest." Thus, we called the location "Hairy Chest Village."

At Hairy Chest's village we were told that the Sikoi village was a good five days away— that's five Sanumá days of trekking through the forest. For the Setenabi (white man), perhaps twice that long. We were on a strict time schedule, and it looked as if the possibility of reaching the Sikoi would prove elusive for Don once again. However, God's providential hand was at work. We were told by Hairy Chest that the Sikoi were probably moving in our direction to take part in a bone-drinking ceremony in honor of a revered individual who had died awhile back in the village. This gave us some hope, so we decided to push on.

Interestingly, there were two Sikois who were at Hairy Chest's village when we arrived. Some men who had been hunting had recently returned, and several of them agreed to be carriers for us. Our times over the next few days were quite enlightening to Norm and me. We eventually came to a beautiful, small stream where we decided to wait for the Sikois to arrive. The two Sikois were sent ahead to announce our desire to meet the people coming our way. The following picks up my memory of that encounter.

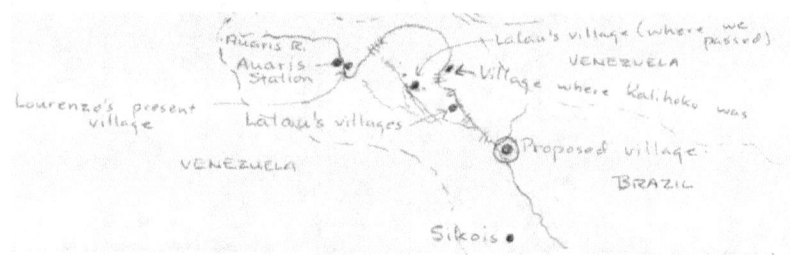

Map of Sikoi Expedition

Day 9, April 20, The Sikois are Near

Up early as usual, we wondered today when or if we would meet the people we had come to find. We decided to wash our clothes. Washi, one of the two we had sent ahead, suddenly showed up, crossed the river and told us that he had met the Sikois on the trail and that they would be arriving the next day. They apparently were very close but wanted to come tomorrow so their women and children would be prepared. That was astounding news which meant all the hardship of the expedition would be fulfilled. Since they were coming tomorrow, it gave us some time for leisure but also preparation for our visitors. We washed our clothes as well as ourselves and spent some time fishing as well as swimming in the rapids. Komak joined Norm and me and seemed to really enjoy the time with us. He had warmed up to us a bit by this point, although he still stuck pretty close to his father.

We finished out the day by continuing our study of Romans, praying awhile, singing, and memorizing more Scripture. We sang a lot on the trail. One that was fairly regular for us was "They That Wait Upon the Lord" which seemed to help a lot while we were hiking. We sang that again at this point. Don then taught us a Sanumá song which he had written and composed. The lyrics with English translation:

> Teus a toita; (God is good)
> Teus a lotete; (God is powerful)
> Samak pi ipa sai;(He loves us much)
> Samak noamay. (He protects us)

Appendix H

"Teus a Toita"

We went to sleep that night wondering what tomorrow would hold for us. We trusted that the Lord had brought us this far for a purpose, but what was in store we could not know. Would the Sikoi be friendly and welcoming or something else? One could not help but think of Jim Elliot and his partners as they had been the first to contact the Aucas. We were the first to contact the Sikoi.

Day 10, April 21, The Sikoi

Morning dawned, and I slept in a little. I got up, walked to the river to wash, and took a picture of it. We then had our Bible study. No sooner had we finished when the first of the Sikoi began appearing across the river—only a few men at first. They crossed the river and approached the shelter but were hesitant to enter. At that point, Don greeted them in Sanumá, and they entered right in. (I think they were as wary of us as we were of them.) Several more came across the river and entered the shelter. We sat in a ring around the fire on logs we had rolled in. As it turned out, one of the older men in the group was the chief. His name was Allabi (pronounced just like Norm's last name). What an interesting coincidence that no one had expected. Incidentally, when the Sanumá heard my last name, they called me Sokonas, which means "sloth claw"! Strange, but quite funny.

The first order of business seemed to be between Allabi and one of the Sanumá men who had accompanied us. They sat facing each other and exchanged formal news from the region. One thing that came out was that the Sikoi had been at war with another tribe—the Waicas. As the discussion progressed, one would talk loudly and go through contortions and gesticulations. The other would just sit quietly and listen, responding in a soft agreeing tone. Then the other would start in.

After a bit, Allabi turned to Lourenzo, and they began what appeared a rather heated discussion. Lourenzo told Allabi that the Sanumá up the river were blaming the malaria outbreak on the Sikoi. Allabi insisted that it was not their fault but the Waicas with whom they were at war presently. Lourenzo brought up several issues with Allabi including the above-mentioned war, the throwing of magic root on the Sanumá (remember back to the Sanumá man who asked Don to tell the Sikoi not to throw magic root on them), and the matter of some killings that had taken place in the past. As we learned, the Sikoi were, in fact, Sanumá people. They had split off some time earlier because Allabi had killed another Sanumá man. His family and others followed him to their new location, and that's where they had resided ever since. I don't know how long before that occurred, but it must have been in the distant past because the Sikoi were considered separate, and Don had never met them. The dialogue between Lourenzo and Allabi became quite tense, but Don assured us that this was nothing serious, just how these people typically engaged each other in situations like this.

As this was going on, I had a Sikoi boy sitting next to me who kept rubbing his hands on my arms and legs and then rubbing them on his own. It was quite strange and a bit unnerving. I asked Don what he was doing. He said that the Sikoi was trying to receive the white man's strength and friendliness. In their minds, the attributes of another could be appropriated in such a manner, sort of like the bone drinking ceremony, I suppose. I guess what impressed this young man was the girth of my thighs and calves in particular, which were much greater than the average Sanumá.

I am sure that the Sikoi had heard of white men from other Sanumá as well as members of other tribes. They had seen our plane fly over and probably had seen many others going back and forth from Boa Vista to Auaris. Nevertheless, after looking at me, Allabi asked Don if we, the white men, were spirits. Don told them, "No," and that we were mere men. But it opened the door for him to tell them about God—that God was the only Spirit and that He made all men and the earth and heavens. They appeared quite interested in all this and had an interesting way of showing awe: they clicked their tongues. Many of them did this, including Allabi, in my recollection. This showed their genuine interest. Don then proceeded to sing them the Sanumá song he had taught us the day before. This was followed by more tongue clicking. (As I have thought about it, I did not hear any type of music, melodic or rhythmic, by the Sanumá.) It's hard to know if they were more amazed by the singing or the words. It was probably a combination of both.

By the time this interchange had ended, the entire traveling village of Sikoi had entered our camp—about 55 to 60 people in all. They were of all ages from babies to the elderly and of both sexes. I do not recall seeing any young teenage girls, which I think was probably not unusual with the way their society was structured. We were informed that there was another village that existed near them. No doubt, this was the village I had seen and told the others about when we had flown over them. While this was all going on, a couple of men showed up with some anteater meat to share with their newfound friends—us! It turned out that the meat was rancid, and Allabi ordered it sent away. The men ate it, nonetheless. Imagine eating rancid anteater meat!

It had been determined that with this first encounter with the Sikoi, we would not stay long. After about an hour or so, we decided it was time to depart. We did do some trading a bit. Don began by giving Allabi a loincloth along with some fishing line and hooks, for which he seemed appreciative. I traded with a Sikoi for a wanas and a bow and some arrows in exchange for a belt buckle. The fellow seemed satisfied at first but then got a little testy about it. I figured that after he had assessed the belt buckle a bit, he got to thinking, "What in the world am I going to do with this?" I felt a little bad about the situation but didn't really have much more to give him. I may have produced a safety pin, but I just don't recall. (A wanas, incidentally, is a small item, made of a cut-off and hollowed out reed, about two to three inches in diameter, and perhaps about a foot long. The wanas is an important accoutrement that Sanumá men carry with them. They are used as containers for extra arrowheads, twine, and anything else that they might like to carry.)

In the wanas I traded for, I found extra arrowheads for larger animals as well as smaller sharpened bone arrowheads to be used for birds. I also found what appeared to possibly be either a claw or small carved bone that might be used as a scraper of some sort. I just don't know what its purpose was. I did find something quite interesting in this fellow's wanas however: a long, narrow, metal rod. I have no idea where he would have gotten this. The Sanumá were essentially Stone Age people, to use a phrase. Since to my understanding the Sikoi had never been contacted by anyone outside of their civilization, I can only conclude that this artifact came to him through a series of trades made from one community to the next. I would imagine that it must have been valuable to him, since there seemed to be no other evidence of metal among these people. I can't remember if I traded for anything else with the Sikoi, even though I did bring home a number of souvenirs from the trip.

Although a gift and not a trade, I seem to recall giving a t-shirt I had been wearing to one of the Indians. (I think it was probably the fellow who carried my pack most of the way.) The t-shirt depicted a mountain climber ascending a snowy peak with a Pepsi machine at the top. (I don't remember if there was any other wording on it.) For a long time afterward I used to wonder what impression that image made on my Sanumá friend or to what extent I had compromised an Indigenous culture. (Imagine a mountain climber scaling a snow-covered peak reaching for a Pepsi in the remote jungle of South America!) He liked the shirt, so I gave it to him.

I recall that Don traded something for a pair of small parrots that were held in a little wooden cage. I'm not sure what Norm may have traded for, but I'm sure he did something, perhaps the same as I. At one point, Norm showed and turned on a flashlight he had brought along. Allabi was frightened of it, thinking it might explode. Norm also tried to take a picture of some of the Sikoi. When he attempted to take the picture, the people he was pointing the lens at all scattered. I noticed that the Sikoi mothers would not allow their young children to look at us. They must have thought that we were from another world. In a very real sense, we were.

It came time to leave. Don and Lourenzo thought it best not to linger, especially after the trading had taken place. Sometimes things could become a bit heated as individuals began to think that they had lost out on a deal or had gotten the short end of the stick. Some might wonder why we needed to trade at all—bringing in some sort of material emphasis to the situation when we were simply trying to get acquainted and bring knowledge of the true God and his gospel. Although it is speculation on my part, I believe it would have been in a way unmannerly to have not engaged with them in this way. I think trading is part of a social pattern that is simply expected. To not have done it may have seemed insulting. I don't know for sure.

At any rate, we made our leave of the Sikoi after doing our trading. Getting our packs together as well as taking down and wrapping up our hammocks, we left the camp by the big river and made our way over the hill back to the spot we had camped only two nights before. I remember turning in for the night with a bit of apprehension. The Sikoi were only a short distance away. Our interaction with them had been friendly, but I did wonder about the fellow who felt he had gotten the raw end of the deal in my trading. What if he were waiting for a chance of reprisal in the middle of the night? What if the entire group of Sikoi descended upon us? Neither Don nor Lourenzo seemed at all concerned nor the Sanumás who were carrying our belongings, thus, I felt there was really no reason to fear. I climbed into my hammock and dozed off pretty quickly.

Appendix I

A Word about Don and Barb Borgman, by Rev. Stan Allaby

I HAVE KNOWN DON Borgman for 66 years and his wife Barb for about 64 years. They are a sterling couple. I met Don when I became the pastor of his church in Bridgeport, Connecticut. We are approximately the same age. When I met him in 1956, I was pastor of my first church, and he was studying linguistics and preparing to become a missionary. I was immediately impressed by him. He was good looking, intelligent, and an athlete. He was soft spoken, friendly, and humble, and it was obvious that he loved the Lord with all his heart. Thus was born a friendship that has lasted for decades.

When he had completed his linguistic studies, he felt led to be ordained to Christian ministry. I was present at his ordination council. He presented a well thought through paper which set forth his beliefs. It was a wonderful paper and left no doubt about his doctrine and his commitment to the Lord and to his calling. He also answered questions thoughtfully and biblically. The council approved him for ordination, and a couple of weeks later I presided at his ordination.

Not long after that Don met Barb and they fell in love. However, the timing did not seem right. Don was committed to leave for Brazil, and there was not enough time to plan and execute a wedding. Several of us from Black Rock and Barb went to the airport to see Don off. It was difficult for Don and Barb to separate, but they both felt that it was the Lord's will, and they were going to do what God wanted them to do.

But that meant that Don went alone for his first missionary assignment. He was flown into the jungle by Mission Aviation Fellowship and served alone for his first term. The natives had never seen a white man before, and of course Don did not know their language. It must have been a very difficult start, but I never heard Don complain about it.

During that first term while he was alone, he cut himself quite seriously. That could have made many people give up, but Don would not. He gave himself first aid and nursed himself back to health.

In 1960, I was invited to speak to the Unevangelized Field Missionaries at their annual retreat in Brazil. I asked for permission to visit Don at his remote station, and permission was granted. I was flown in over hundreds of miles of impenetrable forest by Mission Aviation Fellowship. To my surprise, the pilot was my best friend from high school days, Norm Olson. That week with Don was one of the most interesting weeks of my life. Don always had a notebook and pen with him. When a native would point to something to Don, he would write it in his notebook. That is how, for months, Don learned vocabulary and grammar. It took years to learn enough to be able to translate the Bible into the language of the natives, but in April 2008 Don presented me with a complete New Testament in the language of the Sanumá people. This is a gift I will always cherish. What a marvelous contribution to the Kingdom of God and to the cause of missions!

I don't remember exactly when Don and Barb got married or the circumstances. It may have been in the last part of Don's first term or the beginning of his second term, but they did get married and started a family. We all rejoiced with them, but then something tragic happened. Their little boy, David, was bitten by a snake and he died. This was a devastating thing that happened to them. Our church grieved with them. We offered to bring them home so they could be with family and friends while they grieved. They were devastated by their loss, but even that did not prevent them from returning to the field where God had called them. This demonstrated to all of us the strength of their faith and the determination of their commitment.

There is so much more that I could write, but I will finish by saying that there is no one that I respect more than Don and Barb. They are present day missionary heroes. I am proud to call them my friends.

Stanley Allaby
August 16, 2022

Appendix J

Terms of Service, Furlough Dates, and Continued Work (1958 to 1999)

Terms

First Term, 1958 to 1962:

- Bonfim
- Jungle training
- 9 months at Mucajaí
- 6 months at Georgetown
- 1 year at Surucucu

Second Term, January 1963 to September 1968:

- Atroai Expedition
- Cafuini River with F.A.B.
- Marriage
- Entrance to Sanumás
- Survey from Auaris to Surucucu by river

Third Term, May 1969 to 1972:

- At Auaris
- Start of translation
- Death of David

Fourth Term, July 1973 to April 1978:

- Based in Boa Vista, Don makes month-long trips 3 to 4 times a year and works as consultant
- Barb home-schools in afternoon and is involved in hospitality department at base
- May 1976 to May 1977, Don has responsibilities as Field Leader
- November 1977, Don, Barb, and Darlene plus Lois Cunningham are one year back at Auaris

Fifth Term, May 1979 to August 1983:

- Bible translation
- October to November 1979, Don at Auaris
- 1980, Entrance into Olomai
- Measles at Auaris
- Don and Barb's three kids go to boarding school

Sixth Term, August 1984 to December 1986:

- Christmas conference at Auaris
- February 1985, Blood clots in lung send Don to Bridgeport Hospital
- September and November 1985, Visits to Olomai
- Indian conference at Auaris

Seventh Term, 1987 to 1989:

- Based in Boa Vista
- August 1988, Checking O.T. selections with Moises
- January 1989, Purchase of Tepequem property
- April and June 1989, Bible conferences at Olomai, Baptisms by Lourenzo
- March 1990, Dino and sons at Tepequem

Eighth Term, 1990 to 1992:

- August 1990, Barb teaches at Puraquequara school on Amazon
- At PQQ, Don works on O.T. abridgement and checking, also makes visit to the tribe
- September 6, 1990, Lorenzo and Alberto shot to death by miners
- March 1991, Aborted planned river trip to Olomai due to news of several deaths: Koki (daughter of Lorenzo), Koki's husband, Lorenzo's wife, and another two of Lorenzo's daughters.
- September 1991, 3 months in B.V. for translation checking of Penteteuch with Honai
- March 1992, 5 weeks in Tepequem with Dino and sons
- June 1992, Finish at Puraquequara school

FURLOUGHS

First Furlough, March 1962 to January 1963:

- S.I.L. Oklahoma, third year
- Don and Barb meet

Second Furlough, September 1968 to April 1969:

- S.I.L.
- Work on Sanumá language data

Third Furlough, May 1972 to July 1973:

- S.I.L.
- Grammar write-up
- Teaching phonetics

Fourth Furlough, April 1978 to April 1979:

- Don active in Missionary Conferences
- Barb active in Pioneer Girls and Bible Study Group

Fifth Furlough, August 1983 to August 1984:

- Don's "Deputation" (Conferences at churches)
- Don and Barb purchase their first computer
- Full grammar write-up
- Tons of dental work

Sixth Furlough, November 1986 to December 1987:

- Move to Bradenton, Florida to work with M. Seely on translation
- Translated John
- Finished grammar write-up

Seventh Furlough, May to August 1990:

- Short duration
- Attend Steve's graduation from college

Eighth Furlough and Final Move to U.S., June 1992:

- 1992, Translation work with M. Seely in Bradenton
- Two-month trip to Brazil for translation checking

Continued Work

Continued Work and Travels (1993 to 1999):

- 1993, Five men at Tepequem for translation
- 1994, Two months with Resende and Mateus at Tepequem
- 1995, Ron and Robin Brown join me, Resende and Kanawati at Tepequem
- 1996, Mimica and several from JOCUM (Youth with a Mission) hold forth at Auaris
- Summer 1996, Ron and Robin join Don along with Mateus, Enoki, and Jacó at Tepequem
- June 1997, Translation workshop in Boa Vista

Appendix J

- August 1997, Robbed in Miami
- August to September 1997, at Tepequem with Ron, Robin, Honai, Resende, Carlos, and Geraldo
- 1998, Contact with Wycliffe consultant, Bruce Moore
- 1999, Language survey trip to Kobalis in Venezuela
- Jim Kakumasu of S.I.L checks Acts
- 7 weeks in Tepequem with Shileno, Cláudio, and Manu

Bibliography

"Amazon tribe accuses Brazilian military of genocide." *New York Post*, March 8, 2019. https://nypost.com/2019/03/08/amazon-tribe-accuses-brazilian-military-of-genocide/.

"Black Rock Congregational Church – 1849–1999," Black Rock Church, Fairfield, Connecticut, October 27, 2023, https://blackrock.org/. https://blackrock.org/wp-content/uploads/2021/01/0e7040975_1519772762_br-history.pdf.

Borgman, Donald M. "Sanumá," In *Handbook of Amazonian Languages*, edited by Desmond C. Derbyshire and Geoffrey K. Pullum, 15–248. Berlin: Mouton de Gruyter, 1990.

Born, William G. *God Parts the Clouds*. Unpublished manuscript, 2013.

Cambresis Junior, Manuel. *João Camarão Telles Ribeiro: um notável cidadão brasileiro* [João Camarão Telles Ribeiro: a notable Brazilian citizen]. Rio de Janeiro, Brazil: Instituto Histórico-Cultural da Aeronáutica (INCAER), October 31, 2023. https://www2.fab.mil.br/incaer/images/eventgallery/instituto/Opusculos/Textos/opusculo_tb_camarao.pdf.

Chagnon, Napoleon A. *Yanomamö–The Last Days of Eden*. Orlando: Harcourt, Brace and Company, 1992.

Dowdy, Homer E. *Christ's Jungle*. Gresham, OR: Vision House, 1995.

———. *Christ's Witchdoctor*. New York: Harper and Row, 1963.

———. *Speak My Words Unto Them, a History of UFM International*. Bala Cynwyd, PA: UFM International, Inc., 1997.

Gheerbrant, Alain. *Journey to the Far Amazon*. New York: Simon and Schuster, Inc., 1954.

Hallesby, O. *Prayer*. Translated by Rev Clarence J. Carlsen. Minneapolis: Augsburg, 1931.

Howe, Marvine. "Amazon Indians Kill 3 in Attack." *The New York Times*, January 6, 1975. https://www.nytimes.com/1975/01/06/archives/amazon-indians-kill-3-in-attack-brazilian-agency-evacuates-posts.html.

Migliazza, Ernest C. *Yanomama Grammar and Intelligibility*. Indiana University, 1972.

Peters, Jonathan F. *Amazon Jungle Life Among the Yanomami*, University of Waterloo, Print + Retail Solutions, n.d.

———. *Life Among the Yanomami: The Story of Change Among the Xilixana on the Mucajaí River in Brazil*. Toronto: University of Toronto Press, 1998.

Ramos, Alcida Rita. *Sanumá Memories: Yanomami Ethnography in Times of Crisis*. Madison: The University of Wisconsin Press, 1995.

Sorkness, Thomas J. *Into the Wilds of Brazil–An Account to Contact the Sikois.* Unpublished manuscript, 2018.

Tierney, Patrick. "The Fierce Anthropologist." *The New Yorker*, October 9, 2000. https://www.newyorker.com/magazine/2000/10/09/the-fierce-anthropologist-2.

Subject Index

A

Abel (Sanumá), 163, 165, 183n6, 186, 197–198, 241
Accident, 62, 237
Acculturation, xxvii, xxviiin11, 19n3
Ademir. *See* Mimica.
Adultery, 246, 271, 321
Aica, xx–xxi, 52, 60
Alberto, xiii, 213n6, 214, 226, 229, 244, 247–248, 254, 257–258, 263–269, 290, 371–372, 381
Allaby, Norman, xiii, 213n6, 247n7, 371
Allaby, Stan, xvi, 1n1, 104, 213, 377–378
Alphabet, 154, 156, 160, 252, 274–275, 287
Amazon
　rainforest (jungle), xxii–xxvi, 106, 352
　river, xxiv, 26, 34n4, 132, 136, 215, 222, 269–270, 313, 369, 381
American Bible Society, 159
Anauá River, 28, 30, 32, 34, 42–49, 61, 129
Anderson, Steve, 152, 154, 166, 168, 227
Angels, 57, 101, 261
Animism, xxi, 319
Anthropology, xxn2, 18, 31, 133, 165, 177n4, 294
　anthropologists, xxvii, xxix, 164, 175, 177, 204, 332, 351
Anti-American sentiment, 19, 249, 256, 265, 277–278, 309

Anti-missionary efforts, xxiii, 52, 64, 67, 104, 112, 114, 134, 175, 249–250, 271, 291, 309, 329–330
Apiaú River, xxiv, 52, 61, 62, 66, 335, 338
Apollo program, 179
Arawakan, xxii, 19n3
Army, 48, 138, 278, 287, 344, 348n4, 351
Atheism, 204
Attacks, 133, 138, 166–167, 180, 188, 209, 260, 342, 345
Atroais, xxii, xxx, 129–143, 170, 208–209, 228, 330, 341–348, 379
Auaris River, xx, 68, 70, 115n12, 141–142
Auaris Station, 151, 153, 174, 191, 225, 241, 244, 260, 281, 295, 303

B

Backsliding, 317
Baptism, 27–28, 48, 240, 241, 244, 246, 250, 258, 275–276, 305, 308, 311, 319–322, 380
Beating, 157–158
Birth, 40, 160, 170, 178, 194–196, 198, 199, 229–230, 267, 299
　of Christ, 66
Bonfim, Brazil, 17
Borgman, Arnold, 9n5, 17, 338
Born, William G. (Bill), 230, 352–368
Brazilian Air Force (FAB), xvi, 104–125, 129–131, 141, 152–153, 161, 288
Brazilian Bible Society, 306
British Guiana. *See* Guyana.

387

Brown, Dan, 260, 282
Brown, Dave, 260
Brown, Ron and Robin, 220, 279, 282, 285, 289–290, 382–383
Burgess, Eunice, 210

C
Cable, Bob, 67–68, 72, 75, 78, 79–84, 87–88, 91, 94, 98, 100, 112, 117–118, 227
Cafuini River, 34, 129, 131, 379
Campinas Language School, 149
Carey, William, 17
Carib, xxii, 34, 129–131, 141, 284
Catholicism, 196, 204, 211
Church, 9–10, 17, 33, 99, 147, 171, 223, 234, 330–331
   indigenous, xxiii, xxvii, 27, 29, 48–49, 141, 170, 209, 288, 300, 302, 304, 308–309, 313–315, 321–322, 323–326, 351
   Planting, xxvi–xxvii, 15, 246, 269, 342
Civilization, xxviii, 30, 61, 67, 71, 110, 126, 133–140, 159, 166, 170, 175, 187, 198, 274, 351, 375
Comfort, 31, 44, 57, 85, 122, 151, 189, 193, 206, 234, 263, 356–357, 362–363, 370
Communication, xxviin10, 26, 53, 60–62, 124, 175, 178–179, 253, 339, 343, 348n4, 352–353
Communion. *See* Lord's Supper.
Communism, 152, 206
Conferences, 18, 30, 53, 60, 104, 130, 147, 152, 154, 162, 165, 244–250, 254, 258, 312–313, 319–325, 339, 347, 380–382
Confession, 199, 223, 229, 246, 249, 258, 264, 273–274
   of faith, 16, 308
Conflict, xxi–xxii, 113, 162
Congress for Indigenous Evangelical Pastors and Leaders (CONPLEI), 312–313
Contextualization, xv, xxx, 151, 180, 181

Conversion, xxvi, 8, 16, 109, 131, 158, 165–166, 233, 247, 250–251, 254, 258, 264, 273, 300, 321, 322
Creation, 65, 91, 157, 201, 261, 280, 313,
Crossworld. *See* UFM International.
Cue, Sandy, 107, 125, 144, 183, 227
Cunningham, Lois, 215–216, 219–220, 223, 227, 253, 308, 310, 380

D
Danadarwana, Guyana, 20–21, 24
Danger, 28, 138, 207–208, 266, 282
Darius, King, 48, 155
Death, xi, 6, 42, 55, 126–127, 133, 146, 153, 155, 174, 180, 199, 207, 216, 219, 226, 235–236, 238, 257–260, 257, 263, 266–267, 270, 286, 288, 300, 321, 344, 346, 349, 374, 381
   murder (of Lourenzo and Alberto), 263–265, 270, 275, 381
   of son (David), 187–188, 193, 230n3, 354–368, 369, 378, 379
   suicide, 159
Deconversion, 254
Dedication of New Testament, 309–312
Derbyshire, Des, 231
Diet, 22–23, 38–39, 46, 55, 63, 83, 122, 154, 165, 175, 273, 298
Dino (Sanumá), 226, 229, 241, 244, 247, 258–259, 262, 270
Discipleship, xxvii, 147, 200, 226, 269–270, 287, 304, 308, 320–321
Disease, xxvii, 194, 235
Drug use, 229, 262, 264, 271, 350
Dowdy, Homer, xxiin6, 9n4, 51n1, 105n7, 131, 140n3, 341n1
Dreams, 197, 293, 321
Drunkenness, 216, 274, 321, 326

E
Education, xxxvi–xxviii, 160, 190–191, 201, 207, 215n7, 222, 236, 245, 262, 267, 281, 291–292, 297–298, 318–320, 323, 325, 342, 350–352, 369–370
Elders, 27, 48, 51, 131, 300, 314

Subject Index

Elliot, Elizabeth (*These Strange Ashes*), 299
Elliot, Jim, xi, 373
Elká (Wai Wai), xxvi, 27–29, 41, 51, 131–132, 134, 140, 228, 347
Epidemic, 153, 167, 175, 192, 198, 219, 235–236, 257, 266, 349
Eppler, Darrel, 306–307
Essequibo River, 20
Ethnos360. *See* New Tribes Mission.
Evangelical Mission of the Amazon, 317
Evangelical missions, xii, 277–278
Evangelicalism, 223
Evangelism, xi, 6, 75, 152, 170, 187, 298, 342
Expedition, xi, xiii, xxn2, 10, 30, 34–50, 51–61, 67–105, 109, 113, 129–143, 213–214, 338–340, 342–343, 371–376, 379

F

Faith, xxix, 7–8, 38, 45, 64, 84, 197, 206–208, 225–226, 233, 241, 254–256, 320, 329, 378
Fatigue, 41–42, 122
Fear, 41, 78–79, 90, 94, 117, 124, 126–127, 158, 209, 232–235, 266, 288, 344–345
Fellowship, 26, 40, 83, 85, 130, 140, 169, 229, 245, 279
Fighting, 157, 162, 216–217, 220, 238, 248–249, 350
Financial support, xxiii, 6–9, 285, 318
Foreign Missions Fellowship, 6–7
Forgiveness, 127, 146, 199, 206, 234, 258
Friendship, xxviii, 145, 166, 177, 263, 347, 370
Frustration, 30, 41–42, 206, 210, 228, 256, 343
FUNAI. *See* National Indian Foundation.
Furlough, 127–128, 142–145, 169–174, 227, 244–245, 379–383

G

Gheerbrant, Alain, xxn2
Gordon College, xiii
Gospel, xix, 30–31, 33, 35, 176, 180–181, 223, 246, 329–331
 resistance to, 76, 103, 165, 241, 247, 264
Government permission, 67, 108, 134, 141
Grace, 31, 209, 322
Graham, Billy, 33
Great Commission, xi, xxix, 48–49
Guilt, 127, 234
Guyana (Guiana), xi, xxii, xxiv–xxvi, 9–10, 14–16, 19–20, 42, 64, 73, 104–105, 113–115, 129–131, 206, 245, 342–343

H

Handbook on Amazonian Languages (HAL), 231
Harris, Leonard, 26–28
Hawkins, Bob, xxvi, 10, 28, 51, 68, 76, 202
Hawkins, Neill, xvii, xxii, xxvi, 9–10, 14–15, 18–22, 30, 48, 51, 61, 64, 68, 106, 113–114, 133, 138–141, 149–152, 159, 162, 330, 340
Hawkins, Rader, 9–10, 15, 24, 104, 329–330
Healing, 154–155, 177, 201, 259, 282
Helicopter crash, 111–113
Hell, 38, 57
Hill, Joe, 228, 346
Holy Spirit, 32, 35, 127, 168, 171, 179, 210, 226, 232, 246, 247, 250, 261, 269, 292, 323, 326, 329

I

Illness, xxvii, 137, 143, 149, 167, 213, 216, 218–219, 222, 224, 253, 287
 treatment of the sick, xxvii, 83, 119, 153–158, 174, 176, 185, 198, 219, 257, 259, 266–267, 280, 350–351
 mental, 201
Indian Bible Conference, 165
Indian Protection Services (IPS), 19, 48, 106, 134, 139–140, 175, 342
Indigenous church activities, xxix, 140–141, 168, 187, 220, 227, 253, 255, 281, 313, 321, 325–326, 351

Inter-Varsity Christian Fellowship, 15

J
Jauaperi River, 133
Jesus Film Project, 281, 306–308, 310
José (Sanumá), 218, 222–223, 226, 229, 241, 247, 254, 257, 259, 262
Justice, 248–249, 350

K
Kamoa River, 42
Kanashen, Guyana, 18–19, 21, 25–27, 30, 36–37, 40, 47, 343
Kashi (Sanumá), 312–313, 315, 325
Kirifaká (Wai Wai), 27-28
Klemtu (Wai Wai), 27, 34, 68, 72–73, 77, 80, 87–88, 92, 94, 100–101
Komak. *See* Alberto

L
Language, learning and analysis, xxvii, 53, 71, 84, 140, 143–144, 147, 152, 154, 156, 158–159, 165–166, 169, 170, 172, 173, 175, 183–187, 202, 208, 211–212, 231, 245, 274–276, 278–279, 281–284, 289, 299, 332–334, 350
Leadership, xxvii, 3–4, 130, 141, 167, 204, 206, 209, 217, 244, 247–248, 254, 257–258, 263–267, 269, 272, 276, 280–282, 290, 302–326
Leavitt, Claude, xxvi, 15, 17–18, 28, 30, 49, 52, 55, 60, 64, 214, 338, 342
Lethem, Guyana, 15, 16, 18–20, 104, 154, 162
Lewis, Rod, xxvi, 51, 68, 74, 149, 151, 173–174
Linguistics. *See* Language, learning and analysis.
Loneliness, 26, 65, 146, 168, 192, 231–232, 248, 287, 370
Lord's Supper, 48, 240, 305
Lourenzo, xiii, xxviii, 164–165, 180–182, 185, 192, 196, 213–214, 216–218, 221–226, 229–230, 240–241, 244, 247, 250, 254, 258, 261, 263–267, 269–270, 275, 290, 330, 371, 374, 376, 380

M
Macushi(s), xxii, 22, 206, 209, 275, 284, 292, 297–298, 300, 313
Maiongong, xiii, xxii, xxiv, xxviii, 30, 69–71, 75, 118, 141–142, 153, 155–157, 164–166, 175, 192, 214, 224, 227, 240–241, 330, 333
Malaria. *See* Illness.
Marooned, 338
Marriage, 142
Martyrdom, xi, xxvi, 28
Massacre, 344
Mateus (Sanumá), 275–277, 280–282, 304–305
Maquiritare. *See* Maiongong.
Mawashá (Wai Wai), 27, 29, 51, 68, 71, 73, 79–80, 87–88, 94, 98, 100–102, 131
McCheyne, Robert Murray, 11
McCully, Ed (Edward), xi
McGee, J. Vernon ("Through the Bible"), 233
Medicine. *See* Health *and* Illness.
Migliazza, Ernest, xixn1, 63, 106, 332
Mimica (Brazilian Missionary), 278–279, 281, 287, 294, 303, 305–310, 313, 315–319, 322–325
Missionary Aviation Fellowship (MAF), xii, xxiii, xvi, 10, 15, 18n2, 49, 51–52, 60–65, 68, 107–108, 114, 154, 162, 170, 178, 188, 196, 208, 230, 249–250, 286–287, 295, 309, 339–340, 343, 352–368
Moises (Sanumá), 255–256, 264, 296, 300, 306
Moody Bible Institute, xi, xix, 3–6
Moore, Bruce, 287–288, 299, 305, 383
Mucajaí River, xx, xxiv, 48, 51, 60, 63, 66, 333
Mucajaí Station, 52, 60, 105, 137, 149, 335, 338–339
Museum of the Bible, xii

N
National Indian Foundation (NIF/FUNAI), xxn1, 175n3, 204, 224,

Subject Index

242, 250, 256, 277–278, 287, 295, 297, 342, 344
New Tribes Mission, xii, xxii, 71, 183, 211, 286, 288, 309, 312
Ninam. *See* Yanam.

O
Old Testament, 216, 255, 264, 267, 277, 292, 308–309, 313, 318
Orthography. *See* Language, learning and analysis.

P
Palimi-U Station, xxvi, 115, 227, 334
Parima River, 67–68, 71, 76, 105–106, 108–110, 113, 167
Pastors, 1, 99, 130, 136, 150, 298, 300, 310, 313–314, 321–322
Patience, 5, 32–34, 108, 155–159, 178, 209, 227, 256, 296
Paulo Ilo (Sanumá), 198–200, 216, 220, 229, 264, 266, 296–297
Pedro (Maiongong/Sanumá), 187, 193, 216, 246, 258, 266, 275–276, 281
Pentateuch, 255
Peters, John, xxn2, xxiii, xxvi, 18, 20, 51–53, 60–63, 73, 132, 134, 136, 140, 149–150, 240, 338–339
Pierce, Kitty, 154, 184, 188, 211–212, 355, 357–360, 368
Police, 264
Prayer, xxiii, 7, 12, 17–18, 23, 30–31, 35, 36, 38, 40, 44, 46, 48, 54, 56–57, 64, 73, 79, 83, 108, 110, 113, 131, 137, 146–147, 152, 155–156, 158, 166, 173, 176, 182, 185, 199, 201–202, 205, 210, 213–214, 220, 226, 229–230, 234, 241, 250, 257, 259, 262, 273, 276, 282, 294, 296, 300, 302, 305, 307, 314, 324, 338–339, 347, 354–368, 372
Preaching, 31, 48, 91, 241
Providence, 65, 112, 147
Puraquequara, 215, 262, 295, 347
Purity, 31

R
Ragas, Elizabeth, 286, 288
Ramos, Alcida, 177
Repentance, 200, 249, 258, 321, 323
Revenge, xxii, 180–181, 238, 257, 265
Rezende (Sanumá), 273–274, 276, 279–280, 298–299, 304
Ribeiro, Colonel João Camarão Telles, 105n7,
Rio Branco, xix–xx, xxiii–xxiv, 19, 30, 47, 48
Riedle, Florence, 209, 345
Robbery, 160–161, 284–285
Rupununi River, 24
Ryrie, Charles, 233

S
Saint, Nate, xi
Salvation, xxix, 2, 29, 109, 226, 247, 307–308
  Lordship, 233
Sammy (Wapishana), 20–21, 23–25
Sasscer, Russ, 112, 116, 125
Satan, 31–32, 48, 155, 201, 208, 246, 259, 267, 293, 306, 316, 350
Saula (Sanumá), 180, 184, 197, 202, 219
Seely, Merrill, xxviin10, 212n5, 252, 271, 285, 382
Seely, Louise, xxviin10, 270–271, 285
Scripture Union, 205
Sergio and Nathaly (Natalie), 320, 324
Sermons. *See* Preaching.
Shamanism, xxvi, 35, 126, 158, 229, 233, 254, 258–259, 273
Sickness. *See* Illness.
Silas, Paulo, 184, 187, 209, 220, 253, 257, 267, 274–278, 282, 297, 299–302, 304, 309–310, 351
Sin, 31, 65, 127, 255, 317, 325–326, 335
Social mission, 223
Soldiers. *See* Army.
Sorkness, Tom, 213
Sovereignty, God's, 329–331
Spiritism, 350
Spiritual growth, 198–200
Suffering, 56–57, 131, 197, 207, 224, 239, 259, 293, 362

Subject Index

Summer Institute of Linguistics (SIL), 13, 128, 144–145, 168–169, 210n4, 211, 231n5, 299
Superstition, 106, 126
Surucucu Station, 131, 153, 167, 181
Survey, 142
Survival International, 250
Syncretism, 319

T
Taylor, Hudson, 145
Taylor, Ken, 177–178
Technology, 179, 245–246, 278, 282, 316, 322
Teeter, Dan, 313
Temptation, 125, 132
Testimony, 114, 231, 246, 250, 254, 300, 308, 321, 325
Texas Tech, 164
Theft. *See* Robbery.
Theology, 228
Threats, 233
"Three Freds," xxii, xxvi, 28
Training, 15
Trotman, Dawson, 33

U
Uatumã River, xxx, 131, 133-134, 136, 139
Unevangelized Fields Mission (UFM/ UFM International), xi–xiii, xix, xxii–xxvi, 9–10, 17, 48, 144, 145, 150, 228, 260–261, 270, 304, 330, 346, 378
Uraricoera River, xx, 17, 48, 51–52, 67, 210, 330, 332–334

V
Vaccination, 228, 235–236, 249, 258
Venezuela, xii, xx, 30, 70–71, 104, 114n11, 153, 212, 219, 244–245, 252, 285–288, 290, 295, 309, 332–333, 383
Voth, Dianne, 227, 238, 243, 253, 258, 262

W
Wahne (Wai Wai), 53–54, 59
Wai Wai, xx, xxvi, 9, 17, 19–20, 25–55, 65, 68, 72–73, 83, 98, 129–143, 170, 202, 209, 228, 313, 330, 338–339, 341–348
Waicas *See* Yanomam.
Waica Station, 48, 51, 67–68n6, 104–109, 111, 113, 115n12, 124–125, 140–141, 143, 153, 161, 166–167, 227n2
Waodani, xi
Wapishanas, xxii, xxvi, 18–25, 313
War, 188, 206–207, 374
Watts, Isaac, 45
Weariness, 156, 206, 232, 277, 287, 305
Wheaton College, xi, xix, 3–8
Wheaton Graduate School, 8–13, 330
Will, God's, 33, 143, 149, 246
Word of Life, 149, 153
World Team, 228
Worldwide Evangelization Crusade (WEC), xxii
Wycliffe Bible Translators, xii, xxii, 6–9, 85, 116, 147, 169, 181, 183, 208, 274, 283–288, 299, 304–307, 383

Y
Yakutá (Wai Wai), 27, 34, 37, 53–54, 59, 131, 228, 343
Yanam, xx, xxii, 18n2, 51–52, 60, 104, 211, 332–334
Yancey, Philip (*Where is God When it Hurts?*), 239
Yanomam. *See* Yanomami.
Yanomami, xix–xxix, 6, 10, 17–19, 50–53, 56, 58–59, 62, 66–68, 77, 83, 100, 104–106, 108, 110, 118, 119, 127–129, 136, 139–142, 153, 165–167, 177, 211, 227, 266, 271, 281, 284, 288–289, 295, 303, 313, 329–334
Yanomamö. *See* Yanomami.
Ye'kuanas. *See* Maiongongs.
Youderian, Roger, xi
Young Life, xi, 8, 11, 33
Youth for Christ, 8
Youth with a Mission (YWAM), 279, 382

Scripture Index

OLD TESTAMENT

Deuteronomy
7:1–6	31
7:7–8	32
7:16–27	33
7:22	33
9:4	32
9:5b	32
31:8	129
33:27	41

Joshua
1:9	288

Ruth
1:16b	144

1 Chronicles
29:13	309

Ezra
1:5	48
2:69	48
4:4	48
5:6–7	48
6:14	48
6:22	47
8:21	49
8:31	49

Job
23:8–19	11, 54
23:10	11

Psalms
5:3	320
19:10	54
23:2	22
25:15	12
27:13	190
32:8	359
32:10–11	367
37:23	142
42:1–2	54
42:8	194
63:1–2a, 8a	54
67:1–2	148
73:24–25	13
78:19	65
85:5–7	172
84	189
84:11	145
91	44
91:5	42
91:15	24
107:4	231n6
119:67, 71	239
119:103	54
121	111
121:8	112
128:2	291
146	64

Proverbs

16:9	61, 143, 367
21:1	105
27:1	352
27:7	85
29:25	13, 30

Ecclesiastes

3:4	321
3:11	207

Isaiah

40–43	131
40:3	51, 108
40:5	110
43:2–3	358
43:12–13	131
55:11	269

Lamentations

3:21–23	353

NEW TESTAMENT

Matthew

5:38	194
6:33	239
16:17–19	268
28:18–20	134, 245

Mark

16:15	48

Luke

1:37–38	141
2:30–32	246–247
18:1	305

John

16:33	252

Acts

19:18–19	233
27:25	47
28:28	222

Romans

8:28	45
10:14	vi
10:17	315
12:17–21	181
15:20–21	xi

1 Corinthians

4:8	85–86
7	10
16:9	19, 312

2 Corinthians

1:10–11	64
5:8	186

Galatians

1:24	99
4:19	198
6:9	287

Ephesians

4:16	208

Philippians

1:3–6	17, 229, 251

Colossians

1:28–29	66
3:1–2	239
4:12	67

1 Thessalonians

4:13	216

2 Timothy
1:5–7 1

Hebrews
13:8 297

James
1:2 235
1:5 362

1 Peter
1:13 14

2 Peter
3:18 322

Revelation
7:9–10 331

www.ingramcontent.com/pod-product-compliance
Lightning Source LLC
Chambersburg PA
CBHW072117290426
44111CB00012B/1692